ADMINISTRATION OF TORTURE

ADMINISTRATION OF TORTURE

A Documentary Record

from Washington to

Abu Ghraib and Beyond

Jameel Jaffer and Amrit Singh

COLUMBIA UNIVERSITY PRESS

NEW YORK

Columbia University Press
Publishers Since 1893
New York   Chichester, West Sussex
Copyright © 2007 American Civil Liberties Union Foundation
All rights reserved

A Caravan book. For more information, visit www.caravanbooks.org

Library of Congress Cataloging-in-Publication Data

Jaffer, Jameel.
   Administration of torture : a documentary record from Washington to
Abu Ghraib and beyond / Jameel Jaffer and Amrit Singh.
      p. cm.
   ISBN 978-0-231-14052-2 (cloth : alk. paper)–ISBN 978-0-231-14053-9
(pbk. : alk. paper)–ISBN 978-0-231-51162-9 (e-book)
   1. War on Terrorism, 2001—Law and legislation–United States–Sources.
2. War and emergency powers–United States–Sources. . 3. Military interrogation–
United States–Sources. I. Singh, Amrit. II. Title.

   KF7225.J34 2006
   341.6'5–dc22

   2007024188

Columbia University Press books are printed on permanent and durable acid-free
paper.
Printed in the United States of America
c 10 9 8 7 6 5 4 3 2 1

CONTENTS

Acknowledgments   vii

Foreword   ix

Introduction: Administration of Torture   1

Timeline of Key Events   45

Description of the Documents   53

The Documents   A-1

ACKNOWLEDGMENTS

A large number of people contributed to this project in diverse ways. We would like to thank, first, the many lawyers who have worked with us on *American Civil Liberties Union v. Department of Defense*, the lawsuit that resulted in the release of the documents compiled here—in particular, Ann Beeson, Jennifer Ching, Melanca Clark, Art Eisenberg, Bassina Farbenblum, Bill Goodman, Lucas Guttentag, Beth Haroules, Omar Jadwat, Alexa Kolbi-Molinas, Megan Lewis, Larry Lustberg, Barbara Olshansky, Brigette Pak, Judy Rabinovitz, Michael Ratner, Laura Rotolo, and Steven Watt. We would also like to thank Chris Anders, Nasrina Bargzie, Simon Baumer, Laurie Beacham, Barton Beebe, Karen Curry, Jamil Dakwar, Terence Dougherty, Lee Gelernt, Melissa Goodman, Edwin Grimsley, Chris Hansen, Khaled Fahmy, Scott Horton, Catherine Itaya, Donna Lieberman, Jed Miller, Linda Mills, Lauren Nakamura, Catherine Hounfodji, Pauline Nguyen, Erica Pelletreau, Col. Michael Pheneger, Alice Ristroph, Reid Rowe, Len Rubenstein, John Sifton, Paul Silva, Katie Traverso, Emily Tynes, Alex Vitrak, Allison Walker, Cecillia Wang, Sarah Weiss, Emily Whitfield, and Ben Wizner. Finally, we would like to thank the Center for Constitutional Rights, Physicians for Human Rights, Veterans for Common Sense, and Veterans for Peace, organizations that are co-plaintiffs with the ACLU in the lawsuit. We gratefully acknowledge Peter Dimock and the Columbia University Press team for providing invaluable guidance throughout the publication process.

FOREWORD

The United States has both the oldest written constitution in the world and a long history of ignoring it in times of national crisis. The Alien and Sedition Acts were adopted less than a decade after the U.S. Constitution was ratified. The writ of habeas corpus was suspended during the Civil War and more than 30,000 people were imprisoned without charges or trial. Thousands of people were jailed for opposing U.S. participation in World War I, including such prominent critics as Eugene Debs (who ran for president from jail). More than 120,000 Japanese Americans were "interned" in domestic concentration camps during World War II. And untold numbers of lives were ruined by witch-hunts and blacklists during the Cold War.

As a nation, we look back on each of these incidents with regret. Regretting past mistakes is not the same as learning from them, however. The events of September 11, 2001, were horrific and demanded a response. But that response did not have to include torture. It did not have to include indefinite detention at Guantánamo Bay. It did not have to include secret CIA kidnappings. It did not have to include warrantless wiretaps. And it did not have to include spying on peaceful protestors.

Americans did not authorize any of these actions that were taken in our name. We were not even told about them. Nor, for the most part, was Congress. Now that these practices have come to light, the Bush administration has remained unrepentant. Faced with mounting criticism, it continues to insist that the president can act secretly, and on his own, whenever he chooses because we are engaged in a "war against terrorism" and the president is commander in chief.

That is not the way our democracy works. Having lived under kings, the framers of our Constitution created a system of divided powers. And having lived through war and revolution, they wrote a constitution that was meant to guide us through hard times with our principles secure and values intact.

There are constitutions in the world that can be suspended during periods of national emergency. Our Constitution cannot. As the Supreme Court famously said in 1866, when the country had just survived the gravest threat ever to its survival: "The Constitution of the United States is a law for rulers and people, equally in war and in peace, and covers with the shield of its protection all classes of men, at all times, and under all circumstances."

The Bush administration appears not to share that belief. In an early indication of the administration's approach to the rule of law, then White House Counsel and now Attorney General Alberto Gonzales described the Geneva Conventions as "quaint" and "obsolete" in a memo explaining why they did not have to be obeyed. The administration's attitude toward the Constitution is essentially the same. In the administration's view, civil liberties are a "quaint" luxury we can no longer afford in the "war against terrorism," and any suggestion that the administration should be held legally or politically accountable for its actions reflects an "obsolete" response to the threat we are facing.

The documents collected in these pages help us to understand better where that attitude has led. They tell a story of torture, abuse, and mistreatment of prisoners held in American custody that most of us would have found unimaginable even a few years ago. They also reveal a concerted effort by the Bush administration to deny the scope and extent of those abuses. When that cover-up was no longer possible, the administration used all the resources at its disposal to delay and frustrate meaningful judicial and legislative oversight. Slowly but inevitably, the administration's effort is beginning to unravel. Americans do not want their government to engage in torture. It is not who we are or who we aspire to be.

The ACLU has therefore had a simple and consistent message since September 11: in an increasingly dangerous world, the government's first obligation is to ensure that we remain both "safe and free." Over the past six years, the Bush administration too often has treated these ideas as mutually inconsistent. The framers of the Constitution understood better, and the American people know better. We are not safer today because of the abuses that took place at Abu Ghraib and other less-publicized places. Even the administration does not seriously claim otherwise.

Justice Louis Brandeis once wrote that "sunlight is said to be the best disinfectant." The Freedom of Information Act embodies that principle and this book embodies that hope. The events of September 11, 2001, were so overwhelming, and so tragic, that for a while they stifled any meaningful public debate. Now we are in the midst of an important national discussion about first principles. We cannot possibly know how we want our government to act unless we know what our government has done.

This book is designed to shed light on that question. To borrow a phrase from Watergate, what did senior policymakers know and when did they know it? In our democratic system, all of us have a responsibility to ask. And we have a right to know.

Anthony D. Romero
Steven R. Shapiro

ADMINISTRATION OF TORTURE

INTRODUCTION: ADMINISTRATION OF TORTURE

Let me make very clear the position of my government and our country. We do not condone torture. I have never ordered torture. I will never order torture. The values of this country are such that torture is not a part of our soul and our being.

—*President George W. Bush*
June 22, 2004[1]

When the American media published photographs of U.S. soldiers abusing prisoners at Abu Ghraib prison in Iraq, the Bush administration assured the world that the abuse was isolated and that the perpetrators would be held accountable. In a May 10, 2004 address, President Bush said that the "cruel and disgraceful" abuses were the work of "a small number" of soldiers and that some of those responsible had already been charged with crimes.[2] Defense Secretary Donald Rumsfeld traveled to Iraq and offered similar assurances there.[3] Over the next three years, the Bush administration refined its narrative at the margins, but by and large its public position remained the same.[4] Yes, the administration acknowledged, some soldiers had abused prisoners, but these soldiers were anomalous

---

[1]Remarks by the president during a photo opportunity with Prime Minister Medgyessy of Hungary at the White House Oval Office, June 22, 2004. Available at http://www.whitehouse.gov/news/releases/2004/06/20040622-4.html.

[2]Statement of President George W. Bush, "President Bush Reaffirms Commitments in Iraq," May 10, 2004. Available at http://www.whitehouse.gov/news/releases/2004/05/20040510-3.html.

[3]Remarks by Secretary of Defense Donald H. Rumsfeld at Abu Ghraib Prison, May 13, 2004. Available at http://www.defenselink.mil/speeches/speech.aspx?speechid=121.

[4]See, e.g., the testimony of Alberto Gonzales before the U.S. Senate Judiciary Committee, January 6, 2005: "[The President] does not believe in torture, condone torture; has never ordered torture . . . [a]nd anyone engaged in conduct that constitutes torture is going to be held accountable." Available at http://www.washingtonpost.com/wp-dyn/articles/A53883-2005Jan6.html. See also the Second Periodic Report of the United States of America to the Committee Against Torture, May 6, 2005, ¶ 10: "When allegations of torture or other unlawful treatment arise, they are investigated and, if substantiated, prosecuted." Available at http://www.state.gov/g/drl/rls/45738.htm.

sadists who ignored clear orders. Abuse was aberrational—not systemic, not widespread, and certainly not a matter of policy.

The government's own documents tell a starkly different story. In October 2003, the ACLU, the Center for Constitutional Rights, Physicians for a Human Rights, Veterans for Common Sense, and Veterans for Peace filed a request under the Freedom of Information Act (FOIA) for government records concerning the treatment of prisoners apprehended by the United States in connection with the "war on terror." A lawsuit filed in New York to enforce the FOIA request has since resulted in the release of thousands of government documents. While the government continues to withhold many key records, the documents that have been released show that the abuse and torture of prisoners was not limited to Abu Ghraib but was pervasive in U.S. detention facilities in Iraq and Afghanistan and at Guantánamo Bay, and that the maltreatment of prisoners resulted in large part from decisions made by senior civilian and military officials. These decisions, moreover, were reaffirmed repeatedly, even in the face of complaints from law enforcement and military personnel that the policies were illegal and ineffective, and even after countless prisoners—including prisoners not thought to have any connection to terrorism—were abused, tortured, or killed in custody. The documents show that senior officials endorsed the abuse of prisoners as a matter of policy—sometimes by tolerating it, sometimes by encouraging it, and sometimes by expressly authorizing it.

The Bush administration has professed a commitment to democracy and human rights and claimed solidarity with those who struggle against tyranny. But the documents show unambiguously that the administration has adopted some of the methods of the most tyrannical regimes. Documents from Guantánamo describe prisoners shackled in excruciating "stress positions," held in freezing-cold cells, forcibly stripped, hooded, terrorized with military dogs, and deprived of human contact for months. Documents from Afghanistan and Iraq describe prisoners beaten, kicked, electrocuted, and burned. An autopsy report from Iraq describes a prisoner who was found shackled to the top of a door frame with a gag in his mouth; the report concludes that interrogators beat and asphyxiated the prisoner to death. The documents, besides evidencing conduct that violates U.S. and international law, demonstrate a profound betrayal of the values that President Bush and his administration pledged to uphold.

This book is an effort to make the government's documents and the story they tell more widely known. All of the documents that have been released in response to the FOIA litigation are posted on the ACLU's website, but the sheer number of documents—more than a hundred thousand pages have been released thus far—renders the collection of limited use to anyone not already immersed in the issues. By presenting some of the most significant documents here, we hope to make at least this important subset of the records known to a larger number of people. In this introduction, we have sought to explain the significance of the key documents and place them in context. The introduction relies on the FOIA documents—and on other documents obtained and made public by the news media—to show the connection between the policies adopted by senior civilian and military officials and the torture and abuse that took place on the ground.

I

Few principles are as well settled in international law as those that prohibit the abuse and torture of prisoners. The Universal Declaration of Human Rights, which the United Nations General Assembly adopted at the close of World War II and the United States helped draft, prohibits states from subjecting prisoners "to torture or to cruel, inhuman or degrading treatment or punishment."[5] The International Covenant on Civil and Political Rights, which the United States signed in 1977 and ratified in 1992, uses the same language.[6] The Convention Against Torture, which the United States signed in 1988 and ratified in 1994, requires states to "take effective legislative, administrative, judicial or other measures to prevent acts of torture in any territory under [their] jurisdiction"; to make torture a criminal offense under their domestic laws; and to take affirmative steps to prevent abuse that does not rise to the level of torture.[7] The prohibition against torture is considered to be a *jus cogens* norm, meaning that no derogation is permitted from it under any circumstances.[8]

International humanitarian law—the law of armed conflict—makes clear that the same prohibitions apply with equal force in times of war. Each of the four Geneva Conventions ratified by the United States after the end of World War II includes a provision—known as Common Article 3—that mandates that prisoners be "treated humanely" and specifically protects prisoners from "violence to life and person," including "cruel treatment and torture," and from "outrages upon personal dignity, in particular, humiliating and degrading treatment."[9] The Third Geneva Convention affords

---

[5]Universal Declaration of Human Rights, G.A. Res. 217 A (III), UN G.A.O.R., 3d sess., UN Doc. A/810 (December 12, 1948), art. 5.

[6]International Covenant on Civil and Political Rights, December 19, 1966, 999 U.N.T.S. 171, 6 I.L.M. 368, art. 7.

[7]Convention Against Torture and Other Cruel, Inhuman or Degrading Treatment or Punishment, opened for signature December 10, 1984, 108 Stat. 382, 1465 U.N.T.S. 85, arts. 2, 4, 16.

[8]Some authorities also consider the prohibition against cruel, inhuman or degrading treatment to be a *jus cogens* norm. See, e.g., the Restatement (Third) of the Foreign Relations Law of the United States § 331 cmt. e and § 702(d) cmt. n (1987).

[9]Convention for the Amelioration of the Condition of the Wounded and Sick in Armed Forces in the Field, August 12, 1949, 6 U.S.T. 3114, 75 U.N.T.S. 31, art. 3; Convention for the Amelioration of the Condition of Wounded, Sick and Shipwrecked Members of Armed Forces at Sea, August 12, 1949, 6 U.S.T. 3217, 75 U.N.T.S. 85, art. 3; Convention Relative to the Treatment of Prisoners of War, August 12, 1949, 6 U.S.T. 3316, 75 U.N.T.S. 135 ("Third Geneva Convention"), art. 3; Convention Relative to the Protection of Civilian Persons in Time of War, August 12, 1949, 6 U.S.T. 3516, 75 U.N.T.S. 287, art. 3.

additional protections to detained enemy fighters who qualify as prisoners of war.[10] For almost half a century, the U.S. military's own regulations have expressly required interrogators to abide by the Geneva Conventions' proscriptions against torture and abuse. The 1992 version of Army Field Manual 34-52, which governed military interrogations until September 2006, prohibited "acts of violence or intimidation, including physical or mental torture, threats, insults, or exposure to inhumane treatment as a means of or aid to interrogation." "Such illegal acts," the Field Manual stated, "are not authorized and will not be condoned by the US Army."[11]

This was the legal landscape when the first U.S. military planes landed at Guantánamo Bay with prisoners who had been captured in Afghanistan. By then, however, President Bush and his closest advisors had already begun to envision a new legal framework meant to permit U.S. interrogators to subject prisoners to torture and abuse. In January of 2002, then White House Counsel Alberto Gonzales opined that the war on terror had "render[ed] obsolete Geneva's strict limitations on questioning of enemy prisoners," and he recommended that the president deny al Qaeda and Taliban prisoners the protection of the Third Geneva Convention to "preserve flexibility" and "reduce the threat" that administration officials and military personnel would later be prosecuted for war crimes.[12] Stating that the war against terrorism had "usher[ed] in a new paradigm," President Bush formally endorsed this policy in a memorandum issued on February 7.[13] The same memorandum declared—wrongly, as the Supreme Court held four years later[14]—that al Qaeda and Taliban prisoners were not entitled even to the baseline protections of Common Article 3.[15]

Under this "new paradigm," interrogation policies at Guantánamo Bay began to take shape. Within months of the first prisoners' arrival, interrogators sought authority to use interrogation methods beyond those endorsed by the Field Manual. To develop these new methods, they looked to a program designed to train U.S. military personnel to withstand

---

[10]Under the Third Geneva Convention, arts. 4(A)(1), (3), (4) and (6), "prisoners of war" include "[m]embers of the armed forces of a Party to the conflict, as well as members of militias or volunteer corps forming part of such armed forces," "[m]embers of regular armed forces who profess allegiance to a government or an authority not recognized by the Detaining Power," "[p]ersons who accompany the armed forces without actually being members thereof," and "[i]nhabitants of a non-occupied territory, who on the approach of the enemy spontaneously take up arms to resist the invading forces, without having had time to form themselves into regular armed units, provided they carry arms openly and respect the laws and customs of war."

[11]Department of the Army, Field Manual 34–52 (1992), Intelligence Interrogation, ch. 1, pp. 1–8. In September 2006, the Army announced that it was replacing Field Manual 34-52 with a new manual, Field Manual 2-22.3. The new manual, like its predecessor, expressly references the Geneva Conventions and prohibits torture and abuse. Department of the Army, Field Manual 2-22.3 (2006), Human Intelligence Collector Operations, ch. 5, pp. 5–26.

[12]**A-1–3**: Memorandum from White House Counsel Alberto Gonzales to President George Bush, January 25, 2002.

[13]**A-6**: Memorandum from President Bush to the vice president et al., February 7, 2002.

[14]*Hamdan v. Rumsfeld*, 126 S.Ct. 2749, 2795–96 (2006).

[15]**A-7**: Memorandum from President Bush to the vice president et al., February 7, 2002.

interrogation by enemy captors. Known as "Survival, Evasion, Resistance and Escape" (SERE), the program is administered by the Joint Personnel Recovery Agency ("JPRA") at Fort Belvoir, Virginia.[16] Military personnel who undergo SERE training are deliberately humiliated, subjected to stress positions, forced to exercise to the point of exhaustion, and subjected to various forms of psychological duress—all to prepare them for the possibility of abuse and torture by foreign intelligence services. The program is tightly controlled because the methods used in the program are recognized to be extremely dangerous, but commanders at Guantánamo—and officials at the Pentagon as well—believed that the methods used in the SERE program could be adapted for use against prisoners held by U.S. forces.[17] At the end of the summer of 2002, a review of intelligence collection operations at Guantánamo Bay conducted under the auspices of the Chairman of the Joint Chiefs of Staff concluded that interrogations had not been fruitful and recommended that the Army and FBI develop "a new plan to exploit detainee vulnerabilities."[18] The JPRA, working with the Army Special Operations Command's Psychological Directorate, developed a plan based on SERE methods,[19] and in September 2002 the Army Special Operations Command and JPRA co-hosted a conference at Fort Bragg for Guantánamo interrogation personnel.[20] Instructors from JPRA also traveled to Guantánamo to train interrogators there.[21] By December 2002, the Defense Department had produced a draft

---

[16]Office of the Inspector General of the Dep't of Defense, *Review of DOD-Directed Investigations of Detainee Abuse,* Aug. 25, 2006 ("DOG IG Report"), available at http://www.dodig.osd.mil/fo/Foia/ERR/06-INTEL-10-PublicRelease.pdf, pp. 23–24.

[17]Mark Benjamin, "Torture Teachers," *Salon,* June 29, 2006. See also Jane Mayer, "The Experiment," *The New Yorker,* July 11, 2005; M. Gregg Bloche and Jonathan H. Marks, "Doing Unto Others as They Did Unto Us," *New York Times,* November 14, 2005.

[18]DOG IG Report, p. 25.

[19]Ibid. For reasons that are obscure, the JPRA developed its plan even before the Chairman of the Joint Chiefs of Staff completed his review. Ibid. It is not clear on whose authority the JPRA was operating. Even within the JPRA, notably, there was disagreement about the extent to which the agency should become involved in interrogation operations. A JPRA representative who attended the SERE conference recommended to his commander that the agency not become "directly involved in actual operations." He warned that JPRA "had no actual experience in real world prisoner handling" and questioned why the agency was "assuming" that SERE methods would be effective interrogation techniques. These concerns were ignored. Ibid.

[20]DOD IG Report, p. 25; **A-9**: FBI e-mail re interrogation training at Ft. Bragg, September 9, 2002; **A-15**: Summarized witness statement of Maj. Gen. Geoffrey Miller, March 18, 2005, in which Miller acknowledges that military psychologists, forensic psychologists, and clinical psychologists at Guantánamo trained in SERE techniques but denies that interrogators received such training.

[21]DOD IG Report, p. 26; **A-8**: Summarized witness statement of former Interrogation Control Element chief at Guantánamo, March 22, 2005, in which the witness states that his predecessor "arranged for SERE instructors to teach their techniques to the interrogators at GTMO." The witness also states that Maj. Gen. Geoffrey D. Miller, who became commander of Guantánamo on November 4, 2002, "didn't believe the [SERE] techniques were appropriate for the [Guantánamo] mission." As discussed below, however, the evidence suggests that Miller approved the use of SERE methods at Guantánamo and in fact defended their use even after FBI personnel complained that the methods were counterproductive.

document titled "JTF GTMO SERE INTERROGATION SOP." "SOP" in this context stands for "standard operating procedure."[22]

The government's documents show that the decision to adopt more aggressive interrogation methods—including SERE methods—was made at the highest levels. In February 2002, Defense Secretary Donald Rumsfeld asked Maj. Gen. Michael E. Dunlavey to oversee interrogation operations at Guantánamo.[23] According to a statement that Dunlavey provided in 2005, Rumsfeld told him that the Defense Department "had accumulated a number of bad guys" and that "he wanted a product and he wanted intelligence now." Dunlavey was initially told that he would "answer to" Rumsfeld and to U.S. Southern Command, the Defense Department's command unit responsible for military operations in Central and South America and the Caribbean. Later, however, "the directions changed and [Dunlavey] got [his] marching orders from the President of the United States." Dunlavey was expected "back in Washington D.C. every week to brief [Rumsfeld]."[24]

In his 2005 statement, Dunlavey does not explain what "marching orders" he received from the president, but in October 2002 Dunlavey wrote to the Commander of U.S. Southern Command, Gen. James T. Hill, to request that interrogators be granted permission to use interrogation methods beyond those authorized by the Field Manual. The request was directed, at least in part, at obtaining approval for methods that could be employed against Mohammed al-Qahtani, a prisoner thought to have knowledge of the September 2001 attacks.[25] Stating that the military's interrogation methods "ha[d] become less effective over time," Dunlavey proposed that the military adopt more aggressive methods. He stated that the adoption of such methods would "enhance [interrogators'] efforts to extract additional information,"[26] and to make his case he attached a memorandum that defended the legality of the proposed interrogation methods. The analysis relied on President Bush's February 2002 "new paradigm" memorandum, and in particular on the president's determination that al Qaeda and

---

[22]The Defense Department continues to withhold this document, but it is referenced in a December 2002 memorandum written by the special agent in charge of the Defense Department's Criminal Investigation Task Force at Guantánamo. **A-18**: Memorandum, December 17, 2002.

[23]**A-21**: Summarized witness statement of Maj. Gen. Michael Dunlavey, March 17, 2005. At the time, interrogation operations at Guantánamo were run by Joint Task Force 170 (JTF 170), while detention operations at Guantánamo were run by a separate unit, Joint Task Force 160 (JTF 160). In November 2002, JTF 170 and JTF 160 were merged and redesignated Joint Task Force GTMO, and Maj. Gen. Geoffrey Miller was made commanding general. See Sworn Statement of General James Hill, October 7, 2005, available at http://images.salon.com/ent/col/fix/2006/04/14/fri/HILL.pdf.

[24]**A-21**: Summarized witness statement of Maj. Gen. Michael Dunlavey, March 17, 2005.

[25]**A-30**: Sworn statement of Lt. Gen. Randall Schmidt, August 24, 2005.

[26]**A-85**: Memorandum from Maj. Gen. Michael Dunlavey to commander, U.S. Southern Command, re counter-resistance strategies, October 11, 2002.

Taliban prisoners were not entitled to Enemy Prisoner of War (EPW) status under the Geneva Conventions. "Since the detainees are not EPWs," the analysis stated, "the Geneva Conventions limitations that ordinarily would govern captured enemy personnel interrogations are not binding on U.S. personnel."[27]

Dunlavey's request was sent up the chain of command and ultimately to the Pentagon. General Hill forwarded Dunlavey's request to Gen. Richard Myers, who was then the chairman of the Joint Chiefs of Staff.[28] Myers discussed the request with Defense Department General Counsel William J. Haynes II, who discussed the request with Paul Wolfowitz, the deputy secretary of defense, as well as with Douglas J. Feith, undersecretary of defense for policy. Ultimately Haynes sent the request to Rumsfeld with a recommendation that he endorse it.[29]

On November 12, 2002, Rumsfeld verbally authorized a "special interrogation plan" that permitted interrogators to confine al-Qahtani in an "isolation facility" for up to thirty days, subject him to "20 hour interrogations for every 24-hour cycle," and intimidate him with military working dogs during those interrogations.[30] On the basis of Rumsfeld's authorization, interrogators subjected al-Qahtani to twenty-hour interrogations for forty-eight out of fifty-four consecutive days.[31] Lt. Gen. Randall Schmidt, who with Brig. Gen. John Furlow later oversaw a Southern Command investigation into prisoner abuse at Guantánamo, explained in a sworn statement:

> [al-Qahtani] was being interrogated 20 hours a day. Okay? And then given four hours off. In that four hours, he was taken to a white room. Okay? With all the lights and stuff going on and everything and he was—could set your clock by it, it was meticulously logged. You know this was a crucible that was being used.[32]

The treatment destroyed al-Qahtani both physically and psychologically. On one occasion, al-Qahtani had to be revived at the prisoners' hospital after his heart rate fell to 35 beats per minute.[33] In late November 2002, FBI agents saw al-Qahtani after he had been subjected to "intense isolation for over three months . . . in a cell that was always flooded with light." Al-Qahtani "was evidencing behavior consistent with extreme psychological trauma (talking to non-existent people, reporting

---

[27]**A-87**: Memorandum from Lt. Col. Diane E. Beaver to commander of JTF-170 re legal brief on proposed counter-resistance strategies, October 11, 2002.

[28]**A-84**: Memorandum from Gen. James T. Hill to chairman of the Joint Chiefs of Staff, October 25, 2002.

[29]**A-83**: Memorandum from Defense Department General Counsel William J. Haynes II to the secretary of defense, November 27, 2002.

[30]**A-111, 112, 114, 115, 117**: Army Regulation 15-6: Final report of Lt. Gen. Randall Schmidt and Brig. Gen. John Furlow, *Investigation into FBI Allegations of Detainee Abuse at Guantanamo Bay, Cuba Detention Facility*, July 14, 2005 ("Schmidt-Furlow Report"). The Schmidt-Furlow Report does not identify the subject of the interrogation plan but other documents make clear that the subject was al-Qahtani.

[31]**A-117**: Schmidt-Furlow Report.

[32]**A-49–50**: Sworn statement of Lt. Gen. Randall Schmidt, August 24, 2005.

[33]Bill Dedman, "Can '20th hijacker' ever stand trial?," MSNBC.com, October 26, 2006.

hearing voices, crouching in a corner of the cell covered with a sheet for hours on end)."[34]

Al-Qahtani may have been the first prisoner whom military interrogators subjected to such methods, but he was not the last. On December 2, Rumsfeld issued a written directive that authorized for potential use on all prisoners held at Guantánamo Bay many of the same techniques he had already cleared for use on al-Qahtani. In addition to permitting isolation for thirty days at a time, twenty-hour interrogations, and the exploitation of "individual phobias (such as fear of dogs) to induce stress," Rumsfeld's written directive permitted interrogators to deprive prisoners of light and auditory stimuli, forcibly strip them naked, hood them, and subject them to "stress positions."[35] Some of these methods were adapted from the SERE program,[36] and many of them went far beyond the Army Field Manual. Rumsfeld's directive plainly authorized interrogators to subject prisoners to "humiliating and degrading" treatment and worse—in other words, to subject them to interrogation methods that violated Common Article 3 of the Geneva Conventions. At the time, all violations of Common Article 3 were "war crimes" under U.S. law.[37]

Military interrogators exploited the new authority that Rumsfeld had invested in them. At the same time, they adopted sweeping interpretations of methods outlined in the Army Field Manual—ignoring its prohibition against abuse and construing its listed "interrogation approaches" in the broadest possible way. In late 2002, al-Qahtani was stripped naked and paraded in front of female interrogators, made to wear women's underwear on his head, led around on a leash, and forced to perform a series of

---

[34]**A-128**: Letter from T. J. Harrington, deputy assistant director, FBI Counterterrorism Division, to Maj. Gen. Donald J. Ryder, Department of the Army, July 14, 2004.

[35]**A-83**: Action memorandum endorsed by Secretary of Defense Donald Rumsfeld, November 27, 2002; **A-96**: Memorandum from LTC Jerald Phifer to Maj. Gen. Michael Dunlavey, October 11, 2002.

[36]In a June 2004 press briefing, Gen. James Hill of Southern Command confirmed that the techniques authorized by Rumsfeld for use in Guantánamo in December 2002 were derived from the SERE school. He said that Guantánamo staff working with behavioral scientists, "having gone up to our SERE school . . . developed a list of techniques which our lawyers decided and looked at, said were OK." Remarks of General James T. Hill at Media Availability, June 3, 2004, available at http://www.defenselink.mil/Transcripts/Transcript.aspx?TranscriptID=3153.

[37]See 18 U.S.C. 2441(c) (2004). Rumsfeld left open the possibility that he would approve even more extreme methods on a case-by-case basis, and he approved a special interrogation plan for a second prisoner on August 13, 2003, in response to a request submitted by interrogators in July. A later investigation found that "the techniques were never implemented because the subject of the second special interrogation plan began to cooperate prior to the approval." The same investigation found, however, that the prisoner was confined in a cold cell "referred to as the 'freezer,'" that he may have been beaten by guards, and that an interrogator impersonated a navy captain from the White House and told the prisoner that his mother would be imprisoned by the United States if he did not begin to cooperate. **A-118, 119–123**: Schmidt-Furlow Report. **A-72, 75–76**: Sworn statement of Lt. Gen. Randall Schmidt, August 24, 2005. This second prisoner was probably Mohamadou Ould Slahi, a Mauritanian national. Jess Bravin, The Conscience of the Colonel, *Wall St. Journal*, Mar. 31, 2007.

"dog tricks."[38] The Schmidt-Furlow report found that al-Qahtani's interrogators "believed that they were acting within existing guidance."[39] The interrogators apparently viewed the abusive methods as permissible applications of approaches described in the Army Field Manual as "ego down" ("attacking the source's sense of personal worth") and "futility" ("mak[ing] the source believe that it is useless to resist").[40]

Al-Qahtani's interrogators were decidedly not "rogue soldiers." To the contrary, they were closely supervised by high-level officials, including Rumsfeld himself. In a 2005 interview, Lt. Gen. Schmidt stated that Rumsfeld had been "personally involved" in al-Qahtani's interrogation and that Rumsfeld had maintained a "direct connection" to Maj. Gen. Geoffrey Miller, who became commanding general of Guantánamo in early November 2002.[41] When Schmidt interviewed Rumsfeld, however, Rumsfeld professed to be surprised at the methods that interrogators had used. "My God, you know, did I authorize[] putting a bra and underwear on this guy's head," Rumsfeld asked Schmidt in apparent disbelief. Schmidt did not accuse Rumsfeld of having directly authorized such methods, but he suggested that Rumsfeld should have known that such methods would be used because this was "kind of the way we set it up." "Did [Rumsfeld] say put a bra and panties on this guy's head and make him dance with another man," Schmidt asked rhetorically. "No, you didn't say [it] Sir[.] [B]ut just under that broad technique that was [the] application. Well, where in there was the throttle?"[42]

As for Gen. Miller, at first he assured Schmidt that he "walked the gun line," "knew everything that was going on," and was "always aware of everything that happened to" al-Qahtani.[43] Miller acknowledged that all of the details of al-Qahtani's interrogation were meticulously recorded in hourly interrogation logs. In a second interview, however, Miller denied knowing the specifics of al-Qahtani's interrogation.[44] Schmidt found that Miller had failed to limit the interrogators' authority. In Schmidt's opinion, Miller "was the only one that had the suitable knowledge of what

---

[38]**A-116**: Schmidt-Furlow Report.

[39]**A-117**: Schmidt-Furlow Report.

[40]Ibid. The Field Manual states that the pride and ego down approach "is based on attacking the source's sense of personal worth. . . . The objective is for the interrogator to pounce on the source's sense of pride by attacking his loyalty, intelligence, abilities, leadership qualities, slovenly appearance, or any other weakness. This will usually goad the source into becoming defensive, and he will try to convince the interrogator he is wrong. In his attempt to redeem his pride, the source will usually involuntarily provide pertinent information in attempting to vindicate himself." Army Field Manual 34–52 (1992), Intelligence Interrogation, ch. 3, pp. 3–18. The Field Manual describes "futility" as an approach in which "the interrogator convinces the source that resistance to questioning is futile. When employing this technique, the interrogator must have factual information. He should be aware of and able to exploit the source's psychological and moral weaknesses, as well as weaknesses in his society." Ibid.

[41]**A-62–63**: Sworn statement of Lt. Gen. Randall Schmidt, August 24, 2005.

[42]**A-52**: Sworn statement of Lt. Gen. Randall Schmidt, August 24, 2005.

[43]**A-46, 58**: Sworn statement of Lt. Gen. Randall Schmidt, August 24, 2005.

[44]**A-49**: Sworn statement of Lt. Gen. Randall Schmidt, August 24, 2005.

[Rumsfeld] meant because he talked to the Secretary of Defense. He's the only one that really knew the intent of what a technique was and probably where the line was, and crossing it, and should have [been] watching that."[45] Schmidt observed, "By saying 'ego down' . . . we were going to degrade [the prisoner] in some way. What limit? The lowest limit. But General Miller didn't know and didn't set the limits. He didn't set the boundaries. He didn't say how long it was going to go on."[46] It was "a free for all," Schmidt concluded.[47]

Senior officials in the Bush administration continue to insist that, to the extent that prisoners were abused, they were abused in spite of—rather than because of—government policy. The government's own documents, however, belie this claim. The documents establish that senior officials in Washington, including White House Counsel Alberto Gonzales, constructed a legal framework that would permit the abuse and torture of prisoners. They establish that Secretary of Defense Donald Rumsfeld, relying on this legal framework, expressly authorized the use of interrogation methods—including SERE methods—that went far beyond those endorsed by the Army Field Manual. They establish that Rumsfeld and General Geoffrey Miller oversaw the implementation of the newly authorized interrogation methods and closely supervised the interrogation of prisoners thought to be especially valuable. And they make clear that Rumsfeld and Miller declined to limit interrogators' authority in a way that might have at least mitigated the consequences of their radical departure from pre-existing practice.

All of this would be remarkable in itself, but it is made more so by the fact that, at the time each of the critical policy decisions was made, there was considerable skepticism within the intelligence community about the effectiveness of abusive methods. In sharp contrast to Rumsfeld and Miller, FBI personnel stationed at Guantánamo Bay believed from the outset that the military's aggressive interrogation methods—and the SERE techniques in particular[48]—"were not effective or producing [i]ntel that was reliable."[49] FBI officials also doubted the lawfulness of the methods used by military interrogators, and they feared that judges presiding over war crimes prosecutions would reject information obtained through these methods. One FBI document—a memorandum written by the FBI's Behavioral Analysis Unit (BAU)—states that FBI personnel stationed at

---

[45]**A-53**: Sworn statement of Lt. Gen. Randall Schmidt, August 24, 2005.

[46]**A-80**: Sworn statement of Lt. Gen. Randall Schmidt, August 24, 2005.

[47]**A-60**: Sworn statement of Lt. Gen. Randall Schmidt, August 24, 2005. Schmidt recommended that Miller be reprimanded, but the recommendation was rejected by Schmidt's superiors. Josh White, Abu Ghraib Tactics Were First Used at Guantanamo, *Washington Post*, July 14, 2005.

[48]**A-130**: FBI memorandum re "Detainee Interviews (Abusive Interrogation Issues)," May 6, 2004.

[49]**A-131**: FBI e-mail re instructions to GTMO interrogators, May 10, 2004. FBI personnel raised their concerns in weekly meetings with senior officials at the Criminal Division of the Justice Department. Ibid.

Guantánamo Bay between late October and mid-December 2002 concluded that military interrogators with the Defense Intelligence Agency's Defense Human Intelligence Service ("DIA Humint") "were being encouraged at times to use aggressive interrogation tactics . . . which are of questionable effectiveness and subject to uncertain interpretation based on law and regulation." The memorandum continues:

> Not only are these tactics at odds with legally permissible interviewing techniques used by U.S. law enforcement agencies in the United States, but they are being employed by personnel in GTMO who appear to have little, if any, experience eliciting information for judicial purposes. The continued use of these techniques has the potential of negatively impacting future interviews by FBI agents as they attempt to gather intelligence and prepare cases for prosecution.[50]

DIA Humint personnel in Guantánamo, however, responded to the FBI's arguments "with considerable skepticism and resistance."[51] They were "adamant that their interrogation strategies [were] the best ones to use despite a lack of evidence of their success."[52]

Gen. Miller was apprised of FBI concerns on multiple occasions. At a meeting on November 20, 2002, FBI and DIA Humint personnel met to discuss an interrogation plan that DIA Humint personnel had developed. FBI officials expressed "misgivings about the overall coercive nature" of the plan, questioned the "efficacy" of DIA Humint's "fear-based approach," and registered doubts about the plan's legality. In response to the FBI's concerns, DIA Humint personnel agreed to present a revised plan to FBI headquarters.[53] The next day, however, DIA Humint personnel submitted the original plan to the Pentagon's Office of General Counsel, and according to FBI accounts, "blatantly misled the Pentagon" into believing that the FBI had endorsed it.[54] When FBI personnel learned of this, they wrote to Miller objecting to the submission of the plan without prior review by FBI headquarters. They also complained that the plan had not been reviewed by the chief psychologist of the Navy Criminal Investigative Services, who was scheduled to arrive on November 21 with the specific purpose of evaluating the plan.[55] In a document that appears to have been forwarded to Miller on November 22, 2002, FBI personnel formally objected to the substance of the DIA Humint's interrogation plan. The FBI document states: "Many of [DIA Humint's] methods are considered coercive by Federal Law Enforcement and [Uniform Code of Military Justice] standards." The same document continues: "[R]eports from those knowledgeable about the use of these coercive techniques are highly skeptical as to their effectiveness and reliability."[56]

---

[50]**A-133**: FBI electronic communication re BAU concerns, May 30, 2003.
[51]**A-134**: FBI electronic communication re BAU concerns, May 30, 2003.
[52]**A-135**: FBI electronic communication re BAU concerns, May 30, 2003.
[53]**A-139**: FBI e-mail to General Miller, undated.
[54]**A-135**: FBI electronic communication re BAU concerns, May 30, 2003.
[55]**A-139**: FBI e-mail to Maj. Gen. Miller, undated.
[56]**A-140**: FBI (BAU) draft letter for Maj. Gen. Miller, November 22, 2002.

FBI personnel met with Miller in person in early December to raise their concerns again.[57] Miller was not receptive. The BAU memorandum states: "Although MGEN Miller acknowledged positive aspects of [the FBI's] approach, it was apparent that he favored [DIA Humint's] interrogation methods, despite FBI assertions that such methods could easily result in the elicitation of unreliable and legally inadmissible information."[58] In an e-mail, an FBI agent expresses incredulity at press reports quoting Miller saying that he believed in the "rapport-building approach," which was the approach that FBI personnel had been advocating. The agent's e-mail continues: "[T]his is not what [Miller] was saying at gitmo when [I] was there . . . . [T]he battles fought in gitmo while gen miller . . . was there are on the record."[59]

Miller's inflexibility ultimately led some FBI personnel to conclude that critical decisions about the interrogation of Guantánamo prisoners were actually being made by Miller's superiors, and in particular by Rumsfeld. In one e-mail, an FBI official in Washington states that he and other FBI personnel met with Miller (and earlier with Dunlavey) to explain the FBI's concerns regarding the military's interrogation methods. Both generals, however, dismissed the concerns. The Defense Department "has their marching orders from the Sec Def," the FBI e-mail says.[60] Another FBI e-mail, dated December 16, 2002, expresses frustration at the Defense Department's refusal to modify its interrogation methods. "Looks like we are stuck in the mud with the interview approach of the military vrs. law enforcement," the e-mail complains.[61]

FBI personnel were not alone in voicing unease with these interrogation methods. Similar concerns were expressed by some military personnel, including the Defense Department's Criminal Investigation Task Force (CITF), the unit responsible for investigating crimes committed by prisoners before their capture. CITF personnel met with Miller on two occasions to object to the military's interrogation methods.[62] On December 2, 2002, Colonel Brittain Mallow, CITF's commander at Guantánamo, prohibited CITF agents from "participat[ing] in the use of any questionable techniques" and ordered them to report "all discussions of interrogation strategies and approaches" to CITF leadership.[63] Two weeks later, a

---

[57]**A-142**: FBI e-mail re "Briefing notes for the General Miller," December 2, 2002.

[58]**A-135**: FBI electronic communication re BAU concerns, May 30, 2003.

[59]**A-143**: FBI e-mail re current events, May 13, 2004.

[60]**A-131**: FBI e-mail re instructions to GTMO interrogators, May 10, 2004.

[61]**A-144**: FBI e-mail re GTMO matters, December 16, 2002.

[62]**A-68**: Sworn statement of Lt. Gen. Randall Schmidt, August 24, 2005. According to news reports, CITF personnel also "raised the issue almost weekly in August and September" with the Pentagon general counsel's office. Bill Dedman, "Can '20th hijacker' ever stand trial?," MSNBC.com, October 26, 2006. CITF personnel found the Pentagon's attorneys to be "sympathetic" but determined that they "had limited influence on policy areas handled by the office of the secretary of defense." Ibid.

[63]**A-145**: E-mail from CITF Commander Col. Brittain Mallow re "participation in discussions of interrogation strategies, techniques, etc.," December 2, 2002.

CITF special agent in charge wrote a memorandum questioning the December 10 Defense Department document titled "JTF GTMO 'SERE' INTERROGATION SOP." The memorandum makes clear that CITF personnel shared the FBI's concern that information obtained through SERE techniques would be unreliable and also unusable in court. "Both the military and [law enforcement agencies] share the identical mission of obtaining intelligence in order to prevent future attacks on Americans," the memo states. "However, [law enforcement agencies] ha[ve] the additional responsibility of seeking reliable information/evidence from detainees to be used in subsequent legal proceedings."[64]

Some military personnel had even more serious concerns: they believed that the methods being used by military interrogators could constitute torture. On December 17, CITF personnel informed the navy's general counsel, Alberto J. Mora, that prisoners at Guantánamo were being subjected to "physical abuse and degrading treatment."[65] According to a chronology drafted by Mora, navy personnel stated that the methods used by interrogators "included physical contact, degrading treatment (including dressing detainees in female underwear, among other techniques), the use of 'stress' positions, and coercive psychological procedures."[66] On December 20, Mora approached the Defense Department's general counsel, William Haynes, to express concerns about the abuse and about Rumsfeld's interrogation directive. He warned Haynes that some of the interrogation methods that Rumsfeld had authorized in the directive "could rise to the level of torture," and "expressed surprise that the Secretary had been allowed to sign it."[67] When Haynes disagreed with Mora's characterization of the interrogation methods, Mora "urged him to think about the techniques more closely."[68] Mora later wrote:

> What did "deprivation of light and auditory stimuli" mean? Could a detainee be locked in a completely dark cell? And for how long? A month? Longer? What precisely did the authority to exploit phobias permit? Could a detainee be held in a coffin? Could phobias be applied until madness set in? Not only could individual techniques applied singly constitute torture, I said, but also the application of combinations of them must surely be recognized as potentially capable of reaching the level of torture.[69]

Partly in response to Mora's concerns, Secretary Rumsfeld withdrew the December 2002 directive on January 15th, 2003.[70] He convened a

---

[64]**A-18**: Memorandum from CITF special agent in charge, December 17, 2002.

[65]Memorandum from Alberto J. Mora, general counsel, Department of the Navy, to inspector general, Department of the Navy, July 7, 2004 ("Mora Memorandum") p. 3, available at http://www.aclu.org/moramemo. Mora's memorandum was first published by *The New Yorker. See* Jane Mayer, "The Memo," *The New Yorker*, February 27, 2006.

[66]Mora Memorandum, p. 3.

[67]Ibid., p. 7.

[68]Ibid.

[69]Ibid.

[70]**A-146**: Memorandum from Defense Secretary Donald Rumsfeld to U.S. Southern Command re counter-resistance techniques, January 15, 2003.

working group to reconsider the directive and, if necessary, to authorize a new set of interrogation techniques.[71] Rumsfeld also ensured, however, that the working group would ultimately support the kinds of interrogations that military interrogators had already been conducting. The working group was advised that the Justice Department's Office of Legal Counsel (OLC) would prepare a legal memorandum that the working group would be required to accept as "definitive guidance."[72] According to Mora, the OLC delivered a draft of this memorandum to the working group in late January.[73]

The OLC draft, written by Deputy Assistant Attorney General John Yoo, was modeled on a memorandum that Assistant Attorney General Jay. S. Bybee had written for the CIA in August 2002.[74] The August 2002 Bybee memorandum took the position that abuse does not rise to the level of torture under U.S. law unless it inflicts pain "equivalent in intensity to the pain accompanying serious physical injury, such as organ failure, impairment of bodily function, or even death." The Bybee memorandum, which was plainly meant to permit the use of even the harshest techniques, also argued that U.S. laws banning torture could not constitutionally be applied to interrogations ordered by the president in his capacity as commander in chief of the armed forces, and that, in any event, the defenses of "necessity" and "self-defense" would "potentially eliminate criminal liability."[75] Yoo's memorandum for the working group parroted the legal reasoning of the August 2002 Bybee memorandum.[76]

Not all members of the working group were willing to endorse abusive interrogation methods, and some members urged the group to reject Yoo's analysis. Mora himself argued that the OLC memorandum was "fundamentally in error" and "virtually useless."[77] In February, after the working group began to consider specific interrogation methods, Jack Rives, deputy judge advocate general of the air force, wrote that "[s]everal of the more extreme interrogation techniques, on their face, amount to violations of domestic criminal law and the [Uniform Code of Military Justice]." He continued, "[a]pplying the more extreme techniques during the interrogation of detainees places the interrogators

---

[71]**A-147**: Memorandum from Defense Secretary Donald Rumsfeld to William J. Haynes II, general counsel, Department of Defense, January 15, 2003.

[72]Mora Memorandum, p. 15.

[73]Ibid., p. 16.

[74]The Bybee memorandum reportedly ratified harsh interrogation methods that the CIA was already employing. David Johnston & James Risen, "Aides Say Memo Backed Coercion Already in Use," *New York Times*, June 27, 2004.

[75]Memorandum from Jay. S. Bybee, assistant attorney general, to Alberto Gonzales, White House counsel, re standards of conduct for interrogation under 18 U.S.C. §§ 2340–2340A, August 1, 2002, at 1, 39, available at http://www.gwu.edu/~nsarchiv/NSAEBB/NSAEBB127/02.08.01.pdf. The Bush administration withdrew the August 2002 Bybee memorandum in December 2004. See Mike Allen and Susan Schmidt, "Memo on Interrogation Tactics is Disavowed," *Washington Post*, June 23, 2004.

[76]Mora Memorandum, pp. 16–17.

[77]Ibid., p. 17.

and the chain of command at risk of criminal accusations domestically." The judge advocate generals of the army and navy raised similar objections.[78]

These efforts by individual military officers to prevent the maltreatment of prisoners were admirable but ultimately unsuccessful: the broader working group dismissed the objections and adopted Yoo's legal analysis almost verbatim. On the basis of Yoo's permissive analysis, the group's final report recommended that the Defense Department endorse a set of thirty-five interrogation techniques, some of which extended far beyond those authorized by the Army Field Manual.[79] On April 16, 2003, Rumsfeld approved twenty-four of the thirty-five recommended techniques, including environmental manipulation, sleep adjustment, extended isolation, and false flag—the last of these a technique meant to convince a prisoner that his interrogators were from a country known for its use of torture.[80]

While Rumsfeld's April 2003 directive was broad, it did not authorize all of the interrogation methods that the working group had endorsed. For example, it declined to endorse interrogation methods labeled "face or stomach slap," "removal of clothing," and "mild physical contact." Rumsfeld's April 2003 directive, however, may have been only a feint directed at critics like Mora. Mora and other critics of Yoo's legal analysis were never given a final copy of the working group's report; Mora himself had no idea the report had even been finalized.[81] Because the Defense Department was taking the position publicly that it was rejecting the use of interrogation methods that would violate the Convention Against Torture, Mora assumed that Yoo's analysis had been rejected. Miller and Hill, however, were informed that the working group had completed its report and they were specifically briefed on the report's contents.[82] That the report was withheld from those who had disagreed with Yoo's analysis but briefed to those who were in charge of interrogations at Guantánamo may suggest that it was the working group report— and not the April 2003 directive—that was meant to govern actual interrogations.[83]

In the documents, FBI agents describe interrogations conducted by military personnel at Guantánamo in the months after the issuance of

---

[78]The JAG memos are available at www.aclu.org/jagmemos.

[79]"Working Group Report on Detainee Interrogations in the Global War on Terrorism: Assessment of Legal, Historical, Policy, and Operational Considerations," April 4, 2003, in *The Torture Papers*, ed. Karen J. Greenberg and Joshua L. Dratel (New York: Cambridge University Press, 2005), pp. 346–47.

[80]**A-148–151**: Memorandum from Defense Secretary Donald Rumsfeld to commander, U.S. Southern Command, April 16, 2003.

[81]Mora Memorandum, p. 20.

[82]Ibid., p. 20, n. 14.

[83]*See* Jane Mayer, "The Memo," *The New Yorker*, Feb. 27, 2006. A later memorandum from Acting Assistant Attorney General Daniel Levin to Haynes suggests that the Defense Department relied on Yoo's legal analysis until at least December 2003. See Memorandum from Acting Assistant Attorney General Daniel Levin to Defense Dep't General Counsel, William Haynes, Feb. 4, 2005, available at http://www.aclu.org/levinmemo.

Rumsfeld's April 2003 directive. One e-mail describes interrogations in which military personnel employed "environmental manipulation" in combination with other techniques. The agent writes:

> On a couple of occasions, I entered interview rooms to find a detainee chained hand and foot in a fetal position to the floor, with no chair, food, or water. Most times they had urinated and defecated on themselves, and had been left there for 18–24 hours or more[.] On one occa[s]ion, the air conditioning had been turned down so far and the temperature was so cold in the room, that the barefooted detainee was shaking with cold[.] When I asked the MP's what was going on, I was told that interrogators from the day prior had ordered this treatment, and the detainee was not to be moved[.] On another occasion, the A/C had been turned off, making the temperature in the unventilated room probably well over 100 degrees[.] The detainee was almost unconscious on the floor, with a pile of hair next to him[.] He had apparently been literally pulling his own hair out throughout the night[.] [84]

An FBI agent who served at Guantánamo between July and August 2003—soon after the April 2003 interrogation directive was issued—writes of seeing "strobe lights in interview rooms" and hearing "loud music being played and people yelling loudly from behind closed doors."[85] In another document, an FBI agent describes an interrogation that took place in February 2004:

> [The prisoner] did not recognize the interviewers and when he told them he didn't want to speak to anyone unless they were introduced by his regular interrogators, he was yelled at for 25 minutes . . . was short-shackled, the room temperature was significantly lowered, strobe lights were used, and possibly loud music. . . . After the initial 25 minutes of yelling . . . was left alone in the room in this condition for approximately 12 hours[.][86]

Still another document describes a military interrogation that took place in April 2003. During the interrogation, the interrogator "was repeating the [same] question over and over, in rapid fire fashion, so quickly that the interpreter was not keeping up with the questioning and the detainee would not have been able to answer without interrupting." An experienced Army interrogator who witnessed the interrogation writes,

> [The interrogator] then shouted "down[,]" and the two detainee escorts pushed the detainee to the floor. When I say pushed to the floor I mean they pushed in the back of the detainee's knees with their knees, taking the detainee to his knees. Then holding the detainee by his upper arms they slammed his upper body to the floor. This series of motions was all done in one swift movement, so that the detainee went from a standing position to a prone position all at once. . . . The detainee was slammed to the floor in this manner seven or eight times. . . . The detainee was being slammed to the floor so hard that I was concerned for his safety. The force with which the detainee hit the floor was, in my estimation, adequate to cause severe internal injury.[87]

---

[84]**A-154**: FBI e-mail describing interrogations at Guantánamo, August 2, 2004.
[85]**A-155**: FBI memorandum describing interrogations at Guantánamo, July 13, 2004.
[86]**A-158**: FBI e-mail describing interrogations at Guantánamo, May 6, 2004.
[87]**A-162–163**: Department of Defense memorandum relating to commander's inquiry, April 26, 2003.

FBI personnel continued to believe that the military's methods were ineffective and even counterproductive. In an interrogation that took place in late 2003, military interrogators impersonating FBI agents employed interrogation methods that FBI agents later characterized as "torture." According to the FBI, the military's interrogation methods "produced no intelligence of a threat neutralization nature," and the CITF believed that the techniques had "destroyed any chance of prosecuting the detainee."[88] Another FBI memorandum states, despairingly, "every time the FBI established a rapport with a detainee, the military would step in and the detainee would stop being cooperative."[89] A July 2003 e-mail expresses a similar sentiment: "We're still fighting the battle with [DIA Humint] which routinely has a negative impact on what we're trying to do."[90]

The documents make clear that the cruel treatment of prisoners at Guantánamo was routine. On July 9, 2004, the FBI's Office of Inspections circulated an e-mail asking agents who had been stationed at Guantánamo whether they had "observed aggressive treatment, interrogations or interview techniques ... which [were] not consistent with [FBI] interview policy/guidelines."[91] As of August 17, more than two dozen FBI agents had responded that they had "observed what was believed to be some form of mistreatment."[92] An undated summary states that prisoners were "threatened (either in person or aurally) by dogs" and "subjected to considerable pain."[93] In one case, a prisoner "was told that his family had been taken into custody and would be moved to Morocco for interrogation if he did not begin to talk."[94] One agent wrote that he had seen a prisoner "sitting on the floor of the interview room with an Israeli flag draped around him, loud music being played and a strobe light flashing."[95] Other agents witnessed similar incidents.[96]

Virtually all of the abuse described in the FBI documents stemmed directly from interrogation methods expressly approved by the chain of command. Indeed, FBI agents stationed at Guantánamo repeatedly noted the close connection between high-level Defense Department directives and the abuses they witnessed. One FBI agent observed that, notwithstanding Rumsfeld's "public statements" to the contrary, military interrogators' abusive methods "were approved at high levels

---

[88]**A-159**: FBI e-mail describing interrogations at Guantánamo, December 5, 2003. The impersonation generated concern within the FBI that, though it had been military interrogators who had used "torture techniques," it would be FBI agents who would be "left holding the bag before the public." Ibid.

[89]**A-155**: FBI memorandum describing interrogations at Guantánamo, July 13, 2004.

[90]**A-160**: FBI e-mail describing interrogations at Guantánamo, undated.

[91]**A-165**: FBI e-mail requesting reports of abusive treatment, July 9, 2004.

[92]**A-166**: FBI e-mail re GTMO special inquiry, August 17, 2004.

[93]**A-168**: FBI background, undated.

[94]Ibid.

[95]**A-170**: FBI e-mail describing interrogations at Guantánamo, July 30, 2004.

[96]**A-172**: FBI e-mail describing interrogations at Guantánamo, August 2, 2004; **A-173**: FBI document re "GTMO Issues for SAC Wiley," undated.

w/in DoD."[97] FBI e-mails discussing military interrogators' use of "torture techniques" indicate that these techniques had been approved by the Deputy Secretary of Defense, who at the time was Paul Wolfowitz.[98] After FBI agents reported abuse in response to the Office of Inspection's investigation, the FBI's general counsel concluded that seventeen of the twenty-six reports stemmed from "DOD approved interrogation techniques."[99] In other words, the interrogation methods that FBI agents were identifying as abusive were precisely the methods that had been endorsed by the chain of command.[100]

II

Until April 2004, the interrogation practices of the Bush administration's "new paradigm" remained largely obscured from public view. But in that month, photographs of abuse at Abu Ghraib prison were leaked to the media and widely disseminated. Those now infamous photographs depicted U.S. military personnel using some of the same methods that had been authorized and used at Guantánamo. Some photographs showed naked and hooded prisoners piled on top of one another; others showed prisoners shackled in obviously painful positions to railings, doors, and metal racks; still others showed prisoners cowering in front of unmuzzled military dogs. The photographs showed prisoners being subjected to "stress positions," "removal of clothing," exploitation of "individual phobias"— the same methods that Secretary Rumsfeld had approved. Several photographs showed prisoners wearing women's underwear on their heads and being dragged across the floor with a leash, methods that interrogators at Guantánamo had used against Mohammed al-Qahtani in the fall of 2002.

---

[97]**A-174**: FBI e-mail re "Detainee abuse claims," May 5, 2004.

[98]**A-176**: FBI e-mail describing interrogations at Guantánamo, January 21, 2004; **A-159**: FBI e-mail describing interrogations at Guantánamo, December 5, 2003. Another document indicates that Wolfowitz reviewed the interrogation methods that Rumsfeld authorized in December 2002. **A-83**: Action memorandum endorsed by Secretary of Defense Donald Rumsfeld, November 27, 2002.

[99]**A-166**: FBI e-mail re GTMO special inquiry, August 17, 2004.

[100]Even the Defense Department has abandoned the claim that these abusive methods are effective. In a press conference convened to mark the introduction of a new interrogation Field Manual last year, a Defense Department spokesperson was asked whether a prohibition against "nudity, hooding, [and] that sort of thing" would "limit the ability of interrogators to get information that could be very useful." The spokesperson offered this candid answer: "No good intelligence is going to come from abusive practices. I think history tells us that. I think the empirical evidence of the last five years, hard years, tell us that. Moreover, any piece of intelligence which is obtained under duress, through the use of abusive techniques, would be of questionable credibility, and additionally it would do more harm than good when it inevitably became known that abusive practices were used." See Defense Department News Briefing on Detainee Policies, Sept. 6, 2006, available at http://www.washingtonpost.com/wp-dyn/content/article/2006/09/06/AR2006090601442.html.

The question of how military personnel at Abu Ghraib came to use these methods is one that, more than three years after the publication of the photographs, has still not been satisfactorily answered. But the government's own documents show that these methods—as well as methods even more severe—were routinely employed against prisoners elsewhere in Iraq and Afghanistan. The documents also make clear that interrogation policies applied in Iraq and Afghanistan were to a significant extent derived from policies developed for use at Guantánamo. The contention that the abuse of prisoners was attributable to the transgressions of "rogue soldiers" is largely false. The documents show that, both in Iraq and in Afghanistan, interrogators and other military personnel employed abusive methods because commanders tolerated such abuse and, in some instances, authorized or actively encouraged it.

In Afghanistan, military interrogators began using abusive interrogation methods soon after their arrival in the country in November 2001.[101] Although the commander of coalition forces in Afghanistan issued an order in October 2001 "instructing [that] the Geneva Conventions were to be applied to all captured individuals in accordance with their traditional interpretation,"[102] in January 2002 Defense Secretary Rumsfeld rescinded the order in favor of one that stated that Al Qaeda and Taliban prisoners were not entitled to prisoner of war status.[103] By late 2002, interrogators were employing many of the techniques that Rumsfeld approved for use at Guantánamo in December of that year.[104] As discussed above, those techniques included subjecting prisoners to stress positions, isolating them for prolonged periods, depriving them of light and sleep, forcibly removing their clothing, and terrorizing them with military dogs.[105] Some interrogators went further. A chronology prepared at one Afghanistan detention facility refers to multiple incidents in January 2002 in which prisoners were beaten, kicked, and hit with the butt of a rifle.[106] In December 2002, interrogators at Bagram Collection Point in Afghanistan killed one of their prisoners by shackling him by his wrists to

---

[101]Vice Admiral A. T. Church III, *Review of Department of Defense Detention Operations and Detainee Interrogation Techniques*, submitted March 7, 2005 ("Church Report"), available at http://www.aclu.org/images/torture/asset_upload_file625_26068.pdf, p. 196.

[102]Hon. James R. Schlesinger et al., *Final Report of the Independent Panel to Review DoD Detention Operations*, submitted August 24, 2004 ("Schlesinger Report"), available at http://www.defenselink.mil/news/Aug2004/d20040824finalreport.pdf, p. 80.

[103]**A-177**: Memorandum from Secretary of Defense Donald Rumsfeld to the chairman of the Joint Chiefs of Staff, January 19, 2002. Notably, this memorandum predated President Bush's "new paradigm" memorandum by several weeks.

[104]It is now generally understood that Rumsfeld's December 2002 directive, and a draft report produced by the working group he convened, formed the basis for interrogation policy in Afghanistan. Church Report, p. 201; DOD IG Report, pp. 15–16, 27.

[105]Maj. Gen. George R. Fay, *Article 15–6 Investigation of the Abu Ghraib Prison and 205th Military Intelligence Brigade*, August 23, 2004 ("Fay Report"), available at http://www. defenselink.mil/news/Aug2004/d20040825fay.pdf, p. 29.

[106]**A-179, 181, 183**: Chronology of guard/detainee issues, undated.

the wire ceiling above his cell and beating his legs repeatedly.[107] A post-mortem investigation identified abrasions and contusions on the prisoner's face, head, neck, arms and legs and determined that the death was a "homicide" caused by "blunt force injuries."[108] About six days later, interrogators at the same facility killed another prisoner, this time one whom interrogators themselves believed to be innocent.[109] A subsequent autopsy found that this death, too, was a "homicide" and had been caused by "blunt force injuries."[110]

Senior Defense Department officials knew that interrogators in Afghanistan were using abusive techniques. In January 2003, the acting staff judge advocate for Combined Joint Task Force 180 (CJTF-180)—the coalition force responsible for military operations in Afghanistan—sent a memorandum to U.S. Central Command headquarters in Florida listing and describing many of the interrogation methods that were then being used by military interrogators. A subsequent military investigation found that the list had been developed from two sources. First, interrogators—and particularly personnel associated with the 519th Military Intelligence Battalion—based some techniques on an extraordinarily broad reading of the approaches set out by the Army Field Manual.[111] Second, interrogators borrowed from the list of techniques that Rumsfeld had approved in December 2002 for use at Guantánamo.[112] The memorandum sent to U.S. Central Command in January 2003 listed the techniques that interrogators had been using and "strongly recommend[ed]" that Central Command endorse these techniques as official policy.[113] Central Command forwarded the memorandum to the Joint Chiefs of Staff, and the chairman of the Joint Chiefs in turn forwarded it further up the chain of command—including, apparently, to Rumsfeld's office.[114]

The January 2003 CJTF-180 memorandum put senior military and civilian leaders on notice of at least some of the abusive methods that were being used by interrogators in Afghanistan, and it presented them with an opportunity to place limits on interrogators' authority. Rather than do so, however, the senior leadership simply ignored the memorandum. It was left to military leaders in the field to decide whether interrogators' authority should be limited, and, if so, in what ways. Predictably, CJTF-180 interpreted the silence from headquarters to mean that the techniques then in use "were unobjectionable to higher headquarters and that the

---

[107]Tim Golden, "In U.S. Report, Brutal Details of 2 Afghan Inmates' Deaths," *New York Times*, May 20, 2005.
[108]**A-185–186**: Final report of postmortem examination, December 8, 2002.
[109]Tim Golden, "In U.S. Report, Brutal Details of 2 Afghan Inmates' Deaths," *New York Times*, May 20, 2005.
[110]**A-187**: Excerpt of autopsy report, February 25, 2003.
[111]Church Report, pp. 6, 196, 214.
[112]Ibid., p. 201; Fay Report, p. 29.
[113]Church Report, pp. 196, 201.
[114]Ibid.

memorandum [describing those techniques] could be considered an approved policy."[115]

It was not until February 2003—almost a year and a half after the first U.S. interrogation teams arrived in Afghanistan—that military leaders in the field made any attempt to limit the methods being used by interrogators. In February 2003, Lt. Gen. Dan K. McNeill, then the commander of coalition forces in Afghanistan, revised interrogation policy by eliminating five techniques not found in the Field Manual.[116] Little if any effort, however, was made to enforce the new policy, and in March 2004, CJTF-180 issued a new interrogation directive that restored some of the practices that McNeill had sought to eliminate.[117] The March 2004 directive authorized new techniques as well. These additional techniques were drawn from an unsigned memorandum that was substantively identical to the directive that Rumsfeld had issued at Guantánamo on April 16, 2003.[118]

The Afghanistan documents thus establish several notable and disturbing facts. They show that interrogators were initially left without guidance as to which interrogation techniques were permissible and lawful. They show that interrogation policies for Afghanistan were derived from policies that Rumsfeld had instituted at Guantánamo. And they show that senior military and civilian leaders extended interrogators' authority even after prisoners had been tortured and killed in custody.

The Iraq documents tell a similar story. The first group of interrogators to arrive in Iraq was a detachment of the 519th Military Intelligence (MI) Battalion—the same Battalion that had been implicated in the deaths of prisoners at Bagram in late 2002.[119] In Iraq, as in Afghanistan, the interrogators were initially left to develop interrogation policies on their own.[120] Among the members of the 519th MI Battalion transferred from Afghanistan was Captain Carolyn Wood,[121] who in August 2003 became an interrogations operations officer at Abu Ghraib. In a sworn statement, Wood states that, soon after her arrival at Abu Ghraib, she "saw the situation [at Abu Ghraib] moving to the 'Bagram' model."[122] In the absence of guidance from her superiors,[123] she drew on her experience

---

[115]Ibid., p. 201.

[116]Ibid., p. 7.

[117]Ibid.

[118]Ibid. The March 2004 policy was in place until June 2004, when U.S. Central Command determined that all interrogations should be standardized under a single policy. That policy reportedly relies significantly on Army Field Manual 34–52 but has not been made public. Ibid.

[119]Fay Report, pp. 29, 40.

[120]Ibid., p. 29.

[121]Ibid., p. 28.

[122]**A-196**: Sworn statement of Captain Carolyn Wood, May 21, 2004. Wood's name is redacted from the statement but information from others sources makes clear that the statement is hers.

[123]Fay Report, p. 14 (noting that "[i]nitially, no theater-specific guidance on approved interrogation techniques was published by CJTF-7 for the ITO").

in Afghanistan.[124] But Wood soon felt "mounting pressure" from her superiors for actionable intelligence and, reacting to this pressure, she sought authority to use even more aggressive interrogation methods.[125] An officer at Abu Ghraib acquired a copy of the interrogation rules of engagement for Task Force 121 (TF-121),[126] a special operations unit that had been assigned to search for "high value" targets, including Saddam Hussein.[127] The officer, whose name is redacted from Wood's sworn statement, "plagiarized" the TF-121 interrogation rules and sent them up the chain of command for approval. When the officer did not receive a response, Wood herself submitted the rules for approval. But Wood did not receive a response, either.[128] Interrogators therefore relied on the TF-121 interrogation rules, Maj. Gen. Dunlavey's October 2002 memorandum, and the January 2003 CJTF-180 memorandum.[129] As in Afghanistan, the leadership failed to provide guidance even when interrogators in the field formally requested it, and, lacking guidance, interrogators adopted the abusive techniques that had been approved in other contexts.

The leadership's tolerance of abusive interrogation practices had foreseeable consequences. When the International Committee of the Red Cross (ICRC) visited detention facilities in Iraq in the spring and summer of 2003, it found that abuse of prisoners was pervasive. An ICRC report that was later leaked to the press stated that prisoners at detention centers in Iraq were subjected to a variety of abuses "ranging from insults and humiliation to both physical and psychological coercion that in some cases might amount to torture in order to force them to cooperate with their interrogators." At Abu Ghraib, the ICRC noted, "methods of physical and psychological coercion used by the interrogators appeared to be part of the standard operating procedures by military intelligence personnel to obtain confessions and extract information."[130] During visits to Abu Ghraib in October 2003, the ICRC met with prisoners who presented credible allegations that they had been deprived of sleep, forced to walk the corridors handcuffed and naked, and confined in stress positions.[131] Although the

---

[124]**A-196**: Sworn statement of Capt. Carolyn Wood, May 21, 2004.

[125]Ibid.

[126]Ibid.

[127]Josh White, "U.S Generals in Iraq Were Told of Abuse Early, Inquiry Finds," *Washington Post,* December 1, 2004. According to the *Washington Post,* a December 2003 report authored by retired Col. Stuart A. Herrington found that "[d]etainees captured by TF 121 have shown injuries that caused examining medical personnel to note that 'detainee shows signs of having been beaten'" and concluded that "TF 121 needs to be reined in with respect to its treatment of detainees."

[128]**A-196**: Sworn statement of Capt. Carolyn Wood, May 21, 2004.

[129]Fay Report, p. 83.

[130]*Report of the International Committee of the Red Cross on the Treatment by the Coalition Forces of Prisoners of War and Other Protected Persons by the Geneva Conventions in Iraq During Arrest, Internment and Interrogation, February 2004,* ("February 2004 ICRC Report") available at http://www.globalsecurity.org/military/library/report/2004/icrc_report_iraq_feb2004.pdf, ¶ 24.

[131]Fay Report, pp. 64–65.

ICRC formally reported its findings in November, military commanders neither investigated the allegations nor re-examined their policies with respect to the treatment of prisoners. Indeed, the only formal response that commanders provided to the ICRC was a letter signed by Brig. Gen. Janis Karpinski, who oversaw military police at Abu Ghraib from June 2003 until January 2004. Karpinski's letter, according to a military report, "tend[ed] to gloss over, close to the point of denying the inhumane treatment, humiliation, and abuse identified by the ICRC."[132]

Senior military officials did eventually issue guidance to interrogators in Iraq. When they did so, however, the guidance extended rather than limited the interrogators' authority. At the end of August 2003, Gen. Miller was dispatched to Abu Ghraib to assess interrogation and detention operations there and to make recommendations for improvements.[133] By that time, Miller had been briefed on the report of the working group that Rumsfeld had convened in January 2003; he knew that the working group had concluded that there were few legal limits on the methods that interrogators could use and he knew that the working group had endorsed a slew of extreme interrogation techniques. With that background, Miller concluded that interrogation operations at Abu Ghraib were being "hampered by [interrogators'] lack of active control of the [prisoners] within the detention environment." Miller wanted interrogators to have total control over prisoners' lives—not only during formal interrogation sessions but outside of those sessions as well. He asserted that it was "essential that the guard force be actively engaged in setting the conditions for successful exploitation" of the prisoners. "Detention operations," he argued, "must act as an enabler for interrogation."[134]

Miller gave military leaders in Iraq the list of interrogation methods that Rumsfeld had approved for use at Guantánamo,[135] and his team worked with lawyers for Combined Joint Task Force 7 (CJTF-7), the coalition force responsible for military operations in Iraq, to develop new interrogation policies for Iraq along those lines.[136] Brig. Gen. Karpinski testified in July 2004 that Miller's intention was to "Gitmo-ize" Abu Ghraib.[137] According to Col. Thomas M. Pappas, who was in charge of military intelligence personnel at Abu Ghraib, one of Miller's recommendations was that interrogators should make more aggressive use of military

---

[132]Ibid., p. 67.

[133]A-202: Sworn statement of Tiger Team member, June 4, 2004.

[134]Maj. Gen. Geoffrey Miller, *Assessment of DoD Counterterrorism Interrogation and Detention Operations in Iraq*, undated, available at http://www.aclu.org/torturefoia/released/a20.pdf.

[135]Schlesinger Report, p. 37 (noting that Miller "reportedly" gave Rumsfeld's April 2003 interrogation techniques directive to CJTF-7); Fay Report, p. 58 ("Miller's visit also introduced written GTMO documentation into the CJTF-7 environment").

[136]A-208: Sworn statement of Thomas M. Pappas, May 14, 2004. Pappas's name is redacted from the statement but information from other sources makes clear that the statement is his.

[137]A-219: Excerpt of transcript of interview with Brig. Gen. Janis Karpinski, July 18, 2004 (stating that Miller came to "Gitmo-ize" Abu Ghraib).

dogs. Guards were already using dogs to "control" prisoners outside the context of formal interrogations, but, according to Pappas, Miller thought that military working dogs would be "effective in setting the atmosphere" during interrogations as well.[138] In a sworn statement, one interrogator describes an incident in which a military guard used a dog to terrorize prisoners in a cellblock housing female and juvenile prisoners:

> The dog was a large, black, breed which appeared to be a mix of Labrador Retriever and Belgian Sheppard. It was the only black working dog at [Abu Ghraib]. The dog was on a leash, but was not muzzled. The MP guard and MP Dog Handler opened a cell in which two juveniles, one known as "Casper," were housed. The Dog Handler allowed the dog to enter the cell and go nuts on the kids, barking and scaring them. The kids were screaming, the smaller one hiding behind ***.[139]

This incident took place in late 2003 or early 2004, soon after Miller's visit to Abu Ghraib.[140]

It is important to recognize that the plan to "Gitmo-ize" Abu Ghraib was not Miller's alone. Miller was sent to Abu Ghraib with the "encouragement" of Stephen Cambone, undersecretary of defense for intelligence, under the "auspices" of the Joint Chiefs of Staff.[141] After he left Abu Ghraib, Miller sent Southern Command a written report about his activities. Miller told the Senate Armed Services Committee in May 2004 that he did not brief senior officials about his activities or recommendations,[142] but he later contradicted that testimony, acknowledging that he had briefed both Deputy Defense Secretary Paul Wolfowitz and Undersecretary for Intelligence Stephen Cambone.[143] Miller's project plainly had the support of senior officials, both military and civilian.

Indeed, after Miller left Abu Ghraib, the Defense Department dispatched "Tiger Teams" of analysts and interrogators from Guantánamo Bay to implement Miller's recommendations; these teams were at Abu Ghraib in the fall of 2003.[144] Other teams were sent from Fort Huachuca, Arizona, specifically to train interrogators.[145] Both the Guantánamo Tiger

---

[138]Fay Report, p. 58.

[139]**A-222**: Sworn statement of military interrogator, May 24, 2004.

[140]Ibid.

[141]Testimony of Stephen Cambone, Hearing of the Senate Armed Services Committee on the Treatment of Iraqi Prisoners, May 11, 2004, available at 2004 WL 1053885 (F.D.C.H.); Fay Report, p. 57.

[142]Testimony of Maj. Gen. Geoffrey Miller, Hearing of the Senate Armed Services Committee on the Treatment of Iraqi Prisoners, May 19, 2004, available at 2004 WL 1113660 (F.D.C.H.) ("I submitted the report up to SOUTHCOM. I had no direct discussions with Secretary Cambone or General Boykin.").

[143]Mark Benjamin, "Not so fast, General," *Salon*, March 7, 2006; Mark Benjamin and Michael Scherer, "A Miller Whitewash?," *Salon*, April 25, 2006.

[144]**A-202**: Sworn statement of Tiger Team member, June 4, 2004; **A-209**: Sworn statement of Thomas M. Pappas, May 14, 2004.

[145]Fay Report, p. 62; **A-209**: Sworn Statement of Thomas M. Pappas, May 14, 2004; **A-225**: Sworn statement of interrogator from Fort Huachuca, June 30, 2004. In September 2003, a team from JPRA was sent to train TF 20, a special missions unit operating in Iraq, in the use of SERE techniques. DOD IG Report, p. 28.

Teams and the Fort Huachuca teams pressed interrogators in Iraq to use more aggressive methods. The Fort Huachuca teams instructed interrogators in the use of "strategies outside the ones mentioned in [Field Manual] 34–52" and briefed personnel at Abu Ghraib about interrogation techniques—such as "sleep management" and the use of military working dogs to intimidate prisoners—that had been applied in Afghanistan.[146] One member of the Fort Huachuca team instructed a civilian contractor that "fear works to the interrogator's advantage" and that "[t]he more comfortable a detainee gets with his surroundings, the stronger his resistance becomes." He suggested the possibility of frightening prisoners by showing them photographs of "what appeared to be [military police] in intimidating positions with the detainees." He also told the civilian contractor of an incident in which military interrogators in Afghanistan, intending to humiliate a prisoner, had thrown a Qu'ran on the floor and stepped on it. The Fort Huachuca interrogator stated that the technique was a variant of "pride and ego down," a technique authorized by the Army Field Manual.[147]

Miller's recommendations ultimately led Army Lt. Gen. Ricardo S. Sanchez, who was then the commander of coalition forces in Iraq, to issue a directive formally authorizing interrogators to use techniques beyond those listed in the Field Manual. The directive, issued on September 14, 2003, was informed by the working group report that had been commissioned by Rumsfeld for Guantánamo,[148] but purported to be "modified for applicability to a theater of war in which the Geneva Conventions apply."[149] Of the twenty-nine methods authorized by Sanchez's directive, some were similar to those listed in the Field Manual—these included "pride and ego down," "futility," and "fear up harsh"[150]—but the directive also authorized the use of twelve methods beyond those endorsed by the Field Manual. For example, it authorized interrogators to isolate prisoners for extended

---

[146]Fay Report, p. 63.

[147]**A-226**: Sworn statement of interrogator from Fort Huachuca, June 30, 2004. Military interrogators at Guantánamo appear to have used similar methods. In April 2002, one prisoner told his FBI interrogators that "some of the detainees are feeling that they have nothing to lose and are waiting for a time to cry out." The prisoner said that military police "ha[d] been mistreating the detainees by pushing them around and throwing their waste bucket to them in the cell, sometimes with waste still in the bucket and kicking the Koran." **A-228**: FBI summary of interview with prisoner held at Guantánamo. A later military investigation confirmed five incidents in which military personnel "mishandled" the Qu'ran. See Josh White and Dan Eggen, "Pentagon Confirms Koran Incidents: 'Mishandling' Cases Preceded Guidelines Established in 2003," *Washington Post*, May 27, 2005. In a January 2003 interview summary, a prisoner asserts that suicide attempts by prisoners at Guantánamo were partly a consequence of guards "humiliating" the Qu'ran. **A-230**: FBI summary of interview with prisoner held at Guantánamo. Thirty prisoners attempted suicide between the months of January and August 2002. See "Guantánamo Bay Suicide Attempts," CBS News, August 15, 2002.

[148]Fay Report, p. 14.

[149]**A-231**: Interrogation directive issued by Lieutenant General Ricardo S. Sanchez, September 14, 2003.

[150]Ibid.

periods, to subject them to "stress positions and extreme temperatures, and to deprive them of sleep. It also authorized interrogators to "exploit [ ] Arab fear of dogs" and to deceive prisoners into believing that they were being interrogated by foreign intelligence services.[151]

Central Command objected to the September directive,[152] presumably because of concerns about its lawfulness. As a result, the directive was revised in October 2003.[153] The new directive, issued on October 12, hewed more closely to the Field Manual. It appears that no effort was made, however, to enforce the new directive. On October 16, Capt. Carolyn Wood—one of the interrogators who had come to Abu Ghraib from Afghanistan—created a chart, labeled "Interrogation Rules of Engagement," ostensibly meant to help interrogators understand the differences between the September and October directives. However, the chart failed even to mention some of the techniques that interrogators were using at the time—techniques such as forcibly stripping prisoners, hooding them, bombarding them with loud music, and depriving them of light. As a later military investigation noted, "the failure to list some techniques left a question of whether they were authorized for use without approval."[154]

Commanders in the field also failed to oversee the use of interrogation techniques approved by the Army Field Manual. As the Field Manual itself acknowledges, whether or not the Field Manual techniques conform to the Geneva Conventions depends entirely on how the techniques are implemented. This is particularly true of techniques such as "pride and ego down" and "futility," which can easily become degrading, and "fear up harsh," which can readily become coercive or even violent. The Field Manual acknowledges forthrightly that, of all the methods authorized by the manual, the fear up harsh method "has the greatest potential to violate the law of war."[155] Notably, it was on the basis of "pride and ego down" and "futility" that interrogators at Guantánamo stripped Mohammed al-Qahtani naked, subjected him to repeat strip searches, forced him to wear women's underwear on his head, led him around a room on a dog leash, and forced him to perform dog tricks.[156] The perception that such methods were authorized, combined with the understanding that military

---

[151]**A-234–235**: Interrogation directive issued by Lt. Gen. Ricardo S. Sanchez, September 14, 2003. As noted above, in 2006 the Army replaced Field Manual 34–52 with Field Manual 2–22.3. One notable difference between the two manuals is that the new manual, unlike its predecessor, expressly authorizes interrogators to use an approach called "false flag," the goal of which "is to convince the detainee that individuals from a country other than the United States are interrogating him." However, the new manual prohibits interrogators from using "implied or explicit threats that non-cooperation will result in harsh interrogation by non-US entities." Army Field Manual 2–22.3 (2006), Human Intelligence Collector Operations, ch. 8, pp. 8–18.

[152]**A-208**: Sworn statement of Thomas M. Pappas, May 14, 2004.

[153]**A-238**: Interrogation directive issued by Lieutenant General Sanchez, October 12, 2003.

[154]Fay Report, p. 28.

[155]Army Field Manual 34–52 (1992), ch. 3, pp. 3–16.

[156]**A-112–113**: Schmidt-Furlow Report.

police were expected to "set the conditions" for fruitful interrogations,[157] is almost certainly what led military police to use these methods on prisoners at Abu Ghraib.

Because neither civilian nor military leaders effectively enforced the October 2003 directive, interrogators in Iraq also continued to use methods from the invalidated September 2003 directive. In November 2003, interrogators in Iraq killed Abed Hamed Mowhoush, a fifty-six-year-old Iraqi general, during an interrogation in which they put him into a sleeping bag and tied him up with electrical cord. An autopsy report states:

> This 56 year-old Iraqi detainee died of asphyxia due to smothering and chest compression. Significant findings of the autopsy included rib fractures and numerous contusions (bruises), some of which were patterned due to impacts with a blunt object(s). . . . [T]he history surrounding the death along with patterned contusions and broken ribs support a traumatic cause of death and therefore the manner of death is best classified as homicide.[158]

An Army officer reprimanded for Mowhoush's death asserted that the "sleeping bag technique" was a "stress position" that he considered to have been authorized by a September 10, 2003 "CJTF-7 Interrogation and Counter-Resistance Policy"—presumably a draft of Sanchez's September 14, 2003 interrogation directive—and that "[i]n SERE, this position is called close confinement and can be very effective."[159] While the September 2003 directive authorized the use of stress positions, the October directive, which superseded it, did not.

Special forces units in Iraq were similarly permitted to employ interrogation techniques that were nominally prohibited by the governing interrogation directives. An investigation conducted by Brig. Gen. Richard Formica found that, between February and May 2004, special forces in Iraq subjected prisoners to stress positions, confined them in extreme temperatures (under the rubric of "environmental manipulation"), stripped them naked during interrogations, bombarded them with deafeningly loud music, and fed them only bread and water.[160] Formica's report states that interrogators used the "environmental manipulation" technique "in accordance with the superseded" September 14, 2003 policy, which they "believed to be in effect."[161] The report also suggests that the use of that technique—one variant of which involved soaking prisoners with cold

---

[157]Maj. Gen. Antonio M. Taguba, *Article 15-6 Investigation of the 800th Military Police Brigade*, submitted on February 26, 2004 ("Taguba Report"), available at http://www.aclu.org/torturefoia/released/TR3.pdf, p. 18.

[158]**A-245**: Autopsy examination report, December 18, 2003. Mowhoush's name is redacted but information from other sources makes clear that the report relates to him.

[159]**A-246–247**: Army memorandum re CW3 Lewis E. Welshofer Jr., February 11, 2004.

[160]Brig. Gen. Richard P. Formica, *Article 15-6 Investigation of CJSOTF-AP and 5th SF Group Detention Operations*, released to the ACLU on June 15, 2006 ("Formica Report"), available at http://action.aclu.org/torturefoia/released/061906/FormicaReport.pdf, pp. 73–74.

[161]Formica Report, p. 73. Special forces also used methods listed in the January 2003 CJTF memorandum. DOD IG Report, p. 15.

water and then confining them in freezing-cold cells—might have led to the death of a prisoner in April 2004.[162] An autopsy report supports the theory that the prisoner died because as a result of "environmental manipulation." The report relates to the death in Mosul, Iraq, of a twenty-seven-year-old Iraqi male who had been hooded, flex-cuffed, deprived of sleep, washed down with cold water, and subjected to extreme temperatures. Although the report states that the exact cause of death was "undetermined," it lists hypothermia as a possible contributing factor.[163] A related document notes that the prisoner had been interrogated by Navy Seals and states, cryptically, that the prisoner "struggled/interrogated/died sleeping."[164]

Thus, the October 2003 directive did not curtail the use of abusive interrogation methods; it had little practical effect because the chain of command made little or no effort to police its implementation.[165] When supervising officials did focus on the methods being used by interrogators, they expanded interrogators' authority. One investigative file relates to the detention and interrogation of three individuals who were apprehended together with Saddam Hussein. The file refers to a document titled "Exception to CJTF-7 Interrogation and Counter-Resistance Policy, 14 Dec 03, authorizing pre-approved interrogation approaches for the three detainees captured in conjunction with Saddam Hussein on 13 Dec 03."[166] While this December 2003 interrogation directive is still being withheld by the Defense Department, a sworn statement of a military interrogator explains that "when Saddam was captured, a new section called special projects was developed" and that the new section was informed that, for high-value prisoners, interrogators "already had LTG Sanchez's approval for the use of [interrogation methods that] included sleep deprivation, dietary manipulation, use of guard dogs, sensory deprivation, stress positions etc."[167]

The government's documents thus belie the claim that the abuse of prisoners in Afghanistan and Iraq was attributable to rogue soldiers. The documents show that senior officials—military and civilian—tolerated the abuse, encouraged it, and sometimes expressly authorized it. If the abuse in the Abu Ghraib photographs was aberrational, it was aberrational only in that it was captured on film and made known to the public. But the documents make clear that the abuse of prisoners was the result of decisions made at the very highest levels of the U.S. government.

---

[162]Formica Report, pp. 74–75, n. 31.

[163]**A-250**: Final autopsy report, November 22, 2004.

[164]**A-253**: Detainee autopsy summary, September 23, 2004.

[165]Fay Report, p. 28.

[166]CID Report of Investigation, July 31, 2005, ("July 31, 2005 ROI") available at http://www.aclu.org/projects/foiasearch/pdf/DOD049684.pdf, at DOD 049686.

[167]July 31, 2005 ROI at DOD 049713.

The fact that the Abu Ghraib photographs depicted abuse at a single prison allowed senior administration officials to claim, as they did repeatedly, that the abuse was confined to that facility. This claim was completely false, and senior officials almost certainly knew it to be so. A Defense Department "Information Paper" shows that, three weeks before the Abu Ghraib photographs were leaked to the press, Army leaders were aware of at least sixty-two allegations of prisoner abuse in Afghanistan and Iraq, most of which did not relate to Abu Ghraib. Investigators had already substantiated allegations relating to physical assaults, death threats, and mock executions. Of the sixty-two allegations enumerated in the April 2004 Information Paper, twenty-six related to prisoner deaths, and, according to the Defense Department's own investigators, fourteen of these deaths could not be attributed to natural causes.[168]

In fact, the abuse captured in the Abu Ghraib photographs was far from isolated. The same kind of abuse, and indeed much worse, was inflicted on prisoners at detention facilities throughout Afghanistan and Iraq. The documents supply countless examples—far too many to catalogue here. One navy document describes a "substantiated" incident in which marines in Al Mahmudiya, Iraq, electrocuted one prisoner and set another's hands on fire.[169] Another document—the report of a soldier recently returned from Samarra, Iraq—describes incidents in which soldiers strangled prisoners and placed lit cigarettes in their ears.[170] In a sworn statement, a private contractor who worked with military intelligence in Iraq states that there were approximately ninety incidents of abuse at Al Asamiya Palace, another detention facility in Baghdad. According to the contractor, some of the prisoners "were abused with cigarette burns and electric shocks."[171] A report issued in February 2006 by Human Rights First found that nearly one hundred prisoners had died in U.S. custody since August 2002 and that, of these deaths, thirty-four had been classified by military investigators as suspected or confirmed homicides.[172] Autopsy reports obtained by the ACLU attribute numerous deaths to "strangulation,"[173] "asphyxia,"[174]

---

[168]**A-260–264**: Information Paper, April 2, 2004.

[169]**A-273–274**: USMC alleged detainee abuse cases, June 16, 2004.

[170]**A-280**: FBI urgent report, June 25, 2004.

[171]**A-283**: Sworn statement of contractor stationed at Abu Ghraib.

[172]Hina Shamsi, "Command's Responsibility: Detainee Deaths in U.S. Custody in Iraq and Afghanistan," February 2006, p. 1. Available at http://www.humarights first.info/pdf/06221/-etn-hrf-dic-rep-web.pdf.

[173]**A-284**: Final autopsy report, October 22, 2003.

[174]**A-286**: Excerpt from final autopsy report, April 30, 2004; **A-244**: Autopsy examination report, December 18, 2003.

and "blunt force injuries."[175] An autopsy report relating to a forty-seven-year-old prisoner killed by U.S. personnel at a detention center in Baghdad describes a death that might as easily have taken place in Saddam Hussein's Iraq:

> This 47-year old White male . . . died of blunt force injuries and asphyxia. The autopsy disclosed multiple blunt force injuries, including deep contusions of the chest wall, numerous displaced rib fractures, lung contusions, and hemorrhage into the mesentery of the small and large intestine. . . . According to the investigative report provided by U.S. Army CID "[Criminal Investigation Division"], the decedent was shackled to the top of a doorframe with a gag in his mouth at the time he lost consciousness and became pulseless.
>   The severe blunt force injuries, the hanging position, and the obstruction of the oral cavity with a gag contributed to this individual's death. The manner of death is homicide.[176]

Incidents of this kind cannot be traced directly to publicly available interrogation orders issued by senior civilian or military officials. So far as we know, no senior official directed soldiers to electrocute prisoners, to strangle them, to beat them, to hang them by their arms, or to burn them with cigarettes. But though the interrogation directives issued by Rumsfeld and Sanchez authorized only certain kinds of abuse, they conveyed the message that abuse was acceptable, and they created a climate in which more extreme abuse was foreseeable.

In his memorandum for the navy inspector general, Navy General Counsel Alberto Mora discusses a phenomenon called "force drift." The phrase refers to the danger that "once [an] initial barrier against the use of improper force [has] been breached," the force used to extract information "will continue to escalate." Interrogators permitted to use *some* force, Mora writes, tend ultimately to use *more* force. If the progression is left unchecked, the application of force can readily become the application of torture.[177] Something like this phenomenon took place among Defense Department interrogators. Perhaps senior officials meant to authorize only specific, enumerated types of abuse, but this was certainly not the message heard by interrogators. Without clear statements

---

[175]**A-186**: Final postmorterm report, December 8, 2002; **A-187**: Autopsy examination report, February 25, 2003; **A-288**: Final autopsy report, November 13, 2003; **A-286**: Final autopsy report, April 30, 2004; **A-313**: Final autopsy report, January 9, 2004. All of the autopsy and death reports obtained by the ACLU are catalogued at http://action.aclu.org/torturefoia released/102405.

[176]**A-287**: Final autopsy report, April 30, 2004.

[177]Mora Memorandum, p. 4. The State Department's general counsel, William Howard Taft IV, made a similar point in a March 2005 speech. The conclusion that the Geneva Conventions did not apply, he said, "unhinged those responsible for the treatment of the detainees in Guantánamo from the legal guidelines for interrogation of detainees reflected in the Conventions and embodied in the Army Field Manual for decades. Set adrift in uncharted waters and under pressure from their leaders to develop information on the plans and practices of al Qaeda, it was predictable that those managing the interrogation would eventually go too far." William Howard Taft IV, remarks at American University, Washington College of Law, March 24, 2005, quoted in Joseph Margulies, *Guantánamo and the Abuse of Presidential Power* (2006), p. 232.

of the distinction between permissible and impermissible methods, interrogators seem to have understood only that prisoners could be abused. Interrogators gave effect to that message at Guantánamo, in Afghanistan, and in Iraq.

It was entirely foreseeable that interrogators, especially those who were not trained in the legal standards governing prisoner treatment, would interpret the directives broadly, and indeed would test the limits of their authority. But rather than attempt to check the escalation of force, civilian and military leaders encouraged it—sometimes tacitly, sometimes expressly. When Secretary Rumsfeld signed the December 2002 interrogation directive, for example, he added this handwritten note: "I stand for 8–10 hours a day. Why is standing limited to 4 hours?" Mora later observed that, while he believed the note was meant to be "jocular," the note could be interpreted as "a written nod-and-a-wink to interrogators to the effect that they should not feel bound by the limits set by the memo, but consider themselves authorized to do what was necessary to obtain the necessary information."[178] The White House sent similar signals, only more bluntly. In a September 2001 press interview, Vice President Dick Cheney stated that U.S. intelligence personnel would have to "work . . . sort of the dark side, if you will" and that it would be "vital" for them "to use any means at [their] disposal, basically, to achieve [their] objective." "[W]e need to make certain that we have not tied the hands . . . of our intelligence communities," he said. "It is a mean, nasty, dangerous dirty business out there, and we have to operate in that arena."[179] In an October 2006 interview, Cheney endorsed the use of "water boarding," a practice that involves subjecting prisoners to near drowning. Cheney termed the practice a "no brainer."[180]

The administration message was heard clearly at Guantánamo and in Iraq and Afghanistan. In Iraq, an officer who led a team of interrogators states that Lieutenant General Sanchez encouraged interrogators to "go to the outer limits" to obtain information and that "Headquarters" pressed interrogators to "break" the prisoners.[181] In August 2003, military interrogators in Iraq were informed that the "gloves are coming off," that prisoners were to be "broken," and that the interrogators should propose "wish lists" of "effective" interrogation techniques for review.[182] Instructions

---

[178]Mora Memorandum, p. 8.

[179]Transcript, "The Vice President appears on Meet the Press with Tim Russert," September 16, 2001. Available at http://www.whitehouse.gov/vicepresident/news-speeches/speeches/vp 20010916.html.

[180]Jonathan S. Landey, "Cheney Confirms That Detainees Were Subjected To Water-boarding," McClatchy Newspapers, October 25, 2006.

[181]**A-291**: Defense Intelligence Agency "Report of Conversation," May 19, 2004. Sanchez has denied that he ever used the phrase "outer limits." Joseph L. Galloway, "U.S. General Defends His Adherence To Geneva Conventions In Iraq," Knight Ridder, May 5, 2006.

[182]**A-308**: E-mail stating that "the gloves are coming off," August 14, 2003.

of this kind were understood as a green light for even more aggressive methods.[183] Thus, one response to the "wish list" solicitation read:

> Today['s] enemy . . . understand force, not psychological mind games or incentives. I would propose a baseline interrogation technique that at a minimum allows for physical contact resembling that used by SERE instructors. This allows open handed facial slaps from a distance of no more than about two feet and back handed blows to the midsection from a distance of about 18 inches. Again, this is open handed. I will not comment on the effectiveness of these techniques as both a control measure and an ability to send a clear message. I also believe that this should be a minimum baseline.
>
> Other techniques would include close confinement quarters, sleep deprivation, white noise, and a litany of harsher fear-up approaches . . . fear of dogs and snakes appear to work nicely. I firmly agree that the gloves need to come off.[184]

Other interrogators responding to the "wish list" solicitation sought approval to use, among other techniques, "phone book strikes," "muscle fatigue inducement," "close quarter confinement," and even "low voltage electrocution."[185]

By endorsing some abusive techniques, the chain of command opened the door to others. Some prisoners were forced to perform "ups and downs" in extreme temperatures, sometimes to the point of exhaustion. (An investigative report describes "ups and downs" as a "correctional technique of having a detainee stand up and then sit down rapidly, over and over, always keeping them in constant motion.")[186] A Titan Corporation interpreter stationed at Abu Ghraib recalls seeing a female U.S. soldier make a prisoner clothed in only his underwear "jump up and down and then roll left to right on the ground in what he believed to be a 150 degree Fahrenheit temperature." This went on for about twenty minutes. Afterwards, the prisoner collapsed several times and would vomit every time he attempted to drink water.[187]

Signals from senior military leaders fueled the perception among military personnel that abuse of prisoners was sanctioned at high levels. One file relates to an interrogator in Tikrit who subjected a prisoner to stress positions and beat him with a riot baton.[188] In a signed statement, the staff sergeant who supervised the interrogator criticizes his superiors for having created a "command climate" in which abuse was accepted. He

---

[183]The CIA conveyed similar signals to its agents. See, e.g., Dana Priest and Barton Gellman, "U.S. Decries Abuse but Defends Interrogations": "'Stress and Duress' Tactics Used on Terrorism Suspects Held in Secret Overseas Facilities," *Washington Post*, December 26, 2002 (quoting a CIA official about the interrogation of terrorism suspects: "[I]f you don't violate someone's human rights some of the time, you probably aren't doing your job.").

[184]**A-307**: E-mail responding to request for proposed interrogation techniques, August 14, 2003.

[185]**A-309**: Document titled, "Alternative Interrogation Techniques (Wish List)," undated.

[186]Memorandum for Record re Article 15-6 Investigation into the Death of Abu Malik Kenami, December 28, 2003 ("Kenami File"). Available at http://www.aclu.org/projects/foiasearch/pdf/DODDOA026695.pdf at DODDOA 026695, DODDOA 026698.

[187]**A-312**: Agent's investigative report, June 6, 2004.

[188]**A-310–311**: Sworn statement of prisoner beaten with riot baton during interrogation, October 1, 2003.

refers in particular to the "wish list" solicitation and to the practice of seizing and imprisoning innocent Iraqis as "hostages" to use as leverage against their families—a practice that he suggests was routine.[189] "In hind-sight," he writes, "it seems clear that, considering the seeming approval of these and other tactics by the senior command, it is a short jump of the imagination that allows actions such as those committed by [the interro-gator] to become not only tolerated but encouraged."[190] An army investi-gator reached the same conclusion. "Reference[s] to 'gloves coming off,'" the investigator writes, led interrogators to believe that the chain of com-mand "wanted suggestions of less-than-ethical or less-than-legal nature." The interrogator who beat the prisoner with a riot baton "likely read [these] statements as an endorsement of more violent interrogation methods," the army investigator writes.[191]

An additional problem, at least in Iraq, was that senior civilian and military officials sent conflicting signals concerning the legal status of the prisoners. Administration officials publicly stated that the Geneva Conventions were "fully applicable" in Iraq,[192] and Sanchez's September 2003 interrogation directive took the same position, characterizing Iraq (in contrast to Guantánamo) as a "theater of war in which the Geneva Conventions apply."[193] But according to an investigative report released to the ACLU, soldiers in Iraq were told that the prisoners "are not EPWs [enemy prisoners of war]. They are terrorists and [should] be treated as such."[194] And in a December 2003 letter to the International Committee of the Red Cross, Brig. Gen. Janis Karpinksi, who then commanded the military police at Abu Ghraib, insisted that the Geneva Conventions did not protect "security detainees," a vaguely defined class of prisoners that included those thought to have "significant intelligence value."[195]

Commanders' insistence that not all prisoners were entitled to the protections of the Geneva Conventions led some interrogators to conclude that they could employ methods beyond those contemplated by the Field Manual—and beyond those contemplated by formal interrogation directives.[196] Chief Warrant Officer Lewis E. Welshofer Jr., who was accused of killing Maj. Gen. Abed Hamed Mowhoush by confining him in a sleeping bag and suffocating him to death, defended his actions in this way: "I do not believe interrogation guidelines set forth by CJTF-7 were

---

[189]The CIA is reported to have employed the same method. Olga Craig, "We Have Your Sons: CIA," *Sunday Telegraph*, March 10, 2003.

[190]**A-294**: Supervisor's rebuttal to written reprimand, November 9, 2003.

[191]**A-302**: Memorandum for record concerning Article 15-6 investigation, October 6, 2003.

[192]Douglas Jehl and Neil A. Lewis, "U.S. Disputed Protected Status of Iraq Inmates," *New York Times*, May 23, 2004.

[193]**A-231**: Interrogation directive issued by Lieutenant General Ricardo S. Sanchez, September 14, 2003.

[194]**A-294**: Supervisor's rebuttal to written reprimand, November 9, 2003.

[195]Douglas Jehl and Neil A. Lewis, "U.S. Disputed Protected Status of Iraq Inmates," *New York Times*, May 23, 2004.

[196]**A-294**: Supervisor's rebuttal to written reprimand, November 9, 2003.

written with sufficient understanding of the type of people we are interrogating in Iraq. While current guidelines do mimic rules set forth by the Geneva Convention for questioning Prisoners of War, these guidelines do not clearly address unlawful combatants."[197]

Also contributing to military interrogators' willingness to use extreme methods was the fact that CIA interrogators were using such methods. Very little is publicly known about the CIA's activities in Iraq;—the agency's prisoners at Abu Ghraib were known as "Ghost Detainees," because they were unidentified and unaccounted for,[198] and the CIA continues to resist disclosure under the Freedom of Information Act. One autopsy report that has been released to the ACLU, however, concerns Manadel al-Jamadi, an Iraqi who was captured in Baghdad and died in American custody only hours later. According to news reports, al-Jamadi was suspected of having been involved in an attack on the al-Rashid Hotel during a visit by Deputy Secretary of Defense Paul Wolfowitz in October 2003.[199] Navy SEALS captured him on November 4 and then turned him over to the CIA. During his interrogation by the CIA, al-Jamadi was stripped and doused with cold water and his wrists were shackled behind him and fastened to window bars.[200] According to the autopsy report, al-Jamadi's death was a "homicide" caused by "blunt force injuries compli-cated by compromised respiration." The report also states that "individuals present at the prison during [al-Jamadi's] interrogation indicate that a hood made of synthetic material was placed over the head and neck of the detainee," which further compromised his respiration.[201] A high-level military investigation later found that "CIA detention and interrogation practices led to a loss of accountability, abuse, reduced interagency cooperation, and an unhealthy mystique that further poisoned the atmosphere at Abu Ghraib."[202]

One safeguard against the kind of abuse that took place at detention facilities in Afghanistan and Iraq would ordinarily have been supplied by Article 143 of the Fourth Geneva Convention, which provides that the International Committee of the Red Cross "shall have access to all premises occupied by protected persons and shall be able to interview the latter with-out witnesses, personally or through an interpreter . . . except for reasons of imperative military necessity, and then only as an exceptional and tempo-rary measure." When the ICRC sought to visit Abu Ghraib in January and March 2004, however, Colonel Pappas and Colonel Warren, the staff judge advocate for CJTF-7, invoked the "imperative military necessity" clause to

---

[197]**A-247**: Statement of CWO Lewis E. Welshofer Jr., Feb. 11, 2004.
[198]Fay Report, p. 9.
[199]See John McChesney, "The Death of an Iraqi Prisoner," National Public Radio broadcast, October 27, 2005, available at http://www.npr.org/templates/story/story.php?storyId=4977986.
[200]Ibid.
[201]**A-313–314**: Excerpt from final autopsy report, January 9, 2004. Al-Jamadi's name is redacted but information from other sources makes clear that the report relates to him.
[202]Fay Report, pp. 52–53.

prevent the ICRC from gaining access to several prisoners. In particular, they repeatedly denied the ICRC access to a prisoner who, according to a subsequent investigation, "had been under interrogation for some four months," had been "abused by the use of dogs," and "was detained in a totally darkened cell measuring about 2 meters long and less than a meter across, devoid of any window, latrine or water tap, or bedding."[203]

What did senior military and civilian officials believe was being accomplished by the infliction of such abuse? Administration officials have sometimes sought to justify aggressive interrogation methods by contending that the prisoners are hardened terrorists who have "actionable intelligence"—that is, crucial and time-sensitive information that could be used to prevent imminent attacks. As the ICRC learned when it gained access to the detention facilities, however, many of the prisoners abused by U.S. forces in Iraq had no connection with terrorism or with the insurgency. According to one ICRC report, coalition military intelligence officials estimated that 70 to 90 percent of prisoners detained in Iraq since the beginning of the war "had been arrested by mistake."[204] The government's documents corroborate the ICRC finding. One military commander stationed at Abu Ghraib states:

> It became obvious to me that the majority of our detainees were detained as the result of being in the wrong place at the wrong time, and were swept up by Coalition Forces as peripheral bystanders during raids. I think perhaps only one in ten security detainees were of any particular intelligence value.[205]

In another document, a sergeant assigned to the "Detainee Assessment Board" responsible for screening detainees for release at Abu Ghraib states that "85% to 90% of detainees were of either no intelligence value or were of value but innocent and therefore should [ ] not have remained in captivity."[206] Some of the prisoners were children who appeared to be as young as eight years old. Brigadier General Karpinski, former commander of the 800th Military Police Battalion in Iraq, describes an encounter with one juvenile prisoner at Abu Ghraib: "I saw a kid . . . [who] looked like he was 8 years old. He told me he was almost 12. I asked him where he was from. He told me his brother was there with him, but he really wanted to see his mother, could he please call his mother."[207] In some cases, U.S. forces detained children as leverage against their parents. One interrogator describes an attempt to "break" a prisoner known as "the General":

> When I arrived at Abu Ghraib, I asked to speak to the GENERAL. . . . Some interrogators told me . . . that I could not interrogate the GENERAL because he

---

[203]Fay Report, p. 66.

[204]February 2004 ICRC Report, p. 8, ¶ 7.

[205]**A-316**: Sworn statement of former commander of the 320th Military Police Battalion, May 26, 2004.

[206]**A-317**: Sworn statement of sergeant assigned to the "Detainee Assessment Board," May 18, 2004.

[207]**A-318**: Transcript of interview with Brig. Gen. Janis Karpinski, July 18, 2004.

had just endured a 14-hour interrogation and had been broken. They did not want me to jeopardize their interrogations. I was told that the GENERAL was very concerned about his son due to his age, 17 yrs old. The interrogators . . . took his son and got him wet. They then put mud on his face and drove him around in the back of the Humvee. The boy was very cold. They placed the son in an area where his father could observe him. The GENERAL thought he was going to get to see his son but they just allowed him to see his son shivering and this broke the GENERAL.[208]

There is no indication in the file that the General's 17-year-old son was suspected of having been involved in the insurgency.

Most of the prisoners who were abused had no discernible connection to terrorism or the insurgency. Military personnel, however, operated in an environment in which the abuse of prisoners was accepted as standard practice, even outside the interrogation context. According to one document, "officers and NCOs [noncommissioned officers] at point of capture engaged in interrogations using techniques they literally remembered from movies."[209] Repeatedly, practices that should have been recognized as abusive were accepted as appropriate and routine. A Defense Department memorandum about "Detainees' Basic Rights" under the Geneva Conventions and army regulations states that "[s]ecuring detainees in a cement cell with dimensions of 4 feet long, 3.10 feet high, and 1.5 feet wide secured by a sliding metal door is acceptable for a short duration not to exceed 24 hours."[210] Not surprisingly, a subsequent investigation found that special operations forces in Iraq kept prisoners in "small cells measuring 20 inches (wide) x 4 feet (high) x 4 feet (deep)" while bombarding them with loud music.[211] The same report also found that some prisoners "were fed primarily a diet of bread and water," and that one prisoner was kept on that diet for 17 days."[212]

The abuse of prisoners was considered normal. A Navy corpsman describes a process whereby Iraqis classified as enemy prisoners of war would be taken to an empty swimming pool and handcuffed and leg-cuffed, hooded with burlap bags, and made to kneel for up to twenty-four hours awaiting interrogation. After furnishing this description, the corpsman states that he "never saw any instances of physical abuse."[213] Similarly, a sergeant stationed at Abu Ghraib recalls that the photograph of a hooded prisoner handcuffed to a railing reminded him of another prisoner he had seen in the same position; he states that he did not report the incident because it was common practice to "park" a prisoner in this fashion if the prisoner could not immediately be returned

---

[208]**A-319**: Privacy Act statement of military interrogator, May 13, 2005.
[209]Memorandum for Chief re Army Inspector General investigation, undated. Available at http://www.aclu.org/projects/foiasearch/pdf/DOD015937.pdf, at DOD 15973.
[210]**A-322**: Memorandum for record, June 15, 2004.
[211]Formica Report, p. 45.
[212]Formica Report, p. 33.
[213]**A-323**: Navy Criminal Investigative Service memo, October 7, 2003.

to his cell.[214] Another sergeant stationed at Abu Ghraib states: "While in the Hard Site, we saw the [military police] had two detainees in the middle of the cell. They were naked with a bag over their head, standing on MRE boxes and their hand spread out each holding a bottle in each hand. I asked if this was right. I was told . . . that this was the [military police's] way of disciplining detainees and that it was normal."[215]

If commanders disapproved of such abuses, they expended little effort to stop them. In one document, a soldier stationed at Camp Red in Baghdad states that he observed prisoners subjected to prolonged hooding, exposure to the elements, and excessive restraints. "I saw what I think were war crimes," he says. "[The] chain of command . . . allowed them to happen."[216] Similarly, a psychological assessment conducted as part of a military investigation into the root causes of abuse at Abu Ghraib faults the chain of command for creating an "I can get away with this" mentality. The report states, "detainee abuse was common knowledge among the enlisted soldiers at Abu Ghraib," and that "[a]buse with sexual themes . . . occurred and was witnessed, condoned, and photographed, but never reported." It adds that "officers witnessed abuse on several occasions or had knowledge of abuse" and that "the [Military Intelligence] unit seemed to be operating in a conspiracy of silence."[217]

Contributing to the same climate was the failure of some commanders—and of the Defense Department—seriously to investigate the abuse of prisoners. While some investigations were conducted professionally, many others were not. Investigations were closed summarily, with investigators having failed to interview key witnesses, ask obvious questions, and follow up on leads. In other cases, investigators overlooked or disregarded inconsistencies between the statements of key witnesses. In still other cases, investigators simply ignored evidence corroborating the allegations of abuse.

The failure of investigators seriously to investigate abuses seems to have been a particularly common problem with respect to abuses alleged to have been perpetrated by special forces. One investigative file obtained by the ACLU relates to the detention of a man who sold ice to U.S. forces in Tikrit. The prisoner alleged that, in the fall of 2003, Americans dressed in civilian clothing beat his head and stomach, dislocated his arms, broke his nose, forced an unloaded pistol into his mouth and pulled the trigger, and choked him with a rope.[218] He alleged that he had been beaten so severely

---

[214]**A-324**: Sworn statement of sergeant stationed at Abu Ghraib, May 23, 2004.

[215]**A-329**: Privacy Act statement of sergeant stationed at Abu Ghraib, May 18, 2004.

[216]**A-331**: Sworn statement of soldier stationed at Camp Red, Baghdad, November 14, 2003.

[217]"AR 15-6 Investigation—Allegations of Detainee Abuse at Abu Ghraib, Psychological Assessment," undated, pp. 2–3. Available at http://www.aclu.org/torturefoia/released/t1.pdf.

[218]**A-333**: Agent's investigative report, October 22, 2003; **A-334–335**: Handwitten statement of prisoner alleging abuse, undated.

that he urinated blood.[219] A criminal investigation was initiated "some 40 days after" the prisoner's capture, but the investigation was closed in February 2004, purportedly because the prisoner would not cooperate with the investigation. A later review of the file—a review conducted by the U.S. Army Criminal Investigative Command in Fort Hood—observed that investigators had failed to collect medical evidence; failed to identify, locate, and interview the platoon leader at the time of the capture; and failed to identify other personnel involved in the prisoner's capture and detention.[220] The review also confirmed that while detained at Abu Ghraib, the prisoner was made to sign a statement that read, "I do not want to file a complaint against the American Forces so I can get released. . . . I was not forced or threatened by anyone to write this statement."[221] The review file observed, "This statement, alone, is a prima facie indication of threats."[222]

When investigators reopened this file (along with many others) after the Abu Ghraib photographs were made public in April 2004, the reopened investigation yielded evidence corroborating the prisoner's account. A staff sergeant stated that he had been told that personnel belonging to Task Force 20 (TF 20), a special operations task force, had interrogated the prisoner and that TF 20 personnel wore civilian clothing, as the prisoner said his assailants had done.[223] The Non-Commissioned Officer supporting TF 20 at the time of the prisoner's capture stated that "sometimes the Task Force 20 would come and pick up prisoners from the cell without letting me know they were taking the detainee."[224] A special agent who interviewed the prisoner found him credible, characterizing the prisoner's statement as "pretty detailed" with "good descriptions." In an e-mail to the criminal investigator, the Special Agent wrote, "Interviewed your guy today. . . . Hope this doesn't convolute your investigation, but he was pretty shaken up and also provided medical records as well."[225] The second investigation nonetheless concluded, as the first had done, that the prisoner had not been abused. There is no indication in the file that investigators interviewed TF 20 personnel or that they even attempted to do so.

In fact, the documents suggest that special operations task forces were permitted to abuse prisoners with impunity.[226] One investigative file

---

[219]**A-333**: Agent's investigative report, October 22, 2003.

[220]**A-341**: Memorandum re review of CID investigation, May 19, 2004.

[221]**A-342**: Translation of prisoner's sworn statement, November 25, 2003; **A-341**: Memorandum re review of CID investigation, May 19, 2004; **A-343**: E-mail re possible abuse incident, July 14, 2004.

[222]**A-341**: Memorandum re review of CID investigation, May 19, 2004.

[223]**A-338**: Statement of staff sergeant, July 9, 2004; **A-333**: Agent's investigative report, Oct. 22, 2003.

[224]**A-339**: Statement of NCO in charge of 1/22 Infantry, August 21, 2004.

[225]**A-344**: E-mail from special agent, August 15, 2004.

[226]For a broader discussion of this issue, see Human Rights Watch, "No Blood, No Foul': Soldiers' Accounts of Detainee Abuse in Iraq," July, 2006. Available at http://hrw. org/reports/2006/us0706.

concerns a January 2004 incident in which a prisoner captured in Tikrit alleged that, after he was taken by his captors to Camp Nama at Baghdad International Airport, he was stripped, made to walk into walls blind-folded, punched, kicked in the stomach, and dragged around the room by his interrogators.[227] An investigation was initiated but quickly abandoned after it was determined that the capturing personnel were part of Task Force 6-26 (a successor to TF 20), that members of that unit had been using fake names, and that the unit claimed—implausibly, in the view of a higher-level investigator who reviewed the file a year later—to have had a computer malfunction which resulted in the loss of 70 percent of its files.[228]

In June 2004, the chief of the Defense Intelligence Agency sent a memorandum to Stephen Cambone, undersecretary of defense for intelligence, about other abuses in which TF 6-26 personnel were implicated. The memorandum stated that prisoners delivered by TF 6-26 personnel to a temporary detention facility in Baghdad—probably Camp Nama—were observed to have bruises and burn marks on their backs.[229] It also stated that DIA personnel had observed TF 6-26 personnel punch a prisoner in the face "to the point he needed medical attention." After the incident, task force personnel failed to make a record of the medical treatment and confiscated DIA photos of the injuries.[230] A March 2006 *New York Times* story about Camp Nama reported that, between 2003 and March 2006, Task Force 6-26 personnel were implicated in at least twenty-nine separate allegations of abuse. Only five of the twenty-nine investigations, however, resulted in findings of misconduct.[231]

It is difficult to reconcile files like these with the Defense Department's insistence that allegations of abuse have been aggressively investigated. And, unfortunately, such files are not aberrational. Another file concerns the death of Abu Malik Kenami, a forty-four-year-old man who entered the detention facility in Mosul, Iraq, with no known medical problems but died there after being forced to do "ups and downs" as a punishment for attempting to lift a sandbag off his head.[232] Photographs included in the report show that Kenami had been hooded and had his hands flex-cuffed behind his back. He was seen sweating after the ups and downs.[233] He eventually lay down to sleep among sixty-six detainees packed into a cell for which the maximum capacity was thirty detainees.[234] A sworn

---

[227]**A-346**: Memorandum re CID report of investigation, June 17, 2005.

[228]**A-350**: Memorandum re alleged abuse of prisoner by Task Force 6–26, February 11, 2005. The documents suggest that the investigation was reopened in February 2005, but the Defense Department has not released records concerning the reopened investigation.

[229]**A-351**: Memorandum from L. E. Jacoby, Defense Intelligence Agency, to undersecretary of defense for intelligence, June 25, 2004.

[230]Ibid.

[231]Eric Schmitt and Carolyn Marshall, "In Secret Unit's 'Black Room,' a Grim Portrait of U.S. Abuse," *New York Times*, March 19, 2006.

[232]Kenami File at DODDOA 026695, DODDOA 026698.

[233]Kenami File at DODDOA 026699.

[234]Kenami File at DODDOA 026699.

statement of a medical officer states that Kenami may have died from hypothermia; the medical officer also notes that Kenami had a small scalp laceration and hematoma, "which forces me to entertain trauma as a cause."[235] The investigative report describes Kenami's death as "suspicious or questionable."[236] The report concludes, however, that "[w]hat caused Abu Malik Kenami's death is undetermined . . . because an autopsy was never performed."[237] The report then states that his death was probably due to "natural causes."[238]

Still another file relates to a prisoner who died at Abu Ghraib prison in October 2003. An investigation was opened into the death but closed almost immediately. Many months later, the army's Criminal Investigative Command conducted a review of the investigation. The review disclosed the following deficiencies:

> The investigation did not conduct a crime scene examination or explain why such an examination was not conducted. The investigation did not conduct any interviews to determine the circumstances surrounding the death. There was no investigative effort made to obtain the victim's medical records that could have been used to determine if he was under medical care prior to his death. The investigation was closed without opening a full Report of Investigation (ROI). The case file was closed without any preliminary or final autopsy report, or any information as to whether or not an autopsy was conducted.[239]

Some investigations did lead to findings of culpability. In many cases, however, those found to be culpable for the abuse of prisoners received only nominal punishments. The chief warrant officer who killed Iraqi General Mowhoush by suffocating him inside a sleeping bag was reprimanded and fined $6000.[240] Others implicated in the death received lesser punishments. Punishment in other cases was similarly lenient or nominal. Another file concerns Obeed Hethere Radad, a prisoner who was held by U.S. forces in Tikrit for approximately one week and then shot to death in his cell on September 11, 2003. Radad had been placed in an isolation cell with his hands flex-cuffed in front of him. The specialist who was guarding him claimed that he fired his gun when Radad leaned over the concertina wire at the front of his cell, which he had been instructed not to do.[241] A criminal investigation found that the specialist had failed to use graduated force, as regulations require, and had deliberately shot to kill. The investigation found probable cause to believe that the specialist had committed the offense of murder. Despite this finding, however, the specialist received only non-judicial punishment, a reduction in rank and a discharge.[242]

---

[235]Kenami File at DODDOA 026745.

[236]Kenami File at DODDOA 026696.

[237]Kenami File at DODDOA 026695.

[238]Kenami File at DODDOA 026695.

[239]**A-353**: Memorandum for commander re report of investigation, May 20, 2004.

[240]"Iraq General's Killer Reprimanded," BBC.com, January 26, 2006, available at http://news.bbc.co.uk/2/hi/middle_east/4642596.stm.

[241]**A-355**: Memorandum re preliminary CID investigation, September 16, 2003.

[242]**A-359**: Memorandum re operational review of CID investigation, May 19, 2004.

Yet another file concerns an Iraqi high school student who suffered a broken jaw while detained by U.S. forces in Mosul. U.S. forces seized the boy, the boy's father, and the boy's twenty-five-year-old brother in early December 2003 because the boy's father was "suspected to be an officer in the Fedayeen." According to the investigative file, the boy and his brother were seized as "sub-targets"—that is, not because they were suspected of wrongdoing but because they were "male Iraqi citizens found inside a target's home."[243] U.S. forces brought the boy to a holding area.[244] In the holding area, the boy was flex-cuffed, hooded, doused with cold water, and forced to perform physical exercises until he was exhausted.[245] In a statement dated December 18, the boy alleged that a soldier led him to the side of the room and then kicked him in the face, breaking his teeth and jaw. [246] The boy states that, after he was injured, soldiers took him to another room and told him to say that no one had beaten him but that he had injured himself falling down.[247]

An investigation into this incident corroborated virtually all of the boy's allegations. The investigator found that prisoners in the holding area were "systematically and intentionally mistreated"—hit with water bottles, doused with cold water, deprived of sleep, forced to perform repetitive physical exercises until they could not stand, and "roughly grabbed off the floor" when they collapsed.[248] According to the file, "[t]here [was] evidence that suggests the 311th [Military Intelligence] personnel and/or translators engaged in physical torture of detainees."[249] The investigator states that "[a]buse of the detainees in some form or other was an acceptable practice and was demonstrated to the inexperienced infantry guards almost as guidance."[250] The investigator found, finally, that the boy's jaw had been broken by an "intentional act"—either because the boy had been hit or kicked or because the boy had collapsed after being forced to exercise to the point of exhaustion. The guard who was closest to the boy when he was injured provided inconsistent statements—first stating that he had been assisting the boy when the boy suddenly fell on his jaw and then, in subsequent statements, insisting he did not see the boy fall.[251] The investigating officer recommended that the company commander "as well as anyone else that was involved in the decision to allow the abusive behavior" be disciplined "for allowing abuse of detainees as standard operating procedure."[252] Despite this recommendation, it appears that no one involved in the incident—neither the guard who provided inconsistent

---

[243]**A-368**: Factual summary, undated.
[244]Ibid.
[245]Ibid.
[246]**A-362**: Transcription of prisoner's statement, December 18, 2003.
[247]Ibid.
[248]**A-360**: Untitled memorandum, undated.
[249]**A-363**: Memorandum for record re Article 15-6 investigation, December 31, 2003.
[250]**A-371**: Findings, undated.
[251]**A-368**: Factual summary, undated.
[252]**A-373**: Recommendations, undated.

statements nor the commander who supervised the holding area—was ever disciplined.[253]

The pattern quickly becomes clear. Abuse was condoned rather than condemned. When abuse was investigated, it was investigated halfheartedly. In the relatively few instances in which abuse was actually punished, punishments did not reflect the severity of the crimes. The abuse of prisoners was endorsed, encouraged, and accepted.

IV

The Bush administration promised accountability, but plainly this promise has not been kept. At the senior levels of the administration, there has been no accountability at all; indeed, senior officials who should have been held accountable have been rewarded instead. White House Counsel Alberto Gonzales, who advised the president that the Geneva Conventions' limitations on interrogation were "obsolete," was made attorney general of the United States. Jay Bybee, who as assistant attorney general opined that physical abuse does not amount to torture unless it inflicts pain akin to "organ failure, impairment of bodily function, or even death," was made a federal appellate judge. Maj. Gen. Geoffrey Miller, who oversaw the detention center at Guantánamo Bay and encouraged the adoption of abusive interrogation methods in Iraq, was presented with a Distinguished Service Medal for "exceptionally meritorious service."[254] Deputy Secretary of Defense Paul Wolfowitz, whom FBI personnel accused of having approved "torture techniques," was made president of the World Bank, and he served in that position until June 2007. Donald Rumsfeld, who as Defense Secretary endorsed interrogation methods that amounted to war crimes, served as defense secretary until November 2006 and retired with the president's thanks for his service.

The proposition that leaders should be held accountable for the abuse that they authorized, endorsed, or tolerated is surely not a radical one. The United States Supreme Court recognized the doctrine of command responsibility in 1946, holding that a Japanese commander could be tried for permitting his subordinates to violate the laws of war. Commanders have "an affirmative duty," the Supreme Court said in that case, "to take such measures as [are] within [their] power and appropriate in the circumstances to protect prisoners of war and the civilian population."[255] The Army's Field Manual governing interrogations sets out that the same principle. "The commander is responsible," it says, "for ensuring that forces under his command comply with the Geneva

---

[253]**A-364**: Memorandum for record re Article 15-6 investigation, December 31, 2003.
[254]Robert Burns, "General in Prison Probe Retires," Associated Press, July 31, 2006.
[255]*In re Yamashita*, 327 U.S. 1, 16 (1946).

Conventions."[256] The Military Commissions Act that President Bush signed into law in October of 2006 allows the Defense Department to rely on the doctrine of command responsibility to try prisoners now held at Guantánamo.[257] The principle of command responsibility, in other words, is one that the United States is enforcing against its enemies while ignoring at home.

The administration has insisted that the issue of command responsibility for the abuse of prisoners has already been examined; it points to a dozen or so investigations that have been conducted by the military. But the military investigations have either elided the issue of command responsibility or whitewashed it altogether. One military investigation concluded—in complete disregard of the evidence—that "none of the pictures of abuse at Abu Ghraib bear any resemblance to approved policies at any level, in any theater."[258] Another investigation acknowledged that prisoners at Guantánamo were short-shackled, threatened with dogs, deprived of sleep, and subjected to extreme temperatures, but it nonetheless concluded that "there was no evidence of torture or inhumane treatment."[259] All of the investigations were conducted by officers prohibited by military protocol from making adverse findings about officers of higher rank than themselves. The single investigation that was presented to the public as "independent" was in fact conducted by a panel whose members were handpicked by Rumsfeld, and Rumsfeld expressly directed the panel not to investigate "[i]ssues of personal accountability."[260]

While the U.S. Congress has the power to initiate a bipartisan investigation into the abuse and torture of prisoners, thus far it has declined to do so. One consequence is that a great deal of important information remains secret. Through the FOIA lawsuit, we have learned of the existence of multiple records relating to prisoner abuse that still have not been released by the administration; credible media reports identify others. As this book goes to print, the Bush administration is still withholding, among many other records, a September 2001 presidential directive authorizing the CIA to set up secret detention centers overseas; an August 2002 Justice Department memorandum advising the CIA about the lawfulness of waterboarding and other aggressive interrogation methods; documents describing interrogation methods used by

---

[256]Department of the Army, Field Manual 2-22.3 (2006), Human Intelligence Collector Operations, pp. 5–18. See also Department of the Army, Field Manual 34–52 (1992), Intelligence Interrogation, ch. 1, p. 1.

[257]Military Commissions Act of 2006, s. 950q (stating that "a person is punishable as a principal under this chapter who . . . commits an offense punishable by this chapter, or aids, abets, counsels, commands, or procures its commission [or] is a superior commander who, with regard to acts punishable under this chapter, knew, had reason to know, or should have known, that a subordinate was about to commit such acts or had done so and who failed to take the necessary and reasonable measures to prevent such acts or to punish the perpetrators thereof.").

[258]Church Report, p. 3.

[259]**A-98**: Schmidt-Furlow Report.

[260]Schlesinger Report, appendix B.

special operations forces in Iraq and Afghanistan; investigative files concerning the deaths of prisoners in U.S. custody; and numerous photographs depicting the abuse of prisoners at detention facilities other than Abu Ghraib.

Even more troubling is the fact that senior administration officials, perhaps emboldened by Congress's failure to conduct any serious inquiry into past abuse, continue to advocate the use of interrogation methods that violate domestic and international law. Vice President Cheney defends the use of waterboarding—indeed, he has offered this defense on national television. In a best-selling book, George Tenet, the former Director of the CIA, defends the agency's use of what he calls "enhanced interrogation techniques"—techniques that reportedly include, in addition to waterboarding, depriving prisoners of sleep for extended periods, subjecting them to "stress positions," and locking them in freezing-cold cells to induce hypothermia.[261] In testimony before Congress, a former CIA official defends the agency's "rendition" program, a program under which the CIA kidnaps foreign nationals and sends them to other countries that are known to—and expected to—use torture. Discussing the treatment inflicted on prisoners who have been rendered, the former CIA official states:

> I would not . . . be surprised if their treatment was not up to U.S. standards. This is a matter of no concern, as the rendition program's goal was to protect America, and the rendered fighters delivered to Middle Eastern governments are now either dead or in places from which they cannot harm America. Mission accomplished, as the saying goes.[262]

Secretary Rumsfeld observed three years ago that the standard by which the United States and its government will ultimately be judged is "not by whether abuses take place, but rather [by] how [the] nation deals with them."[263] Rumsfeld was right about this, if little else. The documents compiled here make clear the pressing need for a serious Congressional inquiry into official responsibility for the torture and abuse of prisoners in U.S. custody. It is imperative that senior officials who authorized, endorsed, or tolerated the abuse and torture of prisoners be held accountable, not only as a matter of elemental justice, but to ensure that the same crimes are not perpetrated again.

---

[261] George Tenet: At the Center of the Storm, CBSnews.com, Apr. 29, 2007. Available at http://www.cbsnews.com/stories/2007/04/25/60minutes/main2728375_page3.shtml; Brian Ross & Richard Esposito, "CIA's Harsh Interrogation Techniques Described: Sources Say Agency's Tactics Lead to Questionable Confessions, Sometimes to Death," ABC News, Nov. 18, 2005.

[262] Testimony of Michael Scheuer, Hearing of the International Organizations, Human Rights and Oversight Subcommittee and the Europe Subcommittee of the House Foreign Affairs Committee, April 17, 2007, available at http://ctstudies.com/Document/scheuer_testimony_17apr07.html.

[263] Testimony as prepared by Secretary of Defense Donald H. Rumsfeld, before the Senate and House Armed Services Committees, May 7, 2004, available at www.defendamerica.mil/articles/may2004/a050704e.html.

TIMELINE OF KEY EVENTS

Oct. 2001	United States forces commence hostilities in Afghanistan.
Jan. 2002	Prisoners begin arriving at U.S. naval base at Guantánamo Bay.
Jan. 25, 2002	White House Counsel Alberto Gonzales advises President Bush to deny al Qaeda and Taliban prisoners protection under the Geneva Conventions.[264]
Feb. 7, 2002	President Bush issues directive denying al Qaeda and Taliban prisoners baseline protections under the Geneva Conventions.[265]
Jun.–July 2002	Chief of Staff of the Joint Personnel Recovery Agency ("JPRA") develops a plan with the Army Special Operations Command's Psychological Directorate to train interrogators in Survival Evasion, Resistance, and Escape ("SERE") methods.[266]
End summer 2002	Chairman of Joint Chiefs of Staff review of intelligence operations at Guantánamo Bay concludes that traditional interrogation methods prescribed by Army Field Manual 34–52 had proven to be ineffective.[267]
August 2002	Assistant Attorney General Jay Bybee writes memorandum stating that abuse does not rise to the level of torture

---

[264]**A-1**: Memorandum from White House Counsel Alberto Gonzales to President George Bush, January 25, 2002.
[265]**A-6**: Memorandum from President Bush to the vice president et al., February 7, 2002.
[266]DOD IG Report, p. 25.
[267]Ibid.

	unless it causes pain akin to that caused by organ failure or death.[268]
Sep. 16, 2002	Army Special Operations Command and JPRA co-host a SERE psychologist conference in Fort Bragg for Guantánamo interrogation personnel.[269]
Oct. 11, 2002	Maj. Gen. Michael Dunlavey, Commander of Guantánamo interrogation operations, requests authorization from Southern Command to use interrogation methods beyond those listed in Army FM 34–52.[270]
Nov. 4, 2002	Maj. Gen. Geoffrey Miller becomes Commanding General of Guantánamo.
Nov. 12, 2002	Defense Secretary Rumsfeld verbally authorizes a "special interrogation plan" that permits interrogators to confine Mohammed al-Qahtani in an "isolation facility" for up to thirty days, subject him to "20 hour interrogations for every 24-hour cycle," and intimidate him with military working dogs.[271]
Late 2002	FBI's Behavioral Analysis Unit begins objecting to Defense Department interrogation tactics at Guantánamo Bay. These objections culminate in a May 30, 2003 FBI electronic communication which states that "not only are these tactics at odds with legally permissible interviewing techniques . . . but they are being employed by personnel in GTMO who have little, if any, experience eliciting information for judicial purposes."[272]

---

[268]Memorandum from Jay. S. Bybee, assistant attorney general, to Alberto Gonzales, White House counsel, re standards of conduct for interrogation under 18 U.S.C. §§ 2340–2340A, August 1, 2002, at 39, available at http://www.gwu.edu/~nsarchiv/NSAEBB/NSAEBB127/02.08.01.pdf.

[269]DOD IG Report, p. 25.

[270]**A-85**: Memorandum from Maj. Gen. Michael Dunlavey to commander, U.S. Southern Command re counter-resistance strategies, October 11, 2002.

[271]**A-112, 117**: Schmidt-Furlow Report.

[272]**A-133**: FBI memorandum re "Detainee Interviews (Abusive Interrogation Issues)," May 6, 2004.

Nov. 20, 2002	FBI officials express "misgivings about the overall coercive nature" of an interrogation plan developed by Defense Intelligence Agency ("DIA") Human Intelligence ("Humint") personnel.[273]
Nov. 22, 2002	FBI document criticizing the DIA Humint interrogation plan is forwarded to Maj. Gen. Geoffrey Miller.[274]
Dec. 2, 2002	Rumsfeld issues written directive authorizing Guantánamo prisoners to be subjected to interrogation methods including isolation for thirty days at a time, twenty-hour interrogations, stress positions, removal of clothing, hooding, and exploitation of "individual phobias (such as fear of dogs) to induce stress."[275]
Dec. 2, 2002	Colonel Brittan Mallow, Criminal Investigation Task Force ("CITF") Commander at Guantánamo, prohibits CITF agents from "participating in the use of any questionable techniques."[276]
Late 2002	Interrogators in Afghanistan begin employing many of the techniques Rumsfeld approved in his December 2, 2002 directives.[277]
Dec. 3, 2002	Interrogators at Bagram Collection Point in Afghanistan kill an Afghan prisoner by shackling him by his wrists to the wire ceiling above his cell and repeatedly beating his legs.[278] A post-mortem report finds abrasions and contusions on the prisoner's face, head, neck, arms and legs and determines that the death

---

[273]**A-139**: FBI e-mail to General Miller, undated.

[274]**A-140**: FBI (BAU) draft letter for Maj. Gen. Miller, November 22, 2002.

[275]**A-83**: Action memorandum endorsed by Secretary of Defense Donald Rumsfeld, November 27, 2002; **A-96–97**: Memorandum from LTC Jerald Phifer to Maj. Gen. Michael Dunlavey, October 11, 2002.

[276]**A-145**: E-mail from CITF Commander Col. Brittain Mallow re "participation in discussion of interrogation strategies, techniques, etc.," December 2, 2002.

[277]Fay Report, p.29.

[278]Tim Golden, "In U.S. Report, Brutal Details of 2 Afghan Inmates' Deaths," *New York Times*, May 20, 2005.

was a "homicide" caused by "blunt force injuries."[279]

Dec. 10, 2002 — Interrogators at Bagram Collection Point in Afghanistan kill another prisoner, this time one whom interrogators themselves believed to be innocent.[280] A subsequent autopsy finds that this death, too, is a "homicide" and has been caused by "blunt force injuries."[281]

Dec. 10, 2002 — Defense Department drafts SERE Standard Operating Procedure for Guantánamo.[282]

Dec. 17, 2002 — Naval Criminal Investigative Service ("NCIS") personnel attached to CITF inform Navy General Counsel Alberto Mora that Guantánamo prisoners are being subjected to "physical abuse and degrading treatment."[283]

Dec. 20, 2002 — Mora expresses concerns to Defense Department General Counsel William Haynes regarding prisoner abuse and the December 2002 Rumsfeld interrogation directive.[284]

Jan. 15, 2003 — Rumsfeld withdraws the December 2002 interrogation directive and convenes a working group to review permissible interrogation methods.[285]

Jan. 2003 — The acting staff judge advocate for CJTF-180 in Afghanistan sends a memorandum to U.S. Central Command listing and describing interrogation methods then in use, while "strongly recommend[ing]" that Central Command endorse these techniques as

---

[279]**A-185–186**: Final report of postmortem examination, December 8, 2002.

[280]Tim Golden, "In U.S. Report, Brutal Details of 2 Afghan Inmates' Deaths," *New York Times,* May 20, 2005.

[281]**A-187**: Excerpt of autopsy report, February 25, 2003.

[282]**A-18**: Memorandum, December 17, 2002.

[283]Mora Memorandum, p. 3.

[284]Mora Memorandum, p. 7.

[285]**A-146**: Memorandum from Defense Secretary Donald Rumsfeld to SOUTHCOM commander re counter-resistance techniques, January 15, 2003; **A-147**: Memorandum from Defense Secretary Donald Rumsfeld to William J. Haynes II, general counsel, Department of Defense, January 15, 2003).

	official policy.[286] CJTF-180 receives no response to its request and interprets the silence from headquarters to mean that the techniques then in use "could be considered an approved policy."[287]
Late Jan. 2003	Working group receives as "definitive guidance" a legal memorandum authored by Deputy Assistant Attorney General John Yoo modeled on the August 2002 Bybee memorandum written for the CIA.[288] Mora argues that the Yoo memorandum is "fundamentally in error" and "virtually useless."[289]
Feb. 2003	Lt. Gen. Dan K. McNeill, CJTF-180 commander in Afghanistan, revises interrogation policy by eliminating five techniques not found in the Field Manual.[290]
Mar. 2003	United States forces commence hostilities in Iraq.
April 4, 2003	Working group issues report endorsing thirty-five interrogation techniques, some of which extend far beyond those authorized by the Army Field Manual.[291] Mora does not receive the final report, which Rumsfeld himself signs. Miller and Hill, on the other hand, are specifically briefed on the report's contents.[292]
April 16, 2003	Rumsfeld approves twenty-four of the thirty-five techniques recommended by the working group, including environmental manipulation, sleep adjustment, extended isolation, and "false flag."[293]

---

[286]Church Report, pp. 196, 201, 214; Fay Report, p. 29.
[287]Church Report, p. 201.
[288]Mora Memorandum, pp. 16–17.
[289]Ibid.
[290]Church Report, p. 7.
[291]"Working Group Report on Detainee Interrogations in the Global War on Terrorism: Assessment of Legal, Historical, Policy, and Operational Considerations," April 4, 2003, in *The Torture Papers*, ed. Karen J. Greenberg and Joshua L. Dratel, pp. 346–47.
[292]Mora Memorandum, p. 20, n.14.
[293]**A-148**: Memorandum from Defense Secretary Donald Rumsfeld to commander, U.S. Southern Command, April 16, 2003.

Spring/summer 2003	International Committee of the Red Cross visits detention facilities in Iraq and finds that the abuse of prisoners is pervasive.[294]
Aug. 2003	Captain Carolyn Wood becomes an interrogations operations officer at Abu Ghraib in Iraq. Wood, an officer in the 519th Military Intelligence Battalion, which had been implicated in the deaths of Bagram prisoners in late 2002, draws on her experience in Afghanistan in the absence of guidance from her superiors on interrogation methods. She also submits the TF-121 interrogation rules of engagement for approval, but receives no response.[295]
Aug. 14, 2003	Interrogators in Iraq are invited to submit a "wish list" of techniques that might be used against their prisoners.[296] Interrogators seek approval to use, Among other techniques, "phone book strikes," "muscle fatigue inducement," "close quarter confinement," and even "low voltage electrocution."[297]
End Aug. 2003	Gen. Miller is dispatched to Iraq to advise on interrogation operations. He recommends that "detention operations . . . act as an enabler for interrogation."[298] He also gives military leaders in Iraq documents relating to interrogation policy at Guantánamo.[299]
Sep. 2003	JPRA sends an interrogation team to assist TF 20, a special missions unit operating in Iraq, in the use of SERE techniques.[300]

---

[294]February 2004 ICRC Report, ¶24.

[295]**A-189**: Sworn statement of Captain Carolyn Wood, May 21, 2004.

[296]**A-308**: E-mail stating that "the gloves are coming off," August 14, 2003.

[297]**A-309**: Document titled, "Alternative Interrogation Techniques (Wish List)," undated.

[298]Report of Maj. Gen. Geoffrey Miller, "Assessment of DoD Counterterrorism Interrogation and Detention Operations in Iraq," undated, available at http://www.aclu.org/torturefoia/released/a20.pdf.

[299]Schlesinger Report, p. 37 Fay Report, p. 58.

[300]DOD IG Report, p. 28.

Sep. 14, 2003	Lt. Gen. Ricardo Sanchez, commander of coalition forces in Iraq, issues an interrogation directive that is informed by the Guantánamo working group report.[301] The directive authorizes twenty-nine methods including "stress positions," "exploit[ing] Arab fear of dogs," "fear up harsh" and "pride and ego down."[302]
Oct. 12, 2003	Sanchez issues a new interrogation directive which hews more closely to the Army Field Manual but interrogators in Iraq continue to use abusive methods beyond those listed in the directive.[303]
Nov. 4, 2003	Navy Seals capture Manadel al-Jamadi in Iraq and turn him over to the CIA. He is stripped and doused with cold water and his wrists are shackled behind him and fastened to window bars.[304] An autopsy report describes al-Jamadi's death as a "homicide" caused by "blunt force injuries complicated by compromised respiration," and states that a hood made of synthetic material was placed over his head and neck.[305]
Nov. 26, 2003	Interrogators in Iraq kill Iraqi General Abed Hamed Mowhoush during an interrogation in which they put him into a sleeping bag and tie him up with electrical cord. An Army officer reprimanded for this death asserts that the "sleeping bag technique" was a "stress position" that he considered to have been authorized by a September CJTF-7 order.[306]

---

[301]Fay Report, p. 14.

[302]**A-231, 233–234**: Interrogation directive issued by Lt. Gen. Ricardo S. Sanchez, September 14, 2003.

[303]**A-238**: Interrogation directive issued by Lt. Gen. Ricardo S. Sanchez, October 12, 2003.

[304]See John McChesney, "The Death of an Iraqi Prisoner," National Public Radio broadcast, October 27, 2005, available at http://www.npr.org/templates/story/story.php?storyId=4977986.

[305]**A-313**: Excerpt from final autopsy report, January 9, 2004.

[306]**A-246**: Army memorandum re CW3 Lewis E. Welshofer Jr., February 11, 2004.

Mar. 2004	Relying on an unsigned memorandum that is substantively identical to Rumsfeld's April 16, 2003 directive for Guantánamo, CJTF-180 in Afghanistan issues a new interrogation directive that restores some of the practices that McNeill had sought to eliminate in February 2003.[307]
April 2, 2004	Defense Department issues "Information Paper" listing 62 allegations of prisoner abuse, including 14 prisoner deaths in Iraq and Afghanistan which could not be attributed to natural causes.[308]
April 28, 2004	CBS News broadcasts photographs of U.S. military personnel abusing prisoners at Abu Ghraib prison in Iraq.
Oct. 2006	Vice President Dick Cheney publicly endorses the practice of "water boarding," a practice that involves subjecting prisoners to near drowning.[309]

---

[307]Church Report, p. 7.
[308]**A-260–264**: Information Paper, April 2, 2004.
[309]Jonathan S. Landey, "Cheney Confirms That Detainees Were Subjected To Waterboarding," McClatchy Newspapers, October 25, 2006.

DESCRIPTION OF THE DOCUMENTS

The American Civil Liberties Union (ACLU) and its partners obtained most of the documents compiled here through litigation under the Freedom of Information Act (FOIA). The FOIA requests were filed in October 2003 and May 2004 with the Central Intelligence Agency and the Departments of Defense, Homeland Security, Justice, and State. The ACLU and its partners filed suit in June 2004 because none of the agencies had provided any meaningful response to the requests. In September 2004, Judge Alvin K. Hellerstein of the United States District Court for the Southern District of New York ordered the agencies to search their files and to release all responsive records or explain on a case-by-case basis why those records could lawfully be withheld. That ruling set in motion a process that has thus far resulted in the public release of over 100,000 pages.

The documents collected here are those referenced in the preceding narrative. In a handful of instances, the documents have been transcribed for legibility. In most cases, however, the documents are presented in the same form they were provided to the ACLU.

The following documents are reprinted in this volume.

Page	Date of Document	Document
A-1	Jan. 25, 2002	Memorandum from White House Counsel Alberto Gonzales to President George W. Bush recommending that al Qaeda and Taliban prisoners not be extended the protections of the Third Geneva Convention. [Transcription]
A-6	Feb. 7, 2002	Memorandum from President George W. Bush to the vice president et al. stating that al Qaeda and Taliban prisoners are not entitled to the protection of the Geneva Conventions.
A-8	Mar. 22, 2005	Summarized witness statement of former Interrogation Control Element chief at Guantánamo, stating that predecessor "arranged for SERE instructors to teach their techniques to the interrogators at GTMO."
A-9	Sept. 9, 2002	FBI e-mail re interrogation training at Ft. Bragg.
A-10	Mar. 31, 2005	Summarized witness statement in which Maj. Gen. Geoffrey Miller states that military psychologists at Guantánamo "were trained through SERE."
A-18	Dec. 17, 2002	Memorandum from Criminal Investigation Task Force special agent in charge expressing concern about the use of SERE techniques at Guantánamo.
A-21	Mar. 29, 2005	Summarized witness statement in which Maj. Gen. Michael Dunlavey states that he received "marching orders from the President of the United States."
A-30	Aug. 24, 2005	Sworn statement of Lt. Gen. Randall Schmidt discussing interrogation methods employed at Guantánamo.
A-83	Nov. 27, 2002	Action memorandum from Defense Department General Counsel William J. Haynes II recommending that Defense Secretary Rumsfeld approve certain counter-resistance techniques. The memo was endorsed by Rumsfeld on December 2, 2002.

Page	Date of Document	Document
A-84	Oct. 25, 2002	Memorandum from U.S. Southern Command Comdr. Gen. James T. Hill to Chairman of the Joint Chiefs of Staff forwarding memorandum re recommended counter-resistance techniques. [Transcription]
A-85	Oct. 11, 2002	Memorandum from Maj. Gen. Michael Dunlavey to commander, U.S.Southern Command re counter-resistance strategies. [Transcription]
A-86	Oct. 11, 2002	Memorandum from Lt. Col. Diane E. Beaver to commander of the JTF-170 re legal brief on proposed counter-resistance strategies. [Transcription]
A-96	Oct. 11, 2002	Memorandum from Lt. Col. Jerald Phifer to Maj. Gen. Michael Dunlavey, re request for approval of counter-resistance strategies. [Transcription]
A-98	June 9, 2005	Final report of Lt. Gen. Randall Schmidt and Brig. Gen. John Furlow, investigation into FBI Allegations of Detainee Abuse at Guanánamo Bay, Cuba Detention Facility.
A-127	July 14, 2004	Letter from T. J. Harrington, deputy assistant director, FBI Counterterrorism Division, to Maj. Gen. Donald J. Ryder, Department of the Army, relating three incidents in which military interrogators used "highly aggressive interrogation techniques."
A-130	May 6, 2004	FBI memorandum re "Detainee Interviews (Abusive Interrogation Issues)," describing FBI objections to military interrogators' use of SERE interrogation techniques.
A-131	May 10, 2004	FBI e-mail stating concern that Defense Department techniques "were not effective or producing [i]ntel that was reliable," and stating that concerns were raised with Maj. Gen. Dunlavey and Maj. Gen. Miller.
A-132	May 30, 2003	FBI electronic communication "to document BAU assistance and challenges encountered during TDY assignment

		in Guantánamo Bay." Discusses concerns about legality and effectiveness of techniques used by military interrogators. [Transcription]
A-139	Undated	FBI e-mail to Maj. Gen. Miller expressing "misgivings about the overall coercive nature and possible illegality of elements" of a DIA Humint interrogation plan.
A-140	Nov. 22, 2002	FBI (BAU) draft letter for Maj. Gen. Miller discussing FBI skepticism re effectiveness and reliability of DIA Humint interrogation methods. [Transcription]
A-142	Dec. 2, 2002	FBI e-mail re "Briefing notes for the General Miller" suggesting that FBI officials planned to meet with Maj. Gen. Miller within a few days.
A-143	May 13, 2004	FBI e-mail stating that "battles fought in gitmo while gen miller . . . was there are on the record."
A-144	Dec. 16, 2002	FBI e-mail stating that "looks like we are stuck in the mud with the interview approach of the military vrs. law enforcement."
A-145	Dec. 2, 2002	E-mail from Criminal Investigations Task Force Comdr. Col. Brittain Mallow prohibiting CITF agents from "participat[ing] in the use of any questionable techniques" and ordering them to report "all discussions of interrogation strategies" to CITF leadership.
A-146	Jan. 15, 2003	Memorandum from Defense Secretary Donald Rumsfeld to commander, USSOUTHCOM, rescinding December 2002 interrogation directive.
A-147	Jan. 15, 2003	Memorandum from Defense Secretary Donald Rumsfeld to Defense Department General Counsel William J. Haynes II, directing establishment of working group to consider "legal, policy, and operational issues relating to the interrogations of detainees."
A-148	Apr. 16, 2003	Memorandum from Defense Secretary Donald Rumsfeld approving twentyfour

		interrogation techniques including "environmental manipulation," "sleep adjustment," extended isolation, and "false flag."
A-154	Aug. 2, 2004	FBI e-mail describing interrogations at Guantánamo in which prisoners were subjected to extreme temperatures until they were "almost unconscious" and others in which prisoners were "chained hand and foot in a fetal position to the floor" and left in that position "for 18–24 hours or more."
A-155	Jul. 13, 2004	FBI memorandum describing interrogations at Guantánamo in which interrogators used strobe lights and loud music and complaining that "every time the FBI established a rapport with a detainee, the military would step in and the detainee would stop being cooperative."
A-157	May 6, 2004	FBI e-mail describing February 2004 interrogation at Guantánamo during which a prisoner was "short-shackled, the room temperature was significantly lowered, strobe lights were used, and possibly loud music."
A-159	Dec. 5, 2003	FBI e-mail discussing interrogation at Guantánamo during which military interrogators impersonated FBI agents while using "torture techniques." The e-mail states that the military interrogators "produced no intelligence of a threat neutralization nature," "destroyed any chance of prosecuting the detainee," and potentially left the FBI "holding the bag before the public."
A-160	Undated	FBI e-mail stating that "We're still fighting the battle with [DIA Humint] which routinely has a negative impact on what we're trying to do."
A-162	Apr. 26, 2003	Defense Department memorandum relating to commander's inquiry into incident at Guantánamo during which prisoner was "slammed to the floor"

		seven or eight times with a force "adequate to cause severe internal injury."
A-164	Jul. 9, 2004	FBI e-mail requesting that agents who had been stationed at Guantánamo report whether they had "observed aggressive treatment, interrogations or interview techniques . . . which [were] not consistent with [FBI] interview policy/guidelines."
A-166	Aug. 17, 2004	FBI e-mail stating that twenty-six FBI employees stationed at Guantánamo had "observed what was believed to be some form of mistreatment" and that seventeen of the twenty-six reports stemmed from "DOD approved interrogation techniques."
A-167	Undated	"FBI Background" summarizing FBI agents' knowledge of prisoner abuse in Iraq, Afghanistan, and Guantánamo Bay.
A-170	Jul. 30, 2004	FBI e-mail describing interrogation at Guantánamo during which prisoner was "sitting on the floor of the interview room with an Israeli flag draped around him, loud music being played and a strobe light flashing."
A-172	Aug. 2, 2004	FBI e-mail describing interrogation at Guantánamo during which the prisoner was sitting in a chair, shackled at his feet, and subjected to a flickering strobe light and loud music.
A-173	Undated	FBI document entitled "GTMO Issues," stating that "BAU personnel witnessed sleep deprivation," and "utilization of loud music/bright lights/growling dogs in the Detainee interview process by DOD representatives."
A-174	May 5, 2004	FBI e-mail stating that techniques such as "hooding prisoners, threats of violence," as well as "techniques meant to humiliat[e] detainees," were "approved at high levels with DOD." [Transcription]

Page	Date of Document	Document
A-176	Jan. 21, 2004	FBI e-mail stating that the "imperson-ation" technique and all other tech-niques "used in these scenarios" had been "approved by the Dep. Sec Def."
A-177	Jan. 19, 2002	Memorandum from Defense Secretary Rumsfeld to chairman of the Joint Chiefs of Staff requesting that com-manders in Afghanistan "implement" the determination that al Qaeda and Taliban prisoners are not entitled to prisoner of war status.
A-178	Undated	Chronology of guard/detainee issues referring to multiple incidents in which prisoners were beaten, kicked, and hit with the butt of a rifle.
A-185	Dec. 8, 2002	Final report of postmortem examination relating to "27–28 year old Pashtun male" killed at Bagram Collection Point in December 2002. [Transcription]
A-187	Feb. 25, 2003	Excerpt of autopsy report relating to "35 year old Afghan male detainee" killed at Bagram Collection Point in December 2002.
A-189	May 21, 2004	Sworn statement of Capt. Carolyn Wood, 519th Military Intelligence Battalion, discussing development of interroga-tion techniques in Afghanistan. [Transcription]
A-202	June 4, 2004	Sworn statement of Tiger Team member discussing implementation of Maj. Gen. Miller's recommendations at Abu Ghraib. [Transcription]
A-205	May 14, 2004	Sworn statement of Thomas M. Pappas, commander of 205th Military Intelligence Brigade in Iraq. Describes Maj. Gen. Miller's efforts to develop interrogation policies in Iraq based on those previously adopted at Guantánamo. [Transcription]
A-216	July 18, 2004	Excerpt of transcript of interview with Brig. Gen. Janis Karpinski, com-mander of the 800th Military Police Brigade, discussing Maj. Gen. Miller's

role in developing interrogation policies at Abu Ghraib.

A-221   May 24, 2004   Sworn statement of interrogator who
arrived at Abu Ghraib in October 2003,
discussing use of military dogs against
juvenile prisoners. [Transcription]

A-225   June 30, 2004   Sworn statement of interrogator sent
from Fort Huachuca to conduct train-
ing at Abu Ghraib. Recounts incident
in which interrogators suggested to
civilian contractor that he should scare
prisoners by showing them photographs of "what appeared to be [mili-
tary police] in intimidating positions
with detainees." [Transcription]

A-228   April 6, 2002   FBI summary of interview with prisoner
held at Guantánamo. States that mili-
tary personnel had been seen "kicking
the Koran."

A-229   Jan. 22, 2003   FBI summary of interview with prisoner
held at Guantánamo. States that sui-
cide attempts at Guantánamo were
partly a consequence of guards "humiliating" the Qu'ran.

A-231   Sept. 14, 2003   Interrogation directive issued by Lt. Gen.
Ricardo S. Sanchez, authorizing inter-
rogation methods beyond those
endorsed by Army Field Manual 34–52.
[Transcription]

A-238   Oct. 12, 2003   Interrogation directive issued by Lt. Gen.
Ricardo S. Sanchez to supersede direc-
tive issued in September 2003.
[Transcription]

A-244   Dec. 18, 2003   Excerpt of autopsy examination report
for Abed Hamed Mowhoush, stating
that "the history surrounding the death
along with patterned contusions and
broken ribs support a traumatic cause
of death and therefore the manner of
death is best classified as homicide."

A-246   Feb. 11, 2004   Army memorandum re reprimand of
CWO Lewis E. Welshofer Jr. for death
of Abed Hamed Mowhoush. States that
"[i]n SERE," the technique used against

		Mowhoush "is called close confinement and can be very effective."
A-249	Nov. 22, 2004	Excerpt of final autopsy report relating to "27 year-old male civilian" who died in custody on April 5, 2004, in Mosul, Iraq.
A-251	Sept. 23, 2004	Detainee autopsy summary listing instances in which prisoners died in custody.
A-260	April 2, 2004	Information paper describing allegations of abuse in Iraq and Afghanistan.
A-271	June 16, 2004	Marine Corps document describing abuse cases between September 2001 and June 2004, including "substantiated" incidents in which marines electrocuted a prisoner and set another's hands on fire.
A-279	June 25, 2004	Urgent report from Sacramento FBI office concerning soldier who observed "numerous physical abuse incidents of Iraqi civilian detainees."
A-282	Undated	Sworn statement of screener who arrived at Abu Ghraib in December 2003, indicating that prisoners at Asamiya Palace in Baghdad had been beaten, burned, and subjected to electric shocks. [Transcription]
A-284	Oct. 22, 2003	Final autopsy report relating to death of "52 y/o Iraqi Male, Civilian Detainee" held by U.S. forces in Nasiriyah, Iraq. Prisoner was found to have "died as a result of asphyxia . . . due to strangulation."
A-286	April 30, 2004	Excerpt from final autopsy report relating to death of prisoner held by U.S. forces in Al Asad, Iraq. Prisoner was found to have died from "blunt force injuries and asphyxia."
A-288	Nov. 13, 2003	Final autopsy report relating to death of prisoner held by U.S. forces at Forward Operating Base Gereshk, Afghanistan. Prisoner was found to have died from "multiple blunt force injuries."
A-290	May 19, 2004	Defense Intelligence Agency "Report of Conversation" with officer who led a

Page	Date of Document	Document
		team of interrogators in Iraq. Document states that headquarters "wanted the interrogators to break the detainees" and that Lt. Gen. Sanchez encouraged interrogators "to go to the outer limits to get information." [Transcription]
A-292	Nov. 9, 2003	Excerpt from file relating to Article 15-6 investigation into interrogation in Tikrit, Iraq, in the course of which prisoner was beaten with riot baton. Documents include Memorandum for record concerning Article 15-6 investigation, Oct.6, 2003 (295); E-mail responding to request for proposed interrogation techniques, Aug.14, 2003 (306); E-mail stating that "the gloves are coming off," (307–308); Document entitled "Alternative Interrogation Techniques (Wish List)," undated (309); Sworn Statement of prisoner beaten with riot baton during interrogation, Oct.1, 2003 (310). [Partly transcribed]
A-312	June 6, 2004	Agent's investigative report describing incident in which Titan Corp. interpreter witnessed interrogator forcing prisoner to "jump up and down and then roll left to right on the ground in what he believed to be a 150 degree Fahrenheit temperature."
A-313	Jan. 9, 2004	Excerpt from final autopsy report for Manadel al-Jamadi, prisoner killed in custody at Abu Ghraib, Iraq.
A-315	May 26, 2004	Sworn statement of former commander of the 320th Military Police Battalion, stating "perhaps only one in ten security detainees were of any particular intelligence value." [Transcription]
A-317	May 18, 2004	Privacy Act statement of sergeant assigned to the "Detainee Assessment Board" responsible for screening detainees for release at Abu Ghraib. States that "85% to 90% of detainees were of either no intelligence value or were of value but innocent and therefore should []not have remained in captivity."

Page	Date of Document	Document
A-318	May 5, 2004	Excerpt of transcript of interview with Brig. Gen. Janis Karpinski, commander of the 800th Military Police Brigade, discussing detention of juveniles.
A-319	May 13, 2004	Sworn statement of member of 302nd Military Intelligence Battalion recounting incident in which interrogators abused 17-year-old son of prisoner in order to "break" the prisoner. [Transcription]
A-321	June 15, 2004	Memorandum for record re "Detainees Basic Tenant Rights," which states: "Securing detainees in a cement cell with dimensions of 4 feet long, 3.10 feet high, and 1.5 feet wide secured by a sliding metal door is acceptable for a short duration not to exceed 24 hours." [Transcription]
A-323	Oct. 7, 2003	Navy Criminal Investigative Service memo re interview of corpsman "in regards to . . . knowledge of the abuse of Enemy prisoners of war (EPW) in Iraq."
A-324	May 23, 2004	Sworn statement of sergeant stationed at Abu Ghraib noting that prisoners had been handcuffed to railing. [Transcription]
A-328	May 18, 2004	Privacy Act statement of sergeant stationed at Abu Ghraib noting that prisoners had been "naked with a bag over their head, standing on MRE boxes and their hand[s] spread out . . . holding a bottle in each hand." [Transcription]
A-331	Nov. 14, 2003	Sworn statement of soldier stationed at Camp Red, Baghdad. States that "I saw what I think were war crimes" and that "[the] chain of command . . . allowed them to happen."
A-333	Oct. 22, 2003	Excerpt from file relating to criminal investigation into prisoner's allegation that U.S. forces in Tikrit beat him, broke his nose, choked him with a rope, and subjected him to a mock

Page	Date of Document	Document

execution. Documents include Hand-written statement of prisoner alleging abuse, undated (334–337); Statement of staff sergeant, July 9, 2004 (338); Statement of NCO in charge of 1/22 Infantry, Aug. 21, 2003 (339).

A-340   May 19, 2004   Excerpt from file relating to operational review of criminal investigation. Documents include Translation of prisoner's sworn statement, Nov. 25, 2003 (342); E-mail regarding possible abuse incident, July 14, 2004 (343); E-mail from special agent, Aug. 15, 2004 (344).

A-345   June 17, 2005   Excerpt from file relating to criminal investigation into incident in which prisoner captured in Tikrit alleged that he was stripped, made to walk into walls blindfolded, punched, kicked, and dragged around the room. Documents include Memorandum re alleged abuse of prisoner by Task Force 6-26, Feb. 11, 2005 (350).

A-351   June 25, 2004   Memorandum from L. E. Jacoby, Defense Intelligence Agency, to undersecretary of defense for intelligence. States that prisoners held by Task Force 6-26 personnel were observed to have bruises and burn marks on their backs.

A-353   May 20, 2004   Criminal Investigation Command memorandum stating that earlier investigation was "insufficient" because investigators "did not conduct a crime scene examination" and did not indicate whether autopsy was conducted. [Transcription]

A-354   Sept. 16, 2003   Excerpt from file relating to criminal investigation into killing of Obeed Hethere Radad, who died in U.S. custody at Tikrit. The file notes, "there was probable cause to believe" that the soldier who killed Radad had "committed the offense of [m]urder."

Page	Date of Document	Document
A-358	May 19, 2004	Memorandum re operational review of investigation into death of Obeed Hethere Radad.
A-360	Dec. 31, 2003	Excerpt from file relating to Article 15-6 investigation into incident in which prisoner's jaw was broken. Documents include Transcription of prisoner's statement, Dec. 18, 2003 (362); Memorandum for record re Article 15-6 investigation, Dec. 31, 2003 (363–364); Factual summary, undated (368–369); Findings, undated (370–374).

January 25, 2002

MEMORANDUM FOR THE PRESIDENT

FROM: ALBERTO R. GONZALES

SUBJECT: DECISION RE APPLICATION OF THE GENEVA CON-
VENTION ON PRISONERS OF WAR TO THE CONFLICT
WITH AL QAEDA AND THE TALIBAN

PURPOSE

On January 18, I advised you that the Department of Justice had issued a
formal legal opinion concluding that the Geneva Convention III on the
Treatment of Prisoners of War (GPW) does not apply to the conflict with
al Qaeda. I also advised you that DOJ's opinion concludes that there are
reasonable grounds for you to conclude that GPW does not apply with
respect to the conflict with the Taliban. I understand that you decided that
GPW does not apply and, accordingly, that al Qaeda and Taliban detainees are not prisoners of war under the GPW.

The Secretary of State has requested that you reconsider that decision.
Specifically, he has asked that you conclude that GPW does apply to both
al Qaeda and the Taliban. I understand, however, that he would agree that
al Qaeda and Taliban fighters could be determined not to be prisoners of
war (POWs) but only on case-by-case basis following individual hearings
before a military board.

This memorandum outlines the ramifications of your decision and the
Secretary's request for reconsideration.

LEGAL BACKGROUND

As an initial matter, I note that you have the constitutional authority to
make the determination you made on January 18 that the GPW does not
apply to al Qaeda and the Taliban. (Of course, you could nevertheless, as
a matter of policy, decide to apply the principles of GPW to the conflict
with al Qaeda and the Taliban.) The Office of Legal Counsel of the
Department of Justice has opined that, as a matter of international and
domestic law, GPW does not apply to the conflict with al Qaeda. OLC
has further opined that you have the authority to determine that GPW
does not apply to the Taliban. As I discussed with you, the grounds for
such a determination may include:

- A determination that Afghanistan was a failed state because the
  Taliban did not exercise full control over the territory and people,

was not recognized by the international community, and was not capable of fulfilling its international obligations (e.g., was in widespread material breach of its international obligations).

- A determination that the Taliban and its forces were, in fact, not a government, but a militant, terrorist-like group.

OLC's interpretation of this legal issue is definitive. The Attorney General is charged by statute with interpreting the law for the Executive Branch. This interpretive authority extends to both domestic and international law. He has, in turn, delegated this role to OLC. Nevertheless, you should be aware that the Legal Adviser to the Secretary of State has expressed a different view.

RAMIFICATIONS OF DETERMINATION THAT GPW DOES NOT APPLY

The consequences of a decision to adhere to what I understood to be your earlier determination that the GPW does not apply to the Taliban include the following:

Positive:

- Preserves flexibility:
  - As you have said, the war against terrorism is a new kind of war. It is not the traditional clash between nations adhering to the laws of war that formed the backdrop for GPW. The nature of the new war places a high premium on other factors, such as the ability to quickly obtain information from captured terrorists and their sponsors in order to avoid further atrocities against American civilians, and the need to try terrorists for war crimes such as wantonly killing civilians. In my judgment, this new paradigm renders obsolete Geneva's strict limitations on questioning of enemy prisoners and renders quaint some of its provisions requiring that captured enemy be afforded such things as commissary privileges, scrip (i.e., advances of monthly pay), athletic uniforms, and scientific instruments.
  - Although some of these provisions do not apply to detainees who are not POWs, determination that GPW does not apply to al Qaeda and the Taliban eliminates any argument regarding the need for case-by-case determinations of POW status. It also holds open options for the future conflicts in which it may be more difficult to determine whether an enemy force as a whole meets the standard for POW status.
  - By concluding that GPW does not apply to al Qaeda and the Taliban, we avoid foreclosing options for the future, particularly against nonstate actors.

- Substantially reduces the threat of domestic criminal prosecution under the War Crimes Act (18 U.S.C. 2441).
  - That statute, enacted in 1996, prohibits the commission of a "war crime" by or against a U.S. person, including U.S. officials. "War crime" for these purposes is defined to include any grave breach of GPW or any violation of common Article 3 thereof (such as "outrages against personal dignity"). Some of these provisions apply (if the GPW applies) regardless of whether the individual being detained qualifies as a POW. Punishments for violations of Section 2441 include the death penalty. A determination that the GPW is not applicable to the Taliban would mean that Section 2441 would not apply to actions taken with respect to the Taliban.
  - Adhering to your determination that GPW does not apply would guard effectively against misconstruction or misapplication of Section 2441 for several reasons.
    - First, some of the language of the GPW is undefined (it prohibits, for example, "outrages upon personal dignity" and "inhuman treatment"), and it is difficult to predict with confidence what actions might be deemed to constitute violations of the relevant provisions of GPW.
    - Second, it is difficult to predict the needs and circumstances that could arise in the course of the war on terrorism.
    - Third, it is difficult to predict the motives of prosecutors and independent counsels who may in the future decide to pursue unwarranted charges based on Section 2441. Your determination would create a reasonable basis in law that Section 2441 does not apply, which would provide a solid defense to any future prosecution.

Negative:

On the other hand, the following arguments would support reconsideration and reversal of your decision that the GPW does not apply to either al Qaeda or the Taliban:

- Since the Geneva Conventions were concluded in 1949, the United States has never denied their applicability to either U.S. or opposing forces engaged in armed conflict, despite several opportunities to do so. During the last Bush Administration, the United States stated that it "has a policy of applying the Geneva Conventions of 1949 whenever armed hostilities occur with regular foreign armed forces, even if arguments could be made that the threshold standards for the applicability of the Conventions … are not met."
- The United States could not invoke the GPW if enemy forces threatened to mistreat or mistreated U.S. or coalition forces captured during operations in Afghanistan, or if they denied Red Cross access or other POW privileges.

- The War Crimes Act could not be used against the enemy, although other criminal statutes and the customary law of war would still be available.
- Our position would likely provoke widespread condemnation among our allies and in some domestic quarters, even if we make clear that we will comply with the core humanitarian principles of the treaty as a matter of policy.
- Concluding that the Geneva Convention does not apply may encourage other countries to look for technical "loopholes" in future conflicts to conclude that they are not bound by GPW either.
- Other countries may be less inclined to turn over terrorists or provide legal assistance to us if we do not recognize a legal obligation to comply with the GPW.
- A determination that GPW does not apply to al Qaeda and the Taliban could undermine U.S. military culture which emphasizes maintaining the highest standards of conduct in combat, and could introduce an element of uncertainty in the status of adversaries.

RESPONSE TO ARGUMENTS FOR APPLYING GPW TO THE AL QAEDA AND THE TALIBAN

On balance, I believe that the arguments for reconsideration and reversal are unpersuasive.

- The argument that the U.S. has never determined that GPW did not apply is incorrect. In at least one case (Panama in 1989) the U.S. determined that GPW did not apply even though it determined for policy reasons to adhere to the convention. More importantly, as noted above, this is a new type of warfare—one not contemplated in 1949 when the GPW was framed—and requires a new approach in our actions towards captured terrorists. Indeed, as the statement quoted from the administration of President George Bush makes clear, the U.S. will apply GPW "whenever hostilities occur *with regular foreign armed forces*." By its terms, therefore, the policy does not apply to a conflict with terrorists, or with irregular forces, like the Taliban, who are armed militants that oppressed and terrorized the people of Afghanistan.
- In response to the argument that we should decide to apply GPW to the Taliban in order to encourage other countries to treat captured U.S. military personnel in accordance with the GPW, it should be noted that your policy of providing humane treatment to enemy detainees gives us the credibility to insist on like treatment for our soldiers. Moreover, even if GPW is not applicable, we can still bring war crimes charges against anyone who mistreats U.S. personnel. Finally, I note that our adversaries in several recent conflicts have not been deterred by GPW in their mistreatment of

captured U.S. personnel, and terrorists will not follow GPW rules in any event.

- The statement that other nations would criticize the U.S. because we have determined that GPW does not apply is undoubtedly true. It is even possible that some nations would point to that determination as a basis for failing to cooperate with us on specific matters in the war against terrorism. On the other hand, some international and domestic criticism is already likely to flow from your previous decision not to treat the detainees as POWs. And we can facilitate cooperation with other nations by reassuring them that we fully support GPW where it is applicable and by acknowledging that in this conflict the U.S. continues to respect other recognized standards.

- In the treatment of detainees, the U.S. will continue to be constrained by (i) its commitment to treat the detainees humanely and, to the extent appropriate and consistent with military necessity, in a manner consistent with the principles of GPW, (ii) its applicable treaty obligations, (iii) minimum standards to treatment universally recognized by the nations of the world, and (iv) applicable military regulations regarding the treatment of detainees.

- Similarly, the argument based on military culture fails to recognize that our military remain bound to apply the principles of GPW because that is what you have directed them to do.

UNCLASSIFIED

THE WHITE HOUSE
WASHINGTON

February 7, 2002

MEMORANDUM FOR THE VICE PRESIDENT
      THE SECRETARY OF STATE
      THE SECRETARY OF DEFENSE
      THE ATTORNEY GENERAL
      CHIEF OF STAFF TO THE PRESIDENT
      DIRECTOR OF CENTRAL INTELLIGENCE
      ASSISTANT TO THE PRESIDENT FOR NATIONAL
        SECURITY AFFAIRS
      CHAIRMAN OF THE JOINT CHIEFS OF STAFF

SUBJECT: Humane Treatment of al Qaeda and Taliban Detainees

1. Our recent extensive discussions regarding the status
of al Qaeda and Taliban detainees confirm that the application of the Geneva Convention Relative to the Treatment
of Prisoners of War of August 12, 1949 (Geneva) to the
conflict with al Qaeda and the Taliban involves complex
legal questions. By its terms, Geneva applies to conflicts
involving 'High Contracting Parties,' which can only be
states. Moreover, it assumes the existence of 'regular'
armed forces fighting on behalf of states. However, the
war against terrorism ushers in a new paradigm, one in
which groups with broad, international reach commit horrific
acts against innocent civilians, sometimes with the direct
support of states. Our Nation recognizes that this new
paradigm -- ushered in not by us, but by terrorists --
requires new thinking in the law of war, but thinking that
should nevertheless be consistent with the principles of
Geneva.

2. Pursuant to my authority as Commander in Chief and Chief
Executive of the United States, and relying on the opinion
of the Department of Justice dated January 22, 2002, and on
the legal opinion rendered by the Attorney General in his
letter of February 1, 2002, I hereby determine as follows:

  a. I accept the legal conclusion of the Department of
Justice and determine that none of the provisions
of Geneva apply to our conflict with al Qaeda in
Afghanistan or elsewhere throughout the world because,
among other reasons, al Qaeda is not a High Contracting
Party to Geneva.

  b. I accept the legal conclusion of the Attorney General
and the Department of Justice that I have the authority
under the Constitution to suspend Geneva as between
the United States and Afghanistan, but I decline to

Reason: 1.5 (d)
Declassify on: 02/07/12

UNCLASSIFIED

2

exercise that authority at this time. Accordingly, I determine that the provisions of Geneva will apply to our present conflict with the Taliban. I reserve the right to exercise this authority in this or future conflicts.

   c.   I also accept the legal conclusion of the Department of Justice and determine that common Article 3 of Geneva does not apply to either al Qaeda or Taliban detainees, because, among other reasons, the relevant conflicts are international in scope and common Article 3 applies only to "armed conflict not of an international character."

   d.   Based on the facts supplied by the Department of Defense and the recommendation of the Department of Justice, I determine that the Taliban detainees are unlawful combatants and, therefore, do not qualify as prisoners of war under Article 4 of Geneva. I note that, because Geneva does not apply to our conflict with al Qaeda, al Qaeda detainees also do not qualify as prisoners of war.

3.   Of course, our values as a Nation, values that we share with many nations in the world, call for us to treat detainees humanely, including those who are not legally entitled to such treatment. Our Nation has been and will continue to be a strong supporter of Geneva and its principles. As a matter of policy, the United States Armed Forces shall continue to treat detainees humanely and, to the extent appropriate and consistent with military necessity, in a manner consistent with the principles of Geneva.

4.   The United States will hold states, organizations, and individuals who gain control of United States personnel responsible for treating such personnel humanely and consistent with applicable law.

5.   I hereby reaffirm the order previously issued by the Secretary of Defense to the United States Armed Forces requiring that the detainees be treated humanely and, to the extent appropriate and consistent with military necessity, in a manner consistent with the principles of Geneva.

6.   I hereby direct the Secretary of State to communicate my determinations in an appropriate manner to our allies, and other countries and international organizations cooperating in the war against terrorism of global reach.

SUMMARIZED WITNESS STATEMENT OF Lt Col (b)(6)　former Interrogation Control Element (ICE) Chief, who was interviewed on 22 March 2005 at his home in Alabama.

I was stationed at Guantanamo Bay, Cuba (GTMO) on or about the first week of December 2002 and re-deployed at the end of June 2003. I was the Interrogation Control Element (ICE) Chief.

During the course of the interview I was asked about what I knew about detainee abuse at Guantanamo. I was specifically asked about the following acts: Inappropriate use of military working dogs, inappropriate use of duct tape, impersonation of or interference with FBI agents, inappropriate use of loud music and/or yelling, sleep deprivation, short-shackling, inappropriate use of extreme technique, to include the use of lap dances and simulated menstrual fluids.

I have personal knowledge of the following:

It was my understanding that prior to SECDEF approval of the Special Interrogation Plan for ISN (b)((in early December 2002), the guidance for interrogation procedures was Field Manual 34-52.

(b)(6)

When I arrived at GTMO, (b)(6)　my predecessor, arranged for SERE instructors to teach their techniques to the interrogators at GTMO. The instructors did give some briefings to the Joint Interrogation Group (JIG) interrogators. MG Miller and I didn't believe the techniques were appropriate for the JTF-GTMO mission.

I never heard of any interrogators on my watch impersonating FBI agents. I do know that an interrogator, "LT (b)(6)　on the Middle Eastern Team, impersonated a Department of State agent prior to my arrival at GTMO. I would not have had a problem with an interrogator impersonating any federal agency.

Loud music was used during selected interrogations. The rule on volume was that it should not be so loud that it would blow the detainee's ears out.

Yelling was also used on occasion during interrogations. Like music, the volume was never too loud, just a raised voice.

There were times that interrogators adjusted the air conditioner in an attempt to make the interrogation booth cold. It wasn't like the booth was a "snow storm" but it was cool. The temperature depended on the cooperation of the detainee. It was a technique used to make the detainee uncomfortable. I don't believe this would be in an interrogation plan.

847

DOD JUNE

A-8

From: _____ CW3 (H)
Sent: Monday, September 09, 2002 11:?9 AM
To: _____ CIV(H), _____ CIV (H), _____ Civ (H), _____   b6 -1,2
_____ (H), _____ (E-mail) (E-mail) _____ ' (E-mail) (E-mail)
(E-mail), _____ E-mail) (E-mail) (E-mail), _____ (E-mail) ' (E-mail) (E-   b7C -1,2
mail) (E-mail) _____ E-mail)

Subject: FW Ft Bragg Training

Importance. High

To All

b6 -2   I just received this LTC_____ directed his guys to try and get us slots for this course and apparently
b7C -2   they were successful I know that CITFHQ is cool on this course, maybe we can identify someone else to
           fill the seats since they already got them for us I made some inquiries at DoDPI and they might be
           interested in filling a slot or two if we aren't

_____   b6 -2

                            b7C -2

-----Original Message-----
From: _____ Major (H)
b6 -2   **Sent:** Monday, September 09, 2002 11 55 AM
        To _____ LTC (H)
        Cc _____ Maj (H), _____ CW3 (H), _____ @assochqis01 redasoc socom sml mil
b7C -2 **Subject:** Ft Bragg Training

LTC_____
b6 -2   1 I received approval today for 6 additional slots at the BSCT's upcoming Interrogation Training at Ft
b7C -2 Bragg 16-20 Sept SFC_____ at the USASOC Psychological Applications Directorate needs the
        following information as soon as possible for the additional 6 attendees

              a Name
              b SSN
              c Organization
              d Documentation of security clearance

b6 -2   2 SFC_____ fax is COMM_____ His phone is DSN_____
b7C -2 3 On-post billeting is not available at Ft Bragg Attendees must call the Airborne Inn at DSN_____   b6 -2
        for a nonavailability code and contact SPC_____ at JTF_____ or Ms_____ at DSN_____ for a   b7C -2
        list of local hotels

        4 An e-copy of the training POI is attached

        Respectfully,
b6 -2
b7C -2 MAJ_____

        📄
        JPRA Plan of
        Instruction for E.   ████████████████████████████████

                                    DETAINEES-1194

                                                              1177

SUMMARIZED WITNESS STATEMENT OF MAJOR GENERAL GEOFFREY D. MILLER

MG Miller was interviewed on 18 March 2005 at WFO, Arlington, Virginia. The witness was sworn by LtGen Schmidt. His statement was substantially as follows:

I was the Commanding General for the Joint Task Force, Guantanamo Bay, Cuba from 4 November 2002 to 26 March 2004.

My overall responsibility was interrogation and detention at Guatanamo Bay, Cuba. JTF-160 was set up for detention and JTF-170 was set up for interrogation. My task was to integrate them so that they were in synchronization. USSOUTHCOM wanted to improve intelligence and detention. I was told to fix it. It was broken. I did not perceive that I worked for the SECDEF. General Dunlavey and I had four days of overlap. We had a change over from 4-9 November 2002. We did not have a conversation about whether he had authority beyond GTMO. JTF-180 in Afghanistan was not in my command relationship. It was a coordination and information relationship. The detainees did come from JTF-180. Detainees and interrogators all came through JTF-180. There were no detainees that came from IRAQ or Operation IRAQI FREEDOM when I was there.

The command climate at GTMO was dysfunctional when I arrived. There were two separate organizations with senior leadership that was at odds with each other regarding how they would integrate their missions. My first job was putting that together. The leadership had a single mission focus that was separate. Single unit disparity did not allow the units to be successful. There was no abuse or torture going on. The organization was not working together efficiently. It did not affect the detainees. SOPs needed to be updated. The basic standard was going on. The detainees were treated in a humane manner.

I did receive FM 34-52. The additional techniques that were requested went up to GEN Hill. I was uncomfortable with Category III. I was not comfortable using Category III techniques in interrogations. We were going towards incentives. Category III would not help develop intelligence rapidly and effectively from the detainees there. I did not intend to use them. They were approved, but not directed. I had the latitude to use them. It was an order that came down through the SECDEF. I did not question them about not using the techniques in interrogation. They wanted to do aggressive techniques. Special Interrogation Plans (IPs) had to be done in detail and sent to a higher authority. The purpose of the techniques was to support the nation's effort. There were two Special IPs; they were enormous documents. The IPs were the way to set standards. Everyone understood where the limits were.

How controlling was I? I'll be frank with you, when you put an organization together you say here are the new standards. Some thought they were more aggressive. I would state how to do and what to do. It is part of team building for success. You win the battle one day at a time. Senior leadership got on board right away. That is why GEN Hill asked me to come down to GTMO.

AR 15-6 GTMO Investigation
Exhibit __45__ of 76 Exhibits

We had incidences of good faith mistakes. We stopped them. I would do a Commander's Inquiry and corrective action was done on an interrogator. Retraining was done. The interrogator would go back under the supervisor and then interrogate again. A junior interrogator needed oversight. It was a handful of occurrences. The occurrences did not rise to torture, maltreatment, or inhumane treatment. I had an interrogator that exceeded the bounds. It was a female interrogator who took off her BDU shirt and inappropriately rubbed on the detainee. The female rubbing was brought to my attention by a contract interrogator. We pulled her out. We found she did cross boundaries. She was given an administrative Letter of Reprimand and retained her. One incident, the interrogator asked the MP to help in an interrogation and the MP was actively involved. I got it fixed. We continued to refine the policy. We built the SOPs. It was a continuously evolving operation. We had a weekly meeting that had enormous leadership involvement about staying within standards. Whoever violated the standards received appropriate action. In another incident an MP could not control his temper. He struck a detainee. He was a pretty good soldier. It occurred in the cell block. The standards were well known. If any standards were violated, appropriate action would be taken. When a mistake was made we took appropriate action.

The detainees are ruthless, murderous people. We had to teach interrogators and MPs not to hate. I spent a lot of time with the chain of command and how to control them professionally. We had to talk about this to all interrogators.

There was a high leader touch. We had to lead the led. I was down there engaged at the Camp. I spent enormous amount of time going through the cell block. It was difficult keeping that balance. We had weekly meetings. The lawyer went over the standards. The lawyer would tell the interrogators that if you cross the line call me. It got to be a joke sometimes. I said call ████████ Do not cross those standards.

B 6

General Hill told me that you are the Commander. Here are the basic guidelines, go ahead, and go forward.

We had numerous actions routed through the J2, ████████ I worked for General Hill. A direct line to him would interrupt his command authority. I was very clear of my chain of command. I talked to OSD almost every day. There was lots of talk. I understood for whom I worked for. I had informal conversations with OSD. I sent a report to DEPSECDEF through USSOUTHCOM.

B 6

I have known General Hill for 20 years. If I had a problem, I would call him. We talked once or twice a week. I got guidance and all the support I needed.

The contractors probably made up roughly 50% of the personnel. There were a higher number of contract analysts that supported the interrogation mission. I gave the same talk to the contract analyst, their supervisor, and contract interrogators. I told them they were soldiers without the uniform.

2

The FBI was at the established weekly meeting. I had an FBI agent come down. They had opportunity to come to the meeting every week. We had a meeting and I gave the FBI Special Agent (SA) an hour. I told him it was anything he wanted to talk about. They had a different perspective. They had a law enforcement perspective. There was significant friction between the FBI, CITF and JTF on how interrogations were done. It was the first one and then SSA ▇▇▇▇▇▇▇ came later. I said here are the standards. No FBI SA questioned interrogation methodology. For segregation, we had to go to General Hill for 30 days. No one from the FBI came to talk to me about that. One of the Doctor's of CITF came to talk to me about interrogations. $\cancel{B}$ 6

I am not an expert on detention or interrogation. I spent an enormous amount of time to help me understand how I can do this business better. I had a talk with every leader, CITF, FBI and the JTF and told them that they would follow the standards. We would come in on occasion and look at interrogations.

Nothing placed me in a compromising situation.

There was an interrogation SOP in place when I got there. I split the JIG, ICE, and J2. They were counterproductive. It was the most dysfunctional I've ever seen. I could not believe it. It was senior leader's squabbling on personal matters. It was debilitating to the organization. The JIG did normal 2 stuff.

Military working dogs- No, not in interrogations. They were ▇▇▇▇▇▇▇▇▇▇ $\cancel{B}$ 6
▇▇▇ They were used for detention, not interrogation.

Duct tape – Not that I knew of. After I left I was told that a senior interrogator duct taped someone's mouth. I was told it was ▇▇▇▇▇▇▇ but that is only speculation. I was surprised. I don't know when it happened or the dates.
$\cancel{B}$ 6/
$\cancel{B}$ 7

I knew about the false flag. I don't know any instance. It was an authorized technique in the IP.

Impersonating FBI- No.

Yelling at detainee and loud music - ▇▇▇▇▇▇▇▇▇▇▇▇ It was an approved technique. The interrogator was authorized to do that.

Interference with FBI – There was an FBI and CITF focus on law enforcement on DoD guidance to develop intelligence. Their focus was on evidence. We were developing intelligence. They had a different focus. We followed DoD. FBI followed public law.

Sleep deprivation – ▇▇▇▇▇▇▇▇▇▇▇▇▇▇▇
$\cancel{B}$ 6/
$\cancel{B}$ 1

3

DOD JUNE

A-12

Short shackling. While I was there the detainees were chained to the eye-bolt for security. Every interrogator saw the detainee's legs and feet. I saw hundreds of interrogations. There were no stress positions. I gave guidance.

Food and water we do not use as a weapon. ████████ gained 30 pounds. 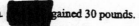 B 6

Hot and cold temperature – Not to my knowledge.

Inappropriate touching is not authorized. It was brought to my attention and we took care of it. The touching was done by a████████ B 6

SGT ██████ ever came to my attention. B 6

Ink and menstrual fluid – No.

There were no ghost detainees that were under the control of JTF-GTMO.

What humane treatment means to me are adequate food, shelter, medical care, and an environment that would not cause physical or mental abuse.

Some interrogation techniques that SECDEF granted authority for was beyond what I was comfortable with.

I never saw a memo or received a memo from the FBI that commented on SIPs.

It was clear to all the standards. The boundaries were for all. FBI and CITF had the same boundaries for all DoD included. In our discussions, everybody understood the standards. We have the same guidance. Everybody was formally notified that the superior commander made the guidance for interrogations.

I recognize the CITF memo objecting to the Special IP. I sent the interim plan up and it was approved by higher headquarters.

My focus was on the relationship between the CITF and the JTF. My focus was to improve it. They were at odds professionally and personally to the detriment of the mission. I called the CITF commander personally. We discussed that they were trying to develop evidence and the JTF position is not to develop evidence, but intelligence. The meeting was attended by General Ryder (the CID Commander), the CITF commander, and myself. We talked about an effective relationship about doing the mission. Subordinates are to work together effectively. An interrogation plan was approved and we followed the plan.

I directed the Director of the JIG to conduct an investigation into the lap dance allegation. I agreed with his recommendations and findings. The Director of the JIG was ████ ████████ was an effective leader and did a good over watch. He was a senior leader down there that would execute the mission. B 6

4

SECRET

The standards were known across the mission. I found out about the duct tape later. It never came to my level. I believe it came to ▮▮▮▮▮▮▮ attention took appropriate action.

I had several counseling sessions with ▮▮▮▮▮▮ He is very fine man. He did o manner that demonstrated what the standards are.

I am a standards guy. If you don't follow the standards, I'll take the appropriate action. When honest mistakes are made, you counsel, coach, and mentor.

I came to a dysfunctional organization not with mission success. I spent a large amount of time fixing it.

I am aware of the 2 May 2003 memo I signed. It was in response to the up and down incident. The letter was signed in response to an AR 15-6. It was a Fear up. The MPs were told not to do it anymore. This particular incident was a single incident. There were some cases of the MPs being actively involved in interrogation; that was not my guidance.

The ICRC brought several general statements for review

The guidance every week revalidated the guidance. It was very important.

The FBI and CIA representative came every 30 days.

Interrogations require that we would restate the standards every time. I knew the contract interrogators. I gave them the same speech for standards.

There was fairly large friction between JTF and ICRC. One of my focuses was to make it effective. It was producing unnecessary friction.

5

~~SECRET~~

I have not been through SERE. I don't believe to my knowledge that the interrogators went through SERE. The Psychologist, Forensic Psychologist, and Clinical Psychologist were trained through SERE.

Most interrogators were school trained on tactical interrogation. Tactical debriefing in strategic interrogation, some were trained. It was a small number. Some picked up training while there at GTMO.

We established the Tiger Team

I have seen several hundred interrogations now. When I showed up at GTMO I had never before witnessed one.

I believe one of the things we found out holistically. Unity of command for success and standards demonstrated success on a regular basis.

JTF-160 and JTF-170 was an ad hoc organization that started from a cold start that we normally would have in our institution. There were a lot of developmental operations and procedures for strategic interrogation on how things should be done.

Abuse problems are simply about discipline setting, standards and developing these standards. You need leadership involvement that clarifies and focuses on the importance of the mission.

GTMO and Iraq are different. I have had a year and a half to look at GTMO. GTMO used standards, how to treat detainee that are not combatants, how to interrogate, and incentive based interrogations. GTMO was successful.

Those interrogations did not involve torture.

GTMOize inappropriately reads bad information. I have heard of it. If you apply a leader and standard there is adherence to the standards. In another context, it brings discredit to all the leaders.

6

On 26 March 2004, I departed the island and went to Iraq three days later.

++

MG Geoffrey Miller was interviewed, via secure telephone, a second time on 31 March 2005 at 1843 EST. At that time Lieutenant General Schmidt advised MG Miller of his rights under Article 31 of the Uniform Code of Military Justice.

Lt Gen Schmidt asked MG Miller several questions regarding events that have been documented in the interrogation logs obtained from GTMO. Lt Gen Schmidt asked MG Miller if he had ever read the interrogation logs and MG Miller responded that he had not. MG Miller responded that he was unaware of the following events:

- on 21 and 23 Dec 02, MPs held down a detainee while ▆▆▆▆▆▆▆▆ straddled the detainee without placing weight on the detainee

- on 4 Dec 02, SGT ▆▆▆▆▆▆ massaged the detainee's back and neck over his clothing

SECRET

3779

that ██████████ showed ██████ fake letter from the White House that spelled out his authorization to make ████ disappear

MG Miller stated that had he known of the threats t██████ his family, he would never have allowed it.

MG Miller stated that he was aware of the following:

- that detainees were yelled at and that music was used in interrogations

that ████ was interrogated for 20 hours a day with 4 hours of sleep from 23 November 2002 until 15 January 2003

- that ████ was separated from the detainee population from 8 August 2002 until 15 January 2003

- that ██████ impersonated a Navy Captain from the White House

I declare under penalty that the foregoing in a true and correct summary of the stateme given by the witness, MG Geoffrey Miller. Executed at Davis-Monthan Air Force Bas., Arizona, on 31 March 2005.

RANDALL M. SCHMIDT
Lieutenant General, USAF
AR 15-6 Investigating Officer

8

SECRET

DEPARTMENT OF DEFENSE
CRIMINAL INVESTIGATION TASK FORCE (DEPLOYED)
GUANTANAMO BAY, CUBA

REPLY TO
ATTENTION OF

CITF-G/SAC

17 Dec 02

MEMORANDUM FOR JTF-GTMO/J2

SUBJECT: JTF GTMO "SERE" INTERROGATION SOP DTD 10 DEC 02

1. On 14 December 02, prior the "Decision Making" brief with the CG, you pro~~~~~~ ~~~ ~ ~~~ b(5)-1
of JTF GTMO SERE INTERROGATION SOP dated 10 Dec 02 and asked me to review it and
provide you my opinion. ██
█████████████████████ However, I do want to reiterate CITF-G's general position on
this matter. As outlined in our memorandum for JTF GTMO dated 15 Nov 02, CITF-G ████
███████████████████████ While the subject SOP clearly does not apply to
LEA (CITF and FBI) interrogators (applicable only to military and civilian interrogators assigned
to JTF-GTMO), LEA in conjunction with the FBI's Behavioral Analysis Unit want to provide
you the following general observations on ██████████████████

2. General Observations: Both the military and LEA share the identical mission of obtaining
intelligence in order to prevent future attacks on Americans. However, LEA has the additional
responsibility of seeking reliable information/evidence from detainees to be used in subsequent
legal proceedings.

3. ██
███
█████████████████████████████████████ b(7)E

4. The SERE methods were designed for use in a battlefield environment as a means of
collecting tactical intelligence (e.g., to uncover enemy plans, determine enemy strength,
movement, weapon capabilities and logistical support, etc.) ████████████
███
██████████ b(5)-1

5. LEA agents are responsible for investigating a wide variety of criminal and
counterintelligence matters around the world. Accordingly, they are highly trained and
experienced in eliciting information from reluctant subjects of diverse cultural and socio-
economic backgrounds. ████████████████████████████

Printed on ♻ Recycled Paper

1318

████████ ███████

109376

A-18

7. Utilizing rapport-based methods, LEA have realized numerous successes during several major terrorism investigations including the bombings of embassies in East Africa, the bombing of the USS Cole and the 1993 World Trade Center bombing. Like most of the GTMO detainees, the perpetrators of these terrorist acts were motivated by a distorted religious doctrine and reinforced by a group/cultural dynamic.

8.

1319

1027H

b(5)

14.

b(7)(c)-1

SPECIAL AGENT IN CHARGE
CRIMINAL INVESTIGATION TASK FORCE
GUANTANAMO

Copy:
JTF-GTMO/SJA
FBI SSA

1320

6937 I

SUMMARIZED WITNESS STATEMENT OF MG (RETIRED) MIKE DUNLAVEY

MG Mike Dunlavey, FORMER COMMANDER, JTF-170, was interviewed and made the following statement on or about 1007 hours, 17 March 2005, at WFO, Arlington, VA:

Appointment memos were shown to this witness. The witness went over the allegations.

Witness sworn by LtGen Schmidt. The witness provided the following testimony:

BACKGROUND:

How I became the JTF-170 Commander? I was working at the National Security Agency. On 14 February 2002, I was contacted to meet with the SECDEF. I received a joint service billet description. I met with the SECDEF on the 20th or 21st of February 2002, along with the Deputy SECDEF, Wolferwitz and a number of other personnel.

The SECDEF told me that DoD had accumulated a number of bad guys. He wanted to set up interrogation operations and to identify the senior Taliban and senior operatives and to obtain information on what they were going to do regarding their operations and structure.

The SECDEF said he wanted a product and he wanted intelligence now. He told me what he wanted; not how to do it.

Initially, I was told that I would answer to the SECDEF and USSOUTHCOM. I did not have to deal with USCENTCOM. Their mission had nothing to do with my mission. Everything had to go up to USSOUTHCOM then to JCS. The directions changed and I got my marching orders from the President of the United States. I was told by the SECDEF that he wanted me back in Washington DC every week to brief him.

I have 35 years of Intelligence experience. I am a trial lawyer and between interrogations in Vietnam, being a CI Commander, and as a trial lawyer, I have done over 3,000 interrogations. The SECDEF needed a common sense way on how to do business.

The mission was to get intelligence to prevent another 9/11.

GTMO Situation:

Mike Lehnert did a miraculous job of getting Camp X-ray set up.

When I got to GTMO the facility consisted of literally a dangling fence. Detainees were right next to one another. In the Seabee hut for example, everyone saw who was being interrogated.

DoD photographers were taking pictures for historical purposes. They published them with no regard for security. My job was to establish it.

(B) 6 [redacted] was the Assistant J2. He worked up the JMD and tried to fill it with bodies to accomplish the interrogation mission.

We have not fought a real war since Vietnam. Except for DHS, our interrogators were virtually inexperienced. It was an OJT situation on the ground at GTMO.

When I arrived, I met the Special Agent in Charge (SAC) for the FBI. He was a SAC out of Miami. Interrogations had started but there was no system. For example, the interrogators thought [redacted] was the big dog. He made a lot of noise in the prison grounds B 6 but he was not the big guy. There simply was no process in place to assess who the real B 6 leaders were.

JTF-160 was losing control of detainees. There was a major riot with the detainees. They were shaking out their blankets and throwing food.

I tried to set up a process that would work for the FBI. [redacted] worked the B 6 U.S.S. Cole incident. He was the best interrogator. He was a native speaker and was very, very good.

The military linguists were worthless. They came out of school and could order coffee, but they were getting smoked by the detainees.

The guards were living no better than the detainees.

The standard was to treat them humanely.

Frankly, the 1992 version of FM 34-52 had a problem with it. It was 18 years old and it was how interrogations were done for POWs.  B1

B1

My people, the interrogators, got briefed on what my task force rules were.

The Geneva Conventions applied. I treated them as human beings, but not like soldiers. They had a significant culture. The rugs and beads were significant to me. I let them practice religion,  B1

The detainees do not control the environment.

2

Everyday we had undercover FBI agents o̶█████████̶ interrogating. We did want to protect the identity of the people. We had news media almost continuously on the island.

██████████████████████████████ **B1**
██████████████████████████████ **B3**
███

We eventually got good information on who the leaders were and then we surprised them with a response team. We grabbed them and took them out to the Brig where the ICRC could see them, but they could not talk to them.

We had detainees that jumped the guards. There was a guy that took the MRE spoon, shaved it down and made a scalpel. We changed their sheets to the sheets in the federal prison system so they can't be torn or tied. They took magnets, welding rods, and fashion them into weapons. We collected a footlocker full of weapons.

INTERROGATIONS:

We built Tiger Teams ██ **B1**

The Combined Investigative Task Force (CITF) brought to the staff and the Joint Commander, a capability to collect evidence to criminally prosecute cases.

Our mission was to stop Americans from being killed. We were trying to work through the ████████████████████████████████ I moved out smartly and met with **B1** the CINC.

CITF ██ They had good investigative skills and had experience dealing with these people. We had mass murderers.

The FBI SAC came every two weeks. They could not decide what to do. They never built up any type of rapport. We had problems from the get go with the FBI. They had the best interrogators. Interrogations were done in my facilities. Any intelligence they got they would share with us.

We had an SOP on how we did business. We knew from the Manchester document that they would accuse us of torture and inhumane treatmen██████████████████ **B 1**
███ **B 5**

3

Exhibit 12
Page 4
Denied in full
Exemption 1

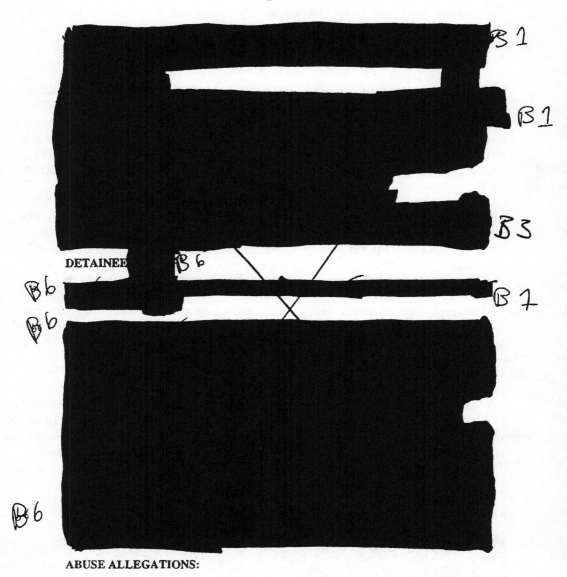

B1

B1

B3

DETAINEE B6

B6

B6

B7

B6

ABUSE ALLEGATIONS:

I would show up unannounced to see what was going on in the interrogations. Someone being out of line is very possible. I won't equate it to NYPD Blue. There were situations where a guy would urinate or jack off on a female interrogator. He did it to offend her. I would not allow them to use religion as a shield. The detainees threw feces at the guards.

DOD JUNE   3742

An Article 15 was given to a guard for hosing down a detainee. The detainee threw a bucket of urine on him.

If something was going wrong, the climate in the command was comfortable for self - reporting.

We all knew the rules; and we followed them period.

I fell on my sword for the guy that was 100 years old. He was 90 to 105 years old and in his 4th lifetime. He had no real good information. If he died we could not do a forensic study. I would violate Sharia. He was not an American soldier that would not come out in one piece. There were two other guys in their 70s to 80s. One was a cab driver that took Al Qaeda to the border. We got him out of there in October. We released 211 detainees. Only Al Qaeda reported abuses. None were abused. If a guy had information, we would focus on him.

The duct tape incident, I remember that. It was in June or July 2002. I did an internal investigation. They sat and screamed at us. I think the MPs helped the interrogators. I don't know if the guard was directed to restrain the detainee from doing something As a judge if they screamed in court, I would tape them to a chair and tape their mouths. In a legitimate detainee facility, you would do it. If we did not, they would do it.

The detainees were treated humanely. They had a high status of care. They were not EPWs. They refused to identify themselves. On the postcards they gave us the wrong name.

Humane is who we are as the American military.

My first lesson was in Vietnam. I went out in the field and the South Vietnamese had two POWs. They got screamed at and kicked around. I watched what was going on. I was a graduate of DLA. There was a big plate of boiled rice with flies on it. I asked one of POWs when he had last eaten. He said, "four days ago and water two days ago". They chained him to a .50 cal and said he would kill him if he ran away. I had a canteen. I drank and gave him a drink. It worked. I got his name.

I employed what worked and did not work.

6

Regarding the use of dogs. The dogs would be used to escort movement of personnel from detention to interrogation facilities. Dogs were there to intimidate. There were only four dogs in the whole facility. They were there to prevent riots and for security

The dogs were under control of the MP handler. They would have the dogs look at the detainees. On the other side of the coin, we do use the dogs as prisoner control in the federal system. We did not let the dogs bark or bite detainees. If ▓▓▓▓ brought dogs to my attention, I probably would have approved it. We did not use the dogs on the prisoners.

Keep in mind, they don't like dogs. Unless the dogs are on patrol, they would be in an interrogation room. Using dogs is equal to the Fear Up technique. It breaks their concentration in their response to the interrogation techniques. They would be thinking about that dog. Is the dog a real threat? Absolutely not.

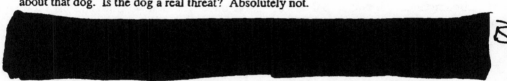

We physically removed an FBI agent when he went across the desk at a detainee. It happened in my first three months. He was a big kind of guy. The detainee said something like he knows his family and that he was going to kill them. I think it happened during my tenure.

FBI impersonation? No, not on a normal course of business. We did not identify who people where. The names and rank were covered. The FBI wore polo shirts and their badge. The CITF did the same thing. It was part of the deception technique. Maybe there was a complaint. I never knew or heard about it. Would CITF and FBI act as DoD? It could have been a technique.

Interfering with FBI; we had a significant difference of opinion. There was a management issue where ▓▓▓▓ would come in and did not coordinate for a detainee because they wanted to talk to the detainee right away. FBI had interrogation plans.

7   ~~SECRET~~

DOD JUNE

3744

They did not brief DoD. CITF was going in without telling us. Every IP had to coordinated for facilities and linguists.

Loud music and yelling was part of a sequence of events to disrupt the detainees thought process.

Chaining the detainee in a fetal position is not a normal procedure to be used in interrogation. If the detainee leaped at an interrogator, it might have been used for security. It is not a normal procedure. The interrogators were instructed not to touch the detainees. They were to leave it to the guards.

If short shackled, the detainee had done an offensive action.

Food and water deprivation I find incredibly hard to believe. BG Baccus would not have tolerated that. Short rations were a disciplinary process. ICRC was there everyday. The Chaplain was there everyday. The average detainee gained 16 pounds. They got medical attention everyday.

The detainees went on a hunger strike. When weight metabolism decreased they went down to the medical facility. They had to give the detainees forcible IVs. They wanted Ensure. We made a joke about it.

There was no lap dance or rubbing up on detainees. There is no doubt the interrogators took off their BDU tops. They wanted to be comfortable. The hardcore detainees did not respond to women. They would not look at women. I did not approve it under any circumstances. It was stupid and offensive under the Geneva Conventions. It does not serve any useful purpose. If that occurred, I want to see the FBI report.

Red ink used as menstrual fluid? I've never heard of that technique. It would disrupt the intelligence and prosecution gathering operations.

Ghost detainees...every person that landed on the island was processed through the MP cycle.

JTF-160 was in disarray when I took over. They had 60 outstanding Inspector General complaints. We tried to clean up as much as we could before MG Miller came.

JTF-170 served two Article 15s to two individuals for personal misconduct. It was not detainee related.

8

SECRET

Other than the incident with FBI contractor that physically went after the detainee, I don't recall any other problems with FBI agents and detainees. LTC ██████ and LTC ██████ might have counseled someone for wrong or inappropriate behavior.

I counseled people on the lack of preparation. I did it as a group. I counseled FBI. I never had information from the IG or JAG that we had a problem. It would stick out.

██████ FBI did separate interviews. I have faith that the ██████ was not abusing detainees. I had a high degree of faith. I had access to anything I wanted.

I also had high faith that the FBI was conducting proper interviews. Physical abuse just does not work. Successful prosecution was their goal. They did not want to jeopardize that.

We had four to six guys in Camp X-Ray. To put a detainee in X-Ray required that we notify USSOUTHCOM and JCS and we would have done a report in writing.

I was interviewed for the Church report.

Virtually no one had a degree of expertise to deal with these people. They do not subscribe to our values legally and morally. We did benefit from some great young people. We had a native Pakistani that was fluent in Arabic.

FBI's approach was that you would stay in jail if you did not talk to us.

Was ██████ tortured? No.

I declare under penalty that the foregoing in a true and correct summary of the statement given by the witness, MG (ret) Mike Dunlavey. Executed at Davis-Monthan Air Force Base, Arizona, on 29 March 2005.

RANDALL M. SCHMIDT
Lieutenant General, USAF
AR 15-6 Investigating Officer

9   ~~SECRET~~

Testimony of LTG RANDALL M. SCHMIDT
Taken 24 August, 2005 at Davis Mountain Air Force Base, Arizona;
between the hours of 0910 and 1055 by ▓▓▓▓▓▓
And ▓▓▓▓▓▓▓▓▓▓▓▓▓▓▓▓▓▓
Department of the Army Inspector General, Investigations Division,
Presidential Towers, Crystal City, Virginia.

▓▓▓▓▓▓▓▓▓ The time is 0910. This tape-recorded interview is conducted
on 24 August, 2005, at Davis Monthan Air Force Base, Arizona.

Persons present are the witness Lieutenant General Randall Marc
Schmidt and the Investigating Officer ▓▓▓▓▓▓▓▓▓▓▓▓▓▓▓▓▓▓
▓▓▓▓▓▓▓

This inquiry is directed by the Vice Chief of Staff of the Army concerning
allegations made against a senior official assigned to the Department of the Army.

An Inspector General is an impartial fact-finder for the Directing Authority.
Testimony taken by an IG and reports based upon that testimony may be used for
official purposes. Access is normally restricted to persons who clearly need the
information to perform their official duties. In some cases, disclosure to other persons
may be required by law or regulation or may be directed by proper authority.

Sir, upon completion of this interview I will ask you whether you consent to
the release of your testimony if requested by members of the public pursuant to the
Freedom of Information Act or FOIA. Since I will ask you to provide your Social
Security Number to help identify you as the person testifying, you've previously been
provided with an explanation of the Privacy Act by ▓▓▓▓▓▓ Sir, do you understand
the Privacy Act?

LTG SCHMIDT: I do.

▓▓▓▓▓▓▓▓▓ You are not suspected of any criminal offense and are not the
subject of any unfavorable information. Before we continue, I was to remind you of the
importance of presenting truthful testimony. It is a violation of Federal Law to knowingly
make a false statement under oath.

Do you have any questions before we begin?

LTG SCHMIDT: No.

▓▓▓▓▓▓▓▓▓: Please raise your right hand so I may administer the oath.

[Lieutenant General Randall Marc Schmidt, US Army Force, was sworn and testified
under oath as follows:]

Q.   You may lower your hand, Sir. Sir, please for the record can you state your full name?

A.   Okay. Randall Marc Schmidt.

Q.   Your rank and component?

A.   Lieutenant General, United States Air Force.

Q.   Your current position and organization?

A.   Commander, 12th Air Force, US Southern Command Air Forces.

Q.   Your Social Security Account Number should you choose to disclose it, Sir?

A.   I'm going to withhold that, the Social Security Number.

Q.   Yes, Sir. And a good address either home or office keeping in mind that the return address on any correspondence from out office will indicate it's from the Department of the Army Inspector General.

A.   Okay, [REDACTED]

Q.   Thank you, Sir, and a phone number?

A.   Okay, it's [REDACTED] is the home phone.

[REDACTED] Okay. Thank you, Sir, [REDACTED] is going to lead off with the questions today.

BY [REDACTED]

Q.   All right, thank you, Sir. Sir, just to start out can you provide us a quick background on why the AR 15-6 Investigation that we now call the Schmidt Furlow Report was initiated?

A.   Well like everybody else I was reading the papers about the abuse allegations at Guantánamo and I passed the papers everyday thanking God that I was not involved in that. I could envision myself with combat operations and training and things like that. I got the phone call from my boss, General Craddock, now the Commander of US Southern Command and he said he had kind of run into a stop on an investigation that was currently undergoing. That General Furlow had been tasked

[REDACTED]

to run it--he had essentially two months underway with a small team looking into these allegations. I was unaware of that. That investigation.

Q.   Okay.

A.   He said that he had been informed by the investigator General Furlow that, he was, in a position where he had to interview officers senior to him. Two, specifically and that unless he received some sort of extraordinary permissions or whatever that, that he'd need some help.

So General Craddock called me said that he needed me to take over the investigation and as he saw it, I didn't have to go back and reinvent the investigation. And-- I'll explain what the investigation was as I got into it, but he needed me to essentially to take over, take it to completion, get the football across the goal line essentially with these two other interviews.

The interviews as he understood it would probably be Major Generals. So he needed a Lieutenant General. Where he only has two assigned there, Lieutenant General Marty Bern, Marine Corps, he's about to retire and me. And I was about to go off to a major exercise. And would I help him. He actually asked and I said I'll find out if I can disengage myself from this exercise.

Q.   Okay.

A.   The largest one that the Air Force and the Army are doing this entire year in the Continental United States. And I was able to get two of my Deputies to take that on and get permission from everybody to do that. So I called him back very quickly and said I would do the investigation. So I was hooked on that. He gave me 30-days.

Q.   Okay.

A.   He said there'd be probably no extensions to that as he has already extended the initial one, and it looked at that time, that there would only be two additional senior officers investigated.

Q.   Okay.

A.   So I convened a small team here. Joined up with the Army team. General Furlow, and his three others, and we set to work on getting that last piece done. What we found was there was a whole lot of other work to be done. The genesis of the investigation was FBI allegations into detainee abuse there--it was pretty well defined and there were essentially a couple of others that were tacked on. Three I believe.

Q.   Okay.

A.   They were tacked by General Craddock to say this clean up. These are things that would beg questions later. So put those into your investigation. Then he also told me that if I saw anything else down there in the course of our investigation that those would also be under my purview to investigate. Any allegations or indications of abuse by any party not just the FBI. So we had those. The FBI allegations were of some number and those are all in my testimony.

Q.   Right.

A   We boiled those down to events and not individual agents. Some agents had seen probably the same thing and it was the same kind of event so we looked to corroborate that. So this thing was actually pretty small. It looked like, let's go just knock these things out one after the other.

Q.   Okay.

A.   What happened was as we began to do these investigations, and I needed the background before I started to do the last interviews. And the last interviews were with, possibly Geoff Miller and JTF-160-170 Commanders that were being combined, Dunlavey.

Q.   Okay.

A.   Major General Dunlavey, a Reservist. So those were the two I think I was being postured to interview. As we got through this, I just needed to understand how the situation got to where it was and why these abuses presented themselves. What was perception or what was ground-truth and that sort of thing.

I went through all of the interviews that had been previously conducted. These were the FBI agents who had actually answered the e-mail queries from the FBI, Department of Justice, saying if you see anything, in the interrogation Protocols down at Guantanamo that conflicted with stand procedure, that—that the Agency would use then respond to this. And there were varied responses. I think it came down to about 26 which melted it down to about there were 11 of which we got down to about nine were actually events that needed to be investigated. And those were the subjects that went through the interviews with all these FBI agents.

Q.   Okay.

A.   There were-- four I believe, FBI agents who has responded out of those 26 that we were unable to contact. For a bunch of reasons. Some were still deployed into combat OPS and that sort of thing and the Agency wasn't about to disclose where they were and that sort of thing. There was another significant, agent that we were just not able to get hold of. And we repeatedly asked the FBI if we could get to them. The FBI was very cooperative. But they were much like an IG charter, they were not going

to say well you contact her at this address. And here's her home--you know they weren't ever going to do that.

Q.   Okay.

A.   As it turned out  She was very sick. They were—it was being sort of a protective sort of thing. And it was none of our business and it wasn't until after the Senate probed this on why—you know, Senator Warner, you know, didn't think very much of this. Why aren't you talking to her. And finally--and the FBI finally said hey she's just now ░░░░░░░░░░░░░░░░░ and we'll make her available now. Obviously things started breaking loose. But we knew what she had alleged.

Q.   Right.

A.   We saw her e-mails, we felt that we had got a complete idea of what she thought she saw and everything.

Q.   Okay.

A.   And so we went that way. So we understood the bubble. So now I'm in the investigation. I have no time. I have 30-days. I went back and relooked the testimony in the interviews. None was sworn. It was a hard to decipher kind of gobblygook. A lot of the testimony was very difficulty to understand.

Q.   This is the FBI testimony that they took?

A.   Our transcribing of the interviews that were done with these agents.

Q.   Oh, I see.

A.   From the time that I took over.

Q.   Okay.

A.   So we spent about a week. We came back to Tucson here with the Army team and the Air Force team, knowing that we got a mindset and started to rebuild and sorted this thing. So we used the interviewer now saying is this was what it meant. Did this person mean this and say this. What's fact. What's opinion and that sort thing. Just sorting that thing out. It took a little of our time. Then I got to the interviews. The interviews, I think actually interviewed seven General officers.

Q.   Okay.

A.   I wanted to cover the entire spectrum of when we stood on operations to include just operations for detention before we got to interrogations at Guantánamo. All the way through today and went down there to interview Jay Hood. Down there today and I had a chance to go down to GTMO again and look at all the things that are going on down there and dig into that.

We found some information that, was very enlightening, in terms of our investigation on that trip.

Q.   Okay.

A.   Those were the interrogation logs that nobody else had even seen for some reason. And they were right three in plain sight kind of thing. Went through it and that's where a lot of our information came from.

Q.   Okay.

A.   At that point, I had already interviewed General Miller.

Q.   Okay.

A.   Okay, and that's what I am trying to, the part that you're concerned about.

Q.   Right.

A.   I had already interviewed General Miller and he has already talked to me about you know what he knew and what he had seen and what was his policies. A lengthy interview. A couple of hours. When I came back, I did a cursory debrief to General Craddock and at that time I came back out and we had to interview General Miller again.

Q.   Okay.

A.   And this time it was point blank. I swore him. And by the way all the testimony after I joined was all sworn testimony.

Q.   And, Sir, just real quick. What made you decided that you needed to interview him again? What caused that?

A.   It was because—now I knew what his policies were.

Q.   Okay.

A.   I knew what he had issued as far as direction. I knew how things had developed as he evolved into what he thought were appropriate detention and interrogation policies and techniques. But I never really sat there on the data that I now

knew and said, did you know--is that part of your policy. Did you know and is this part of your policy? And then I had a chance to do that. So I had two interviews with General Miller.

Q.   Okay.

A.   One was face-to-face. The other one was sworn over the telephone.

Q.   Okay.

A.   And he was very familiar with both of them, and that's--some of the stuff is secret and we had kept that in the secret classification. So when I discuss what we talked about, that will be secret.

Q.   Okay, Sir.

A.   Okay, so at that point is when I started finding out what the disconnect was. So now I investigated all the background mechanics of how guidance as far as techniques for interrogations has come to play and I had to develop all that. And we didn't get that through the FBI interviews.

Q.   Right.

A.   Now I had to figure out how the FBI perceived things to be, abusive, degrading-- one individual even used the word 'torturous' in his assessment of what was going on down there.

Q.   Okay.

A.   So this is what they had seen. Then I had to figure out what they had seen--or what was seen down there was it authorized. Was it torture. Did it mean to be abusive. Did it mean to be degrading. You know, what was the intent of all that and I had to marry that up. Now I'm into the judgment part of this thing.

Q.   Right.

A.   So I finally had the full bubble on that. And here's where it went. What they saw is what they saw. We didn't question the FBI's integrity on this. If they said they saw somebody short shackled to the floor, then somebody was short shackled to the floor. We didn't---that was a given. We didn't question it. There was--what was hard to nail down was when they couldn't tell plus or minus a week or plus or minus a month; or plus or minus two months or three months when they saw this.

Q.   Okay.

A.   Which building they saw it in. Who else was there. When they couldn't put that to it, then it kind of went into the vague we're going to investigate it. We're going to look into that. But it was very hard to nail those down. So we had sort of a spectrum of not credibility but of defining the event.

Q.   Okay.

A.   We were able to prove in fact short shackling did happen. And that covered numerous of the FBI perceptions of what they had seen.

Q.   Okay.

A.   Was short shackling authorized. It was never authorized in interrogation. It was authorized as a security control measure for detention.

Q.   Okay.

A.   The handover from the detention to interrogation is a longer period than you might imagine. They have very, very prescribed, meticulously programmed how to put the manacles on, the detainee turns around, and they do this. It's a check list by the numbers kind of thing. Which it has to be. And they do that today and it's quite impressive. It takes time.

When some of these detainees were brought into the interrogation area, some of the control measures that would be used in detention are still used to get them set-up for the interviews/interrogations. And then, when the interrogation began then the interrogation protocols which did not allow for short-shacking detention, that's where the thing did not allow for some of the control measures.

Q.   Okay.

A.   The strip searches and things like that, where they're done for security control. Were done in detention, for instance. And those were inappropriate. And those were things that we brought out in the investigation. So I had to figure out where all that was. The policy part of this plays heavily, but that was not part of our investigation.

Q.   Right.

A.   But I had to know what was it the policy said you could do in an interrogation. And what the policy said was, Field Manual 34-52 is the overarching guidance for this. The President's guidance for these particular detainees because they were not entitled to Enemy Prisoner of War protocols.

Q.   Okay.

A.   Which if you read the Geneva Conventions and also 34-52, it will tell you that, they're entitled to congregate. They're entitled to elect a leader. They're entitled to have, representation, visits--I mean all kinds of stuff. And the write up it's almost like they're entitled to have a band. You know, and present grievances. And it's pretty crazy. They weren't entitled to that. The President said that they're not entitled to that, but they will be treated humanely and they will be given shelter, security, food, water and medicinal attention. I mean it just laid it out there.

Q.   Okay.

A.   So that became kind of the baseline for what was considered humane treatment. And there is no definition of what is "humane treatment".

Q.   Right.

A.   And I have Senators sending me—you know, answer these questions. What's the difference between inhuman and inhumane. I mean I'm just a dumb fighter pilot that did this investigation. So I said, okay, here's the judgment. The President said this. If they're--and there are no other guidance, if they were Enemy Prisoners of War it would be this. Okay? So somewhere in between. So we have kind of a threshold which I would probably recognize as what's torture. And there is a Convention against torture. I know what that is. There is humane treatment and nobody knows what that is, but there is a general fuzzy line.

Q.   Okay.

A.   And then it's up to me to recognize what abusive or degrading kind of treatment is. That's the protocol we used. The Secretary of Defense, when we started this, took responsibility for providing guidance through US Southern Command down to the JTFs. The JTFs 160 and 170 were set up as independent—

Q.   Right.

A.   Parallel, almost non-cooperative sort of entities.

Q.   Okay.

A.   And the line between the two was really vague. The 160 JTF was detention operations, Military Police. They pretty much knew what they were doing. They were trying to figure out how to deal with the kinds of people they had. Violent people that had written off their lives already. It was like having psychotic murderers row times six hundred. And it remains somewhat like that today, although they did kind of reach a plateau where there was a lot of spitting and things like that and cursing and throwing excrement and things like that are still kind of going on. But it wasn't the violent violence. They've been dummied down quite a bit.

Q.   Okay.

A.   On the interrogations side it was a little bit--and I don't want to say it is out of control, but it was California Avocado Freestyle kind of a thing. Let's figure out what to do and how to interrogate these individuals when they're not Enemy Prisoners of War. They don't have a--they don't have an organizational construct. They're free agents. Dedicated-- they've already signed off their live. There is nothing left to lose kinds of individuals. It's like you have mass murders and said, okay, you know, these are your rules. These are--and they're going we don't do rules. And we don't do your sort of thing.

And the more serious the more influential individuals in that crowd have been trained in what we call "The Manchester Document" the rules of how to resist. They had gone to school on our FM 34-52. They knew we weren't going to torture them. They knew that they had rights. They knew that eventually they'd have the habeas entry into the legal system. They knew all this sort of stuff. And I mean you can--I've read their manual a few times.

Q.   Okay.

A.   And they've been through resistance training and they had a lot of time to think about. And when they sign to go to these missions, they know that if they don't die then they will deal with this and they do pretty well.

The interrogators had to deal with that. Okay? And it was a little chaotic. How they were going to deal with that and how the more structured Military Police side of this, blended together is the subject of several reports.

Q.   Okay.

A.   Every one of these reports made this an issue. The Church Report is probably the best written. The Fay Report is also pretty good on this. It says we got to figure out where the two lines cross. Well, this was kind of chaotic. The lines did cross eventually when General Hill, the Commander of US Southern Command, said, we're going to make this thing JTF-Guantánamo, we're going to combine the two JTFs and have one person have oversight of both of these things and get this act together. That was Geoff Miller that was told to do that.

Q.   Okay.

A.   So he had a chocolate mess on his hands when he got down there as far as discipline and cooperation and our act as national entity, the JTF dealing with this detention problem. Which was starting to create some visibility in the press and other levels. In the Congress as a matter of fact.

Q.   Okay.

A.   So that was the situation. The guidance part of this was the one that was hardest to deduce. The Secretary of Defense got a request from General Dunlavey, saying we now have reached almost a dead-end on exploiting and getting relevant intelligence from people who we know, detainees, who we know in this population that we can get from them. Standard FM 34-52 techniques are not going to work. This was still very close to 2001 and this was approaching 2002 and we didn't know if we were going to get whacked again. We knew at that time we had Mister Khatani.

Q.   Okay.

A.   We knew that he probably had relevant current intelligence about the hijacking operation and who his cohorts were and where the training came from, and the coordination and all that sort of thing. We became aware of the other high value detainee later. And he's obviously the big—he's a bigger fish. A much bigger fish. So this is—other high value detainee is classified, Khatani is not.

Q.   Okay, Sir.

A.   We've laid all that out for everybody. The classified detainee piece is one that comes later because there were two special investigations that were set up. special interrogation plans set up. The only one that was really executed was the one on Khatani started and that one is public knowledge now.

Q.   Right.

A   After our testimony.

Q.   Right.

A.   The Secretary of Defense received a list of interrogation techniques from General Dunlavey.

Q.   Okay.

A.   Who was the JTF Commander at that time. It was still not classified JTF-Guantánamo. It wasn't until General Miller arrived. So he had 170 but he was a domino player. He was senior to 160 Commander. And so—and there were some leadership issues with him.

Q.   Right.

A.   As our investigation reveals pretty chaotic. Pretty dysfunctional as a matter of fact. He looked like he was about ready to die a violent death by the time General Miller came in and took control. And he established good order pretty quickly. He had a lot on his plate.

Q.   Was this General Dunlavey or General Baccus that was

A.   General Baccus was the 160, he was the detention guy.

Q.   Right. In terms of the disorder and about to die a death?

A.   The disorder--he was more the victim I think of General Dunlavey. You're not helping. You're not helpful. You need to do this. You need to do that and he was sticking to his MP discipline in doing, trying to do. General Baccus was a Guardsman.

Q.   Right.

A.   General Dunlavey I believe is a Reservist.

Q.   USAR, yes.

A.   That's right. And there were disconnects there. It was just bad. Really bad. That's the same time that the Secretary received this request for expanded interrogation techniques----

BY

Q.   Excuse me, Sir, but the time was about October of 2002, is that correct?

A.   Yes, that's correct. That's correct. So I think they already the decision to have a JTF-Guantánamo they just hadn't marshaled to people and done the organizational structures.

Q.   Manning document.

A.   Making manning documents and making it one, and get the CONOPS and that sort of stuff, set up the operations and all those kind of normal--

Q.   Sure.

A.   The Secretary of Defense takes this list, vets it out with his General Counsel. The General Counsel goes to the Service General Counsels and they all go through a planning kind of process and that's beyond the report.

BY

Q.   Right.

A.   The report comes back to them. Now, it's important in terms of my report that there were some people omitted from this vetting process. For instance the

Service JAGs. The Service JAGS and the Service General Counsels--whew, just kind of went like that.

Okay.

A.   And that comes to roost later. They came back--to the Secretary of Defense with a-- some recommendations on what could be authorized techniques. And they had done these under what's lawful and unlawful probably. Not what was appropriate or inappropriate which the JAGs kind of had an issue with that later.

He takes it and he chops it down. And he cuts it down to a significant number. Takes out a lot of the stuff that would have really watered your eyes kind of things.

BY

Q.   Right.

A.   If just on the nomenclature of what it looked.

Q.   Okay.

A.   He takes it and chops it down and submits it and says this is approved to be used in special circumstances which I will approve and it's for Mister Khatani number one. So this becomes a special interrogation plan. It's issued now. It is promulgated through US Southern Command with almost no other guidance added to it. It goes to the JTF. The JTF now implements it regarding Mister Khatani.

BY (b)(7)(C)

Q.   Sir, when it came to the JTF, was--this was for General Miller to command, is that correct? When it got down on 2 December I believe? So this---

A.   What happened---

Q.   --was after.

A.   What happened was General Miller was coming in. He wasn't even there when the request went up.

: Yes, Sir.

: Right.

A.   Just deliberated. When it comes down there is--and this is not hugely relevant but it was something that we had to piece together. When was permission

A-42

given to start this special interrogation plan? We're pretty sure it was started about two weeks early. And before the SECDEF actually signed off. And I had this discussion with the Secretary of Defense and he wasn't happy. Okay? And he could not remember--strike that about not being happy. He went around the table to all the people that he could recollect that were in the room for that period. And say did I approve that before I actually signed it? And they all went we don't remember. We just don't remember. The COCOM, General Hill, at that time, had been in D.C. Had been there, and General Hill had been up there. And they had all been together with the Secretary of Defense and they couldn't remember and Craddock as the secretary's Military Assistant was actually in the room and they all couldn't remember.

 Okay.

A.   So rather than to call an entire line of people liars, we said that probably happened. You just can't prove it. So it's unknowable.

BY

Q.   I believe the Church Report found it happened as well.

A.   He deduced that it happened.

Q.   Right.

A.   Based on the same testimony that we got through-- people had no reason not to, you know, say it didn't happen.

Q.   Right.

A.   So we said okay it happened or it didn't happen. All the techniques that were applied in that plan were approved eventually so for us whether it happened two weeks earlier or not wasn't relevant because it was whether they were abusive or not.

Q.   Right.

A.   If they deemed to be abusive intentionally or whatever then they were approved. So it became a non-relevant thing. But it was a point that they dwelled on in the investigation.

 : Yes, Sir.

BY

Q.   And you did talk to the SECDEF, Sir?

A.   Yes. Oh, yes.

Q.   Did you interview General Hill as well?

A.   No, he's the only one we did not interview and that's one where I'd had to bump the investigation again.

Q.   Right.

A.   And I felt like we knew everything that General Hill did.

Q.   Okay.

A.   General Hill, when he promulgated guidance he did it in a very visible transparent way. When he pushed the request forward for instance, when he pushed the quest forward from the JTF to the Secretary of Defense, he was very clear. He did a note on it that was--you know, very clear. He said I find some of these very troubling. And particularly threatening families and--and death threats and things like that. I mean which is something that popped out later.

Q.   Right.

A.   He said I'm not sure we're on solid ground with this. And pushed it forward.

BY

Q.   And we've seen that document?

A.   Yeah. And, so all his correspondence and his chop on everything was clear.

Q.   Okay.

A.   So I didn't have to bump the report again and get another investigating officer--and I'm not sure how they would have done it. But---

Q.   And then just again real quick, Sir, before we let you go on. Did you also talk to Secretary Wolfowitz and/or Cambone?

A.   Did not talk to Wolfowitz or we did not interview Cambone.

Q.   Okay.

A.   Did not find that they were relevant to this. I did not want to investigate the guidance process.

Q.   Right.

A.   That would have taken me beyond my little charter, for the AR 15-6 was to investigate FBI allegations into abuse of detainees.

Q.   Okay.

A.   And now I'm up doing a national level how's policy derived kind of thing. And I got into that about all I needed to.

Q.   Right.

A.   So what I deduced out of all this was when it was promulgated down was the Secretary of Defense, through a vetting of his General Counsels and Service General Counsels said that certain techniques could not be used for a special interrogation plan for a specific person. And it could be used for others if it was requested and laid out; and it wasn't until later when it was done for Classified (b)(7)(C)

So there I knew what the broad techniques were. If you go to the Field Manual what's a technique? What's an approach? You know, they're kind of vague. Ad the guidelines on how vague they should be are unwritten by logic and guidance that pertains to EPWs. Like what's lawful or unlawful. Such broad things as if--if you think that something you're doing to an EPW was done to one of your troops that was held-- was detained, would we consider it torturous? Would we consider abusive or degrading.

Q.   Right.

A.   If it was then don't to it.

Q.   Right.

A.   And that's lawful or unlawful. You can't apply that logic to the status that was accorded to detainees at Guantánamo.

Q.   Okay.

A.   So I had to go back to the President's humane treatment line.

Q.   Okay.

A.   And the obviously the Convention against torture being clear. So this was promulgated down. This guidance was promulgated down from the Secretary of. Defense, through SOUTHCOM to JTF-Guantánamo and now General Miller is there.

Q.   Okay

A.   Okay, he is there. He's new on the ground. Boots on the ground for about two weeks. Two week-ish we think. But this special interrogation had started actually about two weeks earlier because of the verbal that was passed down. Not relevant to our process. General Miller was clear about it. Now, he knew who he had. He also knew in his testimony with me that he knew all aspects of what was going on with the special interrogation plan. He had correspondence with General Hill where he reassured General Hill that he had full knowledge. They were on this. The JTF is on this. We are watching this. This is a very important thing. This is his most important thing he's got going.

BY

Q.   Sir, is that correspondence in your report?

A.   It is. Yes, I think it is. It's one of the annexes.

Q.   I'm aware of the 21 January memo that General Miller wrote back up to Hill.

A.   To General Hill. He says we are--

Q.   Is that the one you're referring to?

A.   Yes.

Q.   Okay.

A.   The special interrogation plan is proceeding. We are watching it meticulously. We're on this.

Q.   Okay.

A.   You know it's under control. We've got it kind of thing. This is reassuring the COCOM that this is important. This is his most important thing. So he's aware of all that.

My first interview with General Miller, I said, were you aware? Oh, yeah. Were you aware of the interrogation plan for Mister Khatani? Oh, yeah. Did you--were you down there for the interrogations? Well, no, not really. Okay. But you were absolutely aware of everything? And he had told us in previous discussions he had "walked the gun line." I think that was a quote. He knew everything that was going on.

I asked him about some of the other things that were kind of spinning off on this. The GTMO-izing thing. I tried to say away from this migration theory.

Q.   Okay.

Q.   Should it have gone to General Miller, Sir, or was it okay not to because they weren't going what they perceived was beyond the guidance in the memorandum as promulgate to them?

A.   The problem was it was hard to go beyond the guidance because there was almost no guidance.

By  Okay.

A.   When the Secretary of Defense says, you go down for futility. When it gets down to a creative application of something. You've seen the menstrual blood thing.

: Yes, Sir.

A.   You've seen the gender coercion stuff.

: Okay.

A.   All that sort of stuff. That never got up to him. He was never--he was not approving that. He never saw that.

BY

Q.   "Him" being General Miller, Sir?

A.   General Miller. He also, well, he told me he was on this. He was watching this. You know, and the time the example I used in our investigation was, "If you're juggling wooden balls and glass balls you really want to watch the glass balls." You know. You can live if you're dropping a wooden one once in a while or a rubber ball. This is one of those ones you have to watch. And he agrees. He agrees.

BY

Q.   Okay.

A.   When I went back through my second interview with him and I said, "Were you aware of this use of dogs?" No, I never would have used dogs. Dogs were used in a special interrogation plan. Okay. It was in it. It was used. I mean here's this guy manacled, chained down, dogs brought in, put his face, told to growl, show teeth, and that kind of stuff. And you can imagine the fear kind of thing. You know at what point-- if that was done our folks then we would have gone--if you had a camera and snapped that picture, you'd been back to Abu Ghraib.

Q.   Right.

A.   You know, the dogs with the guy detained. Here's the dog and with the teeth. We could find that anybody was ever bitten. I don't think anybody was ever bitten.

Q.   Okay.

A.   But now we're also using the Military Police in the interrogation business. Which there was a brig log supposedly. General Miller said there was a brig log; they did facilitate interrogations. There was a detention---these troopers were told these are your wards. Their safety and security are yours. You don't like them. You hate these guys. They hate you. But their safety and security are your responsibility. Then you're in putting a dog in their face.

BY

Q.   Sir, can you elaborate "in their face", that's something I hadn't see before.

A.   Brought into the detention room. Brought up close in the interrogation rooms. These are small rooms. Have you seen the rooms?

BY [REDACTED]

Q.   No, not yet, Sir.

A.   They're little bitty rooms.

Q.   But he was in an interrogation room, he wasn't in his cell?

A.   In the interrogation room. That's right. Not in his cell. The cells are the detention; the interrogation rooms are interrogations operations. Different people.

[REDACTED] Yes, Sir.

A.   Different people. And there's hand-off. There is a bring them, control them, get them down. The interrogators come in. They do their part. They hand them over to the detention folks and then they're returned under a very strict Military Police protocol back to detention operations where they're formally treated. I mean dispassionately these are hated folks, but they are--where safety and security is involved. So that's what I was talking about. When I--

BY [REDACTED]

Q.   So when a detainee is in an interrogation room and he's shackled in some fashion and the dogs---

A-48

A.   And the dogs are out the door and they're brought into interrogation room and they're given--and that's all in my report. And they're brought in and they've told to growl and show teeth, at the detainee. And this guy is restrained. That's sort of a fear factor thing. Anyway, so I asked these about the use. No, I disagree with the use of that. And, and I can get a quote in here but "I would never approve that."

BY

Q.   Okay.

A.   Were you aware of this, this, and this--and I have a whole laundry list here I went through.

Q.   Okay.

A.   And with the exception of only one or two, he said I was not aware. On a couple of them I said "I never would approve that." And now I'm thinking at what point is someone who was 'on this' reassuring the COCOM that he's got eyes on this interrogation thing, this is important, this is the most important thing he's got going on down there. At what point is he checking on this? That's why in my report I didn't say because the dog went in it's his fault. It wasn't because of the-- all, you know, the homosexual stuff going on, the degradation stuff, that he's a fault. It was the cumulative effect of all of that on this particular person that I found him lacking the proper supervision and monitoring of this.

When he told me in the first interview how he was aware of everything and he was responsible. And he was. And I've been a JTF Commander a couple of times and over here where he's not aware of any of this. And then I go down and look through, thumb the interrogation logs and it's all right there. And if you've read the interrogation logs--and I don't know if you've been through those.

Q.   We've read them. They're included in your report.

A.   That's correct.

BY

Q.   Sir, was there evidence that he had reviewed interrogation logs on a regular basis or any time, or----

A.   I told him----

Q.   Or receiving SIDPERs or was----

A.   I asked him, did you look at the interrogation logs that were--not only daily, they're hourly. They're by shift. This individual was being interrogated 20 hours a day.

Okay? And then given four hours off. In that four hours, he was taken to a white room. Okay? With all the lights and stuff going on and everything and he was--could set your clock by it, it was meticulously logged. You know this was a crucible that was being used.

Now this was a bad guy. This was a guy who had information that we needed. Okay? Information that we needed and if he had coerce them in some way that dropped down to the line just above, well above torture, but above humane treatment, where was that line?

He was the guy that I felt should have been at the throttle on this thing. And as it was, he was unaware of all what was surfacing the line. What was going on here. That was entrusted to what I considered some minor level folks. Okay? Important people but minor level.

So for 20 hours a day for at least 54 days, this guy was getting 20 hours a day interrogation in the white cell. In the white room for four hours and then back out. All the stuff that was going on with him--and I won't even go through all the list. You have all that.

BY

    Q.   Okay.

    A.   And I laid it out for the Senate as well. If you read the interrogation logs, I mean you kind of get a little weird feeling. You go, "Man, we're doing that." He--and I asked him point blank. Have you read any of the interrogation logs? No. Where were you getting your feedback to reassure the COCOM that this was all going well? He said we had a meeting at least once a week where we would get the general idea of what was going on and what we were getting from him. And at a point Khatani would in fact break, give us a bunch of stuff, and then kind of come back together again.

The stuff that he gave us, I don't know that all of it was very factual. And I didn't get into the intelligence part of a lot of this. Although I am aware of it.

    Q.   Okay.

    A.   This guy is a hard-nut and he is a bad guy. Okay? And I went down and looked at him and he looks like hell. He was just coming out of this thing.

    Q.   Really.

    A.   He has got black coals for eyes. Now I understand in the last four or five months, he has kind of ballooned up because all of the stuff is off of him. His stress factor has gone way done and he's pounding MREs and he's a 195 pounds.

A.   Because they weren't interviewing witnesses or under these programs, particularly Khatani. Now they had him over in the brig for a long time. And, one-on-one they had total control. Now the other was we also got the brig logs. Nobody else, any previously investigation, had even looked at the brig logs. So we got the ▓▓▓▓ ▓▓▓▓▓▓▓▓▓▓▓▓▓▓▓▓▓▓▓or whatever they call them, who had eyes on these guys during all this. And we found that they were not abused. We found that the amount of interrogation interviews were not very much. And this guy was essentially left alone over in the brig.

So the FBI in their rapport building approach, were unable to establish rapport with Khatani. And they eventually they just left him there and essentially the brig called over and we've got this detainee over here. You know he's sort of a found-on-base item.

Q.   Okay.

A.   And the JTF went over and collected him up. The FBI's approach didn't work. Their rapport building, even this 34-52-ish sort of approach wasn't working on him. And that's when the JTF began and they found out that 34-52 techniques weren't going to work and they requested up.

So, the FBI's approach wasn't working. It was completely dead and I think they recognized it. Then when they saw that the DoD DIA piece of this going on, they went you know that's extreme. And in fact by their standards for evidence it is extreme. By techniques to get intelligence, they were border-line. Okay. They were down there on that--that's why I used the words "abusive and degrading." I didn't use "inhumane" and I absolutely ruled out torture. Okay? I felt that the JTF Commander was the only who had the authority; had the opportunity, and had the responsibility to be at this level. It wasn't above that level. That went on for about 45 days when the JAGs began to up at the higher level, policy level, began to question this. Particularly the ▓▓▓▓▓▓▓ ▓▓▓▓▓▓▓▓▓ said you're way out there and we're finding this thing to be way beyond what we should be doing. And that's when the SECDEF rescinded the guidance that was in the special interrogation plan for Mister Khatani and he went back to the normal 34-52 kind of plan. And he has been a clam ever since.

BY ▓▓▓▓▓▓▓▓▓▓▓

Q.   So we kind of milked all that we could have gotten out of him during that—

A.   But I don't know. We don't because----

▓▓▓▓▓▓▓▓▓▓▓ The guidance changed----

A.   It came down, the guidance changed. And then April, eventually a final, set of guidance on interrogation techniques for the detainees at Guantánamo came

down and that's where we are today. And it has some additional guidance by General Hill that said, okay, this is the guidance, and I as the COCOM now am going to lay-some things on there like what is--what's sleep deprivation.

Q.   Right.

A.   You know it's 16 hours. Blab-blab-blab. No more moving these guys around and doing all this sort of things. I forget what that's called. But moving them around.

Q.   The Frequent Flier Program?

A.   The Frequent Flier Program, moving them around from cell to cell. We found that only happened to a few folks, but it was going on. We don't know it was ever sustained on any individual. A lot of it had to do with moving them around because they were--we know they had developed tap-codes and done all the stuff like we had in Hanoi and those sort of things. So we knew that was all going on. And we couldn't find, even though we knew it happened and was discussed, there was no documentation on it. So we knew it had happened. There were enough witnesses to say, oh, yeah, detainee (b)(6)(c) think was one. (b)(6)(c) was one of the guys who was a frequent flier.

So anyway when it came in April, April 16th, General Hill said also bang, bang, bang, laid a bunch of extra guidance rules on it. And I think it was becoming obvious what was going on down there was going to get looked at pretty hard. So oversight started picked up the pace. Particularly with, after all the discussions at the policy level.

Q.   Right.

A.   The JAGs, the General Counsels, that had all kind of convened and the Secretary of Defense. I thought the Secretary of Defense in good faith was approving techniques. In good faith absolutely after talking to him twice. I know that--and these weren't interrogations or interviews of him. This was our hour and forty-five minute and then another hour and fifteen kind of thing were we sat in there and had these discussions with him. Somewhere there had to be a throttle on this. He was going, my God, you know, did I authorized putting a bra and underwear on this guy's head? You know and make with a male interrogator and tell him all his buddies knew he was a homosexual. Then later he alleged threats of homosexual rape. Well, he could deduce that. You know, I mean's kind of the way we set it up. Collective "we". The Secretary said, yeah, I didn't say that. You know? Well the guy's ego is coming down pretty fast. But I did say put a bra and panties on this guy's head and make him dance with another man? No, you didn't say, Sir, but just under that broad technique that was application. Well where in there was the throttle? It's hard for me to say it was that E5.

Q.   Okay.

A.   The E5 would vet that at the next level up which is ICE, interrogation Control Element. The Interrogation Control Element was good to sign off the interrogation plan. And this stuff was in the plan and then they did it and then they documented what they did in it. And that was a matter of record. And they did it minimum three times a day. There were medical folks watching them the whole time.

This particular individual had a low heart beat condition. There was some concern that, under the temperature control, they'd run the temperature down in the room and everything—he got cold, make him uncomfortable as what maximum it would have been. That this guy was getting hypothermia. He had a low body temperature. His core temperature was pretty low and they kept checking on him. I mean all this stuff is pretty invasive. Somewhere somebody had to be watching that. Who is it? Is a person doing it or is there a perch somewhere. The perch had to be the JTF.

Q.   Okay.

A.   Now I am very aware that NAVBASE issues, the political issues that were going on, and discussions, and all that sort of thing, the organizational issues, the blending of the Military Police detention OPS and the interrogation OPS was still being worked hard. There was a huge facility upgrade. They're building a prison down there essentially.

Q.   Okay.

A.   Getting these folks out of camps. There was a rotational guard force issue they had to keep working. Who knew who was coming in. There were training issues that required a JTF Commander's attention as well. But this was a glass ball right here. This was one that had to be watched. In my opinion the JTF Commander was the only one that had the suitable knowledge of what the SECDEF meant because he talked to the Secretary of Defense. He's the only one that really knew the intent of what a technique was and probably where the line was, and crossing it, and should have watching that. It was not an E5.

Q.   Okay.

A.   And had I not been a JTF Commander like I said a couple of times, I probably have said, no, he's just too busy. There's just not a too busy alibi there for that. And again this was a hard one, because I know Geoff Miller. Geoff Miller's heart absolutely is in the right place. He's a great Soldier and he's a super General Officer. I just found that he should have known about some of this stuff in his opportunity over an extended period of time to the cumulative effect aspect of this on this particular prisoner deserved a little more attention. At least cursory attention and it was not given.

Q.   Okay.

A.   So that's why I found it. And I would have left that alone. That's where a fact-finding AR 15-6 and that's where an investigator stops. Here's the facts. I was directed to not only say it not only the JTF Commander, but it was General Miller, okay because that's where I left it in my report; and then I was directed to say what to do about, and I said because it was not a criminal a failure to monitor appropriately, the cumulative effects, that's not a criminal act.

Q.   Okay.

A.   It doesn't violate policy. Okay? What's the policy? Is there a policy that says what a Commander's responsibilities are? Well there kind of is. You're supposed to—you know you're responsible is what it says.

Q.   Okay.

A.   But what are you responsible for? Everything? You know how much toilet paper is in the 15th stall. You know? I mean there is a common sense line there.

Q.   Right.

A.   So as a guy told to be the investigator and told also to be the evaluator. In the Air Force what we do up to that point if an investigator brings that to me, he's finished. At that point as the Commander it's not only my prerogative it's my responsibility to decide, okay, I now hold this person responsible and this is what I am going to do about it.

       I was directed to do those two things and I did. I submitted my report and General Craddock took it. We had been working with his legal folks. So there were some legal things—and they were good. Good inputs.  to make sure the report read right. And we'd done a huge amount of work getting the testimony from the FBI agents all right. So we thought it was a good report.

       He had a couple of other issues, he held the report because the DOJ was going to do their own report. Now we had collaborating with the DOJ because the genesis of our report was FBI agent's allegations.

Q.   Okay.

A.   So we shared everything we were getting with them. We reconvened back here downstairs in my JAG Office area where we did the bulk of the report in getting it all so it made sense. They were down there with us. So there was daylight between that. If we needed something from DOJ in terms of the FBI they gave it to us.

Q.   Okay.

A.   The two lead investigators. They were directed by Mister Gonzalez, the Attorney General, to do an investigation. So when they went off, we were to stay with them. General Craddock held my report for almost three months while we followed up with them. General Furlow went down to Guantánamo with them and through all the stuff they did, the only thing that was different was they found another piece of paper that had to do with a classified piece, which is the DESKREC by Navy——

Q.   Lieutenant Commander——

A.   Lieutenant Commander, Reservist. We actually found a piece of paper that was the piece of paper used.

Q.   Okay.

A.   That somebody had rat-holed somewhere and didn't produce for us. All that did was corroborate what we already had deduced through all the testimony and actually that the letter itself wasn't nearly as damming as all the testimony of what this guy was told was in the letter.

Q.   Okay.

A.   So that was it. There were no other findings. So again the report was— not it's resubmitted. The legal review is all done. Again, and we knew that was all going to be easy because we has stayed in step with legal review.

We went to— now we're now back to getting ready to go to the Secretary of Defense for the last time, and the day of— it was a Monday, we were going to brief the Secretary of Defense. We went in and General Craddock, we sat down an hour and half before reporting to the SECDEF. And he told me that he disagreed with my recommendations and finding on General Miller. And he said we agree to disagree.

Q.   Okay.

A.   And I just politely said well we haven't really disagreed because I didn't know you were disagreeing with it. You know kind of thing.

Q.   Right.

A.   And we tried to be collegial about. He disagreed for the reason I told you. The same reasons that I had an issue with, that it wasn't criminal because he didn't violate a policy. It wasn't a criminal thing. Particularly on his part. I found him to be responsible and accountable not culpable, but accountable for knowing what was going on in his organization at this level and this important of a project.

Q.   Okay.

A.   He was the only one between the Secretary of Defense and the interrogator that could do it. That actually had the knowledge and the wherewithal to put a throttle on this.

Q.   Okay.

A.   Or look at it and--and it looked like there was almost no attempt. And that's all a matter of record. You read my interviews with him.

Q.   Right.

A.   Okay.

Q.   We've got what is included in the report. Now we don't have---

A.   And that's in the classified report. Did you read the classified report or the unclassified report?

Q.   It's classified, yes, Sir.

A.   It's the unclassified testimony of myself with General Miller the 1st one and the 2nd one.

Q.   Great. Is this a verbatim?

A.   It's the second one is closer to verbatim but it says I asked this question and he answered this.

Q.   Right. Okay, Sir.

A.   That kind of thing and I signed both--I think--yeah, I signed both of those.

Q.   Okay, Sir, and we can take these with us?

A.   Yes and he was sworn both times.

 All right. Thank you, Sir.

BY

Q.   Sir, can I ask you a couple of questions quickly before we go on.

A.   Okay.

Q.   Just administratively you mentioned the name  Can you spell that for us?

A. [REDACTED]

[REDACTED] Oh, [REDACTED]

A. She goes by [REDACTED]

[REDACTED] Okay, Sir, got it.

[REDACTED] I think we'll talk to her.

LTG SCHMIDT: She was the previous [REDACTED]

BY [REDACTED]

Q. Yes, was there any evidence that with respect to the interrogation laws that there techniques being used or events occurring or that occurred that didn't make it into the logs?

A. I got to tell you when you're writing down the level of detail that they did there, they were—they were writing down everything. I can't imagine that they would—that they missed anything. And we wouldn't just presume that they were putting things in there unless we could corroborate a FBI allegation, a date, a time, and a place that was in one of these interrogations and some of those we did. It was so complete that it was an assist to the investigation. It was also so detailed and so well written that I just can't imagine that these weren't being reviewed or read by the JTF.

Q. Yes, Sir.

A. And they weren't. And that's why the logs--and no one had looked at the logs before for some reason. No one had ever even look at the brig logs where Mister Khatani was held for an extended period with the FBI, and then us in the JTF for a while and then he was transferred out.

Q. Were there any written policies, directives or Standing Operating Procedures that were either in place when General Miller took over and that he retained or that he, established and signed and put in place while he was there that you're aware of that would be evidence of supervisory control?

A. He instituted and as they do, all the JTF Commanders, have done the SOPs and those were formative. He had to stand those up himself. The SOPS for the two JTFs were rank gradient. The seams were too wide between the two. And it was the same detainees. The impact on them was the same.

So he had to invent all that stuff. He did a pretty good job of doing that. And again that's part of the caseload he had in addition to this particular individual. And

I was cognizant of that and I tried to put that in the right perspective. And again what he said and what he did were two different things. He said he was all over this. He was watching it. He was aware of everything. As a matter of fact I think it's a quote, "I'm always aware of everything that happened to 063." From the first interview.

The second interview as I went through all the events--[Pounding the desk] that were just booming out of the logs he was essentially not aware of most any of them.

Q. Okay.

A. So, he--

BY

Q. So was----

A. But he did establish policy and he continue to review policy. A lot of it had to do with safety, security, and organizational sort of things. There was some Be Nos in there that he put in there, you know, to-- and there was some that he didn't----

Q. "Be no's", Sir?

A. Yeah, there will "be no" this or "be no" that.

 Oh, okay.

Oh, okay

A. I'm sorry. There were some--he told us that--as far as short shackling. Now he directed there'd be no-- short shackling was inappropriate. Would not be doing that. As a matter of fact they even modified the eye-bolts on the floor so that you couldn't--you couldn't actually put the hand of the--the ones in-- your feet manacles you take a chain, stick in there and do that. But you couldn't do the cuffs the way they were with the locks and everything. You just couldn't get your hands----

Yeah. Okay.

A. --anymore kind of thing.

Q. Okay.

A. So he had said he did a verbal. That was not in the SOPs. We looked that even up to today. I say today, when we--the time of the report. There was no SOP saying no short shackling. It didn't say that. But there was a verbal and every person

we talked to said, no, that you know, that the JTF Commander said none of that. So— some of it wasn't codified. Some of it was.

 All right, Sir.

A.   All right.

BY

Q.   Sir, regarding your finding that you made with respect to General Miller, I just want to make sure we understand it exactly. If you had found that General Miller had been aware of all of those techniques that you went through with him line by line, was aware of them; admitted to it, would you have then come to the same conclusion? Was—was your concern with him more the fact that he didn't know everything that was going or what he should have know that was going on, or was the problem more just abusive and degrading treatment? In other words, if you had—

A.   Yeah, oh, I understand totally.

Q.   Okay.

A.   What I would have said was General Miller was responsible.

Q.   Right.

A.   That would have been a finding. He was responsible for the conduct of interrogations that I found to be abusive and degrading. The intent of those of those might have been to be abusive and degrading to get the information they needed and it might have hovered above the level of inhumane. Above the level which means it didn't—it was not inhumane. And it was certainly not torture.

Q.   It didn't violate anything.

A.   It didn't violate the torture statute.

Q.   Okay.

A.   The Convention against torture. It didn't violate the general premises of humane treatment. Was it abusive and degrading? Find me somebody that will argue that it wasn't.

Q.   Okay.

A.   Was it intentional and did the means justify the ends? That's fine. So he responsible because he was witting and he was responsible.

Q.   Okay.

A.   Recommendation might have been, that's it. You know. The fact that he didn't know what was going on; the fact that it was judged to be abusive and degrading; but that was wasn't the intent or was it the intent? I mean it was just a free for all. That was my finding and my recommendation to hold him to the level of admonishment. Which is about the lowest level that you can get. Was because he didn't know what was going on. And I felt like the JTF Commander or some Commander, him, because he's the one that could be the translator between the SECDEF's guidance because he communicated with the Secretary of Defense; the COCOM; and daily with his—with his interrogator/detention folks.

He was at the appropriate level in my judgment. And asking my opinion and I was told—my opinion and write it down. So I did. I would have, had he been witting of all that, I would have said, still said he's responsible. Because now he is responsible and he always was in my opinion.

Q.   Okay.

A.   But a judgment or an admonishment? No, he was executing what he thought was the Secretary's intent and only he would have been the right guy at that level to know into the action—the application of the technique, and only he would have been the one who should known how it was being applied. He was—

BY

Q.   Well, Sir, even if he had been aware then he would have also been the same position that you were then to make a judgment that the effect of the 54-days, day after day after day, and that the cumulative effect was approaching or perhaps exceeding some line somewhere. Then he would have been in the same position as you then to make judgment. So—

A.   Absolutely. Absolutely. I would have had the same finding. The recommendation would have been different. That's I think what you're asking. The recommendation would have been—now, General Craddock said, you make the recommendation to me. He said to me you make the recommendation and I told him it was inappropriate for me as the investigator to make that—it was a Commander's prerogative. He goes no. You make the recommendation. And I'm being very clear about this. And I don't want to—I'm not going to tube my boss here. I'm just telling you that's why I made a recommendation.

BY

Q.   Right.

A.	And so I said alright. I'm going to tell you that I would admonish your General Officer JTF Commander. He goes fine that's what I wanted to hear. I want to hear what you recommend. And I would have done that. Had General Miller been witting of all this, okay, that means it was deliberately done. It was done with the knowledge of what the technique approved meant in the application process. Instead of going the way it went. I didn't find the threshold of humane crossed.

Q.	Okay.

A.	And torturous—now in the analogy I gave to SASC, you know, there's a level. Is listening to country music, does that bother you? Okay? Now some people say yeah it bothers me. Is that inhumane? Is it torture? No. But if you listen to it for 8-hours, it might go—it's really annoying. But say you listen to it for 24-hours, the same level. Now if it's not so loud he can't stand it, but it's the dominant atmospheric. What if he listened to it for a week? No one ever changed the channel. And you're just hearing. Not there is some of your body that's going to start tuning it out. It becomes background or whatever, but there is a reason, because you're starting to psychologically get whacked with it. Let's say we played that for a month. And that's—you know we just kept playing it. And I mean we did this with Mister Noriega down in Panama. Blasted him with rock and roll. Hard metal and stuff like that.

: Okay.

LTG SCHMIDT: It would drive him nuts and he couldn't think after a while. At what point do you say it's mildly annoying to where it's abusive and what point do you actually say it's torture? Is there a line in there somewhere? Who makes that call? Is it the E-5 who does an 8-hour shift? You know, does three days on; three days off; three days on; three days off? Who makes that call? You know is it—where is the throttle on this stuff?

But you multiply that times all the creative techniques that were done at the lowest level. Supposedly with oversight and it wasn't just applying futility. It wasn't just applying ego down. It—it—you know it was all of them at once. Continuously by different interrogation teams for extended periods of time. There were no limits. There was no limits put on this and there no boundaries. How loud was the music? You know how long did you play it? You know, did you play it just to where it was decibels ear-breaking and you back it off a notch, and then leave it on forever. No end.

When was this special interrogation plan going to end? It was never going to end. Okay? It ended because the SECDEF rescinded his guidance from the policy level and then it shot right down to the JTF, the interrogation level. There was no boundary and there was no limit on all these little creative—and that's what I said in my report. See this was one of those ones, that, I wanted to be right. I was not witch-hunting anybody. I felt no compulsion to go bring a scalp.

I know Geoff Miller and that's when it hit pretty hard. I find him to be a pretty solid guy. But I feel pretty confident that the way I've judged this is the way it should have been handled or--now, again I've got all the details.

BY

Q.   Right.

A.   And that's I felt I should have handled it-- should have been handled.

Q.   Yes, Sir. Sir, would you have made the same recommendation regarding General Miller if you had found that there was no cumulative effect of abusive and degrading treatment regarding ISN 63 but you have found the same lack of involvement in knowledge by General Miller of the interrogations?

A.   I got to tell you if that was the case, there would have been no investigation.

Q.   Right.

A.   And that is---that's so subjective that I can't answer that kind of question.

Q.   I understand.

A.   If nothing had ever been alleged and there had been no abuse, would I have guilty of something?

Q.   Okay.

A.   I can't answer that.

Q.   Okay, but in this case it was more the fact that this was such an important interrogation that it did involve special authority that did push the boundaries perhaps of proper treatment; that that mere fact should have resulted in closer involvement in supervision by General Miller. Is that fair would you say?

A.   Yes, it is.

Q.   Okay, Sir.

A.   This is one that--this wasn't just daily business.

Q.   Okay.

A.   When the Secretary of Defense is personally involved in the interrogation of one person, and the entire General Counsel system of all the Departments of the

Military and the Office of General Counsel and Secretary of Defense, and the Secretary of Defense is personally being briefed on this-- and you mentioned a few names. I know Steve Cambone as well. And he was in there throwing rocks at us. In my staff's testimony. He's real concerned.

Q. Okay.

A. I don't know what element he played because I didn't investigate that.

Q. Right.

A.  is in there.

Q. Okay.

A. I know what level he played at, but I didn't investigate his logic processes.

Q. Right.

A. There were a lot of people that were involved. That was not my job.

Q. Right.

A. And all I wanted to do was find out what was approved and kind of the genesis of how it all kind of came out. How was it promulgated and who was responsible for the promulgation, guidance, and oversight of this.

And I just find it hard to believe, as does anybody, that when the Secretary of Defense has that kind of interest to where he's talking weekly with the JTF Commander and the COCOM, but the JTF Commander too, personally. And General Dunlavey said he didn't even go to the SOUTHCOM, he went directly to the Office of Defense. He dealt with him. He was the Secretary of Defense's person personally on this JTF, and he almost did nothing with JIG-- with SOUTHCOM. He almost ignored them.

When General Miller came in, he understood the chain of command and he went through SOUTHCOM to the Secretary of Defense but there was still a direct connection. And believe me the Secretary of Defense knows who Geoff Miller is.

Q. Yes, Sir.

A. When it's that important and you're asked how is it going and you say we're all over it. We know everything. You know we got this thing tight. Don't worry about it. You know we're-- our oversight is meticulous. I think the word meticulous is in there. He doesn't know anything that's going--and he doesn't even know what they're doing with this guy?

Q.   Okay.

A.   I found that to be lack of sufficient monitoring of this. I mean I'm sorry, don't know how else to call it. And someone can go argue it. That's fine. But I was directed –

Q.   Right, Sir.

A.   –my finding and then the recommendation. Now, in the end, General Craddock, my boss, decided no, he didn't violate a policy. It wasn't criminal. And that's what I said all along. And then he disagreed with it. And then we went and tried to put the face on it. He had, the COCOM, as the Convening Commander, he has the responsibility for making the call. The fact that he asked me and directed me to a make a call is, unfortunately it's a matter of record.

Q.   Right.

A.   Which every Senator–I mean I–you could have seen this one coming. Every Senator and Congressman latched on to it.

Q.   Yes, Sir. Right.

A.   It never should have been in there.

Q.   Yes, Sir.

A.   But it's his responsibility and his prerogative to say in the end I'm the one. His should have been the only judgment on this.

Q.   Yes, Sir.

A.   Otherwise we wouldn't even be having this conversation.

████████████ Sir, I'll tell you what. It is twenty-five after ten I'm going to need to switch over this tape.

LTG SCHMIDT: Okay.

████████████ So let's turn off the tapes for just a second long enough for us to switch this stuff over. So we don't miss a sentence. We don't want to do that.

[Went off tape.]

[Back on tape.]

LTG SCHMIDT: I would also mention that General Furlow was--I don't think I did hardly anything without him.

BY

    Q.   Yes, Sir.

    A.   Latching on. Even though I took over this investigation, the bulk of the interviews were done by him and his team. Then we cleaned up, and edited, and got things so they were actually readable and the intent came out of it. I put a bigger staff on it. He--he was and his team did almost all of the interviews before the General Officer level.

    Q.   Okay.

    A.   And I got involved in a few more as things started popping up. I was there for about four or five-- that we just had-- there were some key people that I just wanted to hear it from.

    Q.   Yes, Sir.

    A.   And then the seven Generals, and actually had to make a call to Kuwait and hook up with one of the--he was the Deputy Commander of Southern Command that was sitting in the saddle before General Hill came on board.

    Q.   Okay.

    A.   So I covered it. I think I hermetically sealed who had knowledge at that level.

    Q.   Sir, can you run through real quickly which General officers you did speak to?

    A.   Phew!

    Q.   The best that you can remember. It was certainly Miller, General Dunlavey, and General Baccus--

    : We may have to ask you questions about---

    A.   Start off with the first JTF 160--oh, gosh! He was Chief of Staff at Southern Command. General-- a Marine Two Star.

BY

    Q.   Pace.

A.   No, no, he was the ▓▓▓▓

BY ▓▓▓▓

Q.   Lehnert?

A.   Lehnert.

BY ▓▓▓▓

Q.   Lehnert. That's right.

A.   We'll start with General Lehnert. Okay? And because he was the guy on the ground that was detention operations. This is before they even started anything to do with interrogations. And we got some good insight on what his marching order was. When he got down there, very quickly it was like how soon can you start interrogations. And that's when they slammed together a JTF 170 team and that's when General Baccus I think was then--and so I interviewed Lehnert and Baccus.

Q.   Okay.

A.   And we started building this bridge.

Q.   Okay.

A.   Dunlavey was then assigned to go down there and be the JTF 170 Commander for interrogations. He and General Baccus were at odds.

Q.   Okay.

A.   Now General Lehnert was the guy that actually build the first facility and got it going and essentially resurrected the--the, Echo, Camp X-Ray, and all that stuff, to go down there for--essentially the migrant camps into detention operations and got those things kind of going So three were--I just wanted to build the bridge as I got there just to kind of figure this thing out.

The next person in was obviously General Miller. And General Miller came in and consolidated into JTF Guantánamo. The oversight for that--and there a lapse because General Pace had left US Southern Command and there was a lapse and General Gary Speer who was the Deputy Commander Two Star-Army, was the interim kind of acting Commander. I also interviewed the J-2, who is not the J-2.

Q.   General Burgess.

A.   Burgess. General Burgess.

A. And everything else. And oh by the way, the Koran abuse thing blew up in the three month interim--

Q. Right.

A. Between my submitting my report to the time I did my final testimony to the SASC. We had seen some things on Koran. You know, handling. And I'm down there and I was dumbstruck. I am really a Middle East guy.

Q. Okay.

A. Five years living in the Middle East.

Q. Okay.

A. Since '83. And I was dumbstruck on the deference given to these detainees' religious sensitivities. Way beyond what I would ever do. And I've lived--like I said I've lived with the Arabs. I was just dumbstruck by it. And then when I heard all the--you know, I watched the Korans all held up on a little doilies kind of thing and they have the prayer rugs and all this sort of thing. I was just blown away by it.

Q. Okay.

A. Because having living in the Middle East that's not how the standard Muslim follows Islam. You know it's their life. Not part of their life. It's their life and then everything else then comes from it.

Q. Okay.

A. But not like that.

Q. Right.

A. And we're giving them a shelter. We gave them a mental and emotional shelter.

Q. Okay.

A. And I was phew! Wow! And then I leave and then I hear all this Koran abuse stuff. I couldn't believe it.

Q. Right.

A. I also had a chance to look at the toilets in those 5 by 8 cells. And I just didn't have the visual of putting one of those in the toilet. Being an engineer it just didn't fit. You know?

Q.   It didn't seem to fit.

A.   Yeah.

Q.   Okay.

A.   Okay. So anyway, those were the General officers and I also—let's see who else did I interview Officer wise? I mean was that five? I think I did seven total.

BY

Q.   I got General Miller, General Hood, General Dunlavey, General Baccus, General Lehnert, General Speer and General Burgess.

A.   That's it. Good to go.

BY

Q.   Okay. Thanks, Sir. Sir, you've actually done a great job of addressing most of our questions that we had for you. I'm just going to go through our list real quick and just pick out a couple that we didn't address directly just to make sure that we cover it.

Sir, what concerns, if any, were raised to General Miller by either GTMO personnel or FBI personnel regarding the interrogation and treatment of Khatani?

A.   Yes.

Q.   In other words, was he ever made directly aware that hey there's some abusive treatment going on? That's what we're trying to pinpoint.

A.   There were I think in our report there were like two occasions where CITF personnel—

Q.   C-I-T-F?

A.   C-I-T-F personnel had meetings with General Miller to say, essentially it was to reiterate the argument about the techniques being used won't help in the prosecution. Evidentiary process of gathering evidence.

Q.   Right.

A.   You know that concern. That's on that was always in their face down there. And it was one that was never going to be understood by the FBI or by the Criminal Intelligence folks or by anybody else. The requirement to get actual

intelligence to stop an attack on the United States or us or wherever else and the information held in the heads of these individuals that we knew about down there, could be the thing that did that. There was just a disconnect. You know everybody has their job. And their job was to get evidence. The FBI and the CIA played another little role down there. That's their thing.

Q.   Okay.

A.   They also had custody by the way and we tried to rule out if something was observed like detainees abuse, it did not automatically say it was while they were in the hands of DoD being DIA or the detention OPS or interrogators, the US Military interrogators, because other people had hands on. Now the FBI probably wouldn't have observed someone in the hands of the FBI being treated that way but we didn't rule it out. You know? You'll get a rogue FBI agent, you know, having enough. And the CIA also had, unfettered access to people that they wanted to have and they had their own area. They didn't use our interrogation facilities because they used their own trailer operation.

Q.   Okay.

A.   But if you know what they were doing over there, it was unlikely that they'd be using anybody but--we didn't assume away anybody having a rogue person. Like we didn't assume away having a rogue, military or DIA person.

Q.   Okay.

A.   So we looked at everything we could.

Q.   Okay.

A.   The question again back to--

Q.   Oh, I was trying to ascertain if allegations of whether we call abuse or whether it was mistreatment were ever raised to General Miller regarding----

A.   We do know because of the evidentiary thing. And again I said I put my hands on and had these detainees for a while. It was raised to him.

Q.   Okay.

A.   And he acknowledges that. There was also--uh--

BY

Q.   Observed by the FBI?

A.   I think it was the FBI agent down there. The senior--the senior agent.

BY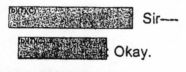

Q.   Do you recall who that was, Sir?

A.   He is called the SAIC. No, I don't.

Q.   You don't know who the guy was. Okay.

A.   No, I don't know. But it wasn't--it wasn't a big slugfest.

Q.   Okay.

A.   Miller said I understand your concerns. And it's exactly what I would have done.

Q.   Right.

A.   There was also one of the other agents down there that had raised this and this wasn't like they said hey they're tearing so and so's hair out. They came to him and said we disagree with your techniques that have been approved. We disagree with your approach that you're taking towards these detention detainees. And that was really the genesis of it and General Miller got that.

 Sir----

Okay.

BY

Q.   Sir, we understand it was because of the differences between getting actual intelligence and evidence to be used for prosecution, but that it also included concerns regarding what they considered to be abusive or even aggressive---

A.   Overly aggressive was the term.

Right, overly aggressive.

A.   We're concerned about your overly aggressive techniques. In those complaints it wasn't that detainee XXX is being abused or tortured or whatever.

Yes, Sir.

A.   It was we're concerned about your methodology here. So he was aware of that. He was very much aware of that

Q.   Sir, in your opinion, should that perhaps have raised a red flag to General Miller?

A.   It would—it would have just got him—well I don't think it would have been a red flag. But it would have said pay attention.

Q.   Right. That's what I'm asking.

A.   Yeah. It means they know that you're the throttle here.

Q.   Okay.

A.   The other agencies because that's where the level of guidance and command came from. He's the authority. I mean he was the authority.

Q.   Right, Sir.

A.   That—you know, yes, he was very much aware of their concerns.

Q.   Okay, well—

[redacted]: Do you know if he took any action regarding it, in response to this meeting?

A.   No, I don't. I know that whenever he had the occasion—and this came out in several interviews. He was very clear that these, that the detainees, would be treated humanely. Now, that's the same broad guidance but there was no definition of humanely that the President promulgated. The President's promulgation was the baseline they used. Which again you know stay secure—

BY [redacted]

Q.   Which is at level one?

A.   Man, it was mass level one right there. And it was medical care, food, water. And in fact food and water it didn't say soda-pop. It didn't say burgers and fries which they're munching on now. I went and watched they're eating fries. It's part of the rapport building now. In those days there was going to be no rapport building. Because fresh from the fight these guys had been swept up off the battlefield. They were going to die. And I mean if it was them and us being the detainees I mean they would have been killing us like that. [Snapped his fingers] You know there is no doubt about it. And they expected the same treatment that they would have given us. It never materialized. The folks that were studied in on the resistance techniques, knew that we weren't going to do anything to them and they were the ones that were going to continue to fight.

BY

Q. Okay, Sir. Just a couple of more things, Sir. Let's just talk and we'll attempt to do this in an unclassified sense or at least up to the secret level. Regarding the classified detainee and the interrogation of him, the interrogation plan, and the report provides a pretty good description of the death threat that was made towards that detainee during the course of an interrogation. But the report also indicated that General Miller was not aware of that death threat. Yet the report did not make a finding regarding General Miller and his supervision of that interrogation as it did with respect to the other interrogations. Just curious why you chose to not do that?

A. The reason—

Q. Okay.

A. First of all the Lieutenant Commander in question here, very clear when we interviewed him that this was his idea and he was the approval authority. He never attempted to vet it up. He did say that he tried to vet it laterally with, another individual a Colonel. A JAG. Both of those are now retired or out and they—we—again, no power of subpoena. We couldn't get corroboration. Both of them pled lawyers.

Q. Okay.

A. They lawyered up" on us.

Q. Okay.

A. And the testimony that we had from the Lieutenant Commander, was enough to tell us that this guy was doing it on his own. He was going to—you know the level that he was going to work this. When I interviewed General Miller he said, he was unaware of it and he never would have approved it. He knew it was not only— not appropriate, it was illegal. He knew that. And that's in my—in the question answer part of the classified piece.

Q. Okay.

A. So what we found there was there was a culpable person at a lower level who was—and I would tell you that Lieutenant Commander was a rogue guy.

Q. Okay.

A. He was sent over there in a capacity that had nothing to do with interrogation really. It had to do with more the process business. He became a zealot

A-72

and he jumped in there and got himself extended. Chopped from his sending organization to the JTF and essentially was having a ball.

Q.   Okay.

A.   I mean he was yakking away when the interview was done by General Furlow. General Furlow came out of there, and his eyes were just watered I guess. This guy was just saying the stuff he was doing. You know? Yeah, we decided to do this, and this, and this. And it was all corroborated by other people.

Q.   Okay.

A.   And he did it alone. General Miller was not accountable for this rogue guy at this point. He would not have approved and done that.

Q.   Okay.

A.   And it was so much that was hidden down there with him. So that's why we recommended a criminal investigation. When we submitted our report that's what it said. We were talked out of that by the legal folks saying well what you really need to do is hand it over to his current Commander in the Reserves for his action. So we kind of liked that. And my JAG who was in this said okay we'll bend to that. Because we don't know that it's criminal, but it needs a further look.

Q.   Right.

A.   The Commander would do that. And we'll put it over to a Commander that has authority over this individual right now. So that's what we did. That was the second point that General Craddock disagreed with me on.

Q.   He liked your first idea?

A.   See he came right back to me, and said no, it needs to be a criminal investigation. You know, so I poked myself in the eye and said you know here we go.

Q.   [Laughter]

A.   So, that s why. So, our recommendation that was negotiated away by the legal team from SOUTHCOM we--he came right back to it. So I'm fine with that.

Q.   Okay.

A.   Either way I would have been fine with it. I prefer the way that he recommended it in the end, General Craddock did.

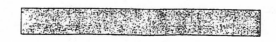

Q.   Did you did not have similar concerns about General Miller's level of participation?

A.   I did not. I did not. I felt like the situation with Khatani was entirely different.

Q.   Okay.

A.   That was one where it was the business execution. Everybody was working in good faith that they were in control at whatever level and whatever they wanted to do. However creative they were going to be. They felt like well we got a green light to do this to whatever level we want to as long as we don't torture this individual.

Q.   Okay.

A.   Essentially was that and that we maintain the level of humane treatment. I think they kind were there. That's why I said I didn't have a finding there. There was question and again I was supposed to look into allegations of abuse.

Q.   Okay.

A.   I think I really want to stop saying "abuse." Was that abusive? Was it degrading? Yes, it was and that's where I labeled it.

Q.   Okay.

A.   I figured that was an echelon above inhumane.

Q.   Okay.

A.   Now, was that the intent? If it was and they didn't violated the level of inhumane or torture. Let's get on with it. Okay? That was our intent.

Q.   Okay.

A.   No one ever said that was our intent.

Q.   Okay.

A.   No one ever put some guidance in there. There was no control.

Q.   Okay.

A. In spite of the fact that people were saying we got this. We know all that. We're in control. There was no control. It would have been easy for what happened with the Lieutenant Commander with the classified detainee to have happened easily.

Q. Okay.

A. It is just luck that it didn't.

Q. Okay.

A. And again I go back to the—you know, they said well a couple of Senators, you know, why did you find this to be "bad", you know?

Q. Okay.

A. Well just for the lack of a camera it would sure look like Abu Ghraib. And I didn't want to draw too much attention there because I had no proof.

Q. Okay.

A. I didn't want to get into this 'migration theory' thing which I'm not going to.

Q. Right.

A. So I didn't chase that one. Could have but that wasn't my charter.

Q. And was the classified detainee interrogated using a special IP?

A. There was a special IP approved for him.

Q. Okay.

A. They never really got into it. They got—they started it, but they didn't get into it because they had this ruse.

Q. Okay.

A. And I don't know that you read that the ruse—the ruse was they were going to put a confederate in with him and they were plant this idea that, well I've had this dream. These guys are very emotional guys. Had this dream that you're going to be buried.

Q. Right.

A. And they had the messengers come to tell him certain things. And then they had the Navy Captain from the White House show up under ruse.

Q. Right.

A. And he had the letter. And we finally got the letter. And the letter wasn't-- the letter was more that we were going to arrest your mother, bring to Guantánamo, and--and that kind of thing.

Q. Okay.

A. And the message that was--the verbal part was that you know, we're going to--you're going to die. You're going away. We are going to erase you and no one is going to miss you.

Q. Right. Okay.

A. And then the last part of the ruse was where he got the boat ride where he thought this is where he goes away. And within a very short time is when he had this epiphany and he joined the global war on terror.

Q. Okay.

A. Which is where he is today.

Q. Right. Hurray for him.

A. Yeah.

Q. Okay, Sir. Thanks. I'm just not going to go into all this other stuff. The report, your report, indicated that there were some personnel that you wanted to interview but were unavailable to you. And you kind of addressed that, earlier, at the beginning of our interview here. Out of that group of folks that, for whatever reasons, you were not able to talk to you--that you were not able to talk to, would you recommend we try to speak to any of them? Do you think they would provide anything that would be useful for our assessment?

A. We've gone back now and we have interviewed all of them as I understand.

Q. Okay.

A. Everything that they say corroborates what they said in their e-mail traffic and no other illuminating sort of stuff.

Q. Okay.

A. The one person was obviou̶ ▓▓▓▓▓▓▓▓▓▓▓▓▓▓▓▓
▓▓▓▓▓▓▓▓▓▓▓▓▓▓▓▓▓▓▓▓

Q.   Right.

A.   She's the one that we finally found out that the reason they wouldn't give us access to her was because of her medical condition.

Q.   Okay.

A.   And supposedly--and there was another one that had--she jumped out of a truck in Afghanistan and broke both of her ankles or something and was getting, you know, some medical kind of treatment, and they wouldn't give us access. They don't tell you why. They just said no you can't have access to them right now. And some of them are involved in very sensitive operations, globally and they weren't going to pull them out.

But after Senator Warner, like I said, you know, got pretty excited about it, we finally got to everybody. Those interviews have now been done. There is nothing in, as I understand from General Furlow, nothing in any of those interviews that changes anything other than adding more discussion to the points we already investigated. The short shackle stuff. The--modifying the temperatures of the rooms. And we found that. Okay? And we addressed. Whether it was policy or not, or used or approved or not. We did all that. So just you know I'm saying it again. When it got to it, it's pretty much airtight.

BY

Q.   Just in case--I'm sorry, but just in case, where are the transcripts for those interviews?

 Who has the interviews? SOUTHCOM?

A.   General Furlow has got it. Took it. It's now an addendum to the report. It's added addendum testimony.

BY (b)(7)(C)

Q.   Okay. We could probably get that from the SJA at SOUTHCOM?

A.   Sure. Yeah, and that's not going to get to the General Miller stuff.

Q.   No.

A.   It just gets to the details of the FBI allegations corroborated or not. So.

Q.   We just want to be able to say we've read everything.

A.   Oh, okay. Yeah, and I would hit those.

Q.   Yes, Sir.

A.   The only one and this is not about General Miller, the only one we just can't get to is this one where ████████████-and she has a couple of e-mails and you've probably read them. Where she actually contradicts herself a little bit and she never saw anything that was really upsetting. And she goes into this thing about this guy was short shackled to the floor. He has pulled his out hair and he was lying in his own excrement and had been denied food or water for several days. When we asked her about it, she goes well, he just looked like he was kind of a thin guy. She translated that into being denied food or water for several days. We could find nothing that said-- and this is on the detention side. Those guards if prisoner so and so wasn't given food and water it was a big deal.

Q.   Okay.

A.   It was documented. We got all the medical records. So we pretty much knew all that. We couldn't find anyone. There was one detainee and he was called "Crazy Bob" and this is a guy who, certifiably crazy. I mean he ate his own excrement.

Q.   Hmm.

A.   I mean this guy did all that kind of stuff. Now ████████████couldn't tell us plus or minus of when she saw this and where she saw it. But she did allude to interrogation. I don't think we had Crazy Bob in the interrogation room. Just a few times because he's so crazy. And we didn't--certifiably crazy and it wasn't an act, but at some point she might have seen Crazy Bob. You know? This guy is a mess. And yeah, to keep him throwing all the excrement on all the guards and doing stuff, he was probably short shackled as a control measure in detention probably. And we just had a real hard time with one. That's the one that the SASC latched on to. That's the one that both the Republican and the Democratic side felt like, there you have it. That's torture. This guy has been shackled to the floor for days deprived of food and water and he is now living in his excrement and, and he has pulled his hair out because he is slowly going crazy. Well, yeah, this guy is crazy. He has been crazy for a while. And detention hasn't helped him.

Q.   Okay, Sir.

A.   Okay, so that's the one left hanging.

Q.   Right.

A.   I don't know that we're ever going to get to it. There are some things that are not known and probably not knowable.

Q.   Right. Okay, Sir.

A.   Okay. Sorry, I dragged that one out. That--

Q.   No. No. That's good.

A.   I just wanted to make it clear to you.

████████████ Yes, Sir. Do you have any other questions?

████████████ No, Ma'am.

BY ████████████

Q.   Sir, is there anything else that you would like to add, perhaps, you know, clarify anything that you may have said previously or would like to add to what you've already said before we begin the read-out and let you go on your way?

A.   No. Yes, there is. One last thing and I did this with the Senate. I said, again, I know Geoff Miller. I'm not finding him and I didn't find him criminally libel for anything.

Q.   Okay.

A.   I didn't find him to be a bad officer, a bad Commander, I think he did some heroic stuff down there. He was given a big job jar. But in the context of this subject and this investigation for--and I'm not walking a mile in his shoes. But having, like I said, having done that, I got to tell you that was probably the most important thing he had for that period of time. And to be unwitting of not small details, but almost everything that was going on with that particular detainee when the Secretary of Defense had eyes on him, and had the entire General Counsels of all the Services ground up into this guy's plan, the not knowing of that and then have all of this creative application of these techniques going on that raised all this concern in my finding of it really being abusive and degrading--which it was. That could have been the intent.

Q.   Okay.

A.   That aside, that's where I found him to come up short. It was his failure to monitor the cumulative effects of this particular detainee. And that's how I listed it. And that's a finding. And someone else can refute that or whatever. I think they would be hard-pressed to do it.

Was that relevant to any kind of behavior or culpability? I would say he was culpable. I said he's the accountable person and because he failed to monitor this and because there was no goal to abuse or goal to degrade, there was probably a goal to not torture and there was a goal to maintain humane treatment. But the rest of it was

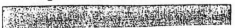

A-79

all left to the creative minds and applications processes of some very low level personnel. That's where I made the recommendation when I was directed to do that. So, that's what I'll say. He's not a criminal.

Q.　　Okay.

A.　　I mean this guy was given a big task and if you put yourself back in the context of the time. And this is where the Republican side was just coming down hard on me. In the context of the times, did we need the information from that person? Yes, no. If within the limits and boundaries that were not defined for the application, but within the limits and boundaries strategically of this detainee, what did the Secretary of Defense mean? Would we degrade this guy? By saying "ego down" my definition we were going to degrade him in some way. What limit? The lowest limit. But General Miller didn't know and didn't set the limits. He didn't set the boundaries. He didn't say how long it was going to go on. In the context of the times knew the country needed that intelligence. Actionable intelligence and I think that's where this thing gets really mushy.

Q.　　Okay

A.　　But absolutely I don't think he watched--he didn't watch this glass ball. By

Q.　　Sir, given that, in your opinion was General Miller derelict in the performance of his duty with respect to the supervision of the interrogation of that detainee?

A.　　I got tell you the word, "derelict" stinks---

Q.　　It's a tough word.

A.　　Yeah, it comes to the wrong level. I'd said, "Failure to monitor".

Q.　　Okay.

A.　　Appropriately, this particular most important interrogation plan.

Q.　　Okay.

A.　　--is where I found him accountable. Not culpable and I'm not going to use the word "derelict".

Q.　　Okay.

A.　　I think that's the wrong level. That's just how I feel about it.

Q.   Gotcha, Sir. All right. Sir, who else do you think we should talk to without-

A.   Senator McCain, Senator Warner, Senator Levin--.

Q.   That might happen.

A.   Yeah, go crazy. everybody has got an interest in this.

Q.   Okay.

A.   Oh, yeah! So my last final word is I felt no pressure to bring back a scalp.

Q.   Okay.

A.   I felt no pressure from General Craddock. I felt no pressure from all the press out there saying hold somebody besides the lower level enlisted person. This is the Abu Ghraib mystique.

Q.   Right.

A.   You know, none of that. None of that. I did not have an agenda. I was told to go do this. And when General Craddock tells me to do the certain task and then he disagreed, I felt no compulsion to change. You know?

Q.   Okay.

A.   He said we've agreed to disagree. And I found out about that at the 11th hour. I was never pressured and I felt like given this investigation and the level that it took, and again it became additive to the 15-6 I felt personally.

Q.   Okay.

A.   I think it's the call that I was directed to make. So I did.

████████████ Okay, Sir. All right. Well, thank you, Sir. Do you have anything else. Bob?

████████████ No, I don't.

████████████ All right then, we'll go ahead and begin the read-out, Sir, and finish up here.

LTGEN SCHMIDT: Okay.

████████████ Sir, we are required to protect the confidentiality of IG Investigations and the rights, privacy, and reputations of all people involved in them.

We ask people not to discuss or reveal matters under investigation. Accordingly, we ask that you not discuss this matter with anyone, except your attorney if you choose to consult one, without permission of the Investigating officers.

Your testimony is part of an official Inspector General Record. Earlier I advised you that while access is normally restricted to persons who clearly need the information to perform their official duties, your testimony may be released outside official channels. Individual members of the public who do not have an official need to know, may request a copy of this record to include your testimony under the Freedom of Information Act. Is there is such a request, do you consent to the release of your testimony outside official channels?

LTG SCHMIDT: Since everything we've discussed here is—was an open forum in the SASC, I would say if there is a FOIA request for it by those kinds of people, then, it could be released.

 Right.

 So that's a yes?

LTG SCHMIDT: Yes.

Do you have any questions?

LTG SCHMIDT: No.

The time is 1055 and the tape-recorded portion of this interview is concluded. Thank you, Sir.

[Testimony of LIEUTENANT GENERAL
RANDALL M. SCHMIDT
Was transcribed and certified by
Certified Court-Reporter, Department of the
Army Inspector General Agency, Crystal City, Virginia.]

UNCLASSIFIED

2002 DEC -2 AM 11: 03

ACTION MEMO

OFFICE OF THE
SECRETARY OF DEFENSE

November 27, 2002 (1:00 PM)

DEPSEC_____

FOR: **SECRETARY OF DEFENSE**

FROM: William J. Haynes II, General Counsel

SUBJECT: **Counter-Resistance Techniques**

- The Commander of USSOUTHCOM has forwarded a request by the Commander of Joint Task Force 170 (now JTF GTMO) for approval of counter-resistance techniques to aid in the interrogation of detainees at Guantanamo Bay (Tab A).

- The request contains three categories of counter-resistance techniques, with the first category the least aggressive and the third category the most aggressive (Tab B).

- I have discussed this with the Deputy, Doug Feith and General Myers. I believe that all join in my recommendation that, as a matter of policy, you authorize the Commander of USSOUTHCOM to employ, in his discretion, only Categories I and II and the fourth technique listed in Category III ("Use of mild, non-injurious physical contact such as grabbing, poking in the chest with the finger, and light pushing").

- While all Category III techniques may be legally available, we believe that, as a matter of policy, a blanket approval of Category III techniques is not warranted at this time. Our Armed Forces are trained to a standard of interrogation that reflects a tradition of restraint.

RECOMMENDATION: That SECDEF approve the USSOUTHCOM Commander's use of those counter-resistance techniques listed in Categories I and II and the fourth technique listed in Category III during the interrogation of detainees at Guantanamo Bay.

SECDEF DECISION:

Approved _____ Disapproved _____ Other _____

Attachments
As stated

*However, I stand for 8-10 hours
A day. Why is standing limited to 4 hours?*

cc: CJCS, USD(P)

D. R. DEC 0 2 2002

UNCLASSIFIED

X04030-02

DEPARTMENT OF DEFENSE
UNITED STATES SOUTHERN COMMAND
OFFICE OF THE COMMANDER
3511 NW 91ST AVENUE
MIAMI, FL 33172-1217

SCCDR   25 October 2002

MEMORANDUM FOR Chairman of the Joint Chiefs of Staff, Washington, DC 20318-9999

SUBJECT: Counter-Resistance Techniques

1. The activities of Joint Task Force 170 have yielded critical intelligence support for forces in combat, combatant commanders, and other intelligence/law enforcement entities prosecuting the War on Terrorism. However, despite our best efforts, some detainees have tenaciously resisted our current interrogation methods. Our respective staffs, the Office of the Secretary of Defense, and Joint Task Force 170 have been trying to identify counter-resistant techniques that we can lawfully employ.

2. I am forwarding Joint Task Force 170's proposed counter-resistance techniques. I believe the first two categories of techniques are legal and humane. I am uncertain whether all the techniques in the third category are legal under US law, given the absence of judicial interpretation of the US torture statute. I am particularly troubled by the use of implied or expressed threats of death of the detainee or his family. However, I desire to have as many options as possible at my disposal and therefore request that Department of Defense and Department of Justice lawyers review the third category of techniques.

3. As part of any review of Joint Task Force 170's proposed strategy, I welcome any suggested interrogation methods that others may propose. I believe we should provide our interrogators with as many legally permissible tools as possible.

4. Although I am cognizant of the important policy ramifications of some of these proposed techniques, I firmly believe that we must quickly provide Joint Task Force 170 counter-resistance techniques to maximize the value of our intelligence collection mission.

Encls

1. JTF 170 CDR Memo
   dtd 11 October, 2002
2. JTF 170 SJA Memo
   dtd 11 October, 2002
3. JTF 170 J-2 Memo
   dtd 11 October, 2002

James T. Hill
General, US Army
Commander

JTF 170-CG   11 October 2002

MEMORANDUM FOR Commander, United States Southern Command, 3511 NW 91st Avenue, Miami, Florida 33172-1217

SUBJECT: Counter-Resistance Strategies

1. Request that you approve the interrogation techniques delineated in the enclosed Counter-Resistance Strategies memorandum. I have reviewed this memorandum and the legal review provided to me by the JTF-170 Staff Judge Advocate and concur with the legal analysis provided.

2. I am fully aware of the techniques currently employed to gain valuable intelligence in support of the Global War on Terrorism. Although these techniques have resulted in significant exploitable intelligence, the same methods have become less effective over time. I believe the methods and techniques delineated in the accompanying J-2 memorandum will enhance our efforts to extract additional information. Based on the analysis provided by the JTF-170 SJA, I have concluded that these techniques do not violate U.S. or international laws.

3. My point of contact for this issue is LTC Jerald Phifer at DSN 660-3476.

2 Encls
1. JTF 170-J2 Memo,
   11 Oct 02
2. JTF 170-SJA Memo,
   11 Oct 02

MICHAEL B. DUNLAVEY
Major General, USA.
Commanding

DEPARTMENT OF DEFENSE
JOINT TASK FORCE 170
GUANTANAMO BAY, CUBA
APO AE 09860

MEMORANDUM FOR Commander, Joint Task Force 170

SUBJ: Legal Review of Aggressive Interrogation Techniques

1. I have reviewed the memorandum on Counter-Resistance Strategies, dated 11 Oct 02, and agree that the proposed strategies do not violate applicable federal law. Attached is a more detailed legal analysis that addresses the proposal.
2. I recommend that interrogators be properly trained in the use of the approved methods of interrogation, and that interrogations involving category II and III methods undergo a legal review prior to their commencement.
3. This matter is forwarded to you for your recommendation and action.

DIANE E. BEAVER
LTC, USA
Staff Judge Advocate

2 Encls
1. JTF 170-J2 Memo,
   11 Oct 02
2. JTF 170-SJA Memo,
   11 Oct 02

DEPARTMENT OF DEFENSE
JOINT TASK FORCE 170
GUANTANAMO BAY, CUBA
APO AE 09860

MEMORANDUM FOR Commander, Joint Task Force 170

SUBJECT: Legal Brief on Proposed Counter-Resistence Strategies

1. (U) ISSUE: To ensure the security of the United States and its Allies, more aggressive interrogation techniques than the ones presently used, such as the methods proposed in the attached recommendation, may be required in order to obtain information from detainees that are resisting interrogation efforts and are suspected of having significant information essential to national security. This legal brief references the recommendations outlined in the JTF-170-J2 memorandum, dated 11 October 2002.

2. (U) FACTS: The detainees currently held at Guantanamo Bay, Cuba (GTMO), are not protected by the Geneva Conventions (GC). Nonetheless, DoD interrogators trained to apply the Geneva Conventions have been using commonly approved methods of interrogation such as rapport building through the direct approach, rewards, the multiple interrogator approach, and the use of deception. However, because detainees have been able to communicate among themselves and debrief each other about their respective interrogations, their interrogation resistance strategies have become more sophisticated. Compounding this problem is the fact that there is no established clear policy for interrogators limits and operations at GTMO, and many interrogations have felt in the past that they could not do anything that could be considered "controversial." In accordance with President Bush's 7 February 2002 directive, the detainees are not Enemy Prisoners of War (EPW). They must be treated humanely and, subject to military necessity, in accordance with the principles of GC.

3. (U) DISCUSSION: The Office of the Secretary of Defense (OSD) has not adopted specific guidelines regarding interrogation techniques for detainee operations at GTMO. While the procedures outlined in Army FM 34-52 Intelligence Interrogation (28 September 1992) are utilized, they are constrained by, and conform to the GC and applicable international law, and therefore are not binding. Since the detainees are not EPWs, the Geneva Conventions limitations that ordinarily would govern captured enemy personnel interrogations are not binding on U.S. personnel conducting detainee interrogations at GTMO. Consequently, in the absence of specific binding guidance, and in accordance with the President's directive to treat the detainees humanely, we must look to applicable International and domestic law

in order to determine the legality of the more aggressive interrogation techniques recommended in the J2 proposal.

a. (U) International Law: Although no international body of law directly applies, the more notable international treaties and relevant law are listed below.

(1) (U) In November of 1994, the United States ratified The Convention Against Torture and Other Cruel, Inhumane or Degrading Treatment or Punishment. However, the United States took a reservation to Article 16, which defined cruel, inhumane and degrading treatment or punishment, by instead deferring to the current standard articulated in the 8th Amendment to the United States Constitution. Therefore, the United States is only prohibited from committing those acts that would otherwise be prohibited under the United States Constitutional Amendment against cruel and unusual punishment. The United States ratified the treaty with the understanding that the convention would not be self-executing, that is, that it would not create a private cause of action in U.S. Courts. This convention is the principal U.N. treaty regarding torture and other cruel, inhumane, or degrading treatment.

(2) (U) The International Covenant on Civil and Political Rights (ICCPR), ratified by the United States in 1992, prohibits inhumane treatment in Article 7, and arbitrary arrest and detention in Article 9. The United States ratified it on the condition that it would not be self-executing, and it took a reservation to Article 7 that we would only be bound to the extent that the United States Constitution prohibits cruel and unusual punishment.

(3) (U) The American Convention on Human Rights forbids inhumane treatment, arbitrary imprisonment, and requires the state to promptly inform detainees of the charges against them, to review their pretrial confinement, and to conduct a trial within a reasonable time. The United States signed the convention on 1 June 1977, but never ratified it.

(4) (U) The Rome Statute established the International Criminal Court and criminalized inhumane treatment, unlawful deportation, and imprisonment. The United States not only failed to ratify the Rome Statute, but also later withdrew from it.

(5) (U) The United Nations' Universal Declaration of Human Rights, prohibits inhumane or degrading punishment, arbitrary arrest, detention or exile. Although international declarations may provide evidence of customary international law (which is considered binding on all nations even without a treaty), they are not enforceable by themselves.

(6) (U) There is some European case law stemming from the European Court of Human Rights on the issue of torture. The Court ruled on allegations of torture and other forms of inhumane treatment by the British in the Northern Ireland conflict. The British authorities developed practices of interrogation such as forcing detainees to stand for long hours, placing black hoods over their heads, holding the detainees prior to interrogation in a room with continuing loud noise, and depriving them of sleep, food, and water. The European Court concluded that these acts did not rise to the level of torture as defined in the Convention Against Torture, because torture was defined as an aggravated form of cruel, inhuman, or degrading treatment or punishment. However, the Court did find that these techniques constituted cruel inhumane, and degrading treatment. Nonetheless, and as previously mentioned, not only is the United States not a part of the European Human Rights Court, but as previously stated, it only ratified the definition of cruel, inhuman, and degrading treatment consistent with the U.S. Constitution. See also *Mehinovic v. Vuckovic*, 198 F. Supp. 2d 1322 (N.D. Geor. 2002); *Committee Against Torture v. Israel*, Supreme Court of Israel, 6 Sep 99, 7 BHRC 31; *Ireland v. UK* (1978), 2 EHRR 25.

b. (U) Domestic Law: Although the detainee interrogations are not occurring in the continental United States, U.S. personnel conducting said interrogations are still bound by applicable Federal Law, specifically, the Eighth Amendment of the United States Constitution, 18 U.S.C. § 2340, and for military interrogators, the Uniform Code of Military Justice (UCMJ).

(1) (U) The Eighth Amendment of the United States Constitution provides that excessive bail shall not be required, nor excessive fines imposed, nor cruel and unusual punishment inflicted. There is a lack of Eighth Amendment case law relating in the context of interrogations, as most of the Eighth Amendment litigation in federal court involves either the death penalty, or 42 U.S.C. § 1983 actions from inmates based on prison conditions. The Eighth Amendment applies as to whether or not torture or inhumane treatment has occurred under the federal torture statute.[1]

(a) (U) A principal case in the confinement context that is instructive regarding Eighth Amendment analysis (which is relevant because the United States adopted the

---

[1] Notwithstanding the argument that U.S. personnel are bound by the Constitution, the detainees confined at GTMO have no jurisdictional standing to bring a section 1983 action alleging an Eighth Amendment violation in U.S. Federal Court.

Convention Against Torture, Cruel, Inhumane and Degrading Treatment, it did so deferring to the Eighth Amendment of the United States Constitution) and conditions of confinement if a U.S. court were to examine the issue is *Hudson v. McMillian*, 503 U.S. 1 (1992). The issue in *Hudson* stemmed from a 42 U.S.C. § 1983 action alleging that a prison inmate suffered minor bruises, facial swelling, loosened teeth, and a cracked dental plate resulting from a beating by prison guards while he was cuffed and shackled. In this case the Court held that there was no governmental interest in beating an inmate in such a manner. The Court further ruled that the use of excessive physical force against a prisoner might constitute cruel and unusual punishment, even though the inmate does not suffer serious injury.

(b) (U) In *Hudson*, the Court relied on *Whitley v. Albert*, 475 U.S. 312 (1986), as the seminal case that establishes whether a constitutional violation has occurred. The Court stated that the extent of the injury suffered by an inmate is only one of the factors to be considered, but that there is no significant injury requirement in order to establish an Eighth Amendment violation, and that the absence of serious injury is relevant to, but does not end, the Eighth Amendment inquiry. The Court based its decision on the "...settled rule that the unnecessary and wanton infliction of pain ... constitutes cruel and unusual punishment forbidden by the Eighth Amendment." *Whitley* at 319, quoting *Ingraham v. Wright*, 430 U.S. 651, 670 (1977). The *Hudson* Court then held that in the excessive force or conditions of confinement context, the Eighth Amendment violation test delineated by the Supreme Court in *Hudson* is that when prison official maliciously and sadistically use force to cause harm, contemporary standards of decency are always violated, whether or not significant injury is evident. The extent of injury suffered by an inmate is one factor that may suggest whether the use of force could plausibly have been thought necessary in a particular situation, but the question of whether the measure taken inflicted unnecessary and wanton pain and suffering, ultimately turns on whether force was applied in a good faith effort to maintain or restore discipline, or maliciously and sadistically for the *very* (emphasis added) purpose of causing harm. If so, the Eighth Amendment claim will prevail.

(c) (U) At the District Court level, the typical conditions-of-confinement claims involve a disturbance of the inmate's physical comfort, such as sleep deprivation or loud noise.

The Eighth Circuit ruled in *Singh v. Holcomb*, 1992 U. S. App. LEXIS 24790, that an allegation by an inmate that he was constantly deprived of sleep which resulted in emotional distress, loss of memory, headaches, and poor concentration, did not show either the extreme deprivation level, or the officials' culpable state of mind required to fulfill the objective component of an Eighth Amendment conditions-of-confinement claim.

(d) (U) In another sleep deprivation case alleging an Eighth Amendment violation, the Eighth Circuit established a totality of the circumstances test, and stated that if a particular condition of detention is reasonably related to a legitimate governmental objective, it does not, without more, amount to punishment. In *Ferguson v. Cape Girardean County*, 88 F.3d 647 (8th Cir. 1996), the complainant was confined to a 5-1/2 by 5-1/2 foot cell without a toilet or sink, and was forced to sleep on a mat on the floor under bright lights that were on twenty-four hours a day. His Eighth Amendment claim was not successful because he was able to sleep at some point, and because he was kept under these conditions due to a concern for his health, as well as the perceived danger that he presented. This totality of the circumstances test has also been adopted by the Ninth Circuit. In *Green v. CSO Strack*, 1995 U.S. App. LEXIS 14451, the Court held that threats of bodily injury are insufficient to state a claim under the Eighth Amendment, and that sleep deprivation did not rise to a constitutional violation where the prisoner failed to present evidence that he either lost sleep or was otherwise harmed.

(e) (U) Ultimately, an Eighth Amendment analysis is based primarily on whether the government had a good faith legitimate governmental interest, and did not act maliciously and sadistically for the very purpose of causing harm.

(2) (U) The torture statute (18 U.S.C. § 2340) is the United States' codification of the signed and ratified provisions of the Convention Against Torture and Other Cruel, Inhuman or Degrading Treatment or Punishment, and pursuant to subsection 2340B, does not create any substantive or procedural rights enforceable by law by any party in any civil proceeding.

(a) (U) The statute provides that "whoever outside the United States commits or attempts to commit torture shall be fined under this title or imprisoned not more than 20 years, or both, and if death results to any person from conduct prohibited by this subsection, shall be punished by death or imprisoned for any term of years or for life."

(b) (U) Torture is defined as "an act committed by a person acting under color of law *specifically intended* (emphasis added) to inflict severe physical or mental pain or suffering (other than pain or suffering incident to lawful sanctions) upon another person within his custody or physical control." The statute defines "severe mental pain or suffering" as "the *prolonged mental harm caused by or resulting* (emphasis added) from the intentional infliction or threatened infliction of severe physical pain or suffering; or the administration or application, or threatened administration or application, of mind-altering substances or other procedures calculated to disrupt profoundly the senses of the personality; or the threat of imminent death; or the threat that another person will imminently be subjected to death, severe physical pain or suffering, or the administration or application of mind-altering substances or other procedures calculated to disrupt profoundly the senses or personality."

(c) (U) Case law in the context of the federal torture statute and interrogations is also lacking, as the majority of the case law involving torture relates to either the illegality of brutal tactics used by the police to obtain confessions (in which the Court simply states that these confessions will be deemed as involuntary for the purposes of admissibility and due process, but does not actually address torture or the Eighth Amendment), or the Alien Torts Claim Act, in which federal courts have defined that certain uses of force (such as kidnapping, beating and raping of a man with the consent or acquiescence of a public official. See *Ortiz v. Gramijo* 886 F.Supp. 162 (D. Mass. 1995)) constituted torture. However, no case law on point within the context of 18 USC 2340.

(3) (U) Finally, U.S. military personnel are subject to the Uniform Code of Military Justice. The primitive articles that could potentially be violated depending on the circumstances and results of an interrogation are Article 93 (cruelty and maltreatment), Article 118 (murder), Article 119 (manslaughter), Article 124 (maiming), Article 128 (assault), Article 134 (communicating a threat, and negligent homicide), and the inchoate offenses of attempt (Article 80), conspiracy (Article 81), accessory after the fact (Article 78), and solicitation (Article 82). Article 128 is the article most likely to be violated because a simple assault can be consummated by an unlawful demonstration of violence which creates in the mind of another a reasonable apprehension of receiving

immediate bodily harm, and a specific intent to actually inflict bodily harm is not required.

4. (U) ANALYSIS: The counter-resistance techniques proposed in the JTF-170-J2 memorandum are lawful because they do not violate the Eighth Amendment to the United States Constitution or the federal torture statute as explained below. An international law analysis is not required for the current proposal because the Geneva Conventions do not apply to these detainees since they are not EPWs.

(a) (U) Based on the Supreme Court framework utilized to assess whether a public official has violated the Eighth Amendment, so long as the force used could plausibly have been thought necessary in a particular situation to achieve a legitimate governmental objective, and it was applied in a good faith effort and not maliciously or sadistically for the very purpose of causing harm, the proposed techniques are likely to pass constitutional muster. The federal torture statute will not be violated so long as any of the proposed strategies are not specifically intended to cause severe physical pain or suffering or prolonged mental harm. Assuming that severe physical pain is not inflicted, absent any evidence that any of these strategies will in fact cause prolonged and long lasting mental harm, the proposed methods will not violate the statute.

(b) (U) Regarding the Uniform Code of Military Justice, the proposal to grab, poke in the chest, push lightly, and place a wet towel or hood over the detainee's head would constitute a per se violation of Article 128 (Assault). Threatening a detainee with death may also constitute a violation of Article 128, or also Article 134 (communicating a threat). It would be advisable to have permission or immunity in advance from the convening authority, for military members utilizing these methods.

(c) (U) Specifically, with regard to Category I techniques, the use of mild and fear related approaches such as yelling at the detainee is not illegal because in order to communicate a threat, there must also exist an intent to injure. Yelling at the detainee is legal so long as the yelling is not done with the intent to cause severe physical damage or prolonged mental harm. Techniques of deception such as multiple interrogator techniques, and deception regarding interrogator identity are all permissible methods of interrogation, since there is no legal requirement to be truthful while conducting an interrogation.

(d) (U) With regard to Category II methods, the use of stress positions such as the proposed standing for four hours, the use of isolation for up to thirty days, and interrogating the detainee in an environment other than the standard interrogation booth are all legally permissible so long as no severe physical pain is inflicted and prolonged mental harm intended, and because there is a legitimate governmental objective in obtaining the information necessary that the high value detainees on which these methods would be utilized possess, for the protection of the national security of the United States, its citizens, and allies. Furthermore, these methods would not be utilized for the "very malicious and sadistic purpose of causing harm," and absent medical evidence to the contrary, there is no evidence that prolonged mental harm would result from the use of these strategies. The use of falsified documents is legally permissible because interrogations may use deception to achieve their purpose.

(e) (U) The deprivation of light and auditory stimuli, the placement of a hood over the detainee's head during transportation and questioning, and the use of 20 hour interrogations are all legally permissible so long as there is an important governmental objective, and it is not done for the purpose of causing harm or with the intent to cause prolonged mental suffering. There is no legal requirement that detainees must receive four hours of sleep per night, but if a U.S. Court ever had to rule on this procedure, in order to pass Eighth Amendment scrutiny, and as a cautionary measure, they should receive some amount of sleep so that no severe physical or mental harm will result. Removal of comfort items is permissible because there is no legal requirement to provide comfort items. The requirement is to provide adequate food, water, shelter, and medical care. The issue of removing published religious items or materials would be relevant if these were United States citizens with a First Amendment right. Such is not the case with the detainees. Forced grooming and removal of clothing are not illegal, so long as it is not done to punish or cause harm, as there is a legitimate governmental objective to obtain information, maintain health standards in the camp and protect both the detainees and the guards. There is no illegality in removing hot meals because there is no specific requirement to provide hot meals, only adequate food. The use of the detainee's phobias is equally permissible.

(f) (U) With respect to the Category III advanced counter-resistance strategies, the use of scenarios designed to convince the detainee that death or severely painful consequences are imminent is not illegal for the same aforementioned reasons that there is a compelling governmental interest and it is not done intentionally to cause prolonged harm. However, caution should be utilized with this technique because the torture statute specifically mentions making death threats as an example of inflicting mental pain and suffering. Exposure to cold weather or water is permissible with appropriate medical monitoring. The use of a wet towel to induce the misperception of suffocation would also be permissible if not done with the specific intent to cause prolonged mental harm, and absent medical evidence that it would. Caution should be exercised with this method, as foreign courts have already advised about the potential mental harm that this method may cause. The use of physical contact with the detainee, such as pushing and poking will technically constitute an assault under Article 128, UCMJ.

5. (U) RECOMMENDATION: I recommend that the proposed methods of interrogation be approved, and that the interrogators be properly trained in the use of the approved methods of interrogation. Since the law requires examination of all facts under a totality of circumstances test, I further recommend that all proposed interrogations involving category II and III methods must undergo a legal, medical, behavioral science, and intelligence review prior to their commencement.

6. (U) POC: Captain Michael Borders, x3596.

DIANE E. BEAVER
LTC, USA
Staff Judge Advocate

DEPARTMENT OF DEFENSE
JOINT TASK FORCE 170
GUANTANAMO BAY, CUBA
APO AE 09860

JTF -J2   11 October 2002

MEMORANDUM FOR Commander, Joint Task Force 170

SUBJECT: Request for Approval of Counter-Resistance Strategies

1. (U) PROBLEM: The current guidelines for interrogation procedures at GTMO limit the ability of interrogators to counter advanced resistance.

2. (U) Request approval for use of the following interrogation plan.

   a. Category I techniques. During the initial category of interrogation the detainee should be provided a chair and the environment should be generally comfortable. The format of the interrogation is the direct approach. The use of rewards like cookies or cigarettes may be helpful. If the detainee is determined by the interrogator to be uncooperative, the interrogator may use the following techniques.

     (1) Yelling at the detainee (not directly in his ear or to the level that it would cause physical pain or hearing problems)

     (2) Techniques of deception:

       (a) Multiple interrogator techniques.

       (b) Interrogator identity. The interviewer may identify himself as a citizen of a foreign nation or as an interrogator from a country with a reputation for harsh treatment of detainees.

   b. Category II techniques. With the permission of the GIC, Interrogation Section, the interrogator may use the following techniques.

     (1) The use of stress positions (like standing), for a maximum of four hours.

     (2) The use of falsified documents or reports.

     (3) Use of the isolation facility for up to 30 days. Request must be made to through the OIC, Interrogation Section, to the Director, Joint Interrogation Group (JIG). Extensions beyond the initial 30 days must be approved by the Commanding General. For selected detainees, the OIC, Interrogation Section, will approve all contacts with the detainee, to include medical visits of a non-emergent nature.

     (4) Interrogating the detainee in an environment other than the standard interrogation booth.

     (5) Deprivation of light and auditory stimuli.

     (6) The detainee may also have a hood placed over his head during transportation and questioning. The hood should not restrict

breathing in any way and the detainee should be under direct observation when hooded.

(7) The use of 20-hour interrogations.

(8) Removal of all comfort items (including religions items).

(9) Switching the detainee from hot rations to MREs.

(10) Removal of clothing.

(11) Forced grooming (shaving of facial hair etc...)

(12) Using detainees individual phobias (such as fear of dogs) to induce stress.

c. Category III techniques. Techniques in this category may be used only by submitting a request through the Director, JIG, for approval by the Commanding General with appropriate legal review and information to Commander, USSOUTHCOM. These techniques are required for a very small percentage of the most uncooperative detainees (less than 3%). The following techniques and other aversive techniques, such as those used in U.S. military interrogation resistance training or by other U.S. government agencies, may be utilized in a carefully coordinated manner to help interrogate exceptionally resistant detainees. Any of these techniques that require more than light grabbing, poking, or pushing, will be administered only by individuals specifically trained in their safe application.

(1) The use of scenarios designed to convince the detainee that death or severely painful consequences are imminent for him and/or his family.

(2) Exposure to cold weather or water (with appropriate medical monitoring).

(3) Use of a wet towel and dripping water to induce the misperception of suffocation.

(4) Use of mild, non=injurious contact, such as grabbing, poking in the chest with the finger, and light pushing.

3. (b) The POC for this memorandum is the undersigned at x3476.

JERALD PHIFER
LTC, USA
Director, J2

Army Regulation 15-6: Final Report

Investigation into FBI Allegations of Detainee Abuse at Guantanamo Bay, Cuba Detention Facility

EXECUTIVE SUMMARY

Detention and interrogation operations at Joint Task Force Guantanamo (JTF-GTMO) cover a three-year period and over 24,000 interrogations. This AR 15-6 investigation found only three interrogation acts in violation of interrogation techniques authorized by Army Field Manual 34-52 and DoD guidance. The AR 15-6 also found that the Commander of JTF-GTMO failed to monitor the interrogation of one high value detainee in late 2002. The AR 15-6 found that the interrogation of this same high value detainee resulted in degrading and abusive treatment but did not rise to the level of being inhumane treatment. Finally, the AR 15-6 found that the communication of a threat to another high value detainee was in violation of SECDEF guidance and the UCMJ. The AR 15-6 found no evidence of torture or inhumane treatment at JTF-GTMO.

INTRODUCTION

In June 2004, the Federal Bureau of Investigation (FBI) began an internal investigation to determine if any of its personnel had observed mistreatment or aggressive behavior towards detainees at Guantanamo Bay, Cuba (GTMO). On 9 Jul 04, the FBI – Inspection Division (INSD), sent an e-mail message to all FBI personnel who had served in any capacity at GTMO. The e-mail stated in relevant part:

"You have been identified as having conducted an assignment at GTMO, Cuba since 9/11/2001. The Inspection Division has been tasked with contacting those employees who have served in any capacity at GTMO and obtain information regarding the treatment of detainees. Employees should immediately respond to the following:

1) Employees who observed aggressive treatment, which was not consistent with Bureau interview policy guidelines, should respond via e-mail for purposes of a follow-up interview.

2) Employees who worked at GTMO and observed no aggressive treatment of detainees should respond via an EC documenting a negative response..."

The above e-mail message was sent by INSD to 493 FBI personnel who had served in GTMO between 9 Sep 01 and 9 Jul 04. INSD received 434 total responses, and 26 agents stated that they had observed aggressive treatment of detainees at GTMO.

In response to FBI agent allegations of aggressive interrogation techniques at Joint Task Force Guantanamo Bay (JTF-GTMO) Cuba, that were disclosed in Dec 04 as a result of FOIA releases, General (GEN) Bantz J. Craddock, Commander United States Southern Command (USSOUTHCOM), ordered an AR 15-6 investigation and appointed Brigadier General (BG) John T. Furlow, United States Army South Deputy Commander for Support, as the investigating officer. BG Furlow was directed to address the following allegations:

a. That military interrogators improperly used military working dogs during interrogation sessions to threaten detainees, or for some other purpose;

b. That military interrogators improperly used duct tape to cover a detainee's mouth and head;

c. That DoD interrogators improperly impersonated FBI agents and Department of State officers during the interrogation of detainees;

d. That, on several occasions, DoD interrogators improperly played loud music and yelled loudly at detainees;

e. That military personnel improperly interfered with FBI interrogators in the performance of their FBI duties;

f. That military interrogators improperly used sleep deprivation against detainees;

g. That military interrogators improperly chained detainees and placed them in a fetal position on the floor, and denied them food and water for long periods of time;

h. That military interrogators improperly used extremes of heat and cold during their interrogation of detainees.

Subsequent to the initial appointment, GEN Craddock directed BG Furlow to investigate two additional allegations concerning a female military interrogator performing a "lap dance" on a detainee and the use of faux "menstrual blood" during an interrogation. Finally, the appointment letter directed BG Furlow to not limit himself to the listed allegations.

On 28 Feb 05, after two months of investigation, BG Furlow advised GEN Craddock that he needed to interview officers senior in grade to himself. On 28 Feb 05 GEN Craddock appointed Lieutenant General (Lt Gen) Randall M. Schmidt, United States Southern Command Air Forces Commander, Davis-

Monthan AFB, AZ, as the senior investigating officer. This report reflects the combined findings and conclusions of the initial investigative efforts and the combined investigative efforts of both BG Furlow and Lt Gen Schmidt.

After submission of the AR15-6 Report of Investigation on 1 Apr 05, CDR USSOUTHCOM directed on 5 May 2005 that the investigation be reopened to consider memos dated 11 Dec 04 and 24 Dec 04, that had recently been discovered, regarding the subject of the second Special Interrogation Plan. Prior to completion of the follow-up, CDR USSOUTHCOM directed on 2 Jun 05 that the investigation should also address new allegations made by the subject of the first Special Interrogation Plan.

SCOPE OF REVIEW

This investigation was directed and accomplished under the "informal procedures" provisions of Army Regulation 15-6, Procedures for Investigating Officers and Boards of Officers, dated 30 Sep 96, (AR 15-6). This AR 15-6 investigation centered on alleged abuses occurring during interrogation operations. This AR 15-6 found incidents of abuse during detention operations; all of which were appropriately addressed by the command. The investigation team conducted a comprehensive review of thousands of documents and statements pertaining to any allegations of abuse occurring at GTMO, to include the complete medical records of the subjects of the first and second Special Interrogation Plan. The team interviewed 30 FBI agents, conducted interviews of over 100 personnel from 6 Jan 05 to 24 Mar 05 and had access to hundreds of interviews conducted by several recent investigations. These interviews included personnel assigned to GTMO, USSOUTHCOM, and OSD during the tenure of JTFs 160, 170, and GTMO. It included nine DIA personnel, including every Joint Intelligence Group Chief and every Intelligence Control Element Chief. It included 76 DoD personnel, to include every General Officer who commanded Joint Task Force 160, Joint Task Force 170 and Joint Task Force GTMO. DoD personnel interviewed also included personnel who served as interrogators at GTMO and instructors at the US Army Intelligence School and Center. During the course of the investigation, the team visited Birmingham, AL; Chicago, IL; Ft Bragg, NC; Ft Devens, MA; Ft Huachuca, AZ; GTMO (twice); Los Angeles, CA; Miami, FL; and Washington D.C. (five times).

The investigation team attempted to determine if the allegations alleged by the FBI, in fact, occurred. During the course of the follow up investigation the AR15-6 also considered allegations raised specifically by detainees the subject of the first and second Special Interrogation Plans. The investigating team applied a preponderance standard of proof consistent with the guidance contained in AR15-6. The team also applied guidance contained in FM 34-52, CDR USSOUTHCOM, and SECDEF memorandums authorizing special interrogation techniques in deciding if a particular interrogation approach fell properly within an authorized technique. In those cases in which the team concluded that the allegation had in fact occurred, the team then considered whether the incident was in compliance with interrogation techniques that were approved either at the time of the incident or subsequent to the incident. In those cases where it was determined the allegation occurred and to have not been an authorized technique, the team then reviewed whether disciplinary action had already been taken and the propriety of that action. On 28 Mar 05, GEN Craddock, as the investigation appointing authority, asked Lt Gen Schmidt to determine accountability for those substantiated violations that had no command action taken.

The team did not review the legal validity of the various interrogation techniques outlined in Army Field Manual 34-52, or those approved by the Secretary of Defense.

BACKGROUND

On 7 Mar 05 Vice Admiral A.T. Church, III submitted his final report of detention operations and detainee interrogation techniques in the Global War on Terror to the Secretary of Defense. (hereinafter "Church Report") That report included a thorough background discussion of detainee operations at GTMO. Our investigation independently researched the genesis and adjustments to policy and interrogation techniques from the origination of GTMO to the present. Our independently derived findings regarding the development and adjustments to policy and interrogation techniques are identical to the Church report. Therefore, I have adopted relevant portions of the Church report to show the development of permissible interrogation techniques.

Interrogation operations at GTMO began in January 2002. Initially interrogators relied upon the interrogation techniques contained in FM 34-52. These techniques were ineffective against detainees who had received interrogation resistance training. On 11 Oct 2002, Major General Michael E. Dunlavey, the Commander of Joint Task Force (JTF) 170, the intelligence task force at GTMO, requested that the CDR USSOUTHCOM, GEN James T. Hill, approve 19 counter resistance techniques that were not specifically listed in FM 34-52. The techniques were broken down into Categories I, II, and III, with the third category containing the most aggressive techniques. On 25 Oct 02 CDR USSOUTHCOM forwarded the request to the Chairman of the Joint Chiefs of Staff, General Richard B. Myers. On 2 Dec 02, the Secretary of Defense approved the use of all Category I and II techniques, but only one of the Category III techniques (which authorized mild, non-injurious physical contact such as grabbing, poking in the chest with a finger, and light pushing). In the approval memorandum, the SECDEF approved the techniques for use by CDR USSOUTHCOM, who subsequently verbally delegated the authority to approve and apply these techniques to CDR JTF-GTMO.

On 15 Jan 03, SECDEF rescinded his approval of all Category II techniques and the one Category III technique leaving only Category I techniques in effect. The SECDEF memo permitted use of Category II and III techniques only with SECDEF approval. No approval was requested or granted.

On 16 Apr 03, the Secretary of Defense issued a new policy accepting 24 techniques, most of which were taken directly from or closely resembled those in FM 34-52. The Secretary's guidance remains in effect today. This policy memorandum placed several requirements on CDR USSOUTHCOM. First, it required all detainees to continue to be treated humanely. Second, it required SECDEF notification prior to the implementation of any of the following aggressive Interrogation techniques: Incentive/Removal of Incentive; Pride and Ego Down; Mutt and Jeff; and Isolation. Third, it specifically limited the use of these aggressive techniques to circumstances required by "military necessity." The memorandum did not attempt to define the parameters of "humane treatment" or "military necessity."

The CDR USSOUTHCOM issued a memorandum on 2 Jun 03 providing further guidance on the implementation of the 16 Apr 03 SECDEF approved techniques. This guidance provided that prior to the use of any of the specified aggressive techniques, the JTF Commander would submit the request in writing to CDR USSOUTHCOM for submission to SECDEF. The guidance also stated that "specific implementation guidance with respect to techniques A-Q is provided in Army Field Manual 34-52. Further implementation guidance with respect to techniques R-X will need to be developed by the appropriate authority." GTMO standard operating procedure on interrogations provides guidance for interrogations.

In addition, the CDR USSOUTHCOM guidance provided the following clarification to the SECDEF's 16 Apr 03 memorandum: **(quoting)**

> (a) Reference Technique B, the Working Group was most concerned about removal of the Koran from a detainee—something we no longer do. Because providing incentives (e.g., McDonald's Fish Sandwiches or cigarettes) is an integral part of interrogations, you will notify me in writing when the provided incentive would exceed that contemplated by interrogation doctrine contained in Army FM 34-52, or when the interrogators intend to remove an incentive from a detainee;

> (b) Reference Techniques I and O, you will notify me in writing when use of these standard interrogation techniques goes beyond the doctrinal application described in Army FM 34-52. When use of the technique is consistent with FM 34-52, you do not need to notify me;

> (c) I define "sleep deprivation", referenced in Technique V, as keeping a detainee awake for more that 16 hrs, or allowing a detainee to rest

briefly and then repeatedly awakening him, not to exceed four days in succession;

(d) Reference Technique X, I do not consider the use of maximum-security units as isolation. A detainee placed in a maximum-security unit is segregated, but not truly isolated;

(e) I define the "least intrusive method" as the technique that has the least impact on a detainee's standard of treatment, while evoking the desired response from the detainee during interrogations;

(f) Except in the case of Techniques B, I, O, and X, I have determined that the first 0-6/GG-15 in the chain of command or supervision, is the "appropriate specified senior approval authority," unless approval authority is withheld from that individual by higher authority.

Lastly, I have told the Secretary of Defense his 16 April guidance applies to all interagency elements assigned or attached to JTF GTMO. **(end quote)**

There have been over 24,000 interrogation sessions at GTMO since the beginning of interrogation operations.

FINDINGS

GENERAL DETAINEE POPULATION

Allegation: That DoD interrogators improperly impersonated FBI agents or Department of State officers during the interrogation of detainees.

Finding #1: On several occasions in 2003 various DoD interrogators impersonated agents of the FBI and the Department of State.

Technique: Authorized: FM 34-52 (p. 3-13); Category I technique approved by SECDEF – Deceiving interrogator identity

Discussion: The Chief of the Special Interrogation Team directed two interrogators to pose as US State Department representatives during an interrogation. In addition another interrogator posed as an FBI agent on one occasion. This impersonation came to the attention of the Senior Supervisory Agent (SSA) of the FBI at Guantanamo Bay when several other agents advised him that detainees were complaining during interviews that the FBI had already asked them the same questions. The SSA approached the Joint Interrogation Group (JIG) Chief, with his agents' concerns. According to the SSA, the JIG Chief did not contest the FBI agents' accusations. In fact, the JIG Chief knew of at least one military interrogator who had impersonated an FBI agent. After the meeting, the JIG Chief agreed to stop the practice of DoD interrogators impersonating FBI agents without prior FBI approval. The SSA made it clear to the investigation team that he did not believe the impersonation interfered with FBI operations and was pleased with the JIG Chief's rapid and thorough response to the situation.

Organizational response: Immediately stopped the practice.

Recommendation #1: The allegation should be closed. The technique, while authorized, was undermining the inter-agency working relationship. No additional corrective action is necessary or appropriate.

Allegation: That a female military interrogator performed a "lap dance" on a detainee during an interrogation. I have expanded this allegation to "That female military interrogators performed acts designed to take advantage of their gender in relation to Muslim males."

Finding #2a: On one occasion between October 2002 and January 2003, a female interrogator put perfume on a detainee by touching the detainee on his arm with her hand;

Technique: Authorized: FM 34-52 (p. 3-11); Category III technique approved by SECDEF – Mild, non-injurious physical touching

Discussion: a. On at least one occasion in late 2002, a female interrogator rubbed perfume on a detainee. The Interrogation Control Element (ICE) Chief stated that he specifically directed the interrogator to go to the PX and purchase rose oil with the intent of rubbing a portion of the perfume on the detainee's arm to distract the detainee. The interrogator admitted to using this approach with a detainee. At the time of the event the detainee responded by attempting to bite the interrogator and lost his balance, fell out of his chair, and chipped his tooth. He received immediate and appropriate medical attention and did not suffer permanent injury.

Organizational response: a. The interrogator was not disciplined for rubbing perfume on a detainee since this was an authorized technique.

Finding #2b: During the month of March 2003, a female interrogator approached a detainee from behind, rubbed against his back, leaned over the detainee touching him on his knee and shoulder and whispered in his ear that his situation was futile, and ran her fingers through his hair.

Technique: Authorized: FM 34-52 technique – Futility – Act used to highlight futility of the detainee's situation.

Discussion: b. On 17 Apr 03, An interrogation supervisor supervised a female interrogator as she interrogated a detainee with her BDU top off[1], and subsequently the interrogator ran her fingers through the detainee's hair. The interrogator also approached the detainee from behind, touched him on his knee and shoulder, leaned over him, and placed her face near the side of his in an effort to create stress and break his concentration during interrogation.

Organizational response: b. The interrogation supervisor was given a written letter of admonishment for failure to document the techniques to be implemented by the interrogator prior to the interrogation. There is no evidence that either activity ever occurred again.

Recommendation #2: Command action was effective and sufficient with respect to the individual interrogators. AR 15-6 recommends that the approval authority for the use of gender coercion as futility technique be withheld to the JTF GTMO-CG.

Allegation: That a female military interrogator wiped "menstrual blood" on a detainee during an interrogation.

Finding #3: In March 2003, a female interrogator told a detainee that red ink on her hand was menstrual blood and then wiped her hand on the detainee's arm.

Technique: Authorized: FM 34-52 technique – Futility – act used to highlight futility of the detainee's situation

Discussion: The female interrogator is no longer in military service and has declined to be interviewed. According to a former ICE Deputy the incident occurred when a detainee spat in the interrogator's face. According to the former ICE Deputy, the interrogator left the interrogation room and was crying outside the booth. She developed a plan to psychologically get back at him. She touched the detainee on his shoulder, showed him the red ink on her hand and said; by the way, I am menstruating. The detainee threw himself on the floor and started banging his head. This technique was not in an approved interrogation plan.

Organizational response: The ICE Deputy verbally reprimanded the interrogator for this incident. No formal disciplinary action was taken. There is no evidence that this happened again.

Recommendation #3: Command action was inadequate with respect to the individual interrogator. The interrogator should have been formally admonished or reprimanded for using a technique that was not approved in advance. Advance approval ensures that retaliatory techniques are not

---

[1] It was common practice at GTMO to conduct interrogations in a t-shirt with the BDU top removed because of the heat and humidity.

employed on impulse. Considering the lapse in time, recommend this allegation be closed.

Allegation: That DoD interrogators improperly played loud music and yelled loudly at detainees.

Finding #4: On numerous occasions between July 2002 and October 2004, detainees were yelled at or subjected to loud music during interrogation.

Technique: Authorized: FM 34-52 technique – Incentive and Futility – acts used as reward for cooperating or to create futility if not cooperating.

Discussion: Almost every interviewee stated that yelling and the use of loud music were used for interrogations at GTMO. On a few occasions, detainees were left alone in the interrogation booth for an indefinite period of time while loud music played and strobe lights flashed. The vast majority of yelling and music was accomplished with interrogators in the room. The volume of the music was never loud enough to cause any physical injury. Interrogators stated that cultural music would be played as an incentive. Futility technique included the playing of Metallica, Britney Spears, and Rap music.

Organizational response: None.

Recommendation #4: The allegation should be closed. Recommend JTF-GTMO develop specific guidance on the length of time that a detainee may be subjected to futility music. Placement of a detainee in the interrogation booth and subjecting him to loud music and strobe lights should be limited and conducted within clearly prescribed limits.

Allegation: That military interrogators improperly used extremes of heat and cold during their interrogation of detainees.

Finding #5: On several occasions during 2002 and 2003, interrogators would adjust the air conditioner to make the detainee uncomfortable.

Technique: Unauthorized prior to 16 Apr 03: SECDEF did not approve exposure to cold in his 2 Dec 02 list of approved techniques

Technique: Authorized after 16 Apr 03: SECDEF approved technique. This technique was officially permitted under 16 Apr 03 SECDEF Memorandum – Environmental Manipulation

Discussion: Two FBI agents indicated that they were aware of DoD interrogators using temperature adjustment as an interrogation technique. Many interviewees, FBI agents and military interrogators, believed the hot climate at GTMO and the detainee's comfort in a hot climate caused a differing in opinions regarding the use of the air conditioning units in the interrogation booths. There were several individuals who were interviewed who acknowledged that certain military interrogators would adjust the air conditioning down (cool) in an attempt to make the detainee uncomfortable for the interrogation. Several witnesses indicated that the practice of adjusting the temperature ceased when CDR JTF-GTMO directed that the practice no longer be employed. The current GTMO SOP still permits interrogators to adjust the temperature. In addition, one interrogator supervisor stated that detainees were interrogated at Camp X-Ray, where the "booths" were not air-conditioned, to make the detainees uncomfortable.

Organizational response: No disciplinary action required.

Recommendation #5: The allegation should be closed.

Allegation: That military interrogators improperly used sleep deprivation against detainees.

Finding #6: During 2003 and 2004 some detainees were subjected to cell moves every few hours to disrupt sleep patterns and lower the ability to resist interrogation. Each case differed as to length and frequency of the cell moves.

Technique: Unauthorized prior to 2 Dec 02 and between 15 Jan 03 and 16 Apr 03: Neither sleep disruption or deprivation is an authorized FM 34-52 technique

Technique: Authorized between 2 Dec 02 and 15 Jan 03 and after 16 Apr 03: The exact parameters of this technique remained undefined until 2 Jun 03 when CDR USSOUTHCOM established clear guidance on the use of sleep adjustment. His guidance prohibited the practice of keeping a detainee awake for "more than 16 hours or allowing a detainee to rest briefly and then repeatedly awakening him, not to exceed four days in succession."

Discussion: Only one FBI agent alleged sleep deprivation; his complaint was that an individual was subjected to 16 hours of interrogation followed by four-hour breaks. He says he was told about these sessions by DoD interrogators and they implied that these 16 hour interrogations were repeated on a 20 hour cycle, but he did not know for certain what in fact occurred. The FBI agent was at GTMO from 2 Jun 03 to 17 Jul 03. Under CDR USSOUTHCOM's 2 Jun 03 guidance, 16 hour interrogations were permitted and do not constitute sleep deprivation if done on a 24 hour cycle. During the course of the investigation of the FBI allegation, the AR 15-6 did conduct a review of the interrogation records to see if there was any evidence that corroborated this allegation. While not directly supporting the FBI's allegation, records indicated that some interrogators recommended detainees for the "frequent flyer program." A current GTMO interrogation analyst indicated that this was a program in effect throughout 2003 and until March 2004 to move detainees every few hours from one cell to another to disrupt their sleep. Documentation on one detainee indicated that he was subjected to this practice as recently as March 2004.

Organizational response: None. Current JTF-GTMO Commander terminated the frequent flyer cell movement program upon his arrival in March 04.

Recommendation #6: The allegation should be closed. Recommend USSOUTHCOM clarify policy on sleep deprivation.

<u>Allegation</u>: **That military interrogators improperly used duct tape to cover a detainee's mouth and head.**

Finding #7: Sometime in October 2002 duct tape was used to "quiet" a detainee.

Technique: Unauthorized

Discussion: In his testimony, the ICE Chief testified that he had a situation in which a detainee was screaming resistance messages and potentially provoking a riot. At the time of the incident there were 10 detainees in the interrogation section and the ICE Chief was concerned about losing control of the situation. He directed the MPs to quiet the detainee down. The MP mentioned that he had duct tape. The ICE Chief says he ultimately approved the use of duct tape to quiet the detainee. The MP then placed a single strand of duct tape around the detainee's mouth. The single strand proved ineffective because the detainee was soon yelling again. This time the MPs wrapped a single strand of duct tape around the mouth and head of the detainee. The detainee removed the duct tape again. Fed up and concerned that the detainee's yelling might cause a riot in the interrogation trailer, The ICE Chief ordered the MPs to wrap the duct tape twice around the head and mouth and three times under the chin and around the top of the detainee's head. According to an FBI agent, he and another FBI agent were approached by the ICE Chief who was laughing and told the agents that they needed to see something. When the first agent went to the interrogation room he saw that the detainee's head had been wrapped in duct tape over his beard and his hair. An interrogator testified that another interrogator admitted to him that he had duct taped the head of a detainee. According to the first agent, the ICE Chief said the interrogator wrapped the detainee's head with duct tape because the detainee refused to stop "chanting" passages from the Koran.

Organizational response: The JTF-170 JAG testified that she became aware of the incident and personally counseled the ICE Chief. The counseling session consisted of a verbal admonishment.[2] The ICE Chief did not receive any formal

---

[2] While the ICE Chief testified that he was counseled by the JTF-GTMO Commander this is not possible. The Commander in question did not arrive until the month following the event. The previous Commander has no recollection of the event.

discipline action. We have no evidence that duct tape was ever used again on a detainee.

Recommendation #7: *Command action was inadequate with respect to the ICE Chief. He should be formally admonished or reprimanded for directing an inappropriate restraint to be used on a detainee.*

Allegation: That military interrogators improperly chained detainees and placed them in a fetal position on the floor

Finding #8: On at least two occasions between February 2002 and February 2003, two detainees were "short shackled" to the eye-bolt on the floor in the interrogation room.

Technique: Unauthorized.

Discussion: Two FBI agents each stated that they witnessed a detainee in an interrogation room that had been "short shackled" to the floor. Short shackling is the process by which the detainee's hand restraints are connected directly to an eyebolt in the floor requiring the detainee to either crouch very low or lay in a fetal position on the floor. The FBI agents indicated that each of the detainees was clothed. Another FBI agent stated she witnessed a detainee short shackled and lying in his own excrement. The AR 15-6 was unable to find any documentation, testimony, or other evidence corroborating the third agent's recollection, to this allegation or her email allegation that one of the detainees had pulled his hair out while short shackled. We also found that 'short shackling' was initially authorized as a force protection measure during the in processing of detainees.[3]

Organizational response: None. JTF-GTMO has implemented SOPs that prohibit short shackling.

Recommendation #8: *The allegation should be closed. The AR 15-6 was not able to find any evidence to adequately assign responsibility for these actions. This practice is now specifically prohibited by current GTMO interrogation policy.*

Allegation: That military personnel improperly interfered with FBI interrogators in the performance of their FBI duties.

Finding #9: We discovered no evidence to support this allegation.

---

[3] During the course of a site visit to GTMO several detention operations personnel indicated that they understood that short shackling was permitted in the early days of GTMO as a force protection measure. They all stated that it was no longer authorized as either a detention measure or during interrogations.

Discussion: This allegation stems from an FBI agent objections to a proposed Special Interrogation Plan. The dispute resulted in a DoD official being rude to the FBI agent. The team did not find any evidence of "interference" with FBI interrogations that extended beyond the dispute over which techniques worked best in interrogation. During the infancy of interrogation operations at GTMO, it was obvious that the different investigative agencies had different interrogation objectives. Law enforcement agencies were primarily interested in interviews that would produce voluntary confessions that would be admissible in U.S. Federal District Courts. Conversely, DoD interrogators were interested in actionable intelligence and thus had greater latitude on the techniques used during the interrogations. These different goals created friction.

Recommendation #9: *The allegation should be closed.*

Allegation: **That military interrogators denied detainees food and water for long periods of time.**

Finding #10: We discovered no evidence to support the allegation that the detainees were denied food and water.

Discussion: This allegation stems from the statement of an FBI Agent. She reports two incidents of observing two detainees in "the fetal position and lying on the floor of interview rooms." And that there were was no "evidence of any food or water." The Agent admits in her statement that she made an assumption that the detainees were denied food and water based solely upon their appearance. The Agent was unable to provide any specific information as to the day she made these observations to permit additional proof or assignment of responsibility.

Recommendation #10: *The allegation should be closed.*

SPECIAL INTERROGATION PLANS

During the course of interrogations certain detainees exhibited refined resistance techniques to interrogations. These detainees were suspected to possess significant current intelligence regarding planned future terrorist attacks against the United States. For these reasons Special Interrogation Plans were proposed and approved for the detainees. A total of two Special Interrogation Plans were carried out. They are referred to herein as the "First Special Interrogation Plan" and the "Second Special Interrogation Plan".

THE FIRST SPECIAL INTERROGATION PLAN

On 23 Nov 02 interrogators initiated the first Special Interrogation Plan. The interrogation plan was designed to counter resistance techniques of the subject of the first Special Interrogation Plan. The memo authorizing the techniques for this interrogation was signed by SECDEF on 2 Dec 02. These techniques supplemented techniques already permitted under the provisions of FM 34-52.

Allegation: That military interrogators improperly used military working dogs (MWD) during interrogation sessions to threaten detainees, or for some other purpose.

Finding #11a: On one occasion in October 2002 a military working dog was brought into the interrogation room and directed to growl, bark, and show his teeth at the subject of the first Special Interrogation Plan.

Technique: Unauthorized prior to 12 Nov 02.

Discussion: a. October 2002 incident: GTMO records indicate that on 01 Oct 02, the Commander of JTF-170 requested Joint Detention Operations Group (JDOG) support for interrogation operations to interrogate the subject of the first Special Interrogation Plan. The dog was requested to assist in the movement of the subject of the first Special Interrogation Plan between Camp X-ray and the GTMO Naval Brig to "discourage the detainee from attempting to escape." The interrogation plan (IP) indicates that the interrogation would begin on the 2nd or 3rd of October 2002. One FBI agent in his statement recalls the MWD being used on or about 05 Oct 02. He indicated that the events were notable for several reasons. He had recently purchased a German Shepard and wanted to get some "tips" from the dog handlers. The FBI agent noticed that there were two working dog teams (one Navy and one Army) present for the interrogation of the subject of the first Special Interrogation Plan. Finally, the FBI agent recalled that he and his partner left the observation room when the MWD was introduced into the interrogation room. The FBI agent's partner corroborates this statement.

In addition an interrogator indicated that she recalled a MWD being brought into the interrogation room during interrogation of the subject of the first Special Interrogation Plan at Camp X-ray, between 02-10 Oct 02. She stated that the dogs were used only "briefly." She stated that the use of the dog was documented on the IP and approved by the ICE Chief and CDR, JTF-GTMO

Finding #11b: In November 2002 a military working dog was brought into the interrogation room and directed to growl, bark, and show his teeth at the subject of the first Special Interrogation Plan.

Technique: Authorized: SECDEF approved the use of Category I and II techniques for the subject of the first Special Interrogation Plan. Category II technique permits the use of dogs to exploit "individual phobias" during interrogations.

Discussion: b. An interrogator testified that the MWD was in the booth on one occasion for the subject of the first Special Interrogation Plan. He testified that he was approached by another interrogator and discussed the use of a MWD in an interrogation session. Specifically, the first interrogator stated that the second interrogator told him that a MWD was brought into the doorway of the interrogation room and ordered by the dog handler to growl, show teeth and bark at the detainee. In addition a psychologist assigned to the Behavioral Science Consultation Team (BSCT) for JTF-170/JTF-GTMO witnessed the use of a MWD named "Zeus" during a military interrogation of the subject of the first Special Interrogation Plan during the November 2002 time period. In his interview, the ICE Chief acknowledged that an MWD had entered the interrogation room of the subject of the first Special Interrogation Plan under the authority of a "special IP" for the subject of the first Special Interrogation Plan. The unsigned but approved interrogation plan for the subject of the first Special Interrogation Plan is from 12 Nov 02. (Church p. 115) It indicates dogs will only be used in interrogation if approved in writing, in advance. Both JTF-GTMO Commanders who were in charge during the execution of the special interrogation plan deny that they authorized the use of MWDs in the interrogation room.

Organizational response: a. and b. None. Current SOPs expressly prohibit the use of MWDs in the interrogation room. There is no evidence that this has ever happened again.

Recommendation #11: The allegation should be closed. While the ICE Chief was aware of and condoned the first use of the MWD, additional corrective action is not necessary. The event occurred on two occasions and was expressly approved after the first occasion for this detainee. This practice is now specifically prohibited by current GTMO interrogation policy.

Allegation: **That a female military interrogator performed a "lap dance" on a detainee during an interrogation. I have expanded this allegation to "That female military interrogators performed acts designed to take advantage of their gender in relation to Muslim males."**

Finding #12a: On 21 and 23 Dec 02, MPs held down a detainee while a female interrogator straddled the detainee without placing weight on the detainee;

Technique: Authorized: FM 34-52 technique – Futility – Act used to highlight futility of the detainee's situation.

Finding #12b: On 04 Dec 02, a female interrogator massaged the detainee's back and neck over his clothing;

Technique: Authorized: FM 34-52 technique – Futility – Act used to highlight futility of the detainee's situation.

Finding #12c: On various occasions between October 2002 and January 2003, a female interrogator invaded the private space of a detainee to disrupt his concentration during interrogation;

Technique: Authorized: FM 34-52 technique – Futility – act used to highlight futility of the detainee's situation.

Discussion: Interrogation logs and MFRs for the subject of the first Special Interrogation Plan document that on both 21 and 23 Dec 02, a female interrogator straddled, without putting any weight on the detainee, the subject of the first Special Interrogation Plan while he was being held down by MPs. During these incidents a female interrogator would tell the detainee about the deaths of fellow Al-Qaeda members. During the straddling, the detainee would attempt to raise and bend his legs to prevent the interrogator from straddling him and prayed loudly. Interrogation MFRs also indicate that on 04 Dec 02, a female interrogator began to enter the personal space of the subject of the first Special Interrogation Plan, touch him, and ultimately massage his back while whispering or speaking near his ear. Throughout this event, the subject of the first Special Interrogation Plan prayed, swore at the interrogator that she was going to Hell, and attempted to get away from her. The female interrogator admitted in her interview that she personally prepared portions of the MFRs of the the subject of the first Special Interrogation Plan interrogations. She asserts that she had permission to employ all these techniques. We have found no evidence of a lap dance ever occurring.

Organizational response: No disciplinary action taken. The ICE Chief approved these techniques at the time.

Recommendation #12: The allegation should be closed. No command action is necessary with respect to the individual interrogators. Their supervisor acknowledged that he approved the approaches at the time of the interrogation. AR 15-6 recommends that the approval authority for the use of gender coercion as futility technique be withheld to the JTF GTMO-CG.

<u>Allegation</u>: **That DoD interrogators improperly played loud music and yelled loudly at detainees.**

Finding #13: On numerous occasions between November 2002 and 15 Jan 03, the subject of the first Special Interrogation Plan was yelled at or subjected to loud music during interrogation.

Technique: Authorized: FM 34-52 technique – Incentive and Futility – acts used as reward for cooperating or to create futility in not cooperating.

Discussion: See above discussion for Finding #4.

Organizational response: No disciplinary action required; technique authorized.

Recommendation #13: The allegation should be closed. Recommend JTF-GTMO develop specific guidance on the length of time that a detainee may be subjected to futility music. Placement of a detainee in the interrogation booth and subjecting him to loud music and strobe lights should be limited and conducted within clearly prescribed limits.

<u>Allegation</u>: **That military interrogators improperly used extremes of heat and cold during their interrogation of detainees.**

Finding #14: On several occasions between November 2002 and January 2003 interrogators would adjust the air conditioner to make the subject of the first Special Interrogation Plan uncomfortable.

Technique: Unauthorized prior to 16 Apr 03: SECDEF did not approve exposure to cold in his 2 Dec 02 list of approved techniques

Discussion. There are no medical entries indicating the subject of the first Special Interrogation Plan ever experienced medical problems related to low body temperature. The subject of the first Special Interrogation Plan's medical records do indicate that he did have a body temperature between 95 and 97 degrees twice. The subject of the first Special Interrogation Plan's medical records do indicate that from 7-9 Dec 02 he was hospitalized for observation after an episode of bradycardia. He was released within forty-eight hours, after the bradycardia resolved without intervention and he maintained stable hemodynamics.[4] He experienced a second episode of bradycardia in Feb 03.

Organizational response: None

Recommendation #14: The allegation should be closed.

<u>Allegation</u>: **That military interrogators improperly used sleep deprivation against detainees.**

Finding #15: From 23 Nov 02 to 16 Jan 03, the subject of the first Special Interrogation Plan was interrogated for 18-20 hours per day for 48 of the 54 days, with the opportunity for a minimum of four hours rest per day.

Technique: Authorized: SECDEF approved technique. This technique was officially permitted under 2 Dec 02 SECDEF Memorandum – The use of 20-hour interrogations

---

[4] Bradycardia is a relatively slow heart; hemo dynamics are mechanics of blood circulation.

Discussion: SECDEF approved 20 hour interrogations for every 24-hour cycle for the subject of the first Special Interrogation Plan on 12 Nov 02. Later, CDR USSOUTHCOM formalized the definition of sleep deprivation in his 02 Jun 03 memorandum "promulgating" SECDEF's interrogation techniques of 16 Apr 03. He defined sleep deprivation as keeping a detainee awake for more than 16 hours, or allowing a detainee to rest briefly and then repeatedly awakening him, not to exceed four days in succession.

Organizational response: None. This was an authorized interrogation technique approved by SECDEF.

Recommendation #15: The allegation should be closed. Recommend USSOUTHCOM clarify policy on sleep deprivation.

Additional Allegations, Re: The subject of the first Special Interrogation Plan: In addition to the FBI allegations addressed above, the following additional interrogation techniques (not all inclusive) were used in the interrogation of the subject of the first Special Interrogation Plan. Each act is documented in the interrogation MFRs maintained on the subject of the first Special Interrogation Plan.

Finding #16a: That the subject of the first Special Interrogation Plan was separated from the general population from 8 Aug 02 to 15 Jan 03.

Technique: Unauthorized prior to 12 Nov 02: SECDEF did not approve movement of detainee to an "isolation facility" for interrogation purposes prior to approval of Category II techniques for the subject of the first Special Interrogation Plan on 12 Nov 02.

Technique: Authorized after 12 Nov 02:

Discussion: The subject of the first Special Interrogation Plan was never isolated from human contact. The subject of the first Special Interrogation Plan was however placed in an "isolation facility" where he was separated from the general detainee population from 8 Aug 02 to 15 Jan 03. The subject of the first Special Interrogation Plan routinely had contact with interrogators and MPs while in the "isolation facility." The SECDEF did not define "isolation facility" when he approved the use of an "isolation facility" for up to 30 days with additional isolation beyond 30 days requiring CDR JTF-GTMO approval on 12 Nov 02. Prior to the SECDEF's approval, placement in an "isolation facility" was not an authorized interrogation technique.

Organizational response to Additional Allegations, Re: The subject of the first Special Interrogation Plan: None taken.

Eight Techniques Below: Authorized: FM 34-52 technique – Ego down and Futility.

Finding #16b: On 06 Dec 02, the subject of the first Special Interrogation Plan was forced to wear a woman's bra and had a thong placed on his head during the course of the interrogation.

Finding #16c: On 17 Dec 02, the subject of the first Special Interrogation Plan was told that his mother and sister were whores.

Finding #16d: On 17 Dec 02, the subject of the first Special Interrogation Plan was told that he was a homosexual, had homosexual tendencies, and that other detainees had found out about these tendencies

Finding #16e: On 20 Dec 02, an interrogator tied a leash to the subject of the first Special Interrogation Plan's chains, led him around the room, and forced him to perform a series of dog tricks.

Finding #16f: On 20 Dec 02, an interrogator forced the subject of the first Special Interrogation Plan to dance with a male interrogator.

Finding #16g: On several occasions in Dec 02, the subject of the first Special Interrogation Plan was subject to strip searches.[5] These searches, conducted by the prison guards during interrogation, were done as a control measure on direction of the interrogators.

Finding #16h: On one occasion in Dec 02, the subject of the first Special Interrogation Plan was forced to stand naked for five minutes with females present. This incident occurred during the course of a strip search.

Finding #16i: On three occasions in Nov 02 and Dec 02, the subject of the first Special Interrogation Plan was prevented from praying during interrogation

Finding #16j: Once in Nov 02, the subject of the first Special Interrogation Plan became upset when two Korans were put on a TV, as a control measure during interrogation, and in Dec 02 when an interrogator got up on the desk in front of the subject of the first Special Interrogation Plan and squatted down in front of the subject of the first Special Interrogation Plan in an aggressive manner and unintentionally squatted over the detainee's Koran.

Finding #16k: On seventeen occasions, between 13 Dec 02 and 14 Jan 03, interrogators, during interrogations, poured water over the subject of the first Special Interrogation Plan head.

---

[5] The subject of the first Special Interrogation Plan alleges that he was subject to "cavity searches." During the course of interrogation, the subject of the first Special Interrogation Plan was strip searched. The AR 15-6 was unable to determine the scope of these strip searches.

Discussion: the subject of the first Special Interrogation Plan was a high value detainee that ultimately provided extremely valuable intelligence. His ability to resist months of standard interrogation in the summer of 2002 was the genesis for the request to have authority to employ additional counter resistance interrogation techniques. The techniques used against the subject of the first Special Interrogation Plan were done in an effort to establish complete control and create the perception of futility and reduce his resistance to interrogation. For example, this included the use of strip searches, the control of prayer, the forced wearing of a woman's bra, and other techniques noted above. It is clear based upon the completeness of the interrogation logs that the interrogation team believed that they were acting within existing guidance. Despite the fact that the AR 15-6 concluded that every technique employed against the subject of the first Special Interrogation Plan was legally permissible under the existing guidance, the AR 15-6 finds that the creative, aggressive, and persistent interrogation of the subject of the first Special Interrogation Plan resulted in the cumulative effect being degrading and abusive treatment. Particularly troubling is the combined impact of the 160 days of segregation from other detainees, 48 of 54 consecutive days of 18 to 20-hour interrogations, and the creative application of authorized interrogation techniques. Requiring the subject of the first Special Interrogation Plan to be led around by a leash tied to his chains, placing a thong on his head, wearing a bra, insulting his mother and sister, being forced to stand naked in front of a female interrogator for five minutes, and using strip searches as an interrogation technique the AR 15-6 found to be abusive and degrading, particularly when done in the context of the 48 days of intense and long interrogations.[6] While this treatment did not rise to the level of prohibited inhumane treatment the JTF-GTMO CDR was responsible for the interrogation of the subject of the first Special Interrogation Plan and had a responsibility to provide strategic guidance to the interrogation team. He failed to monitor the interrogation and exercise commander discretion by placing limits on the application of otherwise authorized techniques and approaches used in that interrogation. The Commander stated he was unaware of the specific details or impacts of the techniques on the detainee for this important interrogation. His failure to supervise the interrogation of the subject of the first Special Interrogation Plan allowed subordinates to make creative decisions in an environment requiring extremely tight controls[7].

Recommendation #16: The Commander JTF-GTMO should be held accountable for failing to supervise the interrogation of the subject of the first Special Interrogation Plan and should be admonished for that failure.

---

[6] The AR 15-6 found no evidence that the subject of the first Special Interrogation Plan was ever physically assaulted. His medical records show no evidence of any physical assaults. A medical examination completed on the subject of the first Special Interrogation Plan on 16 Jan 03 found no medical conditions of note.

[7] The JTF-GTMO Commander's testimony that he was unaware of the creative approaches taken in the interrogation is inconsistent with his 21 Jan 03 letter to CDR USSOUTHCOM in which he asserts that the CJTF approved the interrogation plan in place and it was followed "relentlessly by the command."

Allegation: In addition to the allegations above, the AR 15-6 also considered additional allegations raised specifically by the subject of the first Special Interrogation Plan.

Finding #17: The AR 15-6 was unable to corroborate the subject of the first Special Interrogation Plan's allegations to the point of concluding that they had occurred by a preponderance of the evidence. Specific findings include:

The AR 15-6 did find that the subject of the first Special Interrogation Plan was required to stand for periods of time which he may have interpreted as forced positions.

There is evidence that the subject of the first Special Interrogation Plan regularly had water poured on his head. The interrogation logs indicate that this was done as a control measure only.

There is no evidence that the subject of the first Special Interrogation Plan was subjected to humiliation intentionally directed at his religion. It is however possible that the subject of the first Special Interrogation Plan interpreted many of the interrogation techniques employed to be religious humiliation.

The AR 15-6 found no evidence that the subject of the first Special Interrogation Plan was threatened with homosexual rape. He was told on 17 Dec 02 that he was a homosexual but not threatened in any manner.

There is no evidence, to include entries in his medical records, that either occurred regarding the subject of the first Special Interrogation Plan or any other detainee.

Discussion: In reaching conclusions on the treatment of the subject of the first Special Interrogation Plan the AR 15-6 relied heavily on the interrogations logs. The level of specificity of the logs strongly supports their credibility regarding the interrogation of the subject of the first Special Interrogation Plan and thus they carried considerable weight on the findings.

Recommendation #17: The allegation should be closed

THE SECOND SPECIAL INTERROGATION PLAN

In July 03 interrogators initiated a request for approval of a Special Interrogation Plan for a detainee. This plan was approved by SECDEF on 13 Aug 03. Interrogation logs indicate that the techniques were never implemented because the subject of the second special interrogation plan began to cooperate prior to the approval.

In addition to the interrogation logs, the AR 15-6 also considered allegations of abuse raised by the subject of the second special interrogation, himself. Specifically, after months of cooperation with interrogators, on 11 Dec 04, the subject of the second special interrogation notified his interrogator that he had been "subject to torture" by past interrogators during the months of July to October 2003.[8]

Allegation: That military interrogators improperly used extremes of heat and cold during their interrogation of detainees.

Finding #18: During the summer of 2003, interrogators would adjust the air conditioner to make the subject of the second special interrogation uncomfortable.

Technique: Authorized: SECDEF approved technique. This technique was officially permitted under 16 Apr 03 SECDEF Memorandum – Environmental Manipulation.

Discussion: The interrogation logs of the subject of the second Special Interrogation Plan indicate that on at least two occasions on 10 and 11 Jul 03 the air conditioner was turned off to heat up the room. In addition the subject of the second special interrogation alleges that on repeated occasions from Jul 03 to Oct 03, he was subjected to placement in a room referred to as the "freezer."

Organizational response: No disciplinary action required. Environmental manipulation was expressly permitted in the 16 Apr 03 SECDEF Memorandum. There is no evidence in the medical records of the subject of the second special interrogation being treated for hypothermia or any other condition related to extreme exposure.

Recommendation #18: The allegation should be closed.

Allegation: The subject of the second special interrogation alleges that female military interrogators removed their BDU tops and rubbed themselves against the detainee, fondled his genitalia, and made lewd sexual comments, noises, and gestures.

---

[8] He reported these allegations to an interrogator. The interrogator was a member of the interrogation team at the time of the report. The interrogator reported the allegations to her supervisor. Shortly after being advised of the alleged abuse, the supervisor interviewed the subject of the second special interrogation, with the interrogator present, regarding the allegations. Based upon this interview, and notes taken by the interrogator, the supervisor prepared an 11 Dec 04 MFR addressed to JTF – GTMO JIG & ICE. The supervisor forwarded his MFR to the JTF – GTMO JIG. The JIG then forwarded the complaint to the JAG for processing IAW normal GTMO procedures for investigating allegations of abuse. The JAG by email on 22 Dec 04 tasked the JDOG, the JIG, and the JMG with a review of the complaint summarized in the 11 Dec 04 MFR and directed them to provide any relevant information. The internal GTMO investigation was never completed.

Finding #19: The AR 15-6 was unable to corroborate the allegations to the point of concluding that they had occurred by a preponderance of the evidence.

Discussion: The interrogation logs for the subject of the second special interrogation indicate that on a number of occasions female interrogators used their status as females to distract the subject of the second special interrogation during the interrogation but there is nothing to corroborate the allegation of the subject of the second special interrogation.

Organizational response: No disciplinary action taken.

Recommendation #19: The allegation should be closed.

<u>Allegation</u>: **The subject of the second Special Interrogation Plan alleges that in late summer of 2003 he was hit by guards and an interrogator "very hard" and "with all their strength" he was hit "all over."**

Finding #20: The AR 15-6 was unable to corroborate the allegations to the point of concluding that they had occurred by a preponderance of the evidence.

Discussion: The interrogation logs contain no reference to any physical violence against the subject of the second Special Interrogation Plan. His medical records indicate that in August 2003 the subject of the second special interrogation reported "rib contusions" from an altercation with MPs when moved between camps. During this examination the physician also noted an "edema of the lower lip" and a "small laceration" on his head. There are no other medical entries of any other physical injuries. There are no indications of swelling or contusions to support a conclusion that the subject of the second special interrogation was hit "very hard all over."

Organizational response: No disciplinary action taken. The allegation was not substantiated.

Recommendation #20: The allegation should be closed. There is no evidence to support the subject of the second special interrogation's allegation of physical abuse.

<u>Allegation</u>: **A DoD interrogator improperly impersonated a Navy Captain assigned to the White House.**

Finding #21: The Special Team Chief impersonated a USN Captain assigned to the White House during interrogation of the subject of the second special interrogation.

Technique: Authorized: This technique is permitted under FM 34-52 – Deception.

Discussion: On 2 Aug 03 the Special Team Chief presented himself to the subject of the second special interrogation dressed as a Captain in the USN and indicated he was from the White House in an effort to convince the subject of the second special interrogation that he needed to cooperate with his interrogators. The Special Team Chief presented a letter to the subject of the second special interrogation, which indicated that because of the subject of the second special interrogation's lack of cooperation, U.S. authorities in conjunction with authorities from the country of origin of the subject of the second Special Interrogation Plan would interrogate the mother of the subject of the second Special Interrogation Plan. The letter further indicated that if his mother was uncooperative she would be detained and transferred to U.S. custody at GTMO for long term detention. While the JTF-GTMO Commander acknowledges that he was aware of the intent by the interrogator to wear Captain's rank and purport to be from the White House, he stated that he was not aware of the intention to convey a threat or the plan to use a fictitious letter.

Organizational response: None taken.

Recommendation #21: The allegation should be closed. No further action necessary.

Allegation: That Military interrogators threatened the subject of the second special interrogation and his family.

Finding #22: The Special Team Chief threatened the subject of the second special interrogation and his family in July, August and September 2003.

Technique: Unauthorized: This technique was rejected by SECDEF on   2 Dec 2002

Discussion: During the interrogation of the subject of the second special interrogation, a masked interrogator was used to interrogate the subject of the second special interrogation [9]. On 17 Jul 03 the masked interrogator told that he had a dream about the subject of the second special interrogation dying. Specifically he told the subject of the second special interrogation that in the dream he "saw four detainees that were chained together at the feet. They dug a hole that was six-feet long, six-feet deep, and four-feet wide. Then he observed the detainees throw a plain, pine casket with the detainee's identification number painted in orange lowered into the ground." The masked interrogator told the detainee that his dream meant that he was never going to leave GTMO unless he started to talk, that he would indeed die here from old age and be buried on "Christian... sovereign American soil." On 20 Jul 03 the masked interrogator, "Mr.

---

[9] The interrogator was a DoD interrogator who was masked so as to preserve the identity of the interrogator. This was done in case the interrogation team wanted to use that interrogator later in another role.

X", told the subject of the second Special Interrogation Plan that his family was "incarcerated." On 2 Aug 03, the Special Team Chief, while impersonating a USN Captain from the White House, told the subject of the second special interrogation that he had a letter indicating that the subject of the second special interrogation's family had been captured by the United States and that they were in danger.[10] He went on to tell the subject of the second special interrogation that if he wanted to help his family he should tell them everything they wanted to know. The MFR dated 02 Aug 03 indicates that the subject of the second special interrogation had a messenger that day there to "deliver a message to him". The MFR goes on to state:

> "That message was simple: Interrogator's colleagues are sick of hearing the same lies over and over and are seriously considering washing their hands of him. Once they do so, he will disappear and never be heard from again. Interrogator assured detainee again to use his imagination to think of the worst possible scenario he could end up in. He told Detainee that beatings and physical pain are not the worst thing in the world. After all, after being beaten for a while, humans tend to disconnect the mind from the body and make it through. However, there are worse things than physical pain. Interrogator assured Detainee that, eventually, he will talk, because everyone does. But until then, he will very soon disappear down a very dark hole. His very existence will become erased. His electronic files will be deleted from the computer, his paper files will be packed up and filed away, and his existence will be forgotten by all. No one will know what happened to him and, eventually, no one will care."

Finally, interrogator MFRs dated 08 Sep 03 indicate that the subject of the second special interrogation wanted to see "Captain Collins" and that they "understood that detainee had made an important decision and that the interrogator was anxious to hear what Detainee had to say. Detainee stated he understood and will wait for interrogator's [Captain Collins] return and that the subject of the second Special Interrogation Plan "...was not willing to continue to protect others to the detriment of himself and his family."

In investigating the actions above, the AR 15-6 focused on the threat made by the Special Team Chief.[11] When questioned about the threats to the subject of the second special interrogation, the Special Team Chief indicated that prior to the "threat" to detainee the subject of the second special interrogation he cleared the proposal and the letter with the senior judge advocate who approved the technique as a "deception." As written the letter does contain a threat to detain the subject of the second special interrogation's mother but does not contain any threat on her life or that of her family. The SJA indicated in his initial interview

---

[10] The actual content of the letter simply indicates that his mother will be taken into custody and questioned.

[11] Mr. X's dream story does not rise to the level of a threat. It appears to be a staged prelude to the direct threat made by the Special Team Chief.

that he did not recall the letter. He subsequently elected to exercise his Article 31 rights and declined to answer direct questions about the letter and the threats. The Special Team Chief also indicated that both JIG Chiefs in charge during the promulgation of the Special Interrogation Plan[12] were also aware of the threat letter. The first JIG Chief has retired and was unwilling to cooperate with this investigation. The second JIG Chief indicated under oath that he was unaware of the interrogation events discussed above. He recognizes, that read in conjunction with each other, they indicate a threat. He believes that the Commander of JTF-GTMO was not aware of the threat since the second JIG Chief was not aware of the threat. The second JIG Chief stated that they had weekly meetings with the Commander to discuss interrogations but they would not have covered this level of detail in that meeting. Neither he nor the Commander read interrogation MFRs on a regular basis. Finally, the Commander denies any knowledge of the existence of the threat or the letter. He does not recall ever discussing the issue of threats with the interrogators. He is aware that this is a prohibited practice and would not have permitted it if he had been aware of the plan.

Taken as a whole, it appears that the decision to threaten the subject of the second Special Interrogation Plan was made by the Special Team Chief. He claims that he cleared the plan with the senior judge advocate but not with his supervisors. Considering the actual content of the letter, it is reasonable to conclude that the JAG advised that the letter was a proper deception and therefore additional approval was not required. The Special Team Chief knew that under FM 34-52 deception did not require additional approval.

Despite the fact that the letter may be a proper deception technique under FM 34-52, the interrogation logs clearly indicate that the interrogation went well beyond the "threat to detain" made in the letter, and in fact was a threat to the subject of the second special interrogation and his family that violated the UCMJ, Article 134 Communicating a threat.

Organizational Response: None taken.

Recommendation #22: While the threats do not rise to the level of torture as defined under U.S. law, the facts support a conclusion that the Special Team Chief violated the UCMJ, Article 134, by communicating a threat. Recommend his current commander discipline the Special Team Chief.

---

[12] The first JIG Chief was in charge during the approval process for the second Special Interrogation Plan and then rotated out of JTF-GTMO. The second JIG Chief was in charge during the execution of the second Special Interrogation Plan

SUMMARY OF FINDINGS

The findings above fall into three categories: Techniques that were authorized throughout the interrogation periods; techniques that were never authorized and finally, techniques that were originally unauthorized, and then subsequently authorized. The summary below only outlines the latter two categories of techniques to address whether the findings violated the UCMJ, international law, U.S. Law, regulations or directives.

Techniques that were never authorized: AR 15-6 determined the following acts were NEVER authorized under any interrogation guidance:

   a) On at least two occasions between February 2002 and February 2003, two detainees were "short shackled" to the eye-bolt on the floor in the interrogation room;

   b) Sometime in October 2002 duct tape was used to "quiet" a detainee.

   c) Military interrogators threatened the subject of the second special interrogation and his family;

Techniques that became authorized after the fact: AR 15-6 determined the following acts were initially not authorized under existing interrogation guidance but later authorized as an approved technique.

   a) On several occasions during 2002 and 2003, interrogators would adjust the air conditioner to make the detainees, to include the subject of the first Special Interrogation Plan, uncomfortable. This technique is now permitted under the SECDEF 16 Apr 03 guidance.

   b) On several occasions prior to 2 Dec 02 and between 15 Jan 03 and 16 Apr 03 interrogators had detainees moved from one cell to another every few hours to disrupt sleep patterns and lower the ability to resist interrogation. This technique is now permitted under the SECDEF 16 Apr 03 guidance.

   c) In October 2002 a Military Working Dog was brought into the interrogation room during the course of interrogation of the subject of the first Special Interrogation Plan and directed to growl, bark, and show his teeth at the detainee. This technique is subsequently approved for the interrogation of the subject of the first Special Interrogation Plan by SECDEF on 12 Nov 02.

   d) The subject of the first Special Interrogation Plan was separated from other detainees in an isolation facility away from the general population from 8 Aug 02 to 12 Nov 02. This technique was subsequently approved for the interrogation of the subject of the first Special Interrogation Plan by SECDEF on 12 Nov 02.

In each of the incidents above the violations can best be characterized as violations of policy. The SECDEF's subsequent approval of each of the techniques clearly establishes the ultimate legitimacy of that technique and thus additional corrective action is not necessary.

Additional Matters: In addition to findings outlined above it is important to document some additional findings:

a) The team found no evidence that any detainee at GTMO was improperly documented or unaccounted for at any time. Every agency interviewee clearly indicated that they never knew of any "ghost detainees" at GTMO;

b) Several past interrogators at GTMO declined to be interviewed. In the case of personnel who are currently in a civilian status we had extremely limited authority to compel the individuals to cooperate with this investigation; of particular note was former SGT Erik Saar who has written a book into "activities" at GTMO. Despite repeated requests he declined to be interviewed;

c) During the course of this investigation, JTF-GTMO CG investigated and took action for personal misconduct of senior DoD personnel on GTMO. These allegations were reviewed and it was determined that they were not relevant to this investigation, and did not rise to a level to suggest a leadership environment with any impact on interrogation or detainee operations.

ADDITIONAL RECOMMENDATIONS

This AR15-6 recommends consideration of the following:

a) *Recommendation #23* Recommend a policy-level review and determination of the status and treatment of all detainees, when not classified as EPWs. This review needs to particularly focus on the definitions of humane treatment, military necessity, and proper employment of interrogation techniques. (e.g. boundaries or extremes);

b) *Recommendation #24* Recommend study of the DoD authorized interrogation techniques to establish a framework for evaluating their cumulative impact in relation to the obligation to treat detainees humanely;

c) **Recommendation #25** Recommend a reevaluation of the DoD and Inter-agency interrogation training consistent with the new realities of the requirements of the global war on terror;

d) **Recommendation #26** Recommend a policy-level determination on role of Military Police in "setting the conditions" for intelligence gathering and interrogation of detainees at both the tactical level and strategic level facilities;

e) **Recommendation #27** Recommend an Inter-Agency policy review to establish "standards" for interrogations when multiple agencies and interrogation objectives are involved. Particular emphasis should be placed on setting policy for who has priority as the lead agency, the specific boundaries for the authorized techniques in cases with multiple agencies involved, a central "data-base" for all intelligence gathered at a detention facility, and procedures for record keeping to include historical, litigation support, lessons learned, and successful/unsuccessful intelligence gathering techniques.

US Department of Justice

Federal Bureau of Investigation

Washington, D C 20535-0001

July 14, 2004

Major General Donald J. Ryder
Department of the Army
Criminal Investigation Command
6010 6th Street
Fort Belvoir, Virginia 22060-5506

Re. Suspected Mistreatment of Detainees

Dear General Ryder

      I appreciate the opportunity I had to meet with you last week. As part of a follow up on our discussion on detainee treatment, I would like to alert you to three situations observed by agents of the Federal Bureau of Investigation (FBI) of highly aggressive interrogation techniques being used against detainees in Guantanamo (GTMO). I refer them to you for appropriate action

b6 -1,2
b7C -1,2

    1 During late 2002, FBI Special Agent _____ was present in an observation room at GTMO and observed _____ (first name unknown) _____ conducting an interrogation of an unknown detainee. (SA _____ was present to observe the interrogation occurring in a different interrogation room) _____ entered the observation room and complained that curtain movement at the observation window was distracting the detainee, although no movement of the curtain had occurred She directed a marine to duct tape a curtain over the two-way mirror between the interrogation room and the observation room SA _____ characterized this action as an attempt to prohibit those in the observation room from witnessing her interaction with the detainee Through the surveillance camera monitor, SA _____ then observed _____ position herself between the detainee and the surveillance camera The detainee was shackled and his hands were cuffed to his waist. SA _____ observed _____ apparently whispering in the detainee's ear, and caressing and applying lotion to his arms (this was during Ramadan when physical contact with a woman would have been particularly offensive to a Moslem male). On more than one occasion the detainee appeared to be grimacing in pain, and _____ 's hands appeared to be making some contact with the detainee. Although SA _____ could not see her hands at all times, he saw them moving towards the detainee's lap He also observed the detainee pulling away and against the restraints Subsequently, the marine who had previously taped the curtain and had been in the interrogation room with _____ during the interrogation re-entered the observation room

66F-HQ-A1234210   DETAINEES-3823
TJH.tjh (2)

SECRET

DOJFBI-001914

General Donald J. Ryder

b6 -1,2
b7C -1,2

SA[____] asked what had happened to cause the detainee to grimace in pain. The marine said [____] had grabbed the detainee's thumbs and bent them backwards and indicated that she also grabbed his genitals The marine also implied that her treatment of that detainee was less harsh than her treatment of others by indicating that he had seen her treatment of other detainees result in detainees curling into a fetal position on the floor and crying in pain.

b1
b6 -1,2,5
b7C -1,2,5

2. Also in October 2002, FBI Special Agent[____] was observing the interrogation of a detainee when [____] a civilian contractor, came into the observation room and asked SA[____] to come see something
SA[____] then saw an unknown bearded long-haired detainee in another interrogation room[____] SA[____] asked Mr[____] whether the detainee had spit at the interrogators Mr[____] laughed and stated that the detainee had been chanting the Koran and would not stop Mr[____] did not answer when SA[____] asked[____]   {S}

b6 -4
b7C -4

3 In September or October of 2002 FBI agents observed that a canine was used in an aggressive manner to intimidate detainee[____] and, in November 2002, FBI agents observed Detainee[____] after he had been subjected to intense isolation for over three months During that time period[____] was totally isolated (with the exception of occasional interrogations) in a cell that was always flooded with light By late November, the detainee was evidencing behavior consistent with extreme psychological trauma (talking to non-existent people, reporting hearing voices, crouching in a corner of the cell covered with a sheet for hours on end) It is unknown to the FBI whether such extended isolation was approved by appropriate DoD authorities

b6 -2
b7C -2

These situations were referenced in a May 30, 2003 electronic communication (EC) from the Behavioral Analysis Unit of the FBI to FBI Headquarters. That EC attached, among other documents, a draft Memorandum for the Record dated 15 January 2003 from Capt[____] (USAFR), that refers to the first two events among others in a time line of events related to discussions concerning the use of aggressive interrogation techniques Marion Bowman of the FBI's Office of General Counsel discussed the contents of those communications with Mr Dietz, Deputy General Counsel (Intelligence) and Mr. Del'Orto, Deputy General Counsel of DoD, around the time the EC was received Although he was assured that the general concerns expressed, and the debate between the FBI and DoD regarding the treatment of detainees was known to officials in the Pentagon, I have no record that our specific concerns regarding these three situations were communicated to DoD for appropriate action

2

DETAINEES-3824

DOJFBI-001915

General Donald J. Ryder

If I can provide any further information to you, please do not hesitate to call.

Sincerely yours,

T. J. Harrington
Deputy Assistant Director
Counterterrorism Division

DETAINEES-3825

3

—SECRET—

5/16/04   F   Chris Wray

Detainee Interviews (Abusive Interrogation Issues)

- In late 2002 and continuing into mid-2003, the Behavioral
  Analysis Unit raised concerns over interrogation tactics being
  employed by the U.S. Military. As a result an EC dated
  5/30/03, was generated summarizing the FBI's continued
  objections to the use of SERE (Search, Escape, Resistance and
  Evasion) techniques to interrogate prisoners. This EC is
  attached and includes a collection of military documents
  discussing and authorizing the techniques. We are not aware of
  the FBI participating directly in any SERE interrogations.

- It should be noted that FBI concerns and objections were
  documented and presented to Major General Geoffery Miller, who
  oversaw GTMO operations. MG Miller is now in Iraq serving as
  the commander in charge of the military jails. MG Miller
  appeared in the New York Time on 5/5/04 defending "coercive
  and aggressive" interrogation methods.

- FBI operations in Afghanistan, Iraq and GTMO have each been
  queried and all have reported back that they do not have any
  direct knowledge of any abusive interrogation techniques being
  used. Each location was aware of rumors of abuse which have
  surfaced as a direct result of pending Military investigations
  into abusive interrogation techniques.

- The FBI has participated in the interview of 204 individuals
  in Iraq and 747 in GTMO. Our Afghan operation needs
  additional time to prepare a list of those interviewed in
  theater. Attached are the lists from GTMO and Iraq.

- A key word search of the Iraq interviews identified one
  individual alleging abuse by military personnel. In this
  instance a woman indicated she was hit with a stick and she
  wanted to talk only to German officials.

- FBI personnel assigned to the Military Tribunal effort
  involving GTMO detainees has during the review of discovery
  material seen, on a few rare occasions, documentation of SERE
  techniques being noted in interviews conducted by Military
  personnel. In these instances the material was called to the
  attention of military's Criminal Investigative Task Force
  (CITF), and Office Military Commissions (OMC) personnel.

DETAINEES-3683   CRM 246L

                                   FBI 1836

[redacted] (IR) (FBI) b6 -1 b7C -1

From: [redacted] (Div13) (FBI)
Sent: Monday, May 10, 2004 12:26 PM
To: HARRINGTON, T J. (Div13) (FBI)
Cc: BATTLE, FRANKIE (Div13) (FBI); [redacted] (IR) (FBI); [redacted] (Div13) (FBI); [redacted] (Div13) (FBI); [redacted] (Div13) (FBI); CUMMINGS, ARTHUR M. (Div13) (FBI) b6 -1 b7C -1
Subject: Instructions to GTMO interrogators.

~~SECRET~~//ORCON,NOFORN
RECORD 315N-MM-C99102

TJ,

I will have to do some digging into old files (to see if we specifically told our personnel, in writing, to not deviate from Bureau policy). We did advise each supervisor that went to GTMO to stay in line with Bureau policy and not deviate from that (as well as made them aware of some of the issues regarding DoD techniques). I went to GTMO with Andy Arena early on and we discussed the effectiveness (or lack there of) of the DoD techniques with the SSA. We (BAU and ITOS1) had also met with General's Dunlevey & Miller explaining our position (Law Enforcement techniques) vs. DoD. Both agreed the Bureau has their way of dong business and DoD has their marching orders from the Sec Def. Although the two techniques differed drastically, both Generals believed they had a job to accomplish. It was our mission to gather critical intelligence and evidence (that could be use in a DoD court of law) in furtherance of FBI cases. In my weekly meetings with DOJ we often discussed DoD techniques and how they were not effective or producing Intel that was reliable. Bruce Swartz (SES), Dave Nahmias (SES), Laura Parsky (now SES, GS15 at the time) and Alice Fisher (SES Appointee) all from DOJ Criminal Division attended meetings with FBI. We all agreed DoD tactics were going to be an issue in the military commission cases. I know Mr. Swartz brought this to the attention of DoD OGC.

b6 -1,3,4 b7C -1,3,4 b7D -1 b7F -1

One specific example was [redacted] Once the Bureau provide DoD with the findings [redacted] and other connections to [redacted] et al) they wanted to pursue expeditiously their methods to get "more out of him" [redacted] We were given a so called deadline to use our traditional methods. Once our timeline (that DoD put into place) was up, DoD took the reigns. We stepped out of the picture and DoD ran the operation against [redacted] FBI did not participate at the direction of myself, Andy Arena, and BAU UC [redacted] We would receive IIRs on the results of the process. (S)

b1 b6 -2,3,4 b7C -2,3,4 b7D -1 b7F -1

I went to GTMO on one occasion to specifically address the information coming from the IIRs produced by DoD re [redacted] We (DoD 3 Star Geoff Miller, FBI, CITF [redacted] etc) had a VTC with the Pentagon Detainee Policy Committee. During this VTC I voiced concerns that the Intel produced was nothing more than what FBI got using simple investigative techniques (following the trail of the detainee in and out of the US compared to the trail of [redacted] based on classified info from the Penttbomb investigation). Lt. Col [redacted] was providing the DoD portion of the briefing [redacted] was present at the Pentagon side of the VTC. After allowing DoD (Lt. Col [redacted] to produce nothing, I finally voiced my opinion concerning the information. The conversations were somewhat heated. [redacted] agreed with me. DoD finally admitted the information was the same info the Bureau obtained. It still did not prevent them from continuing the "DoD methods". DOJ was with me at GTMO (Dave Nahmias) during that time.

Bottom line is FBI personnel have not been involved in any methods of interrogation that deviate from our policy. The specific guidance we have given has always been no Miranda, otherwise, follow FBI/DOJ policy just as you would in your field office. Use common sense. Utilize our methods that are proven (Reed school, etc).

If you would like to call me to discuss this on the telephone I can be reached at [redacted] b2 -1

-----Original Message-----

DETAINEES-2709

SECRET

SECRET/ORCON/NOFORN

FEDERAL BUREAU OF INVESTIGATION

(Rev 08-28-2000)

Precedence: ROUTINE   Date: 05/30/2003

To: Counterterrorism   Attn: A/SC Raymond S. Mey,   b6 -1
                                      CTORS
                                      A/UC [   ]   b7C -1
                                      MLDU
        General Counsel   Attn: Marion E. Bowman,
                                      Senior Counsel for National
                                      Security Affairs
        Miami   Attn: SAC Hector M. Pesquera;
                                      ASAC C. Frank Figliuzzi;   b6 -1
                                      SSA [   ]   b7C -1

From: CIRG
                Behavioral Analysis Unit (BAU)   b2 -1
                Contact: SSA [   ]   b6 -1
                                                        b7C -1

Approved By: Wiley Stephen R.
               Battle Frankie
               [   ]   b6 -1
Drafted By: [   ]   b7C -1

Case ID #:   (U)   265A-MM-C99102;   (Pending) 1209

Title: (U)   GTMO-INTEL
               GUANTANAMO BAY, CUBA   ████████ █████
               OO: MIAMI
               MAJOR CASE 188

Synopsis: (U)   To document BAU assistance and challenges encountered during TDY assignment in Guantanamo Bay (GTMO).

        (x)-(U)   Derived From: G-3
                  Declassify On: X1
                                                        b6 -1
Enclosure (s): (U) Enclosed documents provide additional details regarding
issues encountered by SSAs [   ] and [   ] in GTMO: b7C -1

[   ]
                            Referral/Consult DOD
(U) [····X [   ]

████████████████████
██████████████

To: Counterterrorism From: CIRG
Re: (U)   265A-MM-C99102, 05/30/2003

Referral/Consult DOD

3. (LES) FBI (BAU) Letter forwarded to, Major General (MGEN) G.R. Miller, Commander, Joint Task Force-170 on 11/22/2002.

(U) .... ✕

5. (LES) Legal Analysis of Interrogation Techniques by SSA [   ]   b6 -1
[   ] FBI (BAU).   b7C -1

(U) .... ✕   b6 -4
                                                                                 b7C -4
7. (LES) FBI (BAU)/CITF Interrogation Plan for Detainee [   ]
11/22/2002.

(U) .... ✕

9. (LES) Letter from FBI GTMO Supervisor/BAU to MGEN Miller re:
Video Teleconference on 11/21/2002.

12. (LES) FBI (BAU) Interview notes re: Detainee [   ] 11/21/2002.   b6 -4

                                                                            b7C -4

Details: (x) During the TDY assignments of SSA [   ]
b6 -1   (10/27/2002–12/06/2002) and SSA [   ] (11/07/2002–12/18/2002),
b7C -1 to Guantanamo Bay (GTMO), several discussions were held to determine
the most effective means of conducting interviews of detainees. These discussions were prompted by the recognition that members of the Defense
Intelligence Agency's (DIA) Defense Humint Services (DHS) were being
encouraged at times to use aggressive interrogation tactics in GTMO
which are of questionable effectiveness and subject to uncertain interpretation based on law and regulation. Not only are these tactics at odds with
legally permissible interviewing techniques used by U.S. law enforcement
agencies in the United States, but they are being employed by personnel
in GTMO who appear to have little, if any, experience eliciting information for judicial purposes. The continued use of these techniques has the
potential of negatively impacting future interviews by FBI agents as they
attempt to gather intelligence and prepare cases for prosecution.

To: Counterterrorism   From: CIRG
Re: (U)   265A-MM-C99102,   05/30/2003

(U).........✕

Referral/Direct

b1
b6 -1
b7C -1

☒ SSAs [____] and [____] with the concurrence of BAU

(S)   Unfortunately; these arguments were met with considerable skepticism and resistance by senior DHS officials in GTMO, despite several attempts to convince them otherwise. Nonetheless, the DHS have falsely claimed that the BAU has helped to develop and support DHS's interrogation plans.

b6 -1
b7C -1

(U)   During their TDY assignment, SSAs [____] and [____] kept the BAU apprized of details of the above controversy. Additionally, they offered interviewing assistance and provided training on interrogation methods to FBI/CITF personnel.

b6 -1
b7C -1

(U)   On 12/02/2002, SSA [____] sent several documents via e-mail to Unit Chief [____] BAU, Quantico, who advised he would forward them to Marion Bowman, Legal Counsel, FBIHQ. These documents included a letter to the JTF-170 Commanding General, Major General (MGEN), J.G. Miller (Encl 3), a U.S. Army Legal Brief on Proposed Counter-Resistance Strategies supporting the use of aggressive interrogation techniques (Encl 4), and a Legal Analysis of Interrogation Techniques (Encl 5) by SSA [____]

b6 -1
b7C -1

(S)   It is noteworthy that the case agent in GTMO, SA [____] and senior officials from the Criminal Investigative Task Force (CITF), who have been involved in GTMO since the beginning,

b1
b6 -2
b7C -2

(S)

To: Counterterrorism   From: CIPG
Re: (U) 265A-MM-C99102, 05/30/2003

(S) The differences between DHS and FBI interrogation techniques and the potential legal problems which could arise were discussed with DHS officials. However, they are adamant that their interrogation strategies are the best ones to use despite a lack of evidence of their success. The issue regarding the effectiveness of DHS's techniques was amplified during an awkward teleconference between GTMO and Pentagon officials. During this teleconference, the GTMO officer overseeing military interrogations, LCOL _____ USA, blatantly misled the Pentagon into believing that the BAU endorsed DHS's aggressive and controversial Interrogation Plan (Encl 6) for _____ a detainee commonly referred to as _____ Prior to this video teleconference, SSAs _____ and _____ had discussed with DHS the advantages and rationale regarding the FBI's interrogation strategy for _____ (Encl 7), and had made available to them a written draft of this plan.

b6 -1,2,4
b7C - 1,2,4

(U) ················ (S)

Referral/Consult DOD

(U) ········ (S) The military and DHS's inaccurate portrayal to the Pentagon that the BAU had endorsed and, in fact, helped to create DHS's interrogation plan for _____ prompted SSA _____ SSA _____ and the FBI on-scene TDY operations supervisor, SSA _____ to send a letter (Encl 9) to MGEN Miller correcting these misstatements and requesting an opportunity to address the matter with MGEN Miller in person. During a subsequent meeting between MGEN Miller and SSAs _____ and SA _____ details and rationale for the BAU's interviewing approach were presented. Although MGEN Miller acknowledged positive aspects of this approach, it was apparent that he favored DHS's interrogation methods, despite FBI assertions that such methods could easily result in the elicitation of unreliable and legally inadmissible information.

b6 -1,4
b7C -1,4

(U) ········ (S) Subsequent contact with FBI personnel in GTMO has revealed that MGEN Miller remains biased in favor of DHS's interrogation methods, although there is some indication that his attitude may be shifting slightly following a recent visit by Pentagon officials.

Referral/Consult DOD

To: Counterterrorism   From: CIRG
Re: (U) 265A-MM-C99102, 05/30/2003

Referral/Consult DOD

b6 -1

b7C -1

(S) SSAs [ ] and [ ] observed that DHS personnel have an advantage over the FBI as a result of their longer periods of deployment. Currently, DHS personnel are deployed for six months, whereas the FBI on-scene supervisor and interviewing agents are assigned for periods of only 30–45 days. About the time an FBI supervisor or interviewing agent begins to feel comfortable with his/her surroundings and is able to establish meaningful rapport with detainees, he/she must prepare to depart GTMO. There are several examples in which DHS personnel have awaited the departure of an FBI supervisor before embarking on aggressive, unilateral interrogation plans which they knew would not have been endorsed by the FBI. For this reason, SSA [ ] and [ ] suggested to Acting

b6 -1

b7C -1

Unit Chief (A/UC) [ ] that the GTMO Task Force consider extending periods of deployment for the on-site FBI supervisor and for some agents assigned to conduct interviews.

(U) ······ (S) SSAs [ ] and [ ] discussed the above issues not only with BAU management, but also with A/UC [ ] who traveled to GTMO in early December. As part of his visit, A/UC [ ] participated in a second teleconference between MGEN Miller, his staff and the Penta-

b6 -1,2

b7C -1,2

gon. During this teleconference, A/UC [ ] challenged DHS's assertion that the FBI had endorsed DHS's interrogation techniques. This disclosure surprised Pentagon officials who had been led to believe that the FBI and DHS were working as a team. [ ] who was present at the Pentagon during this teleconference, advised that he would follow up on this issue by meeting with senior members of the Department of Defense (DOD) Legal Counsel to provide further background on this issue.

(U) Upon their return from GTMO, SSAs [ ] and [ ] briefed the BAU and provided unit members with copies of relevant documents. During this brief, both explained that although they were compelled by timing and circumstances to devote a considerable amount of time to the above policy issues, they were able, nevertheless, to assist agents conducting interviews

b6 -1,4

b7C -1,4

and provide training to FBI/CITF personnel. Of particular importance were a series of successful interviews which SSA [ ] conducted with [ ] (known as detainee [ ] who had stopped talking to interrogators. Utilizing interviewing techniques taught by the BAU, SSA [ ] was gradually able to re-establish a dialogue (Encl 12) which ultimately led to the detainee's renewed cooperation.

To: Counterterrorism   From: CIPG
Re: (U) 265A-MM-C99102, 05/30/2003

     (S)······(U) SSAs [   ] and [   ] recognize that issues regarding
b6 -1 differences in interrogation techniques may not be encountered by all
b7C -1 BAU agents who travel to GTMO. However, considering the constant
placement and turnover of personnel there, it is an issue which is likely to
surface again. At present, FBI agents and DOD investigators conduct
interviews on a daily basis in response to a steady number of criminal and
intelligence-related leads. Some of the information gathered from these
interviews is likely to be used in military tribunals and, possibly, in federal
court. Therefore, it is essential that FBIHQ, DOJ and DOD provide
specific guidance to protect agents and to avoid tainting cases which may
be referred for prosecution.

To: Counterterrorism   From: CIRG
Re: (U) 265A-MM-C99102, 05/30/2003

LEAD (s):

Set Lead 1: (Discretionary)

COUNTERTERRORISM

AT WASHINGTON, DC

b5 -1

Set Lead 2: (Discretionary)

GENERAL COUNSEL

AT WASHINGTON, DC

b5 -1

Set Lead 3: (Info)

MIAMI

AT MIAMI, FLORIDA

(U) For information only.

cc: SSA [_____] BAU-East   b6 -1
     GTMO Coordinator   b7C -1

b6 -1
b7C -1

From: FBI, Guantanamo Bay
Subject: VTC 21 November 2002
To: Major General Miller

b6 -4
b7C -4

    The purpose of this corresponcence is to bring to the
Commanding General's attention concerns the FBI has regarding
representations that were made about the FBI's position on the
proposed operational approach to[REDACTED]
[REDACTED] at the 21 November VTC.

b6 -4
b7C -4

    At the direction of the Commanding General and in an effort
to find some methodological common ground with respect to an
Interrogation Plan for detainee[REDACTED] the FBI On-site Supervisor
and Supervisors from the FBI Behavioral Analysis Unit met with
JTF GTMO staff members on the evening of 20 November. During
this meeting, DHS presented its draft Interrogation Plan. The
FBI voiced misgivings about the overall coercive nature and
possible illegality of elements of this plan. The FBI also
voiced its strong objections regarding the efficacy of a
fear-based approach.

    The FBI offered in writing an alternative interrogation
approach based on long term rapport-building. This approach was
previously discussed extensively between FBI Behavioral experts
and DHS and JTF staff members. At the 20 November meeting, DHS
and JTF staff members recognized advantages of the FBI's
approach, and decided to revise their plan by incorporating some
of the FBI's rapport-building aspects. Despite the close working
environment of this consultation, JIG and DHS staff never advised
FBI personnel that the revised plan would be presented the
following day to the Pentagon Office of General Counsel.   In
fact, the FBI representatives stated clearly to the JIG and DHS
representatives that the techniques proposed in the plan must be
reviewed and formally approved by FBIHQ and BAU officials prior
to any implementation.

    Had the JIG advised the FBI of his intentions to present the
revised DHS plan to DOD at the 21 November VTC as an FBI/DHS
plan, FBI representatives would have strenuously objected.
Additionally, although all agencies were aware that the NCIS

b6 -2
b7C -2

Chief Psychologist, Dr.[REDACTED] was scheduled to arrive on
21 November for the purpose of evaluating the DHS and FBI plans,
the JIG did not solicit Dr.[REDACTED] professional opinion.

    This matter is brought to the Commanding General's attention
for the purpose of setting an important record straight. The FBI
remains committed to supporting the JTF GTMO mission.

DETAINEES-1232

DECLASSIFIED BY 65179 DMH/STP/LC 04-02-4151
ON 10-19-2006

1235

Drafted by FBI (BAU) personnel at Guantanamo Bay with on-site FBI operations supervisor and forwarded to Commanding General, Joint Task Force-170 on 11/22/2002.

As we approach the one-year anniversary of the confinement of Al Qaeda/Taliban detainees at GTMO, perhaps it is a good time to revisit our interrogation strategies which may be in need of revision.

Since last year, detainees have been interrogated by representatives of the Defense Human Intelligence Services (DHS) and by members of the FBI/CITF in an effort to obtain valuable intelligence. In this sense, the missions appear to be identical. However, both the FBI and the CITF have additional responsibilities. While the FBI is working to obtain information to strengthen existing terrorism investigations for prosecution, the CITF is trying to ensure that incriminating information gathered from the detainees is done in a manner acceptable for military tribunals.

Central to the gathering of reliable, admissible evidence is the manner in which it is obtained. Interrogation techniques used by the DHS are designed specifically for short-term use in combat environments where the immediate retrieval of tactical intelligence is critical. Many of DHS's methods are considered coercive by Federal Law Enforcement and UCMJ standards. Not only this, but reports from those knowledgeable about the use of these coercive techniques are highly skeptical as to their effectiveness and reliability. Since nearly all of the GTMO detainees have been interviewed many times overseas before being sent here, the FBI/CITF would argue that a different approach should be undertaken in terms of trying to elicit information from them. The FBI/CITF favors the use of less coercive techniques, ones carefully designed for long-term use in which rapport-building skills are carefully combined with a purposeful and incremental manipulation of a detainee's environment and perceptions. A model of this approach was offered recently in an FBI/CITF interview plan for detainee ☐

FBI/CITF agents are well-trained, highly experienced and very successful in overcoming suspect resistance in order to obtain valuable information in complex criminal cases, including the investigations of terrorist bombings in East Africa and the USS Cole, etc. FBI/CITF interview strategies are most effective when tailored specifically to suit a suspect's or detainee's needs and vulnerabilities. Contrary to popular belief, these vulnerabilities are more likely to reveal themselves through the employment of individually designed and sustained interview strategies rather than through the haphazard use of prescriptive, time-driven approaches.

b6 – 4
b7C – 4

The FBI/CITF strongly believes that the continued use of diametrically opposed interrogation strategies in GTMO will only weaken our efforts to obtain valuable information.

A second problem with the current interrogation strategy is that detainees are smarter now than when they first arrived. No longer are they susceptible to suggestions for early release or special consideration. Indeed, no one seems to know when the military tribunals will begin. As TDY interrogators continue to interview and re-interview detainees utilizing every theme imaginable, detainees have become increasingly cynical of any offers of concession. Moreover, they appear to have become better conditioned for almost all interrogation approaches with many detainees simply refusing to answer any questions. Complicating matters is the structural set-up of Camp Delta, which enables detainees to exchange counter-interrogation resistance strategies with relative ease while at the same time strengthening their solidarity.

Except for a recently enacted reward system offering minor creature comforts to cooperative detainees, there is a lack of major incentives which could encourage detainees to provide more information. Major incentives are greatly needed. Recently, investigators ⎯⎯ were successful in retriev- (S) ing valuable information and cooperation from some detainees after they were provided with guarantees of judicial leniency.

In addition to a review of interrogation strategies the FBIHQ representatives wish to discuss with the Commanding General the following issues.

1. Projected long term FBI Agent and Professional Support presence in support of JTF GTMO mission
2. FBI continued technical support
3. DOJ prosecutorial interest in GTMO detainees

b6 -1
b7C -1

From:
To: b6 -1
b7C -1
Date: Mon, Dec 2, 2002 11:10 AM
Subject: Briefing notes for the General Miller

b6 -1
b7C -1

b6 -1   We learned that neither _____ nor the Miami ASAC will be coming to GTMO. Instead, only SSA ____
b7C -1   ____ will be coming from FBIHQ . Apparently, FBIHQ is scaling down their presence for the General, so
we on the ground (me, _____ have redesigned our approach and are
preparing to meet with the General in a couple days.

b6 -1,2   Attached are some write-ups prepared by us at the direction of _____ Although we think it not prudent to
b7C -1,2 dwell on lco[____]s style and actions, we belive we that before the General can fully appreciate what the
fFBI has to offer , he must first understand what has transpired. After all, it could easily happen again.

CC: b6 -1
b7C -1

DETAINEES-3305

b6 -1
b7C -1

From:
b6 -1
To:
b7C -1
Date: Thu, May 13, 2004 3:42 PM
Subject: current events

for a better understanding of the issue we spoke about, one should read not only the bau ec, but the
attachments as well.

b6 -1   [____] is here with me and should anyone be interested , he could illuminate a lot about gen miller's views
b7C -1   on interrogation. bc was the the miami case agent for 14 months.

from what cnn reports , gen karpinsky at abu gharib said that gen miller came to the prison several
months ago and told her they wanted to "gimotize" abu gharib. i am not sure what this means. however, if
this refers to intell gathering as i suspect, it suggests he has continued to support interrogation strategies
we not only advised against, but questioned in terms of effectiveness.

yesterday, however, we were surprised to read an article in stars and stripes, in which gen miller is quoted
b6 -1   as saying that he believes in the rapport-building approach. this is not what he was saying at gitmo when i
b7C -1   was there.[__] and i did cart wheels. the battles fought in gitmo while gen miller he was there are on the
record.

b6 -1,2   check out not only the bau ec but one written by miami division [____] should know about this as should
b7C -1,2   [_____] in san francisco. its a must read. [_____] knows these issue quite well and has
also fought battles. has anyone checked with [_____]

b5 -1

b5 -1

b5 -1

b5 -1

talk to you later,

ALL INFORMATION CONTAINED
HEREIN IS UNCLASSIFIED
DATE 11-05-2004 BY 61579 DMH/ECB/ad- (03-CV-4151

DETAINEES-3390

DOJFBI-002604

From:
To:
Date: Mon, Dec 16, 2002 3:23 PM   b6 -1
Subject: Fwd: GTMO matters   b7C -1

Looks like we are stuck in the mud with the interview approach of the military vrs. law enforcement We need to establish a Bureau policy laying out the boundaries for the interview process. Apparently CITF is formulating a policy for their agents.

The attached is a draft that is being worked on down at GTMO   b5 -1
                                                                                           b6 -1
                                                                                           b7C -1

Let·me know what you think.

                        b6 -1
                        b7C -1
CC:

DETAINEES-2859

DOJFBI-001511

FYI guys.

█████████

-----Original Message-----
From: Mallow Brittain   b(7)-(e)2+3
Sent: Monday, December 02, 2002 1:52 PM
To: ████████████ (H) (E-mail);
CC: ████████████LTC: CID001 COS(s); CID001 COMMAND GROUP(s); CID001
SJA(s); ████████ (E-mail); ████████ (E-mail) ' (E-mail)
Subject: CITF Participation in discussions of interrogation strategies,
techniques, etc

All,   b(5)-1

Let me make sure all understand ████████████████████████MG
Ryder, and thru him to MG Miller...
Pls pass this back to ████████and all others down in GTMO.
What follows is my policy.   b(7)-c   b(7)-c

1) CITF elements WILL participate, at the SAC, OPS, or Legal Advisor
level in any and all DISCUSSIONS of interrogation strategies and
approaches. We have to know what is being discussed, and have to be
able to express our views. As per MG Miller, I expect we will be
invited to listen in, and/or give our views.
2) At any point that we disagree with an approach, for its methods,
etc, we should professionaly raise our material/legal, or other
objections, but that does not mean we have to leave the room. The
obligations of our representative at any discussion/meeting are two-
fold: raise a professional objection, and report the issue to CITF
leadership. Our folks should make it clear that our participation in
dialogues related to the aggressive strategies does not amount to an
endorsement of the technique or the interrogation plan. But we MUST
remain engaged with other agencies, and aware of the strategies and
plans relating to all detainees because it will affect our
investigations and our own subsequent interviews.
3) CITF agents and all other personnel will not participate in the use
of any questionable techniques (as defined by law, regulation, and as
interpreted by the SAC there, and any agent has the authority to
withdraw from any environment or action which he/she feels is
inappropriate. Agents must report any such action to the SAC
immediately).

You may share this policy with whomever you need to.

COL M

-----Original Message-----   b(7)c 2+3
From: ████████ (H) [mailto:████████████████████
Sent: Tuesday, November 26, 2002 3:17 PM
To: ████████████ (E-mail) ' (E-mail)

11927

SECRETARY OF DEFENSE
1000 DEFENSE PENTAGON
WASHINGTON, DC 20301-1000

MEMORANDUM FOR COMMANDER USSOUTHCOM   JAN 1 5 2003

SUBJECT: Counter-Resistance Techniques (U)

(S) My December 2, 2002, approval of the use of all Category II techniques and one Category III technique during interrogations at Guantanamo is hereby rescinded. Should you determine that particular techniques in either of these categories are warranted in an individual case, you should forward that request to me. Such a request should include a thorough justification for the employment of those techniques and a detailed plan for the use of such techniques.

(U) In all interrogations, you should continue the humane treatment of detainees, regardless of the type of interrogation technique employed.

(U) Attached is a memo to the General Counsel setting in motion a study to be completed within 15 days. After my review, I will provide further guidance.

SECRETARY OF DEFENSE
1000 DEFENSE PENTAGON
WASHINGTON, DC 20301·1000

JAN 1 5 2003

MEMORANDUM FOR THE GENERAL COUNSEL OF THE DEPARTMENT
OF DEFENSE

SUBJECT: Detainee Interrogations (U)

(U) Establish a working group within the Department of Defense to assess the legal, policy, and operational issues relating to the interrogations of detainees held by the U.S. Armed Forces in the war on terrorism.

(U) The working group should consist of experts from your Office, the Office of the Under Secretary of Defense for Policy, the Military Departments, and the Joint Staff. The working group should address and make recommendations as warranted on the following issues:

- (S) Legal considerations raised by interrogation of detainees held by U.S. Armed Forces.

- (S) Policy considerations with respect to the choice of interrogation techniques, including:
  - (S) contribution to intelligence collection
  - (S) effect on treatment of captured US military personnel
  - (S) effect on detainee prosecutions
  - (S) historical role of US armed forces in conducting interrogations

- (S) Recommendations for employment of particular interrogation techniques by DoD interrogators.

(U) You should report your assessment and recommendations to me within 15 days.

[signature]

Classified by: Secretary Rumsfeld
Reason: 1.5(c)
Declassify on: 10 years

UNCLASSIFIED

♻

Declassify Under the Authority of Executive Order 12958
By Executive Secretary, Office of the Secretary of Defense
By William P. Marriott, CAPT, USN
June 21, 2004

X00175 /03

THE SECRETARY OF DEFENSE
1000 DEFENSE PENTAGON
WASHINGTON, DC 20301-1000

APR 1 6 2003

MEMORANDUM FOR THE COMMANDER, US SOUTHERN COMMAND

SUBJECT: Counter-Resistance Techniques in the War on Terrorism (S)

(U)
(S/NF) I have considered the report of the Working Group that I directed be established on January 15, 2003.

(U)
(S/NF) I approve the use of specified counter-resistance techniques, subject to the following:

(U) a. The techniques I authorize are those lettered A-X, set out at Tab A.

(U) b. These techniques must be used with all the safeguards described at Tab B.

(U)(S) c. Use of these techniques is limited to interrogations of unlawful combatants held at Guantanamo Bay, Cuba.

(U)(S) d. Prior to the use of these techniques, the Chairman of the Working Group on Detainee Interrogations in the Global War on Terrorism must brief you and your staff.

(U)
(S/NF) I reiterate that US Armed Forces shall continue to treat detainees humanely and, to the extent appropriate and consistent with military necessity, in a manner consistent with the principles of the Geneva Conventions. In addition, if you intend to use techniques B, I, O, or X, you must specifically determine that military necessity requires its use and notify me in advance.

(U)
(S/NF) If, in your view, you require additional interrogation techniques for a particular detainee, you should provide me, via the Chairman of the Joint Chiefs of Staff, a written request describing the proposed technique, recommended safeguards, and the rationale for applying it with an identified detainee.

(U)(S) Nothing in this memorandum in any way restricts your existing authority to maintain good order and discipline among detainees.

Attachments:
As stated

classified Under Authority of Executive Order 12958
 Executive Secretary, Office of the Secretary of Defense
Iliam P. Marriott, CAPT, USN
ie 18, 2004

UNCLASSIFIED

Classified By: Secretary of Defense
Reason: 1.5(a)
Declassify On: 2 April 2013

UNCLASSIFIED

TAB A

INTERROGATION TECHNIQUES

(u)
(S//NF) The use of techniques A - X is subject to the general safeguards as provided below as well as specific implementation guidelines to be provided by the appropriate authority. Specific implementation guidance with respect to techniques A - Q is provided in Army Field Manual 34-52. Further implementation guidance with respect to techniques R - X will need to be developed by the appropriate authority.

(u)
(S//NF) Of the techniques set forth below, the policy aspects of certain techniques should be considered to the extent those policy aspects reflect the views of other major U.S. partner nations. Where applicable, the description of the technique is annotated to include a summary of the policy issues that should be considered before application of the technique.

(u)
A. (S//NF) Direct: Asking straightforward questions.

(u)
B. (S//NF) Incentive/Removal of Incentive: Providing a reward or removing a privilege, above and beyond those that are required by the Geneva Convention, from detainees. [Caution: Other nations that believe that detainees are entitled to POW protections may consider that provision and retention of religious items (e.g., the Koran) are protected under international law (see, Geneva III, Article 34). Although the provisions of the Geneva Convention are not applicable to the interrogation of unlawful combatants, consideration should be given to these views prior to application of the technique.]

(u)
C. (S//NF) Emotional Love: Playing on the love a detainee has for an individual or group.

(u)
D. (S//NF) Emotional Hate: Playing on the hatred a detainee has for an individual or group.

(u)
E. (S//NF) Fear Up Harsh: Significantly increasing the fear level in a detainee.

(u)
F. (S//NF) Fear Up Mild: Moderately increasing the fear level in a detainee.

(u)
G. (S//NF) Reduced Fear: Reducing the fear level in a detainee.

(u)
H. (S//NF) Pride and Ego Up: Boosting the ego of a detainee.

Classified By: Secretary of Defense
Reason: 1.5(a)
Declassify On: 2 April 2013

NOT RELEASABLE TO
FOREIGN NATIONALS

UNCLASSIFIED

Tab A

A-149

I. (S//NF) (u) Pride and Ego Down: Attacking or insulting the ego of a detainee, not beyond the limits that would apply to a POW. [Caution: Article 17 of Geneva III provides, "Prisoners of war who refuse to answer may not be, threatened, insulted, or exposed to any unpleasant or disadvantageous treatment of any kind." Other nations that believe that detainees are entitled to POW protections may consider this technique inconsistent with the provisions of Geneva. Although the provisions of Geneva are not applicable to the interrogation of unlawful combatants, consideration should be given to these views prior to application of the technique.]

J. (S//NF) (u) Futility: Invoking the feeling of futility of a detainee.

K. (S//NF) (u) We Know All: Convincing the detainee that the interrogator knows the answer to questions he asks the detainee.

L. (S//NF) (u) Establish Your Identity: Convincing the detainee that the interrogator has mistaken the detainee for someone else.

M. (S//NF) (u) Repetition Approach: Continuously repeating the same question to the detainee within interrogation periods of normal duration.

N. (S//NF) (u) File and Dossier: Convincing detainee that the interrogator has a damning and inaccurate file, which must be fixed.

O. (S//NF) (u) Mutt and Jeff: A team consisting of a friendly and harsh interrogator. The harsh interrogator might employ the Pride and Ego Down technique. [Caution: Other nations that believe that POW protections apply to detainees may view this technique as inconsistent with Geneva III, Article 13 which provides that POWs must be protected against acts of intimidation. Although the provisions of Geneva are not applicable to the interrogation of unlawful combatants, consideration should be given to these views prior to application of the technique.]

P. (S//NF) (u) Rapid Fire: Questioning in rapid succession without allowing detainee to answer.

Q. (S//NF) (u) Silence: Staring at the detainee to encourage discomfort.

R. (S//NF) (u) Change of Scenery Up: Removing the detainee from the standard interrogation setting (generally to a location more pleasant, but no worse).

S. (S//NF) (u) Change of Scenery Down: Removing the detainee from the standard interrogation setting and placing him in a setting that may be less comfortable; would not constitute a substantial change in environmental quality.

T. (S//NF) (u) Dietary Manipulation: Changing the diet of a detainee; no intended deprivation of food or water; no adverse medical or cultural effect and without intent to deprive subject of food or water, e.g., hot rations to MREs.

A-150

U. (S//NF) (u) Environmental Manipulation: Altering the environment to create moderate discomfort (e.g., adjusting temperature or introducing an unpleasant smell). Conditions would not be such that they would injure the detainee. Detainee would be accompanied by interrogator at all times. [Caution: Based on court cases in other countries, some nations may view application of this technique in certain circumstances to be inhumane. Consideration of these views should be given prior to use of this technique.]

V. (S//NF) (u) Sleep Adjustment: Adjusting the sleeping times of the detainee (e.g., reversing sleep cycles from night to day.) This technique is NOT sleep deprivation.

W. (S//NF) (u) False Flag: Convincing the detainee that individuals from a country other than the United States are interrogating him.

X. (S//NF) (u) Isolation: Isolating the detainee from other detainees while still complying with basic standards of treatment. Caution: The use of isolation as an interrogation technique requires detailed implementation instructions, including specific guidelines regarding the length of isolation, medical and psychological review, and approval for extensions of the length of isolation by the appropriate level in the chain of command. This technique is not known to have been generally used for interrogation purposes for longer than 30 days. Those nations that believe detainees are subject to POW protections may view use of this technique as inconsistent with the requirements of Geneva III, Article 13 which provides that POWs must be protected against acts of intimidation; Article 14 which provides that POWs are entitled to respect for their person; Article 34 which prohibits coercion and Article 126 which ensures access and basic standards of treatment. Although the provisions of Geneva are not applicable to the interrogation of unlawful combatants, consideration should be given to these views prior to application of the technique.]

TAB B

GENERAL SAFEGUARDS

(u)

(S//NF) Application of these interrogation techniques is subject to the following general safeguards: (i) limited to use only at strategic interrogation facilities; (ii) there is a good basis to believe that the detainee possesses critical intelligence; (iii) the detainee is medically and operationally evaluated as suitable (considering all techniques to be used in combination); (iv) interrogators are specifically trained for the technique(s); (v) a specific interrogation plan (including reasonable safeguards, limits on duration, intervals between applications, termination criteria and the presence or availability of qualified medical personnel) has been developed; (vi) there is appropriate supervision; and, (vii) there is appropriate specified senior approval for use with any specific detainee (after considering the foregoing and receiving legal advice).

(U) The purpose of all interviews and interrogations is to get the most information from a detainee with the least intrusive method, always applied in a humane and lawful manner with sufficient oversight by trained investigators or interrogators. Operating instructions must be developed based on command policies to insure uniform, careful, and safe application of any interrogations of detainees.

(u)

(S//NF) Interrogations must always be planned, deliberate actions that take into account numerous, often interlocking factors such as a detainee's current and past performance in both detention and interrogation, a detainee's emotional and physical strengths and weaknesses, an assessment of possible approaches that may work on a certain detainee in an effort to gain the trust of the detainee, strengths and weaknesses of interrogators, and augmentation by other personnel for a certain detainee based on other factors.

(u)

(S//NF) Interrogation approaches are designed to manipulate the detainee's emotions and weaknesses to gain his willing cooperation. Interrogation operations are never conducted in a vacuum; they are conducted in close cooperation with the units detaining the individuals. The policies established by the detaining units that pertain to searching, silencing, and segregating also play a role in the interrogation of a detainee. Detainee interrogation involves developing a plan tailored to an individual and approved by senior interrogators. Strict adherence to policies/standard operating procedures governing the administration of interrogation techniques and oversight is essential.

Classified By:	Secretary of Defense
Reason:	1.5(a)
Declassify On:	2 April 2013

NOT RELEASABLE TO
FOREIGN NATIONALS

Tab B

(U)
(S//NF) It is important that interrogators be provided reasonable latitude to vary techniques depending on the detainee's culture, strengths, weaknesses, environment, extent of training in resistance techniques as well as the urgency of obtaining information that the detainee is known to have.

(U)
(S//NF) While techniques are considered individually within this analysis, it must be understood that in practice, techniques are usually used in combination; the cumulative effect of all techniques to be employed must be considered before any decisions are made regarding approval for particular situations. The title of a particular technique is not always fully descriptive of a particular technique. With respect to the employment of any techniques involving physical contact, stress or that could produce physical pain or harm, a detailed explanation of that technique must be provided to the decision authority prior to any decision.

b6 -1
b7C -1

From[   ](INSD) (FBI) b6 -1
To Caproni, Valerie E (OGC) (FBI)   b7C -1
cc
Subject FW GTMO

SENSITIVE BUT UNCLASSIFIED
NON-RECORD

Here is the second summary One more to go
-----Original Message-----
From[   ]BS) (FBI)
Sent Monday, August 02, 2004 10 46 AM   b6 -1
To[   ](INSD) (FBI)   b7C -1
Subject RE GTMO

SENSITIVE BUT UNCLASSIFIED
NON-RECORD

                         b6 -1
Mr[   ]   b7C -1

As requested, here is a brief summary of what I observed at GTMO

On a couple of occassions, I entered interview rooms to find a detainee chained hand and foot in a fetal position to the floor with no chair food or water Most times they had urinated or defacated on themselves and had been left there for 18 24 hours or more On one occassion, the air conditioning had been turned down so far and the temperature was so cold in the room, that the barefooted detainee was shaking with cold When I asked the MP's what was going on, I was told that interrogators from the day prior had ordered this treatment, and the detainee was not to be moved On another occassion, the A/C had been turned off, making the temperature in the unventilated room probably well over 100 degrees The detainee was almost unconcious on the floor, with a pile of hair next to him He had apparently been literally pulling his own hair out throughout the night On another occassion, not only was the temperature unbearably hot but extremely loud rap music was being played in the room, and had been since the day before with the detainee chained hand and foot in the fetal position on the tile floor

Any questions feel free to call or ask via email [   ]   b2 -1
                                                                            b6 -1
-----Original Message-----   b7C -1
From[   ](INSD) (FBI)
Sent Thursday, July 29; 2004 10 58 AM   b6 -1
To[   ](BS) (FBI)   b7C -1
Subject RE GTMO

SENSITIVE BUT UNCLASSIFIED
NON-RECORD

ALL INFORMATION CONTAINED
HEREIN IS UNCLASSIFIED EXCEPT
WHERE SHOWN OTHERWISE

DATE: 11-09-2004
CLASSIFIED BY 61379DMH/BCP/gjg 04-CV-4151
REASON: 1.4 (C)
DECLASSIFY ON: 11-09-2023

SECRET

DETAINEES-1760

1760

5053

FEDERAL BUREAU OF INVESTIGATION

Precedence: ROUTINE   Date: 07/13/2004   b6 -1
                                                                              b7C -1
To: Inspection   Attn: [   ]

From: CIRG
      NCAVC, BAU - 3   b2 -1
      Contact: SSA [   ]   b6 -1
                                                                     b7C -1

Approved By: Tidwell J Stephen   ALL INFORMATION CONTAINED
             Fedarcyk Janice K   HEREIN IS UNCLASSIFIED
             [   ]   DATE 13-07-2004 BY 61579DMH/BCE/.SE CV-04-4151

Drafted By: [   ] gfd   b6 -1
                                                     b7C -1

Case ID #: 297-HQ-A1327669-A   (Pending)

Title: COUNTERTERRORISM DIVISION,
       GTMO,
       INSPECTION SPECIAL INQUIRY

Synopsis: SSA [   ] did not personally witness any   b6 -1
aggressive treatment, interrogations or interview techniques on   b7C -1
GTMO detainees.

Administrative: Reference electronic mailings of AD Steven C.
McCraw, Inspection Division, July 9 and 12, 2004.

Details: SSA [   ] Critical Incident Response Group   b6 -1
(CIRG), Behavioral Analysis Unit 3 (BAU-3) was deployed to GTMO   b7C -1
from July 17, 2003 - August 7, 2003. Members of the BAU Units
were regularly deployed to GTMO to observe interviews of
detainees and provide interview strategies and other behavioral
assistance as needed. During my tenure at GTMO, I never
personally witnessed any aggressive treatment, interrogations or
interview techniques on GTMO detainees.

        On several occasions, I did hear loud music being
played and people yelling loudly from behind closed doors of
interview rooms but I could not say that detainees were present
in those rooms. I also observed strobe lights in interview rooms
on several occasions but never observed those being used on
detainees.

        There were many comments made by investigators during
my tenure at GTMO that every time the FBI established a rapport
with a detainee, the military would step in and the detainee
would stop being cooperative. The military did not stop the
interviews while they were in progress but routinely took control

                        DETAINEES-2447

                        DOJFBI-002959

of the detainee when the interview was completed. The next time
that detainee was interviewed, his level of cooperation was
diminished. There were also accusations made by different
investigators that Military interrogators would present
themselves as FBI Agents to detainees and harass them but that
was never personally observed by SSA[   ]

b6 -1
b7C -1

2   DETAINEES-2448

b6 -1
b7C -1

b6 -1
b7C -1

From [REDACTED] (OGC) (FBI)
To Caproni, Valerie E (OGC) (FBI)
cc Curran, John F (OGC) (OGA) [REDACTED] (OGC) (FBI)
Subject FW reported incidents

Valerie,

b6 -1
b7C -1

Per our conversation, please find attached the e-mail exchange prompted by [REDACTED] s request from his SAs on Wednesday I have asked [REDACTED] to hand carry to you the "A to X memo" related to approved interrogation techniques Further, I inquired about guidance given to SA conducting interviews here, and [REDACTED] replied that no such written guidance exists SA are advised to conduct their interviews in accordance with FBI policy and procedure with the exception of the Miranda requirement According to [REDACTED] he has not recieved any evidence, that SAs have participated in or observed any interviews employing "abusive" interrogation techniques Please let me know if I can be of further assistance

b6 -1
b7C -1

[REDACTED]

AGC [REDACTED]
CTLU/NSLB/OGC
FBI CP
US Naval Base, Guantanamo Bay Cuba

b2 -1
b6 -1
b7C -1

-----Original Message-----
From [REDACTED] (Div13) (FBI)
Sent Fri 5/7/2004 2 03 PM
To [REDACTED] (Div09) (FBI)
Cc
Subject FW reported incidents

-----Original Message-----
From [REDACTED] (Div13) (FBI)
Sent Thursday, May 06 2004 9 54 AM
To [REDACTED] (CG) (FBI)   b6 -1
Cc [REDACTED] (EP) (FBI)   b7C -1
Subject RE reported incidents

Thanks [REDACTED]

As you know, #1 was brought to General Hood's attention by NAE

I consider #2, as you have reported it, unfounded and arguably not credible, based on the source

#3 was observed/supervised by competent JTF medical authority, and as you weren't moved at the time to label it abuse I'm reluctant to do so now

b6 -1
b7C -1

-----Original Message-----
From [REDACTED] (CG) (FBI)
Sent Wednesday, May 05, 2004 11 04 AM
To [REDACTED] (Div13) (FBI)
Cc [REDACTED] (EP) (FBI)

ALL INFORMATION CONTAINED
HEREIN IS UNCLASSIFIED
DATE 11-05-2004 BY 61579DMH/BCK/cjg 04-cv-4151

DETAINEES-1692

1692
DOJFBI-002278

6 -1
7C -1

Subject reported incidents

Per our meeting earlier today, the following information has been brought to my attention

1) ☐
Situation I was told on or about Thursday, 22 April 2004 by ☐ (NAE) that ☐ whom he
debriefs, had provided the following Sometime in the second or third week of February 2004, ☐ was
taken to reservation ☐ was on both FBI and NAE hold) He did not recognize the interviewers and
when he told them he didn't want to speak to anyone unless they were introduced by his regular
interrogators, he was yelled at for 25 mintues ☐ was short-shackled, the room temperature was
significantly lowered, strobe lights were used, and possibly loud music There were two male
interrogators, one stood behind him and the other in front They yelled at him and told him he was never
leaving here The interrogator tried to get ☐ to identify photos After the initial 25 minutes of yelling,
☐ was left alone in the room in this condition for approximately 12 hours At one point, the interrogator
came back in the afternoon to make sure he was still there During the 12 hours, ☐ was not permitted
to eat, pray or use the bathroom One of the interrogators was described as old/late 50's, grey and black
hair, mustache with no beard, short skinny, and wore a blue shirt
My actions verbally informed ☐

                                                                       b6 -1,2,3,4
                                                                       b7C -1,2,3,
                                                                        b7D -1
                                                                        b7F -1

2) ☐
Situation The following information was provided to me by detainee ☐ in approximately January or
February 2004 ☐ was being taken to reservation or medical (something inside Camp Delta, I don't
recall what) While outside near the Brown building, he saw a young Filipino/Asian female with long
dark hair, short tight pants, and a revealing top When the female noticed him, she jumped, laughed,
and ran around the building out of his sight ☐ believed that this was a prostitute
My actions verbally informed ☐ advised this female fit the
description of a prostitute who had previously been working out of the base beauty shop

                                                                        b6 -1,3,4
                                                                       b7C -1,3,4
                                                                        b7D -1
                                                                        b7F -1

3) ☐
Situation I observed the following in early April 2004 ☐ was being debriefed for several hours
(appoximately 15 hours) by NAE Throughout the session, ☐ periodically threw up in a trash can At
the time, I was told he had an ulcer and that the stress was irritating it I was later advised he had a
stomach virus I was told he had been given a shot of Motrin (or something like that) by the medical
staff
My actions Due in part to the fact that ☐ was present and did not object to the situation,
and I never heard ☐ asked to be returned to his cell or request medical assistance, I took no action

Thanks, LL

                                                                        b6 -3,4
                                                                        b7C -3,4
                                                                        b7D -1
                                                                        b7F -1

                                                                        b6 -2,3,4
                                                                        b7C -2,3,4
                                                                        b7D -1
                                                                        b7F -1

b6 -1
b7C -1

b6 -1   **From:**
b7C -1   **To:**   Bald, Gary, BATTLE, FRANKIE, CUMMINGS, ARTHUR, ...
         Date: Fri, Dec 5, 2003 9:53 AM
         Subject: Fwd: Impersonating FBI at GTMO

b6 -1   Frank
b7C -1

I am forwarding this EC up the CTD chain of command. MLDU requested this information be documented to protect the FBI. MLDU has had a long standing and documented position against use of some of DOD's interrogation practices, however, we were not aware of these latest techniques until recently.

b2 -3   Of concern, DOD interrogators impersonating Supervisory Special Agents of the FBI told a detainee that
b6 -4   These same interrogation teams then
b7C -4   The detainee was also told by this interrogation team
b7E -1
b7F -1

These tactics have produced no intelligence of a threat neutralization nature to date and CITF believes that techniques have destroyed any chance of prosecuting this detainee.

If this detainee is ever released or his story made public in any way, DOD interrogators will not be held accountable because these torture techniques were done the "FBI" interrogators. The FBI will left holding the bag before the public.

b6 -1   SSA
b7C -1   CTD/MLDU

         CC: b6 -1
                                                                              b7C -1

                                                     DETAINEES-3168

3977

Close |

📇 **Attached Mail Message (Blind Carbon Copy)**

From: [   ]   b6 -1
To: b7C -1
Subject: Re: GTMO
Message:

Thanks [   ] Sorry I missed your call Your e-mail is very helpful and consistent with some of what I've been told by others re the transition of CITF b6 -1 to the tribunals. I am very concerned about what you report about DHS I will b7C -1 try to call you so we can discuss all of this more directly.

[   ]

>>> [   ] 07/31 12:53 PM >>> b6 -1
Hi [   ]   b7C -1

Things here are in a state of transition. The Bureau and CITF have parted ways as CITF is concentrating on the tribunals. The Bureau is gearing up for the arrival of long term personnel and identifying detainees with a Bureau nexus. Once these detainees are identified, they'll become "projects" and we should have a much greater impact then we have now.

I've been here 2 weeks today and have tagged along and observed approximately 12 interviews. The common theme seems to be the detainees are all extremely frustrated about being asked the same questions, over and over again, by different interrogators. Once the projects are initiated, that should resolve itself. Most of the detainees I've observed have been uncooperative and untruthful and some refuse to speak.

I've met with the BISC (Biscuit) people several times and found them to be a great resource They know everything thats going on with each detainee, who they're talking to, who the leaders are, etc I've encouraged the interview teams to meet with them prior to doing their interviews. We're still fighting the battle with DHS which routinely has a negative impact on what we're trying to do [

[   ]
                                          b5 -1
                                          b6 -2,4
                                          b7C -2,4

I haven't heard anything about the housing situation. A new housing   b6 -1,2
assignment roster came out yesterday and the CA [   ] is   b7C -1,2
assigned to our unit with [   ] told the new Admin CA [   ]
[   ] we had another Agent arriving in mid-August. He said he'd been told we were ending our presence here. I hope that's the case and that would

DETAINEES-2776

DOJFBI-001428

A-160

be my recommendation. During this transitional period, we're having a minimal impact on the interviews that are being conducted and we really don't need to be here Once the projects are identified and we're plugged into them, we can work on the projects from the office and send teams, as needed, to provide assistance.

Let me know what you guys decide and I'll advise them here.. Talk to you later.

Attachments: b6 -1
                               b7C -1

SECRET

DETAINEES 7777

MEMORANDUM FOR RECORD

Date: 4/28/2003
To: ███████████████████████
From: ███████████████████████
Re: INCIDENT ON 22APR03

THE FOLLOWING INCIDENT TOOK PLACE ON 22 APRIL 2003 AT CAMP DELTA, GTMO. AT
APPROXIMATELY 2030 HOURS ████████████████████ AND I WERE IN MONITORING ROOM 5
IN GOLD BUILDING OBSERVING THE APPROACH TECHNIQUE OF ████████████ A FELLOW
INTERROGATOR. ████████████ WAS INTERROGATING IN INTERROGATION ROOM 4.
MONITORING ROOM 5 OVERLOOKS BOTH INTERROGATION ROOM 4 AND INTERROGATION
ROOM 6. AT THIS TIME THERE WAS AN INTERROGATION OF ANOTHER DETAINEE TAKING
PLACE IN INTERROGATION ROOM 6. ████████████████████ AND A YOUNG NAVY
ANALYST WHOSE NAME I DO NOT RECALL WERE ALSO IN MONITORING ROOM 5
OBSERVING THIS INTERROGATION. IN INTERROGATION ROOM 6 I SAW ████████████ A
MILITARY LINGUIST, TWO DETAINEE ESCORTS, AND A DETAINEE. THE DETAINEE WAS
STANDING A LITTLE BACK FROM CENTER OF THE ROOM. ████████████ WAS IN FRONT OF
THE DETAINEE THE TWO ESCORTS WERE ON EITHER SIDE OF THE DETAINEE HOLDING
THE DETAINEE BY HIS UPPER ARMS. THE LINGUIST WAS STANDING IN BACK OF THE
DETAINEE. THE TWO ANALYSTS IN THE MONITORING ROOM HAD A SPEAKER PLUGGED
INTO THE AUDIO OUTPUT FROM ROOM 6 AND ████████████████████   (b)(1)
███████████████████ I HAD ONLY ONE EARPIECE IN SO THAT I COULD TRANSLATE THE
ARABIC ████████████ WAS SPEAKING TO ████████████ WHO DOES NOT SPEAK ARABIC.
OVER THE SPEAKER THAT ████████████ AND THE OTHER ANALYST WERE USING I COULD
HEAR ████████████ BECOMING LOUDER AND LOUDER IN HIS INTERROGATION. ███████
████████████ WAS REPEATING THE SAME QUESTION, "WHAT WERE YOU DOING IN PAKISTAN?"
TO THE DETAINEE. THE DETAINEE IN MY OPINION SEEMED INCOHERENT. (NOTE: AS AN
INTERROGATOR I HAVE SEEN DETAINEES FEIGN INCOHERENCE TO AVOID
INTERROGATION, BUT SUCH WAS NOT THE CASE HERE IN MY ESTIMATION.) ████████████
WAS REPEATING THE QUESTION OVER AND OVER, IN RAPID FIRE FASHION, SO QUICKLY
THAT THE INTERPRETER WAS NOT KEEPING UP WITH THE QUESTIONING AND THE
DETAINEE WOULD NOT HAVE BEEN ABLE TO ANSWER WITHOUT INTERRUPTING HIM.
████████████████████ THEN SHOUTED "DOWN" AND THE TWO DETAINEE ESCORTS
PUSHED THE DETAINEE TO THE FLOOR. WHEN I SAY PUSHED TO THE FLOOR I MEAN THEY
PUSHED IN THE BACK OF THE DETAINEE'S KNEES WITH THEIR KNEES, TAKING THE
DETAINEE TO HIS KNEES. THEN HOLDING THE DETAINEE BY HIS UPPER ARMS THEY
SLAMMED HIS UPPER BODY TO THE FLOOR. THIS SERIES OF MOTIONS WAS ALL DONE IN
ONE SWIFT MOVEMENT, SO THAT THE DETAINEE WENT FROM A STANDING POSITION TO A
PRONE POSITION ALL AT ONCE. THE FORCE WITH WHICH THE DETAINEE'S BODY HIT THE
FLOOR WAS SUCH THAT ████████████████████████████████ IT   (b)(1)
███ WAS
INTERROGATING. IMMEDIATELY BEFORE THE DETAINEE WAS PUSHED TO THE FLOOR,   (b)(1)
███████████████████████████████ AND THE NAVY ANALYST WERE LAUGHING ABOUT THE
TREATMENT OF THE DETAINEE. THE DETAINEE WAS SLAMMED TO THE FLOOR IN THIS

4/28/

23ᵈ

1329

MANNER SEVEN TO EIGHT TIMES. ████████████ WOULD YELL "DOWN" IMMEDIATELY PRECEDING EACH TIME THE DETAINEE WAS SLAMMED TO THE FLOOR. AFTER THE FIRST TWO SLAMS I TOOK OUT MY EARPIECE AND OBSERVED THE HAPPENINGS IN ROOM 6. ████ ████████ WAS ONCE AGAIN ASKING THE DETAINEE, "WHAT WERE YOU DOING IN PAKISTAN?" WHEN, AFTER 5 TO 10 MINUTES OF THIS IMPOSSIBLE-TO-ANSWER, RAPID FIRE QUESTIONINGTHE DETAINEE WOULD NOT ANSWER, ████████████SHOUTED "DOWN," AND THE SLAMMING PROCESS TOOK PLACE APPROXIMATELY TEN TO TWELVE MORE TIMES. THE DETAINEE WAS BEING SLAMMED TO THE FLOOR SO HARD THAT I WAS CONCERNED FOR HIS SAFETY. THE FORCE WITH WHICH THE DETAINEE HIT THE FLOOR WAS, IN MY ESTIMATION, ADEQUATE TO CAUSE SEVERE INTERNAL INJURY. I LEFT THE MONITORING ROOM, ALONG WITH ████████████ TO CALL MY SUPERVISOR AND REPORT THIS INCIDENT. AS WE LEFT I COULD HEAR ████████████ SHOUTING "DOWN" AND I ALSO HEARD IMMEDIATELY FOLLOWING EACH "DOWN" NOISES CONSISTENT WITH THE SOUND THAT WAS MADE WHEN THE DETAINEE WAS SLAMMED TO THE FLOOR. I HEARD THIS COMBINATION OF SHOUTS AND THUDS SIX TO SEVEN MORE TIMES AS I EXITED THE BUILDING. ████████████ AND ████████████ REMAINED AT GOLD BUILDING WHILE I WENT TO MAKE THE PHONE CALLS. WHEN I ARRIVED AT BUILDING 6, I ATTEMPTED TO CALL MY SUPERVISOR, ████████████ BUT GOT NO ANSWER. I THEN WALKED BACK DOWN TO GOLD BUILDING WHERE ████████████ GAVE ME THE NUMBER TO CALL ████████████ I TOLD ████████████ THERE WERE THINGS GOING ON AT THE CAMP THAT COULD ADVERSELY AFFECT THE MISSION AND THAT I NEEDED HIS GUIDANCE ON HOW TO PROCEED. ████████████ TOLD ME HE WOULD COME TO CAMP DELTA, ALONG WITH ████ ████ AND DISCUSS THE MATTER. WHILE WAITING FOR THEM TO ARRIVE I SPOKE WITH ████████████ WHO WAS NOW AT BUILDING 5. ████████████ HAD APPARENTLY BEEN TOLD THAT I WAS REPORTING HIS CONDUCT TO MY SUPERVISOR. I HAD A CONFERENCE WITH ████████████ WHICH LASTED APPROXIMATELY TEN MINUTES DURING WHICH ████████████ TRIED TO CONVINCE ME THAT WHAT HE HAD DONE WAS PROPER. HE TOLD ME THAT WHEN THE GUARDS WERE TAKING THE DETAINEE TO THE FLOOR THEY WERE, AT THE VERY LAST SECOND, PULLING UP ON HIS ARMS TO LESSEN THE IMPACT, AND THAT THE LOUD SOUNDS I HEARD WERE ONLY BOOTS BEING STOMPED ON THE FLOOR. I TOLD ████████████ THAT AS AN EXPERIENCED INTERROGATOR, WHO HAD BEEN TRAINED BY AND SERVED IN THE US ARMY, I HAD NEVER SEEN IN FM 34-52 ANY SECTION DESCRIBING OR PRESCRIBING WHAT HE HAD DONE TO THE DETAINEE. ████████ TOLD ME THAT HE HAD BEEN CALLED IN TO RUN THIS APPROACH ON THIS DETAINEE BECAUSE THE INTERROGATOR RESPONSIBLE FOR THIS DETAINEE HAD RUN "EVRY APPROACH, A TO Z, AND HAS GOTTEN NOWHERE." I TOLD ████████████ THAT I THOUGHT HE HAD JEAPORDIZED THE MISSION AND THAT MOST LIKELY WHOEVER INTERROGATED THAT SOURCE WOULD HAVE TO UNDO THE DAMAGE HE HAD DONE. I LEFT THE OFFICE WHERE WE HAD BEEN TALKING AND WALKED OUTSIDE WHERE I FOUND ████████ AND ████████████ TO WHOM I RECOUNTED WHAT I HAD SEEN.

THE PERSONNEL I COULD NOT IDENTIFY BY NAME, I WOULD BE ABLE TO IDENTIFY BY SIGHT.

████████████████████████████████████

INTERROGATOR, ACS DEFENSE

1330

b6 -1
b7C -1

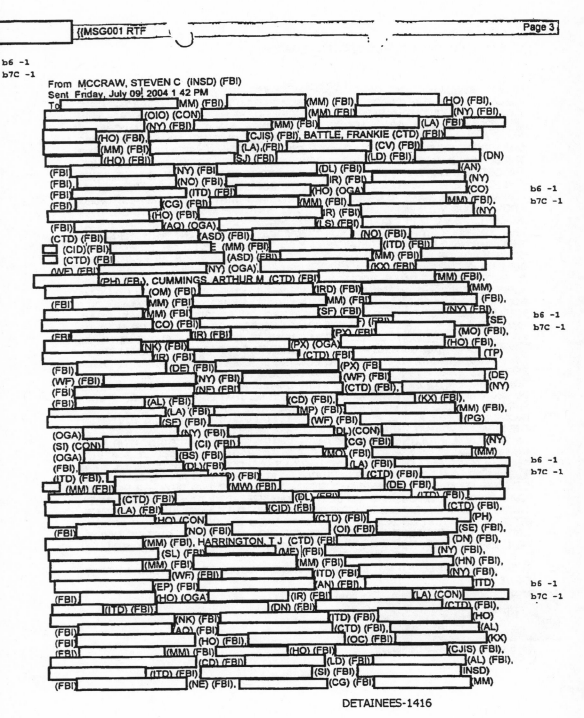

From MCCRAW, STEVEN C (INSD) (FBI)
Sent Friday, July 09, 2004 1 42 PM
To

DETAINEES-1416

1416

DOJFBI-002031

b6 -1
b7C -1

NON-RECORD

You have been identified as having conducted an assignment at GTMO, Cuba since 9/11/01 The Inspection Division has been tasked with contacting those employees who have served in any capacity at GTMO and obtain information regarding the treatment of detainees Employees should immediately respond to the following

1) Employees who observed aggressive treatment, interrogations or interview techniques on GTMO detainees which was not consistent with Bureau interview policy/guidelines, should respond via email for the purpose of a follow-up interview Positive email responses should be directed to

b6 -1
b7C -1

Inspection Division

2) Employees who served at GTMO and observed no aggressive treatment of detainees, should respond via an EC documenting a negative response The EC should include the employee's official Bureau name, title, and tenure of assignment at GTMO

The EC should be titled "Counterterrorism Division, GTMO, Inspection Special Inquiry", file # 297-HQ-A1327669-A The EC should not be uploaded, but only serialized, with a hard copy forwarded to

Inspection Division
Office of Inspections   b6 -1
                                               b7C -1
Room 7837

SENSITIVE BUT UNCLASSIFIED

SENSITIVE BUT UNCLASSIFIED

SENSITIVE BUT UNCLASSIFIED

SENSITIVE BUT UNCLASSIFIED

SENSITIVE BUT UNCLASSIFIED

SENSITIVE BUT UNCLASSIFIED

DETAINEES-1419

1419

DOJFBI-002034

b6 -1
b7C -1

From BALD, GARY M (CTD) (FBI)

b6 -1
b7C -1

To [   ] (INSD) (FBI), HARRINGTON, T J (CTD) (FBI)
cc THOMPSON, DONALD W JR (RH) (FBI), [   ] (INSD) (FBI)
Subject RE GTMO Special Inquiry

UNCLASSIFIED
NON-RECORD

b6 -1
b7C -1

Thanks [   ] - Looks OK to me

-----Original Message-----
From [   ] (INSD) (FBI)
Sent Tuesday, August 17, 2004 9 42 AM
To HARRINGTON, T J (CTD) (FBI)
Cc BALD, GARY M (CTD) (FBI), THOMPSON, DONALD W JR (RH) (FBI), [   ]
(INSD) (FBI)
Subject GTMO Special Inquiry

b6 -1
b7C -1

UNCLASSIFIED
NON-RECORD

This email will provide you with an update of the inquiry As you are aware, an email was sent out to all
personnel who had served in any capacity at GTMO since 9/11/2001 This email required personnel to
respond to INSD and advise if they observed any aggressive treatment of detainees by either DOD or
FBI personnel Those employees who in fact did observe what they perceived to be mistreatment were
to email INSD, provide a short summary of what they observed and be available for a followup interview
Those employees who did not observe any mistreatment were required to document their observation in
an EC format

There were 530 employees who have served in some capacity at GTMO and were notified by email. To
date, 478 have responded Some employees have since retired and others were contractors no longer
employed with the Bureau Of the 478 responses, there were 26 employees who stated they observed
what was believed to be some form of mistreatment These 26 employees provided summaries of what
they actually observed There were no observations of any mistreatment of detainees by FBI personnel

The 26 summaries were provided to General Counsel Caproni, who reviewed each and ascertained that
nine of the respondees would require a followup interview The remaining 17 were deemed to be
appropriate DOD approved interrogation techniques

These nine employees will be interviewed utilizing a set of questions prepared by INSD/CTD and
approved by General Counsel Caproni The questions are attached to this email for your review The
interviews will be conducted this week and be documented via FD-302s Subsequent to the interviews, a
report will be completed and forwarded to General Counsel Caproni, who in turn will notify DOD I will
also forward CTD a copy of the report

UNCLASSIFIED

ALL INFORMATION CONTAINED
HEREIN IS UNCLASSIFIED
DATE 11-03-2004 BY 61579 DMH/PLB/JAC 04-CV-4151

DETAINEES-1412

1412

DOJFBI-002027

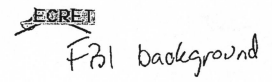

FBI background

Iraq

- Became aware of the abuses at Abu Ghraib when the story broke publicly

- Because of the extremely dangerous conditions that existed at the prison (it was shelled regularly), FBI employees were at the prison only during daytime hours.

- 14 employees were there during the time frame October 1, 2003 through December 31, 2003, the relevant period according to General Taguba's report.

- None of the 14 employees was aware of the sort of mistreatment that has recently been reported, although the following were observed by one or more FBI employee:

  - a detainee, hooded and draped in a shower curtain, was cuffed to a waist high rail. An MP was apparently subjecting the detainee to sleep deprivation, as he was observed slapping the detainee lightly, as if to keep him from falling asleep;

  - a detainee was restrained by military personnel, spread eagle, on a mattress on the floor. The detainee was shouting and flailing about. The military personnel told the agent that the detainee was mentally ill. That conclusion was consistent with the agent's observations,

  - a detainee, either naked or in boxer shorts, lying prone on a wet floor;

  - a detainee being ordered to strip and being placed in an isolation cell;

  - an MP shouting at a detainee, who appeared not to understand the MP's directions and detainees being verbally harassed; and

  - detainees being hooded while being escorted on the prison grounds.

- All employees who were at Abu Ghraib during the October - December time period were asked whether anyone who was interviewed complained of mistreatment. According to our employees:

  - several interviewees complained of abuse occurring prior to being turned over to American authorities (e.g., being kicked, shocked, burned and having family members threatened);

  - one interviewee told of harsh treatment while in American custody, but it did not rise to the level of abuse recently reported. That interviewee reported being held naked and subjected to sleep deprivation. He also reported having been "roughed up" by Americans who were not in uniform and hearing screaming at night. The agent who conducted this interview reported that the interviewee did not have any physical marks, and the agent believed his report of hearing screams at night may

3648

DETAINEES-3648

(P 87)

4645

have been "posturing" on the interviewee's part.

As reported in the press, at least one MP said that the participants in the abuse at the prison included FBI, military intelligence, military criminal investigative division ab1 ▆▆▆▆▆▆▆▆▆▆▆▆▆▆▆▆▆▆▆▆▆▆▆▆▆ The MP's statement provides no specifics and, as indicated above, our review has indicated that FBI employees never spent the night at Abu Ghraib.

Guantanamo Bay

- There have been differences of opinion between FBI and portions of DoD on the desirability of using certain interrogation techniques on the detainees at Guantanamo. The difference of opinion was based partly on differing assessments of the efficacy of harsh interrogation techniques as compared to rapport building techniques, and in part on differing views on the propriety of the harsher techniques.

- Prior to the promulgation of new guidelines, one or more agents observed the following:

    - a detainee's mouth was duct taped for chanting from the Koran; detainee had long hair and a beard; military employee who applied the duct tape found it amusing;

    - an interrogator attempted to block the observation window of an interrogation cell and then rubbed the detainee's arm (this interrogation occurred during Ramadan at a time when contact with an unrelated female is particularly offensive for Islamic men) and did something that could not be observed but that appeared to cause the detainee substantial pain; and

    - a detainee being isolated for substantial periods of time.

- Agents heard of detainees being subjected to considerable pain and very aggressive techniques during interrogations.

- Agents aware of detainees being threatened (either in person or aurally) by dogs.

- Agents have seen documentary evidence that a detainee was told that his family had been taken into custody and would be moved to Morocco for interrogation if he did not begin to talk.

- Agents aware of military screaming in ear of detainee and "manhandling" detainees (e.g., knocking chair from under detainee).

- Agents aware of military misrepresenting themselves as FBI when dealing with detainee.

- In order to know the entire scope of FBI knowledge of treatment of detainees at GTMO, approximately 500 agents would need to be interviewed.

DETAINEES-3649

3649

4646

Afghanistan

- Agents are aware of detainees being subjected to interrogation techniques that would not be permitted in the United States (i.e., stress positions for extended periods of time and sleep deprivation) and to psychological techniques (i.e., loud music).

DETAINEES-3650

3650

4647

b6 -1
b7C -1

From Caproni, Valene E (OGC) (FBI)
b6 -1   To [   ](INSD) (FBI)
b7C -1   cc
Subject RE GTMO

SENSITIVE BUT UNCLASSIFIED
NON-RECORD

-3

-----Original Message-----
b6 -1   From [   ](INSD) (FBI)
b7C -1   Sent Monday, August 16, 2004 2 49 PM
To Caproni, Valene E (OGC),(FBI)
Subject FW GTMO

SENSITIVE BUT UNCLASSIFIED
NON-RECORD

This should be the last one   Let me know followup or not

-----Original Message-----
b6 -1   From [   ](OM) (FBI)
b7C -1   Sent Friday, July 30, 2004 1 56 PM
To [   ](INSD) (FBI)
Subject RE GTMO

ALL INFORMATION CONTAINED
HEREIN IS UNCLASSIFIED
DATE 11-03-2004 [illegible]

SENSITIVE BUT UNCLASSIFIED
NON-RECORD

-1
: -1

    Following a detainee interview exact date unknown, while leaving the interview building at Camp Delta
at approximately 8 30 p m or later, I heard and observed in the hallway loud music and flashes of light I
walked from the hallway into the open door of a monitoring room to see what was going on From the
monitoring room, I looked inside the adjacent interview room At that time I saw another detainee
sitting on the floor of the interview room with an Israeli flag draped around him, loud music being played
and a strobe light flashing I left the monitoring room immediately after seeing this activity I did not see
any other persons inside the interview room with the Israeli flag draped detainee, but suspect that this
was a practice used by the DOD DHS since the only other persons inside the hallway near this particular
interview room were dressed in green military fatigues, similar to the ones worn by DOD DHS and the
DOD MP Uniformed Reservists At no time did I observe any physical assaults take place of this
detainee nor any others while assigned to GTMO
    I understood prior to deployment to GTMO, that such techniques were not allowed, nor approved by
FBI policy While at GTMO no such techniques were never conducted to my knowledge by any of the

DETAINEES-1414

1414

4737

b6 -1
b7C -1

CITF personnel assigned at GTMO
   Approximately one or two days later. DHS tactics were discussed at a weekly held CITF staff meeting. Many of the CITF investigators discussed how some of the DHS tactics had been counterproductive in building rapport with detainees who were being interviewed by CITF members Acting FBI SSA

b6 -1
b7C -1
                         advised that no CITF personnel including FBI agents were to take part in any such interviews or interrogations which fell outside the FBI's policy of interviewing detainees ASSA
                         also advised us that if we became aware of any similar instances where agressive DHS tactics had been observed to notify him, provide details, and he would make these instances known to appropriate GTMO DOD and DOJ officials It should be noted that while at GTMO, ASSA acted in an exemplary manner and represented the FBI as a consumate professional. This summary details the only incident I have to report regarding observing a non-FBI approved tactic being used on a detainee at GTMO

b6 -1
b7C -1

FBI Omaha
Des Moines R A

b2 -1

-----Original Message-----
From   (INSD) (FBI)
b6 -1
b7C -1
Sent Thursday, July 29, 2004 9 59 AM
To   (OM) (FBI)
Subject RE GTMO

SENSITIVE BUT UNCLASSIFIED
NON-RECORD

Could you please provide a short summary of what you observed   Thanks

-----Original Message-----
From   (OM) (FBI)
b6 -1
b7C -1
Sent Friday, July 09, 2004 4 20 PM
To   (INSD) (FBI)
Subject RE GTMO

SENSITIVE BUT UNCLASSIFIED
NON-RECORD

b6 -1
b7C -1

   While at GTMO   observed some non-FBI policy treatment which was conducted by non-Bureau and non-CITF personnel being used on one detainee I did not observe any physical mistreatment of any
b6 -1
b7C -1
detainee

FBI Omaha
Des Moines R A

b2 -1

-----Original Message-----

DETAINEES-1415

1415

4738

A-171

(IR) (FBI)   b7C -1

b6 -1
b7C -1   From: _____ (INSD) (FBI)
          Sent: Monday, August 02, 2004 2:45 PM
b6 -1   To: _____ (IR) (FBI)
b7C -1   Cc: Caproni, Valerie E. (OGC) (FBI)
          Subject: RE: GTMO

SENSITIVE BUT UNCLASSIFIED
NON-RECORD

OK, thanks for the quick response.

b6 -1   ——Original Message——
b7C -1   From _____ (IR) (FBI)
          Sent: Monday, August 02, 2004 2:40 PM
b6 -1   To _____ (INSD) (FBI)
b7C -1   Subject: RE: GTMO

SENSITIVE BUT UNCLASSIFIED
NON-RECORD

I was situated in the observation booth in between two interview rooms, observing an interview which included at least one FBI SA, and possibly a colleague of his from one of the other agencies with invesitgative personnel assigned there at the time. The booth was quite crowded because there were several individuals present who were observing an "interview" in the room on the other side of the booth. In that room, the detainee was seated in a chair and was secured in the same method as I'd seen for all of the other detainees, shackled at his feet so that he could not leave the room. However, there wasn't much talking going on, because the lights had been turned off and a strobe light was flickering on and off, and loud rock music was being played. I estimate that this went on for 30 to 60 minutes. I was told by quite a few FBI personnel that tactics such as this were quite common there at the time. This was the only such event that I observed directly.

b6 -1   ——Original Message——
b7C -1   From _____ (INSD) (FBI)
          Sent: Monday, August 02, 2004 11:03 AM
b6 -1   To _____ IR) (FBI)
b7C -1   Subject: RE: GTMO

SENSITIVE BUT UNCLASSIFIED
NON-RECORD

b6 -1
b7C -1   _____ could you please provide additional information, more specific (short summary) of what you observed on that one incident.

b6 -1   ——Original Message——
b7C -1   From: _____ (IR) (FBI)
          Sent: Friday, July 09, 2004 4:10 PM
b6 -1   To _____ INSD) (FBI)
b7C -1   Subject: GTMO
          Importance: High

SENSITIVE BUT UNCLASSIFIED

DETAINEES-2429

9/20/2004

4482

A-172

CLASSIFIED BY 65179DMH DLF/PLB 10-27-04
REASON: 1.4 (C)
DECLASSIFY ON: X 10072024

GTMO Issues for SAC Wiley

b5 -1

b1
b2 -3
b5 -1
b7E -1

(S)

b1
b2 -3
b5 -1
b7E -1

(S)

b2 -3
b5 -1
b7E -1

* **Department of Defense (DoD) Interrogation Tactics**

   - BAU personnel witnessed sleep depravation _____ and utilization of loud music/bright lights/growling dogs in the Detainee interview process by DoD representatives. These tactics were brought tot the attention of the appropriate DoD legal personnel who requested that BAU members write out "statements" concerning these matters.

   b1

   (S)

* _____ b5 -1

   - _____ b5 -1

* **BAU Vehicle**

   - CIRG/RDLU provided the BAU with an eighteen (18) passenger van for transportation at GTMO. This van is too large for the small roadways/tight turns at GTMO, thereby making it extremely difficult to operate in a safe manner. Additionally, the air conditioner has been/is non-operational after three (3) different service attempts by Motor Pool personnel.

SECRET

DETAINEES-2561

DOJFBI-003045

b6-1

	(IR) (FBI)

b7C-1

From: _____(Div13) (FBI)
Sent: Wednesday, MAY 05, 2004 8:50 AM
To: _____ (Div13)(FBI):_____ (Div13)(FBI) _____   b6
       _____ (Div13)(FBI): _____ (Div13)(FBI): _____ (Div13)(FBI): b7
       _____ (Div13)(FBI): _____ (Div13)(FBI)
Cc: _____ (Div13)(FBI): _____ (Div09)(FBI):
       _____ (IR) (FBI)
Subject: RE: Detainee abuse claims

<u>SENSITIVE BUT UNCLASSIFIED</u>
<u>NON-RECORD</u>

ALCON,
   Based on Rumsfeld's public statements, DoD is against hooding prisoners, threats of violence and techniques meant to humiliating detainees (there is a list of these I have seen). I know these techniques were approved at high levels w/in DoD and used on _____ and _____ Additionally, DoD portrayed b6
themselves as FBI agents in the same time frame these "interrogation tech- b7
niques" were employed on at least _____ An EC outlining these DoD tech-
niques was done by MLDU in November 2003 as to FBI's dissaproval to these DoD "interrogation techniques", regardless of whether they were approved by the Deputy Secretary Defense. DAD Harrington has also been interested in following up on this. The EC regarding _____ has not been uploaded and I provided AGC _____ with another copy of it when I left GTMO on March 30, 2004 so it could go thru the OGC chain. _____
where does that stand?

SSA _____   b6 -1
CTD/ORS/MLDU   b7C -1
JEH, Room 5382
_____ b2 -1

_____**Original Message**_____
From: _____(Div13) (FBI)
Sent: Wednesday, May 05, 2004 8:23 AM
To: _____(Div13) (FBI)_____(Div13) (FBI);
       _____(Div13)   b6
(FBI): _____(Div13) (FBI)_____(Div13)(FBI)   b7
       _____
_____(Div13) (FBI);_____(Div13) (FBI)

Subject: RE: Detainee abuse claims
Importance: High

We need to be very careful here. Everyone should pay particular attention to the distinctions between allegations of abuse and the use of techniques which fall outside of FBI/DOJ training and policy. As I stated in my email yesterday, I am not aware of any credible allegations of abuse by anyone in GTMO.

As it relates to ☐___☐ and ☐___☐ the techniques employed against them in the interrogation process were, based on numerous inquiries I made, in addition to my personal review of the DOD interrogation plans, approved by the Deputy Secretary of Defense.

9/26/2004   DETAINEES-2715

b6 -1
b7C -1

From:	
b6 -1	**To:**	
b7C -1	**Date:**	1/21/04 5:15PM
Subject:	Fwd: Re: Impersonating FBI

When I was in the unit in December, I thought we agreed to take everything out of the EC that doesn't specifically pertain to the "impersonation" issue. All of that other information (including our suggestion
b2 -3   that the detainee was threatened   is still in there, which I think is totally
b7E -1   inappropriate.

Regarding the "impersonation", I'm still not sure what our issue is here. It's fairly clear to me that the "FBI Agent" wasn't successful in gaining the detainees cooperation. Thereafter, (months later)
b2 -3   carried the day with his ruse regarding   Once again, this technique, and all of those
b7E -1   used in these scenarios, was approved by the Dep Sec Def Additionally, the techniques specifically
called into question in the EC were employed months after, and in a different environment from, the "FBI Agent" ruse.

I would request that Spike Bowman, or his designee, review this information and provide us with a definitive opinion before we make an issue of it

Thanks
b6 -1
b7C -1

CC: b6 -1
                                                       b7C -1

ALL INFORMATION CONTAINED
HEREIN IS UNCLASSIFIED
DATE: 12-03-2004 BY 61579DMH/BCE/gjg 04-CV-4151

DETAINEES-3832

DOJFBI-001923

A-176

SECRET UNCLASSIFIED

SECRETARY OF DEFENSE
1000 DEFENSE PENTAGON
WASHINGTON, DC 20301-1000

JAN 19 2002

MEMORANDUM FOR CHAIRMAN OF THE JOINT CHIEFS OF STAFF

SUBJECT: Status of Taliban and Al Qaida

(U) Transmit the following to the Combatant Commanders:

(S) The United States has determined that Al Qaida and Taliban individuals under the control of the Department of Defense are not entitled to prisoner of war status for purposes of the Geneva Conventions of 1949.

(U) The Combatant Commanders shall, in detaining Al Qaida and Taliban individuals under the control of the Department of Defense, treat them humanely and, to the extent appropriate and consistent with military necessity, in a manner consistent with the principles of the Geneva Conventions of 1949.

(U) The Combatant Commanders shall transmit this order to subordinate commanders, including Commander, Joint Task Force 160, for implementation.

(U) Keep me appropriately informed of the implementation of this order.

383σ

14 Jan 02

lassified by: SecDef
reason: 1.5(d)
Declassify on: 01/19/12

DECLASSIFIED ON 4 FEB 2002
PER DOD GENERAL COUNCIL MEMO
Please Notify All Recipients to downgrade this Memorandum to Unclassified

Page 1 of 1

all (b)(6)(4)

Chronology of Guard / Detainee Issues

Jan 5, 2002
- Detainee complains that guard hit him
- Detainee complains that guards are treating him roughly during transport
- 1615Z-0100Z Operations stop due to in-processing
- Observing medic (Rank PFC) struck detainee at approximately 2200 hours, during in-processing, he was kicked out of tent

Jan 6, 2002
- 0130Z-0200Z Operations stop due to drill
- Detainee complained that guards beat him
- 1145Z- Detainee #██████s requested- 1231Z ICE is informed that guards have lost the key to the section of the facility that the detainee was being held-1440Z ICE is informed that the guards have discovered the missing key, and operations resume
- 1600Z until 1700Z Operations stop due to In-processing run-through.

Jan 7, 2002
- Operations stop due to detainee head-count 0115Z until 0300Z.
- Detainees observed ignoring guards.
- 0815Z Operations stop due to re-organization of the facility, projected duration, 4 hours
- Reorganization last from 0815Z until 2000Z.

Jan 8, 2002
- Two detainees arrive at 0200Z. Interrogations continue, but no new guests are brought out for questioning. The two new detainees are in-processed.
- 0608Z requested detainee #████ hold up because guards lost key then they had to stop processing due to feeding. Still waiting for detainee #████ at 0709Z **(Lost keys seems to be an endemic problem for the guards. This is the 4th day in a row where processing was delayed due to lost keys.)**
- Stopped processing due to detainee feeding process 0700Z-0800Z
- Operations stop while MPs move detainees. Projected down time is one hour. Stoppage lasts from 1750Z until 1945Z.
- Detainee ██ arrived 06 JAN 01. No screening record on file. Only reference in ICE database states ██ speaks Pashtu. Name and nationality entered into Master In-Processing Database from Ops info

020550

DOD-043615

A-178

Jan 9, 2002
- At 1010 – 1050Z entire camp shut down due to reaction drill
- In-processing stoppage 1700 until 2130Z.
- In-processing stoppage 2335Z

Jan 10, 2002
- Resumed normal operations at 0500Z
- Requested detainee 323 at 0620Z. At 0723Z we discover that detainee (b)(6) 4 ██ is in the medical tent. It took the MP's one hour and 3 minutes to tell us the disposition of the detainee. **Are the MP's really that unaware of the disposition of their detainees?**
- It is taking upwards of one hour from the time the ICE requests a detainee to the time the detainee is in the booth for debriefing / screening
- (b)(6) 4 Detainee ██ has broken finger due to rough handling by the guards. Guard states that detainee was "giving them a hard time." (In cuffs and shackles "?"
- Took guards 1 hour to *locate* detainee number ███████ (b)(6) 4
- 30 minute delay in screening detainee ██ because guards would not (b)(6) 4 touch the piss bucket or pass it to the group inside the medical tent even though the guards were wearing gloves. Total waiting period was 1 hour.
- 1604 until 2000 stoppage due to reaction to contact. After stand-down MPs move detainees and eat until 2200. In-processing begins at 2300.
- 2330z ICE personnel notice that the JIF has been without lights since base stand-down, MPs on duty with SSG ████ NCOIC, took no initiative (b)(6) 2 to recognize the existence of a problem until ICE personnel brought it to their attention. Lights are turned on approximately 15 minutes later—SSG (b)(6) 2 ██████
- ICE OIC instructed SSG ██████ to inquire about the possibility of (b)(6) 2 conducting a minimal number of interrogations while in-processing was being conducted. He (██████ asked if this was possible and how many (b)(6) 2 MPs are required to run the JIF. After discussing the situation with SSG (b)(6) 2 ██████, JIF MP NCOIC, he stated it was impossible. Upon SSG ██████'s (b)(6) 2 departure SSG ███ used profanity and told him (██████ to leave his (b)(6) 2 area and stop telling him (██████ how to do his job. (b)(6) 2

Jan 11, 2002 (b)(6) 2 (b)(6) 2
- Detainee 374 had deep cut and swelling of right hand, cuts and bruises on face, cuts on ankles. Could not communicate due to language barrier he's around 70 years old, I doubt that he gave them much trouble.
- Night Shift began requesting detainees at approximately 1630. Average wait time for the MPs to bring detainees was at least 30 to 45 minutes. (b)(6) 2 SSG ██████ waited an hour and fifteen minutes for detainee ██████ (b)(6) 4
- 2245Z MPs shut down JIF for incoming detainees. 2335Z ICE is informed detainees will not arrive until 0200Z.

020551

Jan 12, 2002
- Stoppage for incoming detainees 0142Z.
- In-processing begins at 0220Z
- Detainee feeding time-1850 until 1950
- 1950Z—MPs begin contraband search in compound because MREs were not properly broken down. Operations resume at 2330Z.

Jan 13, 2002
- Stoppage 1856Z-Detainee feeding time. MPs shutdown JIF to handle problem inside Det. Operations resume at 2200Z.

Jan 14, 2002   (b)(6)4
- 0715Z, MPs are MIA while retrieving #▆▆, fifty-seven minutes later, source arrives for questioning.

Jan 15, 2002
- Stoppage 0005—MPs shutdown to prep for second incoming group of detainees.
(b)(6)4 - MPs could not locate Detainee ▆▆ after one hour of waiting.
- ▆▆ complains of guards "beating" him during screening.
- Operations resume 0300Z.
- Took MP's 20 minutes to find handcuff key for detainee's cuffs
- 0850Z- Operations reduced to one escort team due to out-processing

Jan 16, 2002
- Special guest in booth 4 requested special device in which to defecate. MP's could not accommodate his request
- ICE is informed the MPs will be conducting 3 exercises throughout the night within the DET. The lights will be turned off for approximately 15 to 20 minutes per exercise and the JIF will be locked down.
- 2145Z-JIF is shut down until 0140Z for exercise and detainee movement.

Jan 17, 2002
- 0710Z- 0729Z Operations halted due to MP support of out-processing
- MP stoppage, 1730Z to move prisoners. Operations resume at 1853Z

Jan 18, 2002
- After MP dayshift leaves the JIF nightshift does not show up for 15 to 20 minutes leaving the JIF unguarded. ▆▆▆▆   (b)(6)2
- 1630Z JIF stoppage for incoming bird. MPs will only run one room until the bird lands. COC informs ICE that once the bird lands that one interrogation would have to stop.
- 1920Z –2030Z MPs feeding prisoners.

020552

DOD-043617

Jan 19, 2002
- 1830Z MPs feeding prisoners, estimate shut down time to be one hour.

Jan 20, 2002
- In-processing from 2005 until 2355.

Jan 21, 2002
- MP shift change stoppage 25 minutes
- At 0530 can only run 4 booths due to MPs sick and one MP on offsite mission
- MP# ███ states that he was roughly treated and beaten by guards during in-processing (Remington)
- MP# ███ was unhurt during in-processing, picture shows no physical damage, upon screening the next day, detainee says he was beaten by the guards, another picture was taken which shows some physical damage
- MP # ███ complains of abuse by guards. After in-processing in the isolation cage an unidentified guard hit ███ with the butt of his or her weapon. Detainee was wearing a hood and could not provide any further information. Detainee head was swollen on the top left side. –

$b (b) (2)$

(b)(6)4

███

Jan 22, 2002

- 0500Z MPs dedicated to the JIF are tasked to count blankets and water, operations are halted
- 2005Z - Operations stopped by MPs at JIF, MPs discover detainees building sand tables and possibly plotting to escape. Reported by ███ (b)(6)2

Jan 24, 2002
- Ceased screening / interrogation operations 0010 – 0450Z due to in-processing. MP's fed detainees from 0500 – 0630Z thereby continuing the work stoppage.
- Approximately 0700Z the MPs misplace the keys to the cages and operation are halted for 10 minutes
- Waited 42 minutes for detainee # ███ from 0925 – 1008 (b)(6)4
- Stopped Screening/ Interrogation operations 1158Z due to in-processing operations.

Jan 26, 2002
(b)(2)3
- Ceased screening/interrogation operations from ███ ue to MP shift change and detainee meal break.
- In-processing begins at 1700. Operations resume at 1800.

020553

DOD-043618

Jan 27, 2002
- 0100 stoppage for feeding of prisoners
- 0600 – 0700Z could only conduct 2 interrogations due to lack of MP guards / escorts

Jan 28, 2002
- 272200ZJAN02 until 280030ZJAN02 In-processing
- MP stoppage 0240Z until 0310.
- MP stoppage from 0400Z - ? due to detainee movement and shake-down
- We arranged with day shift MP's to keep detainee # ▇ in JIF booth (b)(6)4 number 1 on sleep dep beginning 271507ZJAN02. When we came into work on 28 Jan, there were no detainees in the JIF
- There is a new procedures were instituted by the MP night shift for collecting detainees which greatly increases the time it takes to start screenings / interrogations. This is the cycle: ICE calls our rep in the JIF, the rep calls the MP TOC who contacts the MP COC who in turn contacts the JIF MP rep (*who has been sitting next to our rep the entire time*) then the JIF MP rep assigns escorts to fetch the detainee. **Thank you night shift MP OIC/NCOIC.**
- 2000-Stoppage for detainee feeding one hour.

Jan 29, 2002
- 0130-Stoppage for detainee movement. Approximate down-time will be one hour
- Could only operate 4 booths due to lack of MP guards

Jan 30, 2002
- It took nearly 40 minutes from the time we requested detainee # ▇ until (b)(6)4 the time we received him at 0535Z ▇▇▇ (b)(6) 2
- MP guard refused to take the handcuffs off detainee when the interrogator requested it. They think the JIF and detainees in the JIF are property of the MP's even when we are conducting interrogations. MP was dayshift JIF escort NCOIC SSG ▇▇▇ (b)(6) 2
- Able to operate 5 booths at 30 0810Z JAN02
- (b)(6)4 Guard refused to provide interrogation incentive item (additional blanket) to MP# ▇ UBL Drvr to aid in interrogator's rapport building strategy (MP was dayshift JIF escort NCOIC ▇▇▇ (b)(6) 2

Jan 31, 2002
- Operations ceased due to prisoner movement 0250Z – 0500Z

Feb 1, 2002 — (b)(6) 2   (b)(6) 4
- PFC ▇ and SPC ▇ question MP# ▇ notice multiple cuts, bruises, and abrasions on detainees face; detainee complains of

020554

severe headache, and sore ribs. (See picture/statement in Detainee File.)

- 0625Z operations are halted due to shift change and MP escorts working with the doctors in the facility.
- MP SPC ██████ did not loosen ankle cuffs when asked to do so, (b)(6) 2 stating they were not tight. When requested once again, SPC █████ (b)(6) 2 used unnecessary and excessive force with detainee # ██ pulling his (b)(6) 4 feet out from under him by the ankle chains, stepping on his thigh while loosening the cuffs then kicking him in the feet when finished. Later, the MP NCOIC, SSG ███████, barged into the booth, where detainee (b)(6) 2 (b)(6)4 # ██ was being interviewed by the FBI and CID with an MI Interpreter, demanding to know the problem. Detainee asked not to make a fuss over the treatment for fear of further mistreatment .
- In-processing begins at 2200 and ends at 0100.
(b)(6) 4 • Detainee ██ complains that he has not seen the doctor for the last two days. COC is informed that ██ wishes to see medical for frostbite injuries to his foot.   (b)(6) 4

Feb 2, 2002
- 0430, 15 minute delay due to bathing time.
- 1025Z – 1055Z guards unavailable to escort detainees due to their lunch break
- 1900Z-MP inform ICE they can only support three rooms at the JIF. MP NCOIC will attempt to reallocate personnel to support more rooms.

Feb 4, 2002   (b)(6)4
- MP# ██ states that when he was praying the guards asked him a question and when he did not answer, because he was praying, he was punished with physical training. (CPL ██████████ (b)(6) 2

Feb 5, 2002   (b)(6)4
- Detainee ██ still has not seen the doctor for frostbite injuries. MPs stated that they have no record of ██'s request to see the doctor, COC is informed again.   (b)(6)4
- SPC (female medic) is unprofessional and bordering on disrespectful to an officer (interpreter) during medical rounds (LT ██). She is not responsive to detainee needs and appears callous   (b)(6) 2
(b)(6)4 • Detainee ██ complains that the guards interrupted him while praying to bring him to the JIF.

Feb 6, 2002
- Night shift is informed upon arrival to the JIF that the MPs can support a *staggering* 5 booths…. Something is amiss….

020555

DOD-043620

A-183

Feb 7, 2002
- Inprocessing begins at 2145.

Feb 13, 2002
- At 1300Z MP's have enough guards to support only 3 booths
-

020556

ARMED FORCES REGIONAL MEDICAL EXAMINER

LANDSTUHL REGIONAL MEDICAL CENTER
TEL. NO. DSN 486-7492
FAX DSN 486-7502
CIV. 011(49)6371-86-7492
A02-93

FINAL REPORT OF POSTMORTEM EXAMINATION

DATE OF BIRTH:
DATE OF DEATH: 3 December 2002
DATE OF AUTOPSY: 6-8 December 2002
INVESTIGATIVE AGENCY: USACIDC, SSI #
                       0134-02-CID369-23533-5H9B

I. CIRCUMSTANCES OF DEATH: The decedent is a 27-28 year old Pashtun male, who was found unresponsive, restrained in his cell, Bagram Collection Point (BCP), 0015, 4 December 2002. He was dead on arrival at the 339th CSH, Bagram Air Field, Afganistan.

II. AUTHORIZATION: Armed Forces Medical Examiner under Title 10 U.S. Code, Section 1471.

III. IDENTIFICATION: Visual recognition; postmortem dental examination performed; fingerprints and specimens for DNA obtained.

IV. ANATOMIC FINDINGS:
   a. Pulmonary embolism (saddle).
   b. Mild pulmonary congestion and edema; diffuse anthracosis:
   c. Mild chronic passive congestion (agonal change).
   d. Multiple blunt force injuries:
      (1) Head and neck injuries.
         (a) Contusions and abrasions (remote), face & head.
         (b) Linear abraded contusions (3), right neck.
      (2) Torso injuries:
         (a) Abrasions and contusions (non-specific).
         (b) Curvilinear abraded contusions (patterned, left upper abdomen and flank).
         (c) Linear vertical abrasions (brush burn), bilateral back.
      (3) Extremity injuries:
         (a) Abrasions and contusions (non-specific), bilateral arms.
         (b) Linear abrasions and contusions (patterned), bilateral forearms and wrists.
         (c) Elongated contusions, bilateral anterior medial upper thighs (recent).

(d) Contusion, left knee (recent).

(e) Deep contusions with intramuscular hemorrhage and necro-sis (left greater than right), bilateral posterior calves and knees (recent).

(f) Associated patterned abrasions, posterior left calf (recent).

V. TOXICOLOGY: Negative.

VI. CAUSE OF DEATH: Pulmonary embolism due to blunt force injuries.

VII. MANNER OF DEATH: Homicide.

VIII. OPINION: Based on these autopsy findings and the investigative and historical information available to me, the cause of death of this Pashtun male, (b)(6)-4 is pulmonary embolism (blood clot that traveled to the heart and blocked the flow of blood to the lungs). The patterned abrasion on the back of the left calf is consis-tent with the treat of a boot. The severe injury to the underlying calf muscle and soft tissue is most likely a contributing factor. The deceased was not under the pharmacologic effects of drugs or alco-hol at the time of death. Therefore, the manner of death, in my opinion is homicide.

(b)(6)-2

LTC (P), MC, USA
Armed Forces Regional Medical Examiner

HISTORY & PHYSICAL EXAMINATION (SF 504, SF 505, & SF 506)	OPERATION REPORT (SF 516)	NAME	(b)(6)=4	
CONSULTATION SHEET (SF 513)	NARRATIVE SUMMARY (SF 502)	REGISTER NO. PASHTUN, AFGHANISTAN		SSN
CHRON RECORD OF MEDICAL CARE (SF 600)	AUTOPSY PROTOCOL (SF 503)	UNIT	(b)(3)=1	
PROGRESS NOTE (SF 509)		DATE DICT 8 DECEMBER 2002		DATE TYPED 13 JANUARY 2003

MEDICAL RECORD REPORT

OPTIONAL FORM 275 (12-77)
Prescribed by GSA and 1 CMR
FIRMR (41 CFR) 201-45.505
USAPPCV1.00

ARMED FORCES INSTITUTE OF PATHOLOGY
Office of the Armed Forces Medical Examiner
1413 Research Blvd., Bldg. 102
Rockville, MD 20850
1-800-944-7912

Landstuhl Regional Medical Center
Landstuhl, Germany, APO AE 09180
DSN 486-7492
CIV 011 (49) 6371-86-7492

AUTOPSY EXAMINATION REPORT

Name: [(b)(6)-4]

SSAN:

Date of Birth: Unknown, age approx. 35 yrs.
Date/Time of Death: 10 Dec 2002/0200z

Date/Time of Autopsy: 13 Dec 2002/1000
Date of Report: 25 Feb 2003

Autopsy No.: A02-95 (Landstuhl
R.M.C. Autopsy Number)
AFIP No.: 2859183
Rank: Civilian, Afghani national
Place of Death: Bagram Collection
Point, Bagram Air Field, Afghanistan
Place of Autopsy: Bagram Air Field
Afghanistan

Circumstances of Death: Approximately 35 year old Afghan male detainee who was found unresponsive restrained in his cell in the Bagram Collection Point, and pronounced dead on arrival at the 339th CSH, Bagram Air Field, Afghanistan.

Authorization for Autopsy: The Armed Forces Medical Examiner, IAW 10 USC 1471.

Identification: Visual; Post mortem dental examination performed; Fingerprints and DNA specimen obtained.

CAUSE OF DEATH: Blunt force injuries to lower extremities complicating coronary artery disease

MANNER OF DEATH: Homicide

FINAL AUTOPSY DIAGNOSES:

I. Blunt force injuries to bilateral lower extremities with rhabdomyolysis
   a. Extensive soft tissue hemorrhage with muscle necrosis
      i. Involving bilateral legs, extending from upper thighs to upper calves and bilateral inguinal regions
      ii. Nearly circumferential muscle damage, from subcutis to level of periosteum of femurs
      iii. Histologically, extensive muscle destruction with necrosis

MEDCOM - 29

DOD 003156

(b)(6)-4

1.3 cm; interventricular septum thickness 1.2 cm; right ventricle thickness 0.4 cm; grossly unremarkable myocardium; myocardial sections demonstrate no significant histopathologic changes.

Coronary arteries: Normal ostia; right dominant circulation; focal moderate-to-severe atherosclerosis; remaining gross arteries demonstrate 35% lumen area narrowing of the left main and 25% lumen area narrowing of the proximal left anterior descending; submitted histologic sections demonstrate 70% lumen area narrowing of the proximal left anterior descending."

OPINION: This approximately 35-year-old Afghan male detainee died of blunt force injuries to the lower extremities, complicating underlying coronary artery disease. The blunt force injuries to the legs resulted in extensive muscle damage, muscle necrosis, and rhabomyolysis. Electrolyte disturbances, primarily hyperkalemia (elevated blood potassium level) and metabolic acidosis can occur within hours of muscle damage. Massive sodium and water shifts occur, resulting in hypovolemic shock and vasodilatation, and later, acute renal failure. The decedent's underlying coronary artery disease would compromise his ability to tolerate the electrolyte and fluid abnormalities, and his underlying malnutrition and likely dehydration would further exacerbate the effects of the muscle damage. The manner of death is homicide.

(b)(6)-2

MAJ, USAF, MC, FS
Assistant Medical Examiner

(b)(6)-2

LTC, MC, USA
Regional Medical Examiner

SWORN STATEMENT

For use of this form, see AR 190–45; the proponent agency is ODCSOPS

PRIVACY ACT STATEMENT

AUTHORITY: Title 10 USC Section 301; Title 5 USC Section 2951; E.O. 9397 dated November 22, 1943 *(SSN)*.

PRINCIPAL PURPOSE: To provide commanders and law enforcement officials with means by which information may be accurately identified.

ROUTINE USES: Your social security number is used as an additional/alternate means of identification to facilitate filing and retrieval.

DISCLOSURE: Disclosure of your social security number is voluntary.

1. LOCATION Metro Park Springfield, VA	2. DATE(*YYYYM-MDD*) 2004/05/21 ███	3. TIME 1 9 4 5 ███	4. FILE NUMBER
5. LAST NAME, FIRST NAME, MIDDLE NAME ███	6. SSN ███		7. GRADE/STATUS CPT

8. ORGANIZATION OR ADDRESS
A/304TH Military Intelligence Battalion, Fort Huachuca, AZ

9. ███ WANT TO MAKE THE FOLLOWING STATEMENT UNDER OATH:

I have been assigned to the 519th Military Intelligence (MI) Battalion (BN) since 01 MAY 2000. I deployed to Afghanistan for six months with A Company, 519th MI BN on 20 Jul 02. I served as the Operations Officer of interrogation operations at a facility in Bagram until I redeployed on 28 Jan 03. I then deployed to Kuwait on 12 Mar 04, with HHS, 519th MI BN where I served as the Battle Captain/Assistant S-3. I crossed into Iraq on 4 Apr 04, first arriving at LSA Bushmaster, to conduct initial coordination with the 720th Military Police (MP) Battalion who was establishing a detainee facility or "cage". I remained at Bushmaster for approximately 12 days. I then moved forward to LSA Dogwood, where the 720th MP BN established a second cage, and I remained there for 10 days to two weeks at the end of Apr 03. I moved to Camp Speicher (North Tikrit) where the 519th MI BN established its Headquarters. From early May to early June, I served as the 519th MI Bn Liaison Officer to the 4th ID for Tactical Humint Operations. During the June timeframe, I served at the Camp Cropper detention facility as the Senior Intelligence Officer and battalion level representative for the

519th. In early July, I returned to Camp Speicher as a Battle Captain, and it was shortly after returning to Speicher that the 519th received the Warning Order to establish interrogation operations at Abu Ghraib (AG) in support of the upcoming operation Victory Bounty. On or about 23 Jul 03, I was a member of the 519th MI Bn site survey team to conduct an assessment of the AG facility and then returned to Camp Speicher. Due to the overwhelming requests for updates, ███████████ requested additional higher level assistance from the 519th MI Bn so that he could focus on his company command duties and to provide much necessary life support. I arrived at AG on 4 August, and my position was as the Interrogation OIC responsible for supervising the interrogation operations and personnel. I was responsible for screening, interrogations, and reporting of intelligence information. I departed Iraq on 4 Dec 03 on "Rest and Relaxation" leave and unexpectedly received redeployment orders while on leave. I returned to Kuwait to out-process on 24 December 2003 and departed Kuwait 25 December en-route to Fort Bragg. I never returned to AG. While at Camp Cropper, I had various conversations with my two warrant officers, ███████████ interrogation ops, and ███████████ the Operations Officer. All were frustrated with the overcrowded conditions at the Cropper detention facility. For example, the facility was intended to house approximately 200 detainees, and there were anywhere from 700 to 1,000 detainees. Many of the detainees were brought to Cropper for minor infractions, and most of the detainees were "low value detainees". Several detainees were what was referred to as "50 meters detainees", because they had been in the general vicinity of the target of a US raid and had been picked up essentially for being in close proximity. The "low value detainees" did not warrant long term interrogation effort or retention, and Cropper lacked facilities for proper interrogation operations. The conditions were similar at the facilities at Bushmaster and Dogwood. Bushmaster and Dogwood did not have sufficient logistical support—for example there were no tents for detainees and water was rationed. Cropper, however, had tents, which were routinely overcrowded ███████████ voiced his concerns with the overpopulation and the disgruntled mood of the detainees with no response. He published an Information Intelligence Report (IIR) in an effort to alert leadership of the situation and the problems within the facility. I am prior enlisted and served for ten years as an Interrogator/HUMINT Collector (MOS 97E) and am qualified as a "Strategic Debriefer". As a Commissioned Officer. I have served in various positions involving tactical HUMINT Collection Operations. I served as a Tactical HUMINT Team (THT) Leader in Bosni-Herzegovinia for six months (SFOR-8), as an Analysis and Control Team (ACT) leader in Bosnia (SFOR 9), and as an Interrogation operations officer in Afghanistan with the 519th MI BN for six months. I consider myself very knowledgeable of Interrogation Operations and techniques. With the exception of what I discuss below, during my time in Iraq, I never witnessed any interrogation methods or operations that were outside normal procedures and observed nothing contrary to Army Field Manuals, Regulations, Doctrine, or the established curriculum presented at the 97E MOS producing school at the US Army Intelligence Center and School at Fort Huachuca, AZ. The interrogation environment in Iraq was challenging because the current US Army interrogation training and doctrine is rooted in and geared toward a conventional, cold war threat and not toward the Arab mindset. When I arrived at AG, there were approximately 50 to 150 inmates being held on criminal offenses. The 72nd MP Company was manning AG and was significantly undermanned and under resourced. The 519th received the mission for AG in late July, when AG was designated as the detention facility for individuals detained during Operation VICTORY BOUNTY (OVB). OVB was a nation-wide sweep to pick up approximately 1,80█████████ and the 320th MP Battalion started operations there about the same time. While the military constructed a mass holding area (Holding area GANCI), the Coalition Provisional Authority (CPA) was simultaneously renovating the hard-site within AG prison. There was no suitable location to establish an interrogation facility and operations area. The 519th established the interrogation and administrative area in the vicinity of Holding Area VIGILANT, using a ARFABs, DRASH tents. The 205th MI BDE coordinated with the CPA to utilize 10 cells of cell block "1A". As a result of the renovation effort, Iraqi National workers employed for the CPA sponsored renovations utilized the courtyard immediately next to cell block 1A as a center of gravity for their welding and construction operation. The 519th initially used the outside portions of AG, not the hard site, due to the ongoing renovation project. The 205th MI BDE, specifically ████████ COL PAPPAS, █████████████████████████ were Bde battle captains and constantly requested updates, kept pressuring the 519th to utilized the hard-site, but the site was not acceptable for use until about three weeks after our arrival (3rd week in Aug 03) because of the following reasons: the proximity of the construction workers could allow communication with detainees, insufficient numbers of MPs to guard detainees housed in the area, the MPs did not have locks, and the wing did not have electricity or running water. Camp Ganci was constructed within the confines of AG as an outside, main holding facility intended to hold up to 4000 "criminal detainees". Camp Vigilant was an outside facility intended to house general population of "security detainees". Although AG had been designated as the repository of the OVB detainees, we received only approximately 180 OVB detainees. Of those, approximately 62 were on the original list of 1,800, and only about 20 provided information, and that information was not particularly "actionable intelligence". About two weeks into OVB, AG started receiving "security detainees" from operations other than OVB and mission creep began as AG started becoming a general security detainee facility and eventually became the central, consolidated detention facility. I did not believe AG was the best place to use as a central facility, and during a meeting focused on

consolidating assets on at AG in late Aug 03 with ███████████████
███████████████████████████████ (Co Cdr, 325th MI Bn), and
███████████████████████ (325th MI Bn Commander), I voiced
concerns about the defensibility of the facility, man-power shortage,
location, and the stigma attached to AG. On or about 2 Sep 03, MG
Miller and representatives from the joint Task Force (JTF) at Guantanamo
Bay (GTMO), Cuba, arrived at AG. It appeared that LTG Sanchez was
not satisfied with the amount of actionable intelligence resulting from
the interrogation operations at AG, and he had requested MG Miller
review and assess the AG operations and provide recommendations
learned from the detention facility at JTF-GTMO. I had discussions
with MG Miller on a couple of occasions and these conversations centered on renovations and improvements of the facilities, challenges of
interrogation operations, and the need for increased MP/MI cooperation. Specifically, I recall he discussed the implementation of dedicated
MP support to MI. The purpose of dedicated MP support, for example,
was to transport detainees to the designated interrogation booth, observe
detainees while in holding and provide feedback to the interrogators.
I never discussed specific methods or techniques with MG MILLER.
The JTF-GTMO focus was more strategic than the tactical screening
and operational environment of Iraq, and I believed the JTF-GTMO
model could not be replicated in the Iraqi environment and experience.
Although I attempted to express the concept, I do not know if MG
MILLER understood my position and he appeared to press forward with
his JTF-GTMO recommendations. I recommended a central facility
could be constructed at Camp Speicher rather than AG, however
I understood the reason behind the decision was an immediate demand
for a facility. I never saw the final Miller Report, nor ███████████
received any direct feedback as a result of the visit. The only feedback I
saw was from the 205th following the recommendations from MG
MILLER's visit. I do believe that the Miller visit propelled AG to become
a "mini-mo". Shortly after MG MILLER departed AG, ██████████
arrived at AG on approximately 10 September, approximately the same
time as the 325th MI Bn personnel. He was the Senior Intelligence Officer (SIO) to AG. I believe ████████████ role was to be the 205th representative at AG, provide guidance, and implement a mandate from COL
PAPPAS and ██████████ to replicate the JTF-GTMO model in the
form of the Joint Detention and Interrogation Center (JDIC) at AG,
beginning with the introduction of the Tiger Team interrogation concept and strategic level collection (knowledgeability briefs, for example).
Prior to ████████ arrival, I had one chief warrant officer and approximately 12 active duty HUMINT collectors (97E, 97B), an analyst and
a Trojan communications team working for me. I continued to send
operational reporting through the 519th MI Bn Tactical Humint Operations (THOPS) to the 205th MI Bn and COL PAPPAS. It was at this
time (10 September) that the interrogator personnel from the 325th
MI began arriving and the process of merging the 519th and 325th

MI assets began. The 325th initially sent five "Tiger Teams", with one interrogator and one analyst per team. Because I needed leaders for the new arrivals, I pulled one NCO from the five teams to act as a section leader. To facilitate the integration of the 519th and 325th, I then broke up the original teams and merged the personnel of the two units. As the 519th did not have analytical assets, the reorganization benefited the collection mission. The resulting structure was four sections with an NCO in change of each, and at least one analyst per section. This organization did not follow the "GTMO Model" and I receive pressure from the 205th leadership to maintain an interrogator/analyst structure. I believe the structure implemented (two collectors per team and analytical support to the entire section) was more efficient and effective for our operational working environment and available manning. After the close of Cropper (approximately 5–7 days later), the 325th provided additional personnel who became the Operations section. ███████████ arrived at AG on or about 15 Sep 03 and I understood him to be the "new boss". His original title was "Chief of JDIC," but he stated that he did not like the title and changed it to "Director of JDIC". I understood that ██████████ was in charge of the JDIC at AG. ██████████ was fairly uninvolved with interrogation operations within AG and never provided interrogation guidance, Standard Operating Procedures (SOPs), or directives, probably because he was not overly familiar with interrogation operations. At the end of Sep 03 (I do not recall the exact date), the first of the CACI contracted civilian interrogators ████████████████████████████████ arrived. Although I had been told to eventually expect contract augmentees, the three CACI contractors arrived out of the blue. I never received official guidance or perimeters from higher as to how to employ them. I briefly interviewed each contractor, provided in-brief information, and standards of conduct and interrogation rules of engagement and paired them up with a military interrogator since I knew my soldiers capabilities but did not know that of the contractors. At this time I created a three to four page initial counseling statement which each contractor signed. The statement essentially covered the standards of conduct, performance expectations, informed them of the military chain of command and to whom to report any incidents, operational security awareness. About five days later, seven more CACI contractors arrived, and then one's and two's arrived periodically over the next couple of months. I presented each CACI contractor with a new arrival briefing and had each sign an initial counseling statement and acknowledge his understanding of the operation and IROE ████████████████ a contractor who arrived in the second group of seven ██████████ contractors, was the CACI "site manager" at AG, and became my POC for CACI issues and personnel. I relied heavily on ██████████ to manage the CACI personnel and I did not personally interview each contractor individually and knew very little about their qualifications, trusting that higher echelons had validated their qualifications. Most contractors had prior military or police experience.

I basically would rely on ▆▆▆▆▆▆▆ my military section chief, ▆▆▆▆▆▆▆▆ feedback from section leaders and interrogations to judge a contactor's abilities and qualifications. I had only one performance issue with a CACI analyst ▆▆▆▆▆▆▆▆ the analyst continually interjected and attempted to dominate the interrogation. I discussed this issue with ▆▆▆▆▆▆ and the analyst was relocated to another section within the JIDC. ▆▆▆▆▆ 323rd MI Bn (I believe his original unit is within the Utah National Guard), arrived approximately 30 Sep (very unsure of the date, after the mortar attack on 20 Sep and about the same time we began using the hardsite room for interrogation operations) after ▆▆▆▆▆ and ▆▆▆▆▆▆▆ had arrived. He had been the OIC/SIO at Camp Bucca. When Camp Bucca closed its collection mission, the 205th brought 323rd asserts to AG as part of the centralization process. The majority of 323rd personnel became the Command and Control/staff/headquarters element and were not used in interrogation operations. ▆▆▆▆▆ 323rd MI, became the screening OIC and ▆▆▆▆▆ became the CM&D NCOIC. ▆▆▆▆▆ (originally from the 141st MI, Utah National Guard) attached to the 323rd MI BN, became the Headquarters Commander. ▆▆▆▆▆ became the Operations Officer and I worked closely with him. ▆▆▆▆▆ and ▆▆▆▆▆ worked closely together. I took most guidance from ▆▆▆▆▆ who provided oversight to the interrogation operation. During this time period, COL PAPPAS's visits increased from visiting every week or two, to 2–3 visits a week, to occasional overnighting, until late mid Nov mid he moved out to AG. At the beginning of Nov 03, LTG SANCHEZ and MG FAST visited AG for a briefing and to assess the situation. This was the second visit to AG LTG Sanchez made following the 20 Sep mortar attack. The first was on approximately 30 September, when LTG Sanchez's focus was primarily the force protection and defensive posture of AG. LTG Sanchez toured the entire facility, to include a short brief on interrogation operations, which took place in the building recently aquired for use by the JIDC. LTG Sanchez expressed concern about the interrogation operation to COL PAPPAS and indicated that the issue would be further discussed "later". Shortly after the second visit in November, LTG SANCHEZ issued a FRAGO on 19 Nov 03, which appointed COL PAPPAS as the FOB Commander, giving him responsibility for all assigned at AG. In discussion with COL PAPPAS, it was my opinion that this was not a good situation and that there should remain a clear delineation between MI and MP, and that COL PAPPAS should recommend against the appointment. I believed that MI should not become involved in detainee or prison operations. As a result of the OPORD, my understanding was that COL PAPPAS would take control of AG security and force protection, but not "warden responsibilities". After the OPORD, COL PAPPAS assigned AG Force Protection responsibility to ▆▆▆▆▆ 165th MI BN Commander. ▆▆▆▆▆ was a good choice because of his tactical knowledge, and he brought in fragments of the 165th Long Range Surveillance (LRS)

Company to provide a more robust force protection posture and guidance than the MP could provide. The MPs had had many breaches of security and poor installation access control, and frequently allowed private vehicles and taxis on the base without escort. The FRAGO generated tension between MI and the MPs. The MP chain of command pulled the MP detail dedicated to MI for transportation of detainees between their holding area and the interrogation booths. By this time, Camp Vigilant and the hard site (Block 1A and 1B) were overcrowded, so security ████████████ detainees and MI Holds were put in to Camp Ganci and thus scattered throughout all three AG sites. By the time of my departure, the AG population had swollen to about 6,500, and locating and rounding up detainees for interrogation became problematic. With the pulling of the MP detail, the interrogators had to track down and transport the detainees themselves, wasting a considerable amount of valuable time. The MPs also pulled the MP overwatch from the interrogations, putting the interrogators at greater risk. For clarification purposes, a "Security Detainee" was an individual perceived to be a threat to Coalition Force, i.e. detained for weapons possessions, IED involvement, etc. An "MI Hold" is anyone of interest to MI and can include a Security Detainee. This category would also include Al Qaeda types, individuals possessing information regarding foreign fighters, infiltration methods, or pending attacks on Coalition Forces. A "Criminal Detainee" is, as the name indicates, an individual simply involved in criminal activities unrelated to Coalition Forces. All three groups were treated equally. Our interrogation approaches and selected techniques were driven by the individuals circumstances of capture and placement/access, and not determined by their status as one of these categories. The "hard site" consisted of Cell Block "1A" and "1B" as two man cells, and several other wings which were utilized as they became available, which were 4 or 8 man cells. The hard site, like the rest of AG, was under MP control. MI had no say so or influence over inmates or activities in Cell Block 1B, which primarily housed criminal female and juvenile inmates or any of the 4/8 man cell wings. Cell Block "1A" was primarily designated as the holding area for "Security Detainees" and "MI Holds". While the MPs controlled "1A", MI requested and had influence over who would be placed and housed in "1A". "1A" consisted of 40 cells, situated on two levels, with twenty cells on either side of a central corridor. Each cell had two bunks, but efforts were made to have only one detainee at a time in each cell. No detainee could be kept in "1A" longer than 30 days without LTG Sanchez approving an extension. If I, or one of my interrogators, wanted a detainee to remain in "1A" longer than 30 days, the interrogator would write up a justification and request, forwarded from the section leader to myself, which I would forward up through the 205th MI BN for LTG Sanchez's approval. We maintained an electronic dossier folder on each detainee of MI interest, and I placed the approval request and final approval documents in the affected detainee's e-file. The final signed copies were placed in the detainee's paper dossier. Although "1A" was primarily designated as an MI holding area, on occasion, the MPs placed other detainees in "1A". These might include unruly or "problem" detainees and detainees of interest to CID or OGA. However, "1A" was never so crowded that we could not get a cell for an MI detainee. I did not, nor did any other MI personnel to my knowledge, track non-MI detainees for status or release after 30 days, as they were not my responsibility. The MPs were the "inn keepers", specifically an MB ███████████ We began interrogation operations at AG using accepted Field Manual 34-52 norms and techniques. We were moving from a tactical to an operational or insurgent environment and it increasingly felt to me like my experience in Afghanistan. I did not want my folks to loose sight of their boundaries and their left and right limits. I saw the situation moving to the "Bagram" model. Pressures were increasing from overpopulation, the mission creep from bona fide Security Detainees to others who probably really didn't need to be detained for a long period, and the realization that Iraq was evolving into a long standing mission. I increasing felt the need to draw on my experience in Afghanistan. We had used "sleep adjustment" and "stress positions" as effective techniques in Afghanistan. Although I never saw written authorization, the techniques had SJA and CJTF-180 C-2X/C2 review and approval on a case by case basis. Because we had used the techniques in Afghanistan, and I perceived the Iraq experience to be evolving into the same ███████████ operational environment as Afghanistan, I used my best judgment and concluded they would be effective tools for interrogation operations at AG. Because the winds of war were changing, and the mounting pressure from higher for "actionable intelligence" from interrogation operations, I requested more options that FM 34-52 provided. ███████████ acquired a copy of TF-121 IROE and essentially "plagiarized" it, changing the letterhead on the MFR, incorporating some general editing, and then submitted the IROE MFR for approval through the 519th MI BN to the 205th MI BDE for approval. ███████████ never received a response. Shortly after my arrival, I resent the IROE MFR request to the 205th, cc'd the 519th MI Bn. I received no response and again sent out the document to the CJTF-7 C-2X shop. I discussed the issue with ███████████ at the C-2 shop, and he opined that the approval should be sent up through command channels rather than intelligence channels. While the MFR was being staffed, we continued to use FM-34-52 procedures, as well as sleep management and stress positions from our experience in Afghanistan, as I believed these to be reasonable, given the similarity of the situations. However, at AG, sleep management was requested only a few times, and it never exceeded the limit of 72 hours. Stress positions were used a little more frequently, but always in a very controlled manner. All usages of these techniques were documented in Interrogation Plans. Due to the fact the interrogations were conducted in open tents, anyone could observe the actions conducted therein. Concerning administration of the sleep management prior to the actual interrogation, the MPs implemented the procedure.

The MPs would keep the detainees awake by saying "stand up" or "wake up". I did not, nor did any MI personnel to my knowledge, have a conversation or provide written instruction to the MPs as to how to exactly implement the procedure. No MP ever inquired of me as to how the procedure should be implemented. Concerning the administration of stress positions, interrogators could not utilize a stress positions for more than a total of 45 minutes within a given four hour period (meaning the total time a detainee could be in any stress position could not exceed 45 minutes. That did not mean one position could be held for 45 minutes, then move to another position for another 45 minutes.) The time keeping was the responsibility of the two interrogators in the booth, so I can not say for certain that these limitations were not exceeded. However, I never received any reports of excessive use of the technique. The next milestone in the effort to have the IROE approved. On or about 25 Aug 03, two Coalition lawyers ███████████████████████ (Australia) (I am not 100% sure of the US SJA rep's name.), came to AG as a result of providing the IROE draft to ███████████ and requesting assistance and feedback. They came to AG to review operations. The lawyers informed me that my IROE MFR seemed to be within legal purview and authority, and the Australian lawyer even commented that the techniques were rather soft. They indicated the IROE MFR would be pushed higher for CJTF-7 review. The Miller Tiger Team arrived at AG on 2 Sep 03, and remained at AG for three to four full days. On the second day, I participated in a meeting with several members of the Miller Team, COL PAPPAS, and maybe ███████████ It was during that meeting that the Team had a copy of my IROE MFR and someone from the team stated that it was a "good start", but that CJTF-7 should consider something along the lines of what's approved for use in CJTF-170, although no specific tools or techniques were discussed. Shortly thereafter, on 10 Sep 03, the CJTF-7 MFR providing IROE (possibly the result of my MFR and the CJTF-170 approved IROE) was signed. I do not recall seeing a copy of the 10 September, however was provided a copy of the 14 September IROE. At about the same time, on or about 10 Sep 03, the 325th MI BN arrived and I began the integration of the 519th and 325th personnel. During a shift change meeting which included both 519th and 325th personnel, I handed out copies of the 14 Sep IROE approval MFR ███████████ interrogators took turns reading the MFR aloud as others followed along. I am 90% certain that all interrogators and analysts read the IROE MFR, while it is possible due to sick call or some other reason, that some might have missed the meeting. I had each soldier sign a roster stating that he or she had read and understood the IROE. I also created a slide which synopsized the 14 September IROE and posted the IROE in numerous locations throughout the working area as a constant reminder. This original slide contained three columns—the first column general interrogation techniques IAW FM 34-52. Techniques outside of the FM were place in a second column which I titled "OIC approval required prior to use", this was to ensure the interrogators did not have 'carte blanche', and sought guidance with more involved approaches. The third column was titled "CG's approval required for use on EPW's". After the subsequent IROE MFR was signed by LTG Sanchez on 12 Oct 03, I created a second slide to reflect the changes from the 14 September to the 12 October IROEs. Within the body of the main memorandum, it stated that any approach not listed in the policy required the CG's signature. It was explained to me (I cannot remember by who, but the guidance was from higher) that those approaches removed from the 14 Sep version were not necessarily out of reach, that they had to be approved by the CG prior to use. I therefore placed those approaches which were removed were placed under the title "Requires CG's approval in writing". In retrospect, the phrase "all other approaches require the CG's approval" would have been better verbage. This slide was posted about the interrogation operations room about the same time as the CACI contractors arrived. Following the incident involving three soldiers conducting unauthorized activities within 1B, I drafted a "memorandum of understanding" in MFR format (approximately 20 Oct) which not only outlined the approaches approved for use, but also added that all interrogations will be conducted in a humane manner, interrogations involving female detainees required another female's presence, detainees will not be maliciously humiliated, detainees will not be touched in an unwanted or malicious manner, cultural boundaries will be respected, unscheduled interrogations will not be conducted and the understanding of these rules and the requirement to report any violations of these rules to the OIC. I had each member of the JIDC who was in contact with detainees, which included interrogators, analysts, contractors and interpreters, read the MFR and sign indicating their understanding. The IROE has always applied to other agencies as well and I mandated that if other agencies wished to use AG facilities, they were required to follow US Army IROE. Other agency reps were requested to also sign the IROE prior to any interview beginning approximately the beginning of November. COL PAPPAS told me that the CJTF-7 CG delegated to him the authority to approve sleep deprivation and sleep management, but I do not recall if he specifically stated he had received authority to approve use of stress positions. The IROE slide was posted prior to COL PAPPAS's arrival at AG on 16 Nov 03 (in preparation for taking command of the FOB on 19 Nov 03), and there was a conflict between the IROE slide, which stated these techniques required CG's approval, and COL PAPPAS's claim that he had the authority to approve such techniques. COL PAPPAS never stated to me the basis of that authority other than to state that the CG had delegated it to him. I never saw anything in writing granting that authority. Regarding my experience with OGA, I first had limited contact with OGA while at Cropper. It was during the end of Aug 03/beginning of Sep 03 timeframe, everyone started shifting their operations to AG. OGA occasionally coordinated for interrogation space. I instructed OGA representatives that they must abide by the Army IROE while at AG. Most of my contact was with an individual we knew only as ████████ who appeared to be in charge of the OGA interrogation operations. I never endorsed the practice of "overnight parking" of OGA "ghost" detainees and expressed my disapproval to COL PAPPAS ████████████ and ████████████████ but I was overridden. ████████████████ and ████████████ then authorized several interrogations be conducted without the presence of Army interrogators and I did not have visibility or knowledge of what transpired during those interrogations. At the beginning to mid Oct 03, ████████████████ as one of my interrogators sat in on their interrogations. This responsibility was picked up by the operations section, and any other agency requesting to conduct operations at AG coordinated with OPS. It was shortly thereafter that an incident occurred in which an OGA "ghost" detainee died during the course of an interrogation. JIDC personnel were not present during this interrogation. I have no knowledge of any OGA abuses or violations. The practice of housing "ghosts" continued and was still in practice at the time of my departure on 4 Dec 03, and I do not know if LTG Sanchez was aware of the practice or not. . . .

████████████ the first officer in the "interrogation chain", I was comfortable that my subordinates knew their boundaries and believed they would have informed me of any violations or infringements of the IROE or any abuses they might witness. I did not have any concerns about any specific subordinates. The first incident of abuse of which I was aware was the "unauthorized interrogation" incident in early Oct 03. I was notified the following morning and only have second hand knowledge. Three soldiers ████████████████████ were involved in an incident at about 0200 when the three soldiers conducted an unscheduled interrogation of a female criminal detainee in Cell Block "1B", who was not an MI Hold. CID investigated the incident, but I never saw the report. All three soldiers were immediately removed from JIDC duties, received Article 15 punishment under UCMJ and were reduced in rank. ████████████ immediate corrective action was to call a mass formation the next morning at which all personnel were present. He informed the formation that there had been an "altercation" and "unauthorized interrogation". He stated that "such action won't be tolerated", and reiterated the JIDC mission. The second incident of inappropriate actions during interrogation of which I was aware involved ████████████ during the first or second week of Nov 03. She had submitted an Interrogation Plan in which the primary approach was the "direct approach", but I do not recall her secondary approach plan. I gathered that ████████████ viewed the detainee as having a flippant attitude in response to her questioning, perhaps not cooperating because she was female. She then decided to strip the detainee and apparently did so down to his underwear. ████████████ who was the analyst sitting in on the interview passed a note to ████████████ which he asked her "are you sure we can do this ████████████ "yes". After the interrogation, the inmate was escorted

semi-naked back to VIGILANT. ███████████████████████
overheard MPs talking about the incident and inquired as to what
happened and immediately reported the incident to ██████████████
section leader to confronted ████████████ claimed that she did not
know she had █████████ wrong. ████████████ notified me, and I in
turn informed COL PAPPAS and ████████████ I recommended at
██████████ receive an Article 15 to both COL PAPPAS and ████████
but she merely received a written reprimand from ████████████ the
interrogation NCOTC, recommended she be returned back to her
parent unit for the non-compliance. ███████████████████████
were immediately removed from interrogation duties and re-assigned
within the JIDC. I was not aware of any incidents of abuse involving
███████████████████████ I was not █████ any visits to AG by the
International Red Cross. I heard after the fact that they had visited, but
I have no knowledge of the results or findings of those visits. Such visits
would have been coordinated with the MPs. I was unaware of any incident involving administering cold showers to detainees, or the throwing
of cold water on naked detainees, possibly in support of sleep deprivation efforts. I was unaware of any incident in which a naked detainee
was forced to stand on a box with a hood over his head holding bottles
in outstretched hands. I walked through the hard site, more often during
the day or early evening hours than in the late hours of the night, but
I never saw or heard of any naked detainees or any incidents involving
women's underwear.

Q. Is there anything else you would like to add to this statement?
A. No.

End of Statement

AFFIDAVIT

I, ████████ HAVE READ OR HAVE HAD READ TO ME THIS
STATEMENT WHICH BEGINS ON PAGE 1, AND ENDS ON PAGE
9 ████████ UNDERSTAND THE CONTENTS OF THE ENTIRE
STATEMENT MADE BY ME. THE STATEMENT IS TRUE. I HAVE
INITIALED ALL CORRECTIONS AND HAVE INITIALED THE
BOTTOM OF EACH PAGE CONTAINING THE STATEMENT.
I HAVE MADE THIS STATEMENT FREELY WITHOUT HOPE OF
BENEFIT OR REWARD, WITHOUT THREAT OF PUNISHMENT,
AND WITHOUT COERCION, UNLAWFUL INFLUENCE OR
UNLAWFUL INDUCEMENT.

(Signature of Personal Making Statement)

WITNESSES:

Subscribed and sworn to before me, a person authorized by law to administer oaths, this <u>21</u> day of <u>May</u>, <u>2004</u> at <u>Metro Park, Springfield, VA</u>

_____

_____

█████████████████████████

(Signature of Person Administering

ORGANIZATION OR ADDRESS

██████████████████████

_____

(Typed Name of Person administering Oath)

_____

_____

UCMJ, ARTICLE 136

_____

(Authority To Administer Oaths)

ORGANIZATION OR ADDRESS

SWORN STATEMENT

For use of this form, see AR 190-45; the proponent agency is ODCSOPS

PRIVACY ACT STATEMENT

AUTHORITY: Title 10 USC Section 301; Title 5 USC Section 2951; E.O. 9397 dated November 22, 1943 *(SSN)*.

PRINCIPAL PURPOSE: To provide commanders and law enforcement officials with means by which information may be accurately identified.

ROUTINE USES: Your social security number is used as an additional/alternate means of identification to facilitate filing and retrieval.

DISCLOSURE: Disclosure of your social security number is voluntary.

1. LOCATION Metro Park, Alexandria, VA	2. DATE (*YYYYMMDD*) 2004/06/04	3. TIME 1455	4. FILE NUMBER
5. LAST NAME, FIRST NAME, MIDDLE NAME ▮▮▮▮▮▮▮	6. SSN ▮▮▮▮▮▮		7. GRADE/ STATUS E-6/USAR

8. ORGANIZATION OR ADDRESS
3401st Strategic Military Intelligence Detachment, Gaithersburg, MD

9. ▮▮▮▮▮▮▮ _____ WANT TO MAKE THE FOLLOWING STATEMENT UNDER OATH:

I was a member of the Guantanamo TIGER TEAM (TT) which deployed from Guantanamo Bay, Cuba (GTMO) to Abu Ghraib, Iraq from early October 2003 until mid December 2003. I am a US Army reserve solider assigned to the 3409th Strategic Military Intelligence Detachment, Gaithersburg, MD. I was activated from January 2003 to December 2003 and other than my time in Iraq functioned as an analyst in GTMO. My TT was tasked to train personnel in Abu Ghraib on the GTMO TIGER TEAM concept. My team was led by ▮▮▮▮▮▮▮ and consisted of ▮▮▮▮▮▮▮ and myself. We arrived at Abu Ghraib circa early October 2003 (exact date unrecalled) and departed circa the middle of December 2003. We were the second of two groups sent from GTMO to Abu Ghraib. The first visit included MG Miller and focused on assessing interrogation and detention operations in Iraq and formulating recommendation for changes/improvements. ▮▮▮▮▮▮▮ were part of this first team. Our team arrived about 2 weeks after the first had departed to assess the status of implementation of MG Miller's recommendations and how well the TIGER TEAM concept was being assimilated into operations. Almost immediately on arrival our team was split up operationally. ██████████████ worked primarily with the command/leadership at Abu Ghraib and didn't get involved with operations/interrogations within Tier 1A. ██████████ and I were assigned to one or more of the five interrogation teams and for the duration of our time there did not work together directly. We all were, however, billeted together and saw each other on a daily basis. We all worked on the day shift from 0600-0600. We convened ad-hoc meetings at least every two to three days where we discussed our experiences, observations and recommendations and then we "briefed" (discussed) these with ██████████████. All of our observations/discussions concerned how well the GTMO TIGER TEAM concept was being integrated or employed. We were not at Abu Ghraib to teach interrogation; simply to implement the TT concept. I don't recall our team ever discussing specific interrogation techniques employed, abuse, or unauthorized interrogation methods. My job was as an analyst. I worked with two different teams and rotated between their analysts. Sometimes I'd spend only a day with one analyst and sometimes several. At times I accompanied the analyst (as part of the TT) into interrogations and at times I only helped focus and prepare the analyst prior to an interrogation. I didn't actively involve myself in the interrogation process or preparation other than its link to analysis. I observed about 1-2 interrogations per week. Interrogations were conducted in the interrogation booths or the stairwell or shower room of Tier 1A. I did observe the interrogators providing plans for review and approval before their interrogations. These went to ██████████████ for approval. She would review, discuss as necessary with the interrogator and then initial the plan signifying her approval. I don't ever remember a plan coming back disapproved. Interrogation techniques I observed included mild "fear up" and "ego down." These were all verbal in nature and involved no humiliation or physical abuse. I never observed detainees who were naked although I once heard from an MP (name unrecalled) about a detainee in Tier 1B who had been stripped down and of another detainee who was often shackled in his cell naked because he spread feces on himself and/or ate it. I never heard or saw anyone physically abuse a detainee. Sleep deprivation was a technique I saw employed. It was approved by ██████████████ and would not exceed a 36–48 hour period. I'm not certain of the specifics as it was an interrogator responsibility but I do know that there were limitations (NFI) on this techniques and it was also used in GTMO. I never observed dogs in Abu Ghraib. They were used in GTMO during in-processing. I think it was a "fear up" technique. I had no involvement in the "shooting incident." I heard about it after from ██████████████ as the interrogators had been called to assist. I never saw or heard about anyone taking photos in Abu Ghraib. The only stress positions I observed or heard about were to make a detainee stand and if he was uncooperative to make him sit/stand/sit repeatedly. On occasion I did see MPs and interrogators touch a detainee but it was never abusive; usually a hand on a shoulder or arm to guide. Overall, my impression of interrogations (techniques) at Abu Ghraib was that they didn't differ much from GTMO.

Q: Do you have anything else to add to this statement? ████████████
A: No.

End of Statement

10. EXHIBIT	11. INITIALS OF PERSON MAKING STATEMENT
	████████████

SWORN STATEMENT

For use of this form, see AR 190-45; the proponent agency is ODCSOPS

PRIVACY ACT STATEMENT

AUTHORITY:	Title 10 USC Section 301: Title 5 USC Section 2951: E.O. 9397 dated November 22, 1943 *(SSN)*.
PRINCIPAL PURPOSE:	To provide commanders and law enforcement officials with means by which information may be accurately identified.
ROUTINE USES:	Your social security number is used as an additional/alternate means of identification to facilitate filing and retrieval.
DISCLOSURE:	Disclosure of your social security number is voluntary.

1. LOCATION OSJA, DARMSTADT, GERMANY	2. DATE (YYYYMMDD) 2004/05/14 ■■	3. TIME 1758 ■■■	4. FILE NUMBER
5. LAST NAME, FIRST NAME, MIDDLE NAME ■■■■	6. SSN ■■■■■		7. GRADE/STATUS LTC
8. ORGANIZATION OR ADDRESS 205TH MILITARY INTELLIGENCE BRIGADE, HEIDELBERG, GERMANY APO AE			

9. I ■■■■■■ _____. WANT TO MAKE THE FOLLOWING STATEMENT UNDER OATH:

On 1 July 2003, I assumed command of the 205th MI BDE in Balad, Iraq. My rater was MG WOJDOWKOSKI, Deputy Cdr, CJTF-7 and my senior rater was ■■■■■■ I submitted an OER Support form to MG WOJDOWKOSKI within the first one to two weeks. I do recall discussing the OER support form but I can't remember specifically what we discussed. A copy of the support form is provided at enclosure 1. At the time I took command, there were eight battalions under my command. Under previous agreements made pre-dating my arrival, I did not rate any commander not organic to the brigade with the exception of the reserve component battalion commanders.

Battalions subordinate to my headquarters were located as follows: the 165th, the 223d, the 224th, and the 325th in Balad; the 302d was located at the Palace on Camp Victory working for V Corps and CJTF-7; the 323d resided at Baghdad International Airport; the 519th was located at Camp

Speicher, near Tikrit; and the 1st MI Bn remained in Wiesbaden. Some elements of the brigade were located at Camp Bucca as well. The mission of the brigade was to conduct intelligence and electronic warfare operations in support of V Corps and CJTF-7. The Brigade had numerous intelligence collection activities ongoing in support of this mission. There were UAV operations at two different locations, Balad and al Assad Airbases. The Brigade had an aerial, SIGINT mission ongoing with Guardrail. The CJTF-7 had the Prophet Hammer organic to the divisions. Upgrades were ongoing with Guardrail as well. The Brigade's focus was primarily on HUMINT. There were 48 Tactical HUMINT Teams dispersed throughout Iraq. The Brigade was also heavily involved with the Mujhadeen E Khalq (MEK) mission. The focus with MEK was maintaining surveillance and conducting initial screenings. CENTCOM and the CJTF-7 wanted to register them with the Biometric data systems in order to identify whom the terrorists were. The MEK mission proved more challenging than expected because of arrangements made during the initial phases of combat operations. As a result, only the biometric screening had been accomplished when the Brigade departed theater in February 2004. The 205th MI Bde no longer had organic interrogation assets, because they had been eliminated from the MTO&E sometime between 1993 and 1995. However, there were three battalions task organized to the brigade with interrogation capability. The Brigade's interrogation operations were initially conducted at Camp Bucca, Camp Cropper, and Camp Ashraft. Approximately two or three weeks (mid to late July) after I took command, BG HAHN directed me to provide LTG SANCHEZ a briefing on how the Brigade conducted interrogation operations from the lowest to highest levels. LTG SANCHEZ was not satisfied that the CJTF-7 was getting information from interrogations which could be turned into Actionable Intelligence. Representatives from the 325th MI Bn, the 519th MI Bn and I briefed LTG SANCHEZ as well as representatives from the Military Police and CJ2 on the process that was in place at that time. LTG SANCHEZ expressed concern over the system in place for conducting interrogations and exploiting information derived from them. During the briefing that LTG SANCHEZ directed the Brigade to establish an interrogation site to exploit actionable intelligence from a list of approximately 3000 to 6000 Saddam Fedayeen members that had been provided to the CJTF-7 from 1st Armored Division. At the briefing all parties decided to conduct this operation at Abu Ghraib that facility offered some segregation capability, an appropriate guard force and the ability to house large numbers of detainees. This was despite the inherent dangers of Abu Ghraib caused by ███████ in the Sunni Triangle. I directed the 519th MI Bn to establis operations there after discussing the situation with ██████████ the Battalion Commander. We conducted a site reconnaissance and ████████████████ laid out a general plan to conduct operations. My first impression of Abu Ghraib was "holy mackerel." Not only was the place a decrepit prison, but there were significant force protection concerns and an apparent lack of standards being enforced by the supporting Military Police.

Especially troubling was the lack of uniform standards including soldiers walking around the prison in civilian clothes. I approved the plan laid out for me by ████████████ to conduct the Saddam Fedayeen interrogations. I never spoke to MP personnel on the ground regarding the conduct of the specific operation or the matter of standards. I left on-site coordination to the 519th MI Bn. During the initial phases of the operation the 519th left a field grade officer on site, but eventually left the mission in the hands of ████████████ an experienced interrogator. The operation was not as successful as had been hoped. The CJTF did not get the number of Fedayeen members that the list indicated would be captured and the through C2 channels the Brigade was informed that LTG SANCHEZ was not happy with the quality of reporting. This viewpoint was confirmed when LTG SANCHEZ directed that I provide him an update on interrogation operations toward the end of September ████████████.

████████ Brigade's 53, ████████████ and I went to the CG's office on a Sunday to lay out what we had collected during the Saddam Fedayeen mission and what we thought was needed to improve the quality of interrogations throughout my areas of responsibility. LTG SANCHEZ expressed dissatisfaction from the information collected, was dubious about some of the suggestions made to improve interrogations and directed that the Brigade link up with MG MILLER during his assessment visit to IRAQ to determine a way ahead for interrogation operations. MG MILLER conducted his assessment from 31 August to 9 September 2003. The purpose of his visit was to discuss the ability of CJTF-7 to rapidly exploit internees for actionable intelligence. The team focused on three areas: intelligence synchronization, integration and fusion; interrogation operations; and detention operations. Various members of the team spent around 3-4 days at Abu Ghraib. The Brigade's involvement with the team was in regards to interrogation operations. MG MILLER spent time with BG KARPINSKY and her staff regarding detention operations. As his team made recommendations, I took notes and began to contemplate how to implement some of his recommendations. Essentially, the team's recommendation was for the CJTF-7 to create an interrogation facility along the lines of that which MG MILLER was running at Guantanamo Bay Cuba. The decision was also made to centralize all interrogation operations at Abu Ghraib as a result of MG MILLER's visit. Although the force protection challenges of Abu Ghraib remained, the fact that segregation facilities offered an available guard force, the requisite real estate to establish interrogation facilities was present, and CPA was funding construction there led MG MILLER, MG FAST, COL BOLTZ, BG KARPINSKI and I to support the Abu Ghraib facility. Other facilities although considered were discarded because of their distance from Baghdad or the lack of adequate resources. I cannot recall any specific discussions of force protection at Abu Ghraib during this time. LTG SANCHEZ had the final decision. However, I don't know if he was given a decision brief on Abu Ghraib by anyone in his staff. On 11 September, LTG SANCHEZ again called me to his office and wanted to know what my plan was for implementing the recommendations of the MG MILLER report. It was at this time I showed him some initial design configurations for a Joint Interrogation and Debriefing Center. He asked me how I was going to source that organization and I showed him my plan for consolidating interrogation facilities and using people from the Brigade. He told me that filling these slots was not only the Brigade's problem, but a "national one" and directed me to draft a request for forces (RFF) within 48 hours. Another key development that came out of the MG MILLER assessment was the need to have specific written guidance on interrogation policies and authorities. MG MILLER'S worked with the CJTF-7 legal team on developing a CJTF-7 Interrogation and Counter-Resistance Policy along the lines of the rules approved by the Department of Defense for Guantanamo Bay. Prior to the drafting of the Counter-Resistance policy, as the MILLER assessment noted, there was no written guidance addressing interrogation policy and authority for the entire CJTF. Individual units used internal SOPs at each facility. At Abu Ghraib that was the SOP of the 519th MI Bn. I believed their SOP was adequate from the lack of complaints about interrogations, my confidence in their commander, ███████████████ and their experience in Afghanistan. However, the SOP's tactical focus made it inadequate for the conduct of operational/strategic level interrogations that the Brigade was directed to perform. On 14 September, the CJTF-7 SJA published its first Interrogation and Counter-resistance policy signed by LTG SANCHEZ. This policy was revised on 12 October because of objections from CENTCOM. The 12 October policy eliminated several techniques that were previously approved by LTG SANCHEZ. The Interrogation Rules of Engagement (IROE) was a JIDC published poster based on the 12 October policy created so soldiers and civilians working in the JIDC could have an easy to follow set of rules. It was meant to provide an unclassified reminder that emphasized approved approaches in accordance with the 12 October counter-resistance policy. The IROE was never intended to be, nor was it in fact an approved CJTF-7 policy on the conduct of interrogations. The legally binding document was the approved 12 October policy. To my knowledge, nothing in the IROE violated the 12 October policy. Although the Miller Team had a broad mandate with regard to their assessment, visits to the Brigade did not focus on care and well being of the detainees. Rather, they focused primarily on turning the results of interrogations into actionable intelligence. Discussions on the well being of detainees were discussed with BG KARPISNIKI and the 800th MP BDE as part of the discussions on detention operations. I know that MG MILLER spent time with her and units in the 800th. BG KARPISKI had mentioned to me that they had a very nasty discussion on his findings relative to detainee operations and I believe this included the welfare of detainees. In my opinion, MG MILLER saw many things that had to be done to meet his mandate; improvement to interrogation operations was one of them. I believe that it was MG MILLER'S intention that the person responsible for synchronizing would be located at the CJTF-7 level. I also believe there was pressure from the Department of Defense to produce actionable intelligence from the thousands of security internees the CJTF-7 was capturing. I base my assessment on the discussions with the C2 staff that indicated a tremendous amount of interest in what we were receiving as well as an ever increasing number of "high level" visits to Abu Ghraib. The 205th was given the mission to stand up a joint interrogation and debriefing center as the result of the 11 September meeting. Three critical tasks were involved: completing work on the Request For Forces (RFF), training, and the collapsing of three interrogation facilities into one at Abu Ghraib. The Brigade finished the RFF in concert with the C2 and C3 staff and sent the document out within 72 hours. Training was arranged with Fort Huachuca and TF Guantanamo to begin in October. GTMO would assist with implementing the Tiger Team concept from 5 October through 3 December and Fort Huachuca sent a mobile training team for 21 days in early October to help train soldiers to conduct strategic level interrogations. The movement of personnel to the JIDC was an iterative process because of the need to close old facilities and bring new assets, such as analysts, into the facility that had not been traditionally part of the Brigade's tactical intelligence capability. Initially, ████████████ was designated as the senior MI Officer at Abu Ghraib. We discussed his roles and responsibilities, though I do not recall the specifics. The CG had been specific in his direction to me at the 11 SEP meeting that we needed a LTC to run the facility. I went to ████████████ and told him I needed a LTC to run operations at Abu Ghraib. ████████████ to the Brigade to perform that mission ████████████

I spoke with ████████████ about my concept for operations and intent on the evening of 20 SEP. A mortar attack interrupted our discussions. There was no doubt in my mind that ████████████ was the Joint Interrogation debriefing Center (JIDC) OIC. I know that ████████████ understood this because he sent an e-mail out which specified that ████████████ was the JIDC Chief and that he was the JIDC Operations Officer. Other organization charts that I received from the JIDC always had ████████████ as the person in charge at Abu Ghraib. Commanders maintained their command authority over their soldiers assigned to their units. The arrangement would be somewhat analogous to an Analysis and Control Element in today's intelligence doctrine. ████████████

████████ Until the middle of November when I went to Abu Ghraib on a permanent basis, I saw ████████████ as my guy on the ground and I thought ████████████ was pretty clear on what he was supposed to do as well. After I became engaged in day to day operations of the JIDC and ████████████ Commander of the 165th MI Bn came down to assist in force protection and security, ████████████ did take on more of a liaison role. I did not rate him because he belonged to CJTF-7 and I assumed he was being rated by the C2 chain. This was a similar arrangement to that which was described earlier in this statement for LTC-level commanders. ████████████ would attend the daily meetings with the MPs and the other tenant units. I was under the impression that he was satisfied with the way the MPs were running things on Tier 1A and in generally supporting the interrogation mission. There were other things like relations with MPs in the LSA and post security where there were concerns. However, I was led to believe that he had most of these issues under control. ████████████

████████████████ also identified equipment shortfalls with the JIDC organization. The Brigade staff worked to fill these needs but as in trying to standup any operation without an already established MTOE, there were shortfalls. ████████████████ provided information concerning soldiers showing up without their personal equipment. I believe that they took corrective action on the ground and the Brigade followed up with the Battalions of these soldiers. I do not recall ████████████ discussing with me any issues ████████████ had relayed to him on equipment although I do recall several discussions with the DCO, ████████████ I was not aware that ████████████ had told ████████████ to stay out of operations; in fact I thought the exact opposite to be the case ████████████ and ████████████ would be in a better position to discuss answer your questions on this issue. ████████████

Ultimately, the JIDC was to be filled primarily from a Joint Manning Document (JMD) based on the RFF that was developed as a result of ████████████ visit. The work of writing and filling the JMD was being done by ████████████ from the Brigade and ████████████ from CJTF-7. CJTF-7 was responsible for managing and filling this document. Although the JIDC was technically a joint operation, most of the JMD remained unfilled throughout my tour in Iraq. Specific exceptions included some Air Force medical personnel and some Navy personnel, but these arrived much later. The JIDC was essentially an Army run operation with soldiers and civilians. The decision to use civilians was made because the Brigade ████████████ had no more assets that it could provide to fill the slots. I was consulted concerning this decision and provided favorable feedback. The Brigade S3 and DCO worked with the CJTF-7 headquarters in developing specific requirements. I am unfamiliar with the specifics of the contract and do not recall when the first contractors arrived. However, two requirements were to have a clearance and to have experience. I received positive feedback on the contributions of the contractors from ████████████ and other members of the JIDC. I was never given reason to doubt their competency and no issues were brought to my attention. ████████████

████████████ the first week of November, the CG paid a visit to Abu Ghraib and he was still not happy with operations. In private discussions with the CG and MG FAST I decided to move to Abu Ghraib. My actual movement to Abu Ghraib was sometime in the middle of November. Closely following my movement MG Fast visited me and expressed concerned about the level of force protection at the facility. She indicated that because I was now the senior commander on the ground I might have to take additional responsibility for the force protection mission. The 205th MI Bde was named Forward Operating Base commander on 19 November. Although I didn't ask for the job, I did not fight it because I realized that unless the Brigade assumed this role, things would never get better. The 19 NOV FRAGO designating the Brigade with FOB command responsibility gave TACON of the 320th MP

Bn for force protection and security of detainees as well. The FRAGO did not delineate any responsibilities. My understanding of this FRAGO was to protect all personnel from external threats. To me this meant that the MPs would continue to run confinement and security operations in the prison camps and facilities, while the JIDC would continue to perform interrogations. I brought the 165th MI Bn to oversee base security operations, assist with the implementation of base security policy, and provide forces to enhance perimeter security and conduct reconnaissance and surveillance outside the walls of Abu Ghraib. After the 19 NOV FRAGO my discussions with ██████████████ Commander of the 320th MP Bn were positive. He expressed the opinion that his unit would be able to focus their efforts on confinement operations. This FRAGO did nothing to alter the mission of the MPs to maintain control over all of the detention facilities located at Abu Ghraib, even those where internees of intelligence value were housed. At some point, near the end of November the MPs decided to stop escorting detainees between the CAMP VIGILANT, CAMP GANCI and the interrogation facility. Military Intelligence took over this function. ██████████████ were to ensure that a group of intelligence soldiers were trained on escorting duties and to my knowledge this was done to standard. As a result of the 19 NOV FRAGO I became more involved with base operations at Abu Ghraib. As always, I relied on battalion commanders and the Brigade staff to assist in daily operations of the Brigade. ██████████████ ██████████████ As discussed earlier in this statement, the JIDC created and posted IROE on their bulletin board. The IROE identified presence of working dogs and sleep management as requiring CG approval. However, the 12 October Interrogation and Counter-Resistance Policy General Safeguards (enclosure 2) allowed that dogs present at interrogations were to be muzzled and under the control of a handler. Likewise the Brigade Staff Judge Advocate opined that sleep management could be permitted at the JIDC as long as ██████████████ detainees were allowed adequate sleep. Adequate sleep was defined as "4 hours in a 24 hour period" based on conversations with personnel from Guantanamo Bay. Any sleep of less than 4 hours in a 24 hour period would have required ██████████████ signature. We did submit requests concerning interrogations to ██████████████. I believe these were mostly requests for segregation of detainees in excess of 30-days, but I cannot recall the total number or specifically what they were. The requests were kept on file at Abu Ghraib until January when they were maintained on softcopy. ██████████████ would know where they were kept. As for sleep management, the interrogators had to write down their plan and then give it to the MPs who would maintain and implement it. Additionally, these plans were to be monitored by our resident doctor. I do not know what the MPs did to implement the plan. I do not know of any training that was provided to the MPs on what MI could do with detainees or if MI trained on what MPs could do with detainees. 20/20 Hindsight, it should have been done. ██████████████

██████████████ and that they not have to go through the normal inprocessing procedures. ██████████████ could tell you more. I went to speak to ██████████████ about my concerns over this arrangement and asked if we were going to continue this. He said yes to facilitate their request. They would drop off detainees without notifying us. I do not remember any staff officer voicing any concerns about OGA concerning these practices although they may have. In fact I was under the impression that ▓▓▓▓▓▓▓▓▓▓ established good relations with this organization and that the problem had been reduced to a manageable level. With regards to the specifics of a dead detainee I can relate the following: AN OGA rep and ▓▓▓▓▓▓▓▓▓▓ notified me that a detainee was dead; we reported this information to the C2. I was informed by the OGA representative on the scene that the detainee died during an interrogation while an OGA interrogator was yelling at him. The detainee apparently collapsed while he was being interrogated. The body appeared to have been in a fight. ▓▓▓▓▓▓▓▓▓▓ told me that the detainee received the injuries during the take down in operations the night before. The operation was a combination of ▓▓▓▓▓▓▓▓ I saw injuries to the left side of the head. It was decided that the body would be placed in a bag and iced to prevent rotting. The body was removed that evening/next day quietly making it appear as if a detainee was injured in order to prevent unnecessary panic among the other detainees. OGA investigated the incident and decided that they would comply with inprocessing requirements after the ▓▓▓▓▓▓▓▓▓▓ advised them to do so. Likewise when TF-121 asked to use our facility months later I recall we required them to follow established policy as well. ▓▓▓▓▓▓▓▓

▓▓▓▓▓▓▓▓▓▓ have no knowledge of any MI person abusing detainees by pushing them off a truck or on the ground. I would think that if a ISG in my Brigade knew about the use of excessive force, he would let me know No one ever told me about such an incident. ▓▓▓▓▓▓▓▓▓▓

▓▓▓▓▓▓▓▓ The International Community Red Cross (ICRC) visited Abu Ghraib twice. Once before I was FOB commander and once after. They did not meet with me the first time. I did receive a copy of the results and noted there were allegations of maltreatment and detainees wearing women underwear on their heads. I did not believe it. I felt some ▓▓▓▓▓▓▓▓ detainees just simply wanted to get some sympathy. I truly believed our guys were not doing this. I recall I might have relayed to the staff that this stuff couldn't have been happening. I cannot specifically recall telling the staff this stuff better not be happening, but I might have said words to the effect. When the ICRC came by the second time, the FOB invoked GCIV/Article 143, for eight detainees to prevent them from talking to the ICRC while undergoing an active interrogation. ▓▓▓▓▓▓▓▓ informed me that I had the authority to do this. Before I became FOB commander, I was told there was a shortage of jumpsuits, but I was never told about the women's underwear issue. I occasionally walked down Tier 1A and 1B and I never saw any naked detainees. ▓▓▓▓▓▓▓▓

▓▓▓▓▓▓▓▓ The training on IROE was established at Abu Ghraib after we had an incident with A/519th soldiers on or about 6 OCT. It was reported to me that three male soldiers had gone in to interrogate a female detainee and had some sexual motives and had touched the females. I told ██████████████ we needed to suspend the individuals from interrogation operations and remove them from contact with detainees. A CID investigation was initiated but there were not enough evidence to prosecute them for detainee abuse or sexual misconduct so I gave them Article 15s for dereliction of duty. Two soldiers were reduced in rank and fined and another was fined and taken away from interrogation operations. I was told that a TITAN Linguist was also involved, but that he did not participate. ████████████ thought there were some initial problems with the linguists statement and went back to clarify the situation. When he came back ██████████████ told me we had a true statement and I took the recommendations from my staff as to the disposition of the three soldier interrogators. We did not fire the linguist and ██████████████. I do not know what happened to him after he transferred. Everyone was brought eventually together and the IROEs were reiterated. I had no suspicion that the incident went beyond these individuals or that night. Another time, it was reported to me that an interrogator had inappropriately taken the clothes from a detainee and led him back to the compound. I spoke to ██████████████ and he recommended the individuals be suspended form interrogations, orally reprimanded, counseled and given training. I concurred. I didn't think this presented a pattern. We had many interrogations take place between the two incidents without any notification of problems. I believe that the entire chain of command and supervision believed this was an unusual occurrence; and that suspension and retraining would send the appropriate message to everyone. The shooting in the Hard Site was brought to my attention when BG KARPINSKI called to tell me about it. She asked if I knew there had been a shooting in Tier 1A. After notification I went down to the hard site and my immediate concern was to check on everyone and notify higher headquarters. ██████████████ walked me around and explained to me what happened. There was a Syrian detainee who had a handgun. Another detainee had told someone of the presence of the weapon. When I arrived, MPs were conducting a "shakedown" of the Iraqi Police and preparing for a cell search of the Cell Block 1A. I recall witnessing a small part of the cell search. The detainees would be taken out of their cells and the dogs would go in the cell to search for weapons. This was done one by one. As far as I could tell, the guard dogs were being led by their dog handler. An MP captain was in charge of the search. I am sure there were some MI personnel there but I do not remember who they were. ██████████████ told me that our MI personnel were interrogating the Iraqi Police in support of the MPs. I didn't see it. I do not remember any civilians at the site. At no time did I see dogs being used during interrogations. I was not aware that a dog might have bitten a linguist. The first time I found out about it was when I read the CID report. If this happened, someone should have told me. I never witnessed any detainee abuse. I was satisfied with the level of knowledge MI personnel had and that they were in compliance with the policy on counter-resistance, IROE and the Geneva Convention ██████████████ was very competent as the ICE Chief and

A-213

had implemented a system to train personnel coming into the JIDC. I also had the GTMO assistance visit from early October through the beginning of December looking at all facets of operations and they never reported anything inappropriate. During our Fort Huachuca MTT we did a left/right seat ride and was provided only positive feedback about the ongoing operations. I had seen nothing to doubt that things weren't being done right. I was able to identify one of the linguists in one of the photos shown to me ███████████ is standing in one of the TIERS with several soldiers around a naked detainee on the floor. I was also able to identify a female linguist with a civilian (did not recognize him). They were with a detainee who appeared to be in an unauthorized stress position. Taking the photos was a violation. If an NCO did not report an incident he was aware of, there was a break down. There is no justification for any abuse of detainees and the leadership did not condone it. In all cases where abuse was brought to my attention I took action to discipline soldiers. I believe that the vast majority of leaders and soldiers were acting in good faith to do the right thing and that prudent actions were taken to conduct training with teams from GTMO and FT Huachuca. However, clearly a more rigid inspection of operations, less confidence in civilians working in interrogation, and closer attention to ICRC report of abuse may have enabled earlier detection and prevention of some of this. I also believe that the difficult conditions of Abu Ghraib, the lack of established doctrine and little collective training for JIDCs, as well as the Army decision to migrate the Brigade's interrogators into the Reserve Components after Desert Storm were all contributory factors to the situation that occurred at Abu Ghraib. ████████████

Q. Do You have anything else to add to this statement?
A. No ███████████

End of Statement

10. EXHIBIT	11. INITIALS OF PERSON MAKING STATEMENT

AFFIDAVIT

I ███████████ HAVE READ OR HAVE HAD READ TO ME THIS STATEMENT WHICH BEGINS ON PAGE 1 AND ENDS ON PAGE ███████████ FULLY UNDERSTAND THE CONTENTS OF THE ENTIRE STATEMENT MADE BY ME. THE STATEMENT IS TRUE. I HAVE INITIALED ALL CORRECTIONS AND HAVE INITIALED THE BOTTOM OF EACH PAGE CONTAINING THE STATEMENT. I HAVE MADE THIS STATEMENT FREELY

WITHOUT HOPE OF BENEFIT OR REWARD, WITHOUT THREAT OF PUNISHMENT AND WITHOUT COERCION, UNLAWFUL INFLUENCE, OR UNLAWFUL INDUCEMENT

_____ ███████████

(Signature of Person Making Statement)

WITNESSES

_____

_____

ORGANIZATION OR ADDRESS

_____

_____

_____

ORGANIZATION OR ADDRESS

Subscribed and sworn to before me, a person authorized by law to administer oaths this 14th day of May 2004 at DARMSTADT, GERMANY

███████████

_____
Signature of Person administering oaths

_____
*(Typed Name of Person
Administering Oaths)*

UCMJ. ARITCLE 136
_____
(Authority To Administer Oaths)

1   RC: So was it a consensus that they were all yes, release

2 or no, release?

3   WIT: It had to be an agreement to release them.

4   RC: So all three had to vote the same?

5   WIT: Right.

6   DC: But that's only for release.

7   WIT: For hold, we could recommend release and she could

8 override us.

9   RC: So now often did that happen where she overrode?

10   WIT: Often. Especially in the first four weeks of the

11 process. She was looking at it from a responsibility

12 perspective. If anybody had a question when the recommendation

13 got to SENTCOM, they called her back. They didn't call me, they

14 didn't call ███████████████, they didn't ask us to get together

15 and review the file again: they called her.

16   Q. Major General Miller and his visit--when was the first

17 time that you met Major General Miller in country there in Iraq

18 that you recall?

19   A. Whenever he visited Iraq, at the in brief--that was the

20 first time I had----

125

A-216

1   Q. So that would have been--he first arrived in the latter

2 part of August. He was there the last week of August, the first

3 week of September. Is that when you--?

4   A. Right. That was the first time I ever met him.

5   Q. And were you at Victory when you met him or did you

6 meet him at Abu Ghraib?

7   A. No. I met him at Victory.

8   Q. And what did he tell you his mission was when he

9 appeared there in Iraq?

10   A. He gave an in brief. I really don't know if that was

11 the first day he was there or if that was the day of the in

12 brief, but it was very close to the beginning of his trip. He

13 said that he was there to help with the interrogation effort to

14 see what he could do to help Barbara Fast improve the

15 interrogations and the resulting actionable intelligence--he

16 made his own invented expression. And he said he was going to

17 take a look at our different prison facilities.

18   He knew for sure he was going up to the MEK, he was

19 going up to Abu Ghraib, might go down to Bucca, he was going to

20 go down to Cropper--unless it wasn't necessary. If they found

21 someplace early on that served the purpose. I said--I made a

22 comment about the MEK compound. But that was outside of

23 Baghdad, that that was actually the property of the people who

126

1   we were securing up there, and there would be a long discussion

2   about putting any kind of Guantanamo Bay type of an operation up

3   there.

4   Other people were kind of interjecting or asking

5   questions during these in briefs, so I just made a couple of

6   points the same way. And it takes a little bit of time to

7   understand the MEK mission, and if he didn't need to know that

8   and he wasn't going to use that facility--I was actually trying

9   to discourage him, I suppose. But it was under U.S. control, so

10   that was an advantage unlike some of the other facilities. He

11   said they would see; they were going to visit them. I asked if

12   he was there to take a look at detention operations. He said,

13   "No, but if we're looking at detention facilities, then I have a

14   lot of people that do that kind of work in their civilian job,"

15   and he pointed out a couple of people on the team and he said

16   that they might make recommendations. He said that they would

17   work with the interrogators. It was kind of like a generic

18   brief. It was clear, to me, during that in brief, that he was

19   really there to work with the C-2. But you couldn't do any of

20   those--you couldn't setup an operation anywhere in the existing

21   facility, because they all belong to me. So that's why they

22   included us in the in brief. And he made a comment about--one

23   of the interrogators asked the question about what made

                                127

1 Guantanamo Bay so different--or so good that they were going to
2 import those techniques. He said that it was the plan to
3 "GITMOize" the operation. That they had developed techniques
4 and they had so much success in Guantanamo Bay that they were
5 asked to come in and apply those techniques and teach
6 interrogation teams how to apply those techniques.

7   And I said, "Sir, I was down in Guantanamo Bay very
8 quickly, but I do know that the situation in Guantanamo Bay is
9 vastly different than the situation here in Iraq. All of our
10 facilities are routinely attacked. Contrary to wise judgment,
11 you don't run a detention operation in the middle of a hostile
12 firestone, which is what Abu Ghraib is right now." And he said,
13 you know, that they would make the determination and it really
14 wasn't so much different. I mean, I see completely different--
15 black and white differences between Guantanamo Bay and--but I
16 thought, you know, when you drive around Iraq a little bit and
17 you can see and you can feel and you can sense the tension,
18 you'll understand that it's different here.

19   And another interrogator asked him about the--I don't
20 remember the exact question, but it was something about
21 maintaining control. And it might have been the subsequent
22 question to my comment that in Guantanamo Bay they 800 MPs to
23 guard 640 prisoners, and I had--at Abu Ghraib, I had 300 MPs to

128

AG0000126

DOD 000214

A-219

1   guard more than 7,000 prisoners. Then he said, "You have to

2   have full control, and the MPs at Guantanamo Bay know what--they

3   know what that means. A detainee never leaves the cell if he's

4   not escorted by two MPs in leg irons, and hand irons, and a

5   belly chain. And there was no mistake about who's in charge.

6   And you have to treat these detainees like dogs. If you treat

7   them any differently and they get the idea that they're making a

8   decision or they're in charge, you've lost control of your

9   interrogation."

10   Q. Was that a quote? Did he specifically say to treat

11 them like dogs?

12   A. Absolutely.

13   Q. And who else was present at that time when he made that

14 statement?

15   A. Everybody that was in that in brief.

16   Q. Can you give me some names?

17   A. General Fast, Colonel Pappas, maybe ▓▓▓▓▓▓▓▓▓▓▓▓-I

18 believe ▓▓▓▓▓▓▓▓▓ was there, and I--he was there when

19 General Boikan (phonetic) was there. I don't really remember if

20 he was there when General Miller was in briefing. There were a

21 couple of people in civilian clothes that were interpreters--I

22 thought that they were interpreters. Now I don't know if they

AG0000127

DOD 000215

SWORN STATEMENT

For use of this form, see AR 190-45; the proponent agency is ODCSOPS

PRIVACY ACT STATEMENT

AUTHORITY: Title 10 USC Section 301: Title 5 USC Section 2951: E.O. 9397 dated November 22, 1943 *(SSN)*.

PRINCIPAL: To provide commanders and law enforcement officials with means by which information may be accurately identified.

ROUTINE USES: Your social security number is used as an additional/alternate means of identification to facilitate filing and retrieval.

DISCLOSURE: Disclosure of your social security number is voluntary.

1. LOCATION Metro Park Springfield, VA	2. DATE (*YYYYMMDD*) 2004/05/24 ███	3. TIME 0900	4. FILE NUMBER
5. LAST NAME, FIRST NAME, MIDDLE NAME ███	6. SSN ███		7. GRADE/STATUS SPC/E4

8. ORGANIZATION OR ADDRESS
B Company. 2d Military Intelligence Battalion, 66th Military Intelligence Group, Darmstadt. Germany

9. ███ _____ WANT TO MAKE FOLLOWING STATEMENT UNDER OATH:

I am a Human Intelligence (HUMINT) Collector/Interrogator (MOS 97E) assigned to B Co, 66th Military Intelligence (MI) Group, Darmstadt, Germany, currently attached to the 202nd MI Battalion (BN) at Abu Gurayb (AG), Iraq. I deployed to Kuwait along with 11 other 66th MI Group personnel on 15 Oct 03. I arrived at AG on 19 Oct 03. I was on a Rest and Relaxation leave from 5 to 25 Apr 03. Upon arrival at AG, we received a briefing concerning the breakdown of AG operations, the Tiger Team configuration being used at AG, and Interrogation Rules of Engagement (IROE). I read the IROE slide and nothing, other than the presence of military working dogs, surprised me. We were then split up into various sections and paired up with interrogators who were already experienced with AG operations. I conducted my first interrogation on 21 Oct 03. I can not recall my first section leader because it was for only about a week. My second section leader was ███ while I was assigned to A Section. I then moved to the Special Projects Team and my supervisor was ███ I predominately worked with interpreters ███ ███ While with A Section, I was paired up with a staff sergeant from the Guantanamo way (GTMO), Cuba, named ███

known as ▆▆▆▆ I personally observed three incidents which I believe were incidents of detainee abuse. I provided this information in a sworn statement to Army CID on 21 Jan 03 (CID File Number 0003-04-CID 149-83130), and more details can be found in that sworn statement. The first incident was what I believed at the time to be an accident when a Military Policeman (MP) named ▆▆▆▆▆▆▆▆▆ was escorting a detainee down a flight of stairs in the AG hard site. The detainee was hand-cuffed, leg-shackled, and had a sandbag over his head. As ▆▆▆▆▆ was bringing him down the stairs, the inmate appeared to trip and fall on the stairs. This incident was reported to ▆▆▆▆▆▆ and ▆▆▆▆▆ by ▆▆▆▆▆▆▆▆ The second incident also involved ▆▆▆▆▆▆▆ and a cooperating detainee named ▆▆▆▆▆▆▆▆▆▆ was a Lebanese national raised in Syria. ▆▆▆▆▆▆▆ who resided in either Ganci or Vigilant, requested isolation, apparently concerned for his safety because he was cooperating with Coalition Forces. When I arrived at the hard site with ▆▆▆▆▆▆▆▆ asked "is this your guy?" and roughly put a sand bag over ▆▆▆▆▆ head and began to pull him roughly into the hard site. I was caught of guard by the harsh treatment, but then intervened and asked what ▆▆▆▆▆▆ was doing. ▆▆▆▆▆▆ then responded with something to the effect "is the one of the good guys". When I said he was ▆▆▆▆▆ then took the ▆▆▆▆▆▆▆▆ head and calmed down. ▆▆▆▆▆▆ then said that he was going to strip ▆▆▆▆▆▆ down, but did not have a jump suit to issue him. I notified ▆▆▆▆▆ and ▆▆▆▆▆ my Officer-in-Charge (OIC), and ▆▆▆▆▆▆ intervened to have ▆▆▆▆▆ clothes returned to him. ▆▆▆▆▆ remained my detainee and he never mentioned any further abuse after this incident. The third incident occurred in late Dec 03 or early Jan 04 and involved a reluctant Baath Party General Officer named ▆▆▆▆▆ also know as ▆▆▆▆ I had a sleep management plan which was approved by COL PAPPAS (205th MI BDE Commander). I was in Cell Block 1B of the hard site, which was the area of the hard site dedicated to female and juvenile detainees. I had ▆▆▆▆▆▆ held in the shower area of 1B when I witnessed an MP guard and an MP Working Dog Handler with his dog entered 1B. I do not know either of their names, however, investigators showed me digital photographs this day of an MP Working Dog Handler. The MP Handler involved in the incident was the same as the MP Handler in digital photographs numbered as 0196/CG LAPS, 0094/CG LAPS, and 0213 CG LAPS. The dog was a large, black, breed which appeared to be a mix of Labrador Retriever and Belgian Sheppard. It was the only black working dog at AG. The dog was on a leash, but was not muzzled. The MP guard and MP Dog Handler opened a cell in which two juveniles, one known as ("Casper") were housed. The Dog Handler allowed the dog to enter the cell and go nuts on the kids, barking and scaring them. The kids were screaming, the smaller one hiding behind ▆▆▆▆▆▆ The Handler allowed the dog to get within about one foot of the kids. Afterward, I heard the Dog Handler say that he had a competition with another Handler to see if they could scare detainees to the point that they would defecate. He mentioned that they had already made some urinate, so they appeared to be raising the competition. This happened about 0100 and I returned to my quarters for the night. I forgot about reporting it the next day and did not remember it until the CID investigators came to talk to my in Jan 03. Incidentally ████████ died in the mortar attack on Abu Garayb on Apr 03. I never witnessed, nor ever heard of anyone taking unauthorized photographs or videotape of detainees. I never heard anyone talking about "softening up" detainees in preparation for interrogations. I was told by ████████ from the GTMO Team that I was permitted as the interrogator to strip a detainee completely naked in the interrogation booth, although I never used this technique personally. The only incident I ever heard of involving such a technique involved ████████ and I do not have any first hand knowledge of that incident ████████ also told me that I could use working dogs and said that he had used them previously, although he was unclear if he had used then at GTMO or AG. I never used dogs and do not know of any instance in which dogs were used as an interrogation technique. I never questioned the veracity of ████████ statements. I spent a considerable amount of time in the hard site area talking to detainees and giving them cigarettes, building rapport. While there, I would occasionally see inmates without jump suit standing in their cells. I inquired about this and was informed by the MPs that they did not have enough jump suits for all the detainees. I did see some detainees in women's underwear, but this appeared to be by their choice, not as a punishment or harassment. There simply was not enough men's underwear to go around. Since Cell Block 1B of the hard site housed the female detainees, the hard site received shipments of women's underwear and apparently had extra reserves that were offered to the males as better than nothing at all. I had few dealings with OGA and do not know the term "ghost detainee". I know that there are OGA detainees that were off limits for Army interrogators and that some OGA detainees have waited for months for OGA interrogators to see them, violating the 30 isolation limit rule. On only one occasion I recommended a detainee for an extension past the 30 days. The inmate was an Iranian named ████████ and I suggested that he be extended in isolation due to his mental instability ████████ had gotten into a fight in Ganci for no apparent reason and continued to show a tendency toward violence while in isolation. It was reported to me by ████████ had been bitten by police dogs while his cell was being searched. I went to check on ████████ and saw that he had bites on his thighs. When I asked ████████ what had happened he said that the dog bit him, started to cry, and asked to be sent back to Iran. He was present in digital photograph 0178/CG LAPS, shown to me this day by investigators.

End of Statement

10. EXHIBIT	11. INITIALS OF PERSON MAKING STATEMENT

AFFIDAVIT

██████████████ HAVE READ OR HAVE HAD READ TO ME THIS STATEMENT WHICH BEGINS ON PAGE 1 AND ENDS ON PAGE <u>2</u> ███ UNDERSTAND THE CONTENTS OF THE ENTIRE STATEMENT MADE BY ME. THE STATEMENT IS TRUE. I HAVE INITIALED ALL CORRECTIONS AND HAVE INITIALED THE BOTTOM OF EACH PAGE CONTAINING THE STATE-MENT. I HAVE MADE THIS STATEMENT FREELY WITHOUT HOPE OF BENEFIT OR REWARD, WITHOUT THREAT OF PUNISHMENT, AND WITHOUT COERCION, UNLAWFUL INFLUENCE OR UNLAWFUL INDUCEMENT.

_____
(Signature of Person Making Statement)

WITNESSES

_____

Subscribed and sworn to before me a person authorized by law to administer oaths, this <u>25</u> day of <u>May</u>, <u>2004</u> at Alexandria, VA

_____

_____

ORGANIZATION OR ADDRESS

██████████
Signature of Person Administering Oath

██████████
(Typed Name of Person Administering Oath)

_____

_____

_____

ORGANIZATION OR ADDRESS

██████████

UCMJ. ARTICLE 136
(Authority To Administer Oaths)

SWORN STATEMENT

For use of this form, see AR 190–45: the proponent agency is ODCSOPS

PRIVACY ACT STATEMENT

AUTHORITY:Title 10 USC Section 301; Title 5 USC Section 2951; E.O. 9397 dated November 22, 1943 *(SSN)*.

PRINCIPAL PURPOSE: To provide commanders and law enforcement officials with means by which information may be accurately identified.

ROUTINE USES: Your social security number is used as an additional/alternate means of identification to facilitate filing and retrieval.

DISCLOSURE: Disclosure of your social security number is voluntary.

1. LOCATION Fort Huachuca MID, Fort Huachuca, AZ	2. DATE *(YYYYMMDD)* 2004/06/30	3. TIME ▮▮▮ 0830	4. FILE NUMBER
5. LAST NAME, FIRST NAME, MIDDLE NAME ▮▮▮▮▮▮	6. SSN ▮▮▮▮▮▮▮▮		7. GRADE/ STATUS Civilian
8. ORGANIZATION OR ADDRESS B Co, 309th MI Bn, Fort Huachuca, AZ			

9. ▮▮▮▮▮▮▮ _____ WANT TO MAKE THE FOLLOWING STATEMENT UNDER OATH:

I am making this statement as an addition to the statement executed on 10 Jun 03 at 1037. This subsequent statement relates a conversation I had with ▮▮▮▮▮▮ and relevant background information. From 27 Sep to 5 Oct 03 I was deployed to Afghanistan to observe interrogation operations and offer advice and assistance. We provided suggestions on how to improve the effectiveness of interrogation planning, approaches, questioning technique, reporting and the use of interpreters. Our training was limited to small group discussion as the operations were already established and the interrogators were conducting interrogations around the clock. While there, I observed the inprocessing procedures for incoming detainees. The operation was very efficient and professional. The whole process took less than one hour from intrial reception to the time the detainee was seen by an interrogator. This had an advantage as the detainee was still disoriented from the capture and would be more likely to answer questions posed by the interrogators. On 7 Oct 03, I arrived in Abu Ghraib

(AG) to assess interrogation operations and conduct the training I referenced in my previous statement. After observing ███████ conduct at least two interrogations, and prior to the start of the training, I had an offline conversation with ████████████ He approached me asking for ideas as to how to get "these detainees to talk" referring to those who were believed to know the source of the incoming mortars. During the conversation I told ███████████ about the Interrogation Rules of Engagement (IROE) to ensure he knew of their existence. I told ████████ a story I heard in Afghanistan of a dog used during an interrogation. The dog was trained to bark on cue and would bark any time the interrogator had reason to believe the detainee was lying during the interrogation. I told him that this would probably not be allowed, but that the presence of barking dogs in the prison might be effective. I told him of a story of an interrogator using a Pride and Ego Down approach. The interrogator took a copy of a Koran and threw it on the ground and stepped on the Koran, which resulted in a detainee riot. I explained to him that an adjusted sleep schedule was used on detainees in Afghanistan. The process was closely monitored and used to disorient the detainee. Subsequently, I explained that basic approach strategies would be most effective within the first few hours of capture and that they needed to do timely interrogations. The more comfortable a detainee gets with his surroundings, the stronger his resistance becomes. I described the fear that I imagined a detainee might experience in that environment. I also said that the MP's need to understand that this fear works to the interrogator's advantage and that the MP's shouldn't get friendly with the source by trying to converse or offer cigarettes and the like that the interrogator might use as incentives to establish rapport. This type of friendly MP interaction was claimed to be a hindrance to interrogation in Afghanistan. I also suggested the possibility of showing the detainees pictures of what appeared to be MP's in intimidating positions with detainees. I did not describe pictures of MP's actually abusing detainees. If the MP's were actually allowed to abuse the detainees, there would be no reason to have the pictures. The purpose of the pictures was to allow the detainee's initial fear to persist until the interrogator relieved that fear and established rapport. At this point, I described detainee inprocessing as I observed it in Afghanistan. I never personally witnessed the above incidents, but heard about them from other interrogation facility personnel. I encouraged ███████████ to attend the upcoming training. I also made sure ███████████ knew that any interrogation approach or detainee handling technique had to be included into the interrogation plan and had to be approved by the chain of command. I am sure that ████████████ understood that no technique could be used outside the interrogation Rules of Engagement (IROE) and required chain of command approval prior to implementation. ████████████ only attended portions of the training that we provided at AG. I did not participate in or hear about

any other member of the MTT participating in any other offline conversations with the assigned interrogation facility personnel. I never
advocated the physical abuse of detainees and I am sure that
████████████████ understood that my intent was to only take advantage of the detainees pre-existing fear ██████████

Q: Do you have anything to add to this statement?
A: No. ████████████

End of Statement

10. EXHIBIT	11 INITIALS OF PERSON MAKING STATEMENT
	████████████████████

SECRET

I2MS Object Details

DATE: 01-19-2005
CLASSIFIED BY: 61579DMH/BCE/gjg 04-CV-4151
REASON: 1.4 (C).
DECLASSIFY ON: 01-19-2030

Page 1 of 3

Activity Contents

b6 -3,4
b7C -3,4
b7D -1
b7F -1

ID: 00735040300937	Title: ORCON 302 20020406

Narrative:

04/06/2002

b1
b6 -1,3,4
b7C -1,3,4
b7D -1
b7F -1

On 04/06/2002, [ ] detained at Guantanamo Bay (GTMO) Naval Base, Cuba, was re-interviewed by Special Agent [ ] and Special Agent [ ]. After being advised of the identity of the interviewing agents, [ ] provided the following information: ($)

[ ] was questioned regarding information about going on in Camp X-Ray as far as what he has heard the detainees talking about. He advised that the military guards had a demonstration on how the detainees will be moved to the new prison and the prisoners are worried. He also noted that there are some problems in the camp regarding their personal hygiene.

b6 -3,4
b7C -3,4
b7D -1
b7F -1

b6 -2,3,4
b7C -2,3,4
b7D -1
b7F -1

[ ] stated that the detainees are tired of being moved so many times to include Bagram, Qandahar and Camp X-Ray. He also advised that the Military Police (MP's), named [ ] have been mistreating the detainees by pushing them around and throwing their waste bucket to them in the cell, sometimes with waste still in the bucket and kicking the Koran. He also noted that in the Muslim culture, people do not get dressed, shower or use the bathroom in front of others; however, they are being forced to do so.

[ ] stated that the multiple moves, the mistreatment and hygiene issues may force some of the detainees to cause problems during the move. He advised the interviewers to warn the guards that they should take extra precautions during the move because some of the detainees are feeling that they have nothing to lose and are waiting for a time to cry out. The move might be that time. He is aware that other detainees feel that they would rather die than live the way they are living and he has heard an unknown detainee say "Death before I live like this". He noted that he has no specific information about any one particular detainee who may cause a problem but this was his personal feeling. He also stated that having demonstrations on how they are to be moved gives the detainees time to think of a way to possibly cause problems.

b6 -3,4
b7C -3,4
b7D -1
b7F -1

b6 -3,4
b7C -3,4
b7D -1
b7F -1

[ ] explained that some of the detainees are Mujahideen and they feel that when it is time to die it is their time to die and they will not care about taking someone else around them with them when they die.

[ ] advised that the detainees who have been talking and the detainees who have not been talking are all being treated the same; therefore, there is no incentive to talk or cooperate.

b6 -3,4
b7C -3,4
b7D -1
b7F -1

In other Camp X-Ray news, [ ] stated that detainees in Camp X-Ray have heard that the Americans are still fighting in Afghanistan.

b6 -3,4
b7C -3,4
b7D -1
b7F -1

b6 -3,4,5
b7C -3,4,5
b7D -1
b7F -1

[ ] He noted the following:

b6 -3,4
b7C -3,
b7D -1
b7F -1

b6 -3,4
b7C -3,4
b7D -1
b7F -1

[ ] believes that he may be at Camp X-Ray.

b6 -3,
b7C -3
b7D -1
b7F -1

SECRET

DETAINEES-3836

http://148.124.63.24/pls/iol_prod/i2ms.obj_doc_web.Doc_Detail?pS

2

DOJFBI 003190

01/22/2003   204

b6 -1,3,4
ON 1/22/2003   b7C -1,3,4
WAS INTERVIEWED AT CAMP DELTA, GUANTANAMO BAY, CUBA. THE INTERVIEW   b7D -1
WAS CONDUCTED BY FEDERAL BUREAU OF INVESTIGATIONS SPECIAL AGENT   b7F -1
THE INTERVIEW WAS CONDUCTED IN THE ARABIC LANGUAGE AND
TRANSLATED BY CONTRACT LINGUIST   AFTER BEING
INFORMED OF THE IDENTITY OF THE INTERVIEWING AGENT,   PROVIDED THE
FOLLOWING INFORMATION:

b6 -3,4
b7C -3,4   WHEN ASKED IF HE HAD ANY KNOWLEDGE REGARDING
b7D -1   REPLIED THAT HE
b7F -1   HAD NO IDEA AND WANTED TO BE ASKED DIRECT QUESTIONS REGARDING HIMSELF.
            HE WOULD NOT ANSWER ANY QUESTIONS ABOUT HIS

            IN REPLY TO BEING ASKED
                                                                              b6 -3,4,5
                                                                              b7C -3,4,
                                                                              b7D -1
                                                                              b7F -1

                                                  HE WAS UNABLE TO PROVIDE A
            DESCRIPTION OF

b6 -3,4
b7C -3,4
b7D -1
b7F -1

                        DENIED BEING A MEMBER OF   HE   b6 -3,4
            KNEW OF ITS EXISTENCE AND STATED THAT IT WAS SOME TYPE OF A POLITICAL   b7C -3,4
            ORGANIZATION. THERE WAS NEVER ANY NEED FOR HIM TO HAVE ANY TYPE OF   b7D -1
            DEALING WITH THEM   WAS ALSO UNAWARE OF ANY RELATIONSHIP BETWEEN   b7F -1
                        AND AL-QAEDA.

                        DENIED BEING A MEMBER OF AL-QAEDA, WORKING FOR THEM IN ANY
            CAPACITY OR EVER TRANSFERRING MONEY ON THEIR BEHALF.
                                                                              b6 -3,4
            HE FURTHER NOTED NEVER HEARING OF AL-QAEDA UNTIL HE WAS IN AFGHANISTAN   b7C -3,4
                                                                              b7D -1
                                                                              b7F -1

DATE: 12-10-2004
CLASSIFIED BY 61579DMH/BCE/edc 04-CV-4151   SECRET   DETAINEES-4082   ALL INFORMATION CONTAINED
REASON: 1.4 (C)   HEREIN IS UNCLASSIFIED EXCEPT   -2
DECLASSIFY ON: 12-10-2029   WHERE SHOWN OTHERWISE
file://C:\Documents%20and%20Settings\   \Application%20Data\ORION\mar... 10/6/2004 b7C -2

FURTHER DENIED ANY KNOWLEDGE OF UBL'S ASSOCIATION WITH AL-QAEDA.

b6 -3,4
b7C -3,4
b7D -1
b7F -1

COULD NOT RECALL HIS NAME
AND WAS UNABLE TO PROVIDE A DESCRIPTION.

b1
b6 -3,4
b7C -3,4
b7D -1
b7F -1

(S)

b6 -3,4   WAS THEN ASKED IF HE WAS ENCOUNTERING ANY PROBLEMS OR KNEW OF
b7C -3,4   ANYTHING WHICH SHOULD BE BROUGHT TO THE INTERVIEWER'S ATTENTION. HE
b7D -1   STATED THAT A LOT OF THE BROTHERS WERE STILL UPSET ABOUT THE DETAINEE
b7F -1   WHO HAD ATTEMPTED SUICIDE SIX DAYS EARLIER. SEVERAL OF THE BROTHERS
WERE STILL SAYING THAT HE WAS BEATEN BY THE GUARDS. HE WANTED TO KNOW
IF HIS BROTHER WAS STILL ALIVE AND WONDERED IF A COUPLE OF BROTHERS COULD
VISIT HIM TO ENSURE THAT HE WAS NOT DEAD. HE FURTHER COMMENTED THAT
SEVERAL OF THE BROTHERS WERE EXTREMELY UPSET, AND HE WAS AFRAID THAT
OTHERS MIGHT ATTEMPT SUICIDE. HE NOTED THAT SEVERAL OF THE BROTHERS   b6 -3,4
WERE BECOMING WEAK AND BEGINNING TO LOSE THEIR FAITH.   STATED THAT   b7C -3,4
SEVERAL BROTHERS BECAME EXTREMELY AGITATED WHEN GUARDS REPORTEDLY   b7D -1
TOLD SEVERAL OF THE DETAINEES THAT THEIR BROTHER HAD ATTEMPTED SUICIDE b7F -1
BECAUSE HIS FELLOW BROTHERS WERE NOT NICE TO HIM AND HE DID NOT FIT IN.

STATED THE ISSUES REGARDING THE KORAN LED TO THIS. IT WAS JUST A   b6 -3-4
MATTER OF TIME BEFORE SOMETHING LIKE THIS OCCURRED. HE COMMENTED THAT   b7C -3 4
THE KORAN SHOULD NOT BE USED AS A FORM OF PUNISHMENT. ALSO, THE   b7D -1
SEARCHING OF THE KORAN NEEDS TO BE LOOKED INTO. THE GUARDS NEED TO BE   b7F -1
MADE AWARE OF HOW THEY ARE HUMILIATING THE KORAN.

SECRET

DETAINEES-4083

b6 -2
b7C -2

DOJFBI 003437

A-230

DEPARTMENT OF THE ARMY
HEADQUARTERS, COMBINED
JOINT TASK FORCE SEVEN
CAMP VICTORY, BAGHDAD, IRAQ
APO AE 09335

CJTF7-CG   14 SEP 2003

MEMORANDUM FOR Commander. U.S. Central Command, 7115 South Boundary Boulevard, MacDill Air Force Base, Florida 33621-5101

SUBJECT: CJTF-7 Interrogation and Counter-Resistance Policy

Enclosed is the CJTF-7 Interrogation and Counter-Resistance Policy, modeled on the one implemented for interrogations conducted at Guantanamo Bay, but modified for applicability to a theater of war in which the Geneva Conventions apply. Unless otherwise directed, my intent is to implement this policy immediately.

Encl
as

RICARDO S. SANCHEZ
Lieutenant General, U.S. Army
Commanding

UNCLASSIFIED

HEADQUARTERS
COMBINED JOINT TASK FORCE SEVEN
Baghdad, IRAQ
APO AE 09335

CJTF7-CG

14 SEP 2003

MEMORANDUM FOR

C2, Combined Joint Task Force Seven, Baghdad, Iraq 09335
C3, Combined Joint Task Force Seven, Baghdad, Iraq 09335
Commander, 305th Military Intelligence Bdgada, Baghdad, Iraq 09335

SUBJECT: CJTF-7 Interrogation and Counter-Realisation Policy

1. (U) This memorandum establishes the interrogation and counter-resistance policy for CJTF-7.
2. (U) I approve the late of specified interrogation and counter-resistance techniques A-DD, as described in enclosure 1, subject to the following:
   a. (U) These techniques must be used within safeguards described in enclosure 2.
   b. (U) Use of these techniques is limited to interrogations of detainees, security internees and enemy prisoners of war under the control of CJTF-7.
   c. (U) Use of techniques B, I, O, X, Y, AA and CC on enemy prisoners of war must be approved by me personally prior to use. Submit written requests for use of these techniques, with supporting rationale, to me through the CJTF-7 C2. A legal review from the CJTF-7 SJA must accompany each request.
3. (U) CJTF-7 is operating in a theater of war in which the Geneva Conventions are applicable. Coalition forces will continue to treat all persons under their control humanely.
4. (U) Requests for use of techniques not listed in enclosure 1 will be submitted to me through the CJTF-7 C2, and include a description of the proposed techniques and recommended safeguards. A legal review from the CJTF-7 SJA must accompany each request.
5. (U) Nothing in this policy limits existing authority for maintenance of good order and discipline among detainees.
6. (U) POC is ███████████ DNVT ██████ DSN ████████████

2 Encls
1. Interrogation Techniques
2. General Safeguards

RICARDO S. SANCHEZ
Lieutenant General, USA
Commanding

CF. Commander, US Central Command

UNCLASSIFIED

INTERROGATION TECHNIQUES

(U) The use of techniques A-CC are subject to the general safeguards as provided below as well as specific implementation guidelines to be provided by 205th MI BDE Commander. Specific implementation guidance with respect to techniques A-CC is provided in U.S. Army Field Manual 34-52. Further implementation guidance will be developed by 205th MI BDE Commander.

(U) Of the techniques set forth below, the policy aspects of certain techniques should be considered to the extent they reflect the views of other Coalition contributing nations. The description of the techniques is supported to include some policy issues that should be considered before application of the technique.

A. (U) Direct: Asking straightforward questions.

B. (U) Incentive/Removal of Incentive: Providing a reward on removing a privilege, above and beyond those that are required by the Geneva Convention, from detainees. [Caution: Other nations that believe detainees are entitled to EPW protection may consider that provision and retention of religious items (e.g. the Koran) are protected under international law (ucc, Geneva III, Article 34).]

C. (U) Emotional Love: Playing on the love a detainee has for an individual or group.

D. (U) Emotional Hate: Playing on the hatred a detainee has for an individual or group.

E. (U) Fear Up Harsh: Significantly increasing the fear level in a detainee.

F. (U) Fear Up Mild: Moderately increasing the fear level in a detainee.

G. (U) Reduced Fear: Reducing the fear level in a detainee.

H. (U) Pride and Ego Up: Boosting the ego of a detainee.

I. (U) Pride and Ego Down: Attacking or insulting the ego of a detainee, not beyond the limits that would apply to an EPW. [Caution: Article 17 of Geneva III provides, "Prisoners of war who refuse to answer may not be threatened, insulted, or exposed to any unpleasant of disadvantageous treatment of any kind". Other nations that believe detainees are entitled to EPW protections may consider this technique inconsistent with the provisions of Geneva.]

J. (U) Futility: Invoking the feeling of futility of a detainee.

K. (U) We Know All: Convincing the detainee that the interrogator already knows the answers to questions he asks the detainee.

UNCLASSIFIED

L. (U) Establish Your Identity: Convincing the detainee that the interrogator has mistaken the detainee for someone else.

M. (U) Repetition: Continuously repeating the same question to the detainee within interrogation periods of normal duration.

N. (U) File and Dossier: Convincing detainee that the interrogator has a damning and inaccurate file, which must be fixed.

O. (U) Mutt and Jeff: A team consisting of a friendly and harsh interrogator. The harsh interrogator might employ the Pride and Ego Down technique. [Caution: Other nations that believe that EPW protections apply to detainees may view this techniques as inconsistent with Geneva III, Article 13 which provides that EPWs must be protected against acts of intimidation. Consideration should be given to these views prior to application of the techniques.]

P. (U) Rapid Fire: Questioning in rapid succession without allowing detainee to answer.

Q. (U) Silence: Staring at the detainee to encourage discomfort.

R. (U) Change of Scenery Up: Removing the detainee from the standard interrogation setting (generally to a location more pleasant, but no worse).

S. (U) Change of Scenery Down: Removing the detainee from the standard interrogation setting and placing him in a setting that may be less comfortable; would not constitute a substantial change in environmental quality.

T. (U) Dietary Manipulation: Changing the diet of a detainee; no intended deprivation of food or water; no adverse medical or cultural effect and without intent to deprive subject of food or water, e.g., hot rations to MREs.

U. (U) Environmental Manipulation: Altering the environment to create moderate discomfort (e.g. adjusting temperature or introducing an unpleasant smell). Conditions may not be such that they injure the detainee. Detainee is accompanied by interrogator at all times. [Caution: Based on court cases in other countries, some nations may view application of this technique in certain circumstances to be inhumane. Consideration of these views should be given prior to use of this technique.)

V. (U) Sleep Adjustment: Adjusting the sleeping times of the detainee (e.g. reversing sleep cycles from night to day). This technique is NOT sleep deprivation.

W. (U) False Flag: Convincing the detainee that individuals from a country other than the United States are interrogating him.

UNCLASSIFIED

X. (U) Isolation: Isolating the detainee from other detainees while still complying with basic standards of treatment. [Caution: the use of isolation as an interrogation technique requires detailed implementation instructions, including specific guidelines regarding the length of isolation, medical and psychological review, and approval for extensions of the length of isolation by the 205th MI BDE Commander. Use of this technique for more than 30 days, whether continuous or not, must be briefed to 205th MI BDE Commander prior to implementation.

Y. (U) Presence of Military Working Dog: Exploits Arab fear of dogs while maintaining security during interrogations. Dogs will be muzzled and under control of MWD handler at all times to prevent contact with detainee.

Z. (U) Sleep Management: Detainee provided minimum 4 hours of sleep per 24 hour period, not to exceed 72 continuous hours.

AA. (U) Yelling, Loud Music, and Light Control: Used to create fear, disorient detainee and prolong capture shock. Volume controlled to prevent injury.

BB. (U) Deception: Use of falsified representations including documents and reports.

CC. (U) Stress Positions Use of physical postures (sitting, standing, kneeling, prone, etc.) for no more than 1 hour per use. Use of technique(s)) will not exceed 4 hours and adequate rest between use of each position will be provided.

GENERAL SAFEGUARDS

(U) Application of these interrogation techniques is subject to the following general safeguards: (i) limited to use at interrogation facilities only; (ii) there is a reasonable basis to believe that the detainee possesses critical intelligence; (iii) the detainee is medically and operationally evaluated as suitable (considering all techniques to be used in combination); (iv) interrogators are specifically trained for the techniques(s); (v) a specific interrogation plan (including reasonable safeguards, limits on duration, intervals between applications, termination criteria and the presence or availability of qualified medical personnel) has been developed; (vi) there is appropriate supervision; and, (vii) there is appropriate specified senior approval as identified by 205th MI BDB Commander for use with any specific detainee (after considering the foregoing and receiving legal advice).

(U) The purpose of all interviews and interrogations is to get the most information from detainee with the least intrusive method, always applied in a humane and lawful manner with sufficient oversight by trained investigators or interrogators. Operating instructions must be developed based on command policies to insure uniform, careful, and safe application of interrogations of detainees.

(U) Interrogations must always be planned, deliberate actions that take into account factors such as a detainee's current and past performance in both decoration and interrogation; a detainee's emotional and physical strengths and weakness; assessment of possible approaches that may work on a certain detainee in an effort to gain the trust of the detainee; strength and weakness of interrogators; and augmentation by other personnel for a certain detainee based on other factors.

(U) Interrogation approaches are designed to manipulate the detainee's emotions and weaknesses to gain his willing cooperation. Interrogation operations are never conducted in a vacuum; they are conducted in close cooperation with the unit detaining the individuals. The policies established by the detaining units that pertain to marching, silencing and segregating also play a role in the interrogation of the detainee. Detainee interrogation involves developing a plan tailored to an individual and approved by senior interrogations. Strict adherence to policies/ standard operating procedures governing the administration or interrogation techniques and oversight is essential.

UNCLASSIFIED

(U) It is important that interrogators be provided reasonable latitude to vary techniques depending on the detainee's culture, strengths, weaknesses, environment, extent of training in resistance techniques as well as the urgency of obtaining information that the detainee is believed to have.

(U) While techniques are considered individually within this analysis, it must be understood that in practice, techniques are usually used in combination. The cumulative effect of all techniques to be employed must be considered before any decisions are made regarding approval for particular situations. The title of a particular technique is not always fully descriptive of a particular technique. 205th MI BDE Commander is responsible for oversight of all techniques involving physical contact

UNCLASSIFIED

HEADQUARTERS
COMBINED JOINT TASK FORCE SEVEN
BAGHDAD, IRAQ
APO AE 09335

CJTF7-CG   12 OCT 2003

MEMORANDUM FOR
C2, Combined Joint Task Force Seven, Baghdad, Iraq 09335
C3, Combined Joint Task Force Seven, Baghdad, Iraq 09335
Commander, 205th Military Intelligence Brigade, Baghdad, Iraq 09335

SUBJECT CJTF-7 Interrogation and Counter-Resistance Policy

1. (U) This memorandum establishes the interrogation and counter-resistance policy for security internees under the control of CJTF-7. Security internees are civilians who are detained pursuant to Articles 5 and 78 of the Geneva Convention Relative to the Protection of Civilian Persons in Time of War of August 12, 1949 (hereinafter, Geneva Convention).

2. (U) I approve the use of specified interrogation and counter-resistance approaches A-Q, as described in Enclosure 1, relating to security internees, subject to the following:

    a. (U) Use of these approaches is limited to interrogations of security internees under the control of CJTF-7.

    b. (U) These approaches must be used in combination with the safeguards described in Enclosure 2.

    c. (U) Segregation of security internees will be required in many instances to ensure the success of interrogations and to prevent the sharing of interrogation methods among internees. Segregation may also be necessary to protect sources from other detainees or otherwise provide for their security. Additionally, the Geneva Convention provides that security internees under definite suspicion of activity hostile to the security of Coalition forces shall, where absolute military necessity requires, be regarded as having forfeited rights of communication. Accordingly, these security internees may be segregated. I must approve segregation in all cases where such segregation will exceed 30 days in duration, whether consecutive or nonconsecutive. Submit written requests with supporting rationale to me through the CJTF-7 C2. A legal review from the CJTF-7 SJA must accompany each request.

    d. (U) In employing each of the authorized approaches, the interrogator must maintain control of the interrogation: The interrogator should appear to be the one who controls all aspects of the interrogation, to include the lighting, heating and configuration of the interrogation room, as well as the food, clothing and shelter given to the security internee.

3. (U) Requests for use of approaches not listed in Enclosure 1 will be submitted to me through CJTF-7 C2, and will include a description of the proposed approach and recommended safeguards. A legal review from the CJTF-7 SJA will accompany each request.

4. (U) Nothing in this policy limits existing authority for maintenance of good order and discipline among persons under Coalition control.

5. (U) This policy supersedes the CJTF-7 Interrogation and Counter-Resistance Policy signed on 14 September 2003.

6. (U) POC is ███████████ DNVT ███████████ DSN ███████████

2Encls
1. Interrogation Approaches (SI)
2. General Safeguards

RICARDO S. SANCHEZ
Lieutenant General, USA
Commanding

CF: Commander, US Central Command

Enclosure 1

INTERROGATION APPROACHES
(Security Internees)

(U) Use of the following approaches is subject to the application of the general safeguards provided in enclosure (2). Specific implementation guidance with respect to approaches A-Q is provided in U.S. Army Field Manual 34–52. Brigade Commanders may provide additional implementation guidance.

A. (U) Direct: Asking straightforward questions. The most effective of all approaches, it is the most simple and efficient approach to utilize.

B. (U) Incentive Removal of Incentive: Proviging a reward or removing a privilege, above and beyond those required by the Geneva Convention. Possible incentives may include favorite food items, changes in environmental quality, or other traditional or regional comforts not required by the Geneva Convention.

C. (U) Emotional Love: Playing on the love a security internee has for an individual or group. May involve an incentive, such as allowing communication with the individual or group.

D. (U) Emotional Hate: Playing on the genuine hatred or desire for revenge a security internee has for an individual or group.

E. (U) Fear Up Harsh: Significantly increasing the fear level in a security internee. F. (S/NF) Fear Up Mild: Moderately increasing the fear level in a security internee.

G. (U) Reduced Fear: Reducing the fear level in a security internee or calming him by convincing him that he will be properly and humanely treated.

H. (U) Pride and Ego Up: Flattering or boosting the ego of a security internee.

I. (U) Pride and Ego Down: Attacking or insulting the pride or ego of a security internee.

J. (U) Futility: Invoking the feeling in a security internee that it is useless to resist by playing on the doubts that already exist in his mind.

K. (U) We Know All: Convincing the security internee that the interrogator already knows the answers to questions being asked.

L. (U) Establish Your Identity: Convincing the security internee that the interrogator has mistaken the security internee for someone else. The security internee is encouraged to "clear his name."

M. (U) Repetition: Continuously repeating the same question to the security internee during an interrogation to encourage full and candid answers to questions.

N. (U) File and Dossier: Convincing security internee that the interrogator has a voluminous, damning and inaccurate file, which must be corrected by the security internee.

O. (U) Mutt and Jeff: An interrogation team consisting of a friendly and a harsh interrogator. This approach is designed to cause the security internee to have a feeling of hostility toward one interrogator and a feeling of gratitude toward the other.

P. (U) Rapid Fire: Questioning in rapid succession without allowing security internee to answer questions fully.

Q. (U) Silence: Staring at the security internee to encourage discomfort.

GENERAL SAFEGUARDS

(U) Application of these interrogation approaches is subject to the following general safeguards:

(i) limited to use by trained interrogation personnel; (ii) there is a reasonable basis to believe that the security internee possesses information of intelligence value; (iii) the security internee is medically evaluated as a suitable candidate for interrogation (considering all approaches to be used in combination); (iv) interrogators are specifically trained for the approaches; (v) a specific interrogation plan, including reasonable safeguards, limits on duration, intervals between applications, termination criteria and the presence or availability of qualified medical personnel has been developed; and (vi) there is appropriate supervision.

(U) The purpose of all interviews and interrogations is to get the most information from a security internee with the least intrusive method applied in a humane and lawful manner with sufficient oversight by trained investigators or interrogators. Interrogators and supervisory personnel will ensure uniform, careful, and safe conduct of interrogations.

(U) Interrogations must always be planned, deliberate actions that take into account factors such as a security internee's current and past performance in both detention and interrogation; a security internee's emotional and physical strengths and weaknesses; assessment of approaches and individual techniques that may be effective; strengths and weaknesses of interrogators; and factors which may necessitate the augmentation of personnel.

(U) Interrogation approaches are designed to manipulate the security internee's emotions and weaknesses to gain his willing cooperation. Interrogation operations are never conducted in a vacuum; they are conducted in close cooperation with the detaining units. Detention regulations and policies established by detaining units should be harmonized to ensure consistency with the interrogation policies of the intelligence collection unit. Such consistency will help to maximize the credibility of the interrogation team and the effectiveness of the interrogation. Strict adherence to such regulations, policies and standard operating procedures is essential.

(U) Interrogators must appear to completely control the interrogation environment. It is important that interrogators be provided reasonable latitude to vary approaches depending on the security internee's cultural background, strengths, weaknesses, environment, extent of resistance training, as well as the urgency with which information believed in the possession of the security internee must be obtained.

(U) Interrogators must ensure the safety of security internees, and approaches must in no way endanger them. Interrogators will ensure that security internees are allowed adequate sleep and that diets provide adequate food and water and cause no adverse medical or cultural effects. Where segregation is necessary, security internees must be monitored for adverse medical or psychological reactions. Should military working dogs be present during interrogations, they will be muzzled and under control of a handler at all times to ensure safety.

(U) While approaches are considered individually within this analysis, it must be understood that in practice, approaches are usually used in combination. The title of a particular approach is not always fully descriptive of a particular approach. The cumulative effect of all approaches to be employed must be considered before any decision is made regarding approval of a particular interrogation plan.

ARMED FORCES INSTITUTE OF PATHOLOGY
Office of the Armed Forces Medical Examiner
1413 Research Blvd., Bldg. 102
Rockville, MD 20850
1-800-944-7912

AUTOPSY EXAMINATION REPORT

Name: (b)(6)-4
SSAN
Date of Birth: 1947
Date/Time of Death: 26 Nov 2003
Date/Time of Autopsy: 2 Dec 2003

Autopsy No.: ME03-571
AFIP No.: 2901039
Rank: (b)(6)-4
Place of Death: Al Qaim, Iraq
Place of Autopsy: BIAP Mortuary, Baghdad, Iraq

Date of Report: 18 Dec 2003

Circumstances of Death: This Iraqi (b)(6)-4 died while in U.S. custody. The details surrounding the circumstances at the time of death are classified.

Authorization for Autopsy: Armed Forces Medical Examiner, per 10 U.S. Code 1471

Identification: Visual by 3rd Armored Cavalry Regiment, postmortem fingerprint and DNA obtained

CAUSE OF DEATH: Asphyxia due to smothering and chest compression

MANNER OF DEATH: Homicide

MEDCOM - 93

DOD 003220

A-244

(b)(6)-4

Brain: Section shows no significant pathologic abnormality

Right omohyoid muscle: Section shows no significant pathologic abnormality.

Contusion of the right buttock: Sections shows extravasation of erythrocytes without a significant inflammatory response and no significant hemosiderin deposition by H and E stain.

SEROLOGY

Postmortem serologic testing for antibodies to human immunodeficiency virus (HIV) and hepatitis C virus were non-reactive (negative).

Spleen was positive for hepatitis B DNA by PCR.

TOXICOLOGY

Toxicologic analysis of blood and liver was negative for carbon monoxide, cyanide, ethanol (alcohol), and illicit substances (drugs).

OPINION

This 56 year-old Iraqi detainee died of asphyxia due to smothering and chest compression. Significant findings of the autopsy included rib fractures and numerous contusions (bruises), some of which were patterned due to impacts with a blunt object(s). Another finding of the autopsy was an enlarged heart, the etiology of which is uncertain. Other findings included a fatty liver, which can be seen most commonly with obesity or alcohol abuse. The spleen was positive for hepatitis B DNA by polymerase chain reaction (PCR). There were scars in the chest cavity most likely due to an old infection. Scars were noted in the abdominal cavity due to prior surgical removal of the gallbladder.

Although an enlarged heart may result in sudden death, the history surrounding the death along with patterned contusions and broken ribs support a traumatic cause of death and therefore the manner of death is best classified as homicide.

(b)(6)-2

MAJ, MC, USA
Deputy Medical Examiner

DOD 003227

DEPARTMENT OF THE ARMY
66th Military Intelligence Company
3d Squadron, 3d Armored Cavalry Regiment
Camp Rifles Base
Al Asad, Iraq

AFZC-R-K-MI

Death was from asphyxiation! I expect better adherence to standards in the actual future!

11 February 2004

MEMORANDUM FOR Commander 82d ABN DIV, Champion Base, Iraq 09320

SUBJECT: CW3 Welshofer, Lewis E. Jr., 292-58-7040, Rebuttal to General Letter of Reprimand

1. I take responsibility for all actions concerning the interrogation of MG Mowhoush on 26 November 2003. However, I do not believe that my actions led to the death of the General. I have served as an Interrogator for seventeen years, and the methods I have used have never been deemed excessive. Contrary to what one may believe based on autopsy photographs; I did not beat the General. I believe I used acceptable methods in conducting the interrogations. For the reasons set forth below, I respectfully request that you not place the Letter of Reprimand (LOR), dated 22 January 2004, in my Official Military Personnel File (OMPF). If you decide that a LOR is warranted, I ask that you place it in my local file. I also request that you consider setting aside the LOR.

2. MG Mowhoush was potentially a valuable intelligence source and his death set back our collection efforts. I have not been provided with a copy of the autopsy report concerning the death, so I cannot comment on what killed the General. However, I am aware that the General's body had bruises indicating he had been severely beaten during interrogation. Members of ODA and OGA were involved in this interrogation. However, considering the lack of command relationship between our organizations and circumstances that I was placed in, I did not believe that I had the authority to intervene. Although I truly want all the facts to be known, upon advice of my legal counsel, I am unable to further discuss the specifics of the OGA interrogation.

3. In my attempt to gather intelligence to protect the lives of soldiers, I used stress positions that included kneeling, standing, and placing the detainee in a close confinement stress position that I considered acceptable. This stress position previously aided intelligence collection that targeted anti-Coalition forces and helped further develop the threat picture. The "sleeping bag technique" is a stress position I considered authorized by CJTF-7 in their memo; "CJTF-7 Interrogation and Counter-Resistance Policy"; dated 10 SEP 03 which allows "Stress Positions: Use of physical postures (sitting, standing, kneeling, prone etc)". Although a sleeping bag was sometimes used during interrogations, this sleeping bag was porous. The sleeping bag is of Iraqi manufacture and was not much thicker than an ordinary blanket. A cord was used to limit movement within the bag and help bring on claustrophobic conditions. The cord was never placed above the shoulder area. The zipper was broken so the bag was always open from the back allowing air into the bag. The bag is not used to prevent breathing.

A-246

In fact, detainees would probably be able to breathe better in the sleeping bag than they would in the sandbag-hooded conditions in which they are frequently brought to the facility. This position is designed to see if a person is claustrophobic.

4. In SERE, this position is called close confinement and can be very effective. While stationed in Hawaii, I was part of a cadre that taught U.S. soldiers how to survive in captivity and what to expect during an enemy interrogation. We frequently used close confinement positions, both as a group and as an individual stress position. The sleeping bag had been used on prior occasions on other detainees without incident. This position capitalizes on the subject's fear of tight places. Anyone who is claustrophobic gives an almost immediate response. While using the sleeping bag technique, someone who squirms or screams and is obviously having an adverse reaction is allowed out as soon as they start to provide information (incentive). Those who are not claustrophobic are able to control their breathing. When the sleeping bag was used on the General, he was able to control his breathing. He was closely monitored and I opened the bag on several occasions to determine what the General was saying during the interrogation. He did not appear to be in any distress. I believe the technique used was acceptable. Again, while I have not examined the autopsy report, I do not believe that the sleeping bag was responsible for his death.

5. I do not believe interrogation guidelines set forth by CJTF-7 were written with sufficient understanding of the type of people we are interrogating in Iraq. While current guidelines do mimic rules set forth by the Geneva Convention for questioning Prisoners of War these guidelines do not clearly address unlawful combatants who do not follow the Laws of Land Warfare. I always treated detainees humanely; keeping in mind that many detainees, such as the General, concealed information that could potentially save the lives of soldiers. Admittedly, that was my primary concern. It certainly was not my intent to harm the General.

6. Some detainees were questioned through vigorous methods. I always used my best judgment and seventeen years of experience, including what I learned during interrogation operations in Afghanistan, and weighed that against what was acceptable and necessary. I do not believe that I ever operated outside acceptable methods of intelligence collection. While an outside spectator may view the interrogation techniques as being tough, I would point out that these techniques were meant to elicit information from resistant sources.

7. I need to point out that I was in Qatar during the incident involving the death of LTC Jallel. After my return, I learned that LTC Jallel was accused of emplacing IED's. Subsequent questioning by ODA confirmed that suspicion. LTC Jallel took ODA to an IED site where there were three emplaced 155mm artillery shells daisy-chained together. Had LTC Jallel been able to detonate these powerful IEDs, there is no doubt that U.S. soldiers would have died. Additionally, LTC Jallel took ODA to a weapons cache where there were between 50-60,000 pieces of various types of explosives. This cache was capable of providing thousands of potential IEDs and was probably the origin of previous bombs. The bottom line is that what interrogators do is a dirty job but saves lives;

2

interrogators obtain no pleasure in eliciting information using stress positions. However, I reiterate that these positions are not designed to end lives. They are used to acquire critical information.

8. I fully understand the need to try and bring a civility to this country after the years of oppression. However, I cannot overstate the General's complicity in crimes against humanity. From the intelligence that was set forth by the OGA and ODA during their interrogation, it was revealed that the General was involved with massacres in Basrah that killed thousands of Iraqis Our own reporting indicated that the General was a leading anti-Coalition figure in the al Qaim area. He and members of his tribe and family were also responsible for calculated and deliberate attacks on U.S. soldiers; some of which cost the lives of U.S. Servicemen. I am aware of what techniques were used during the interrogation of the General. However, based on my own conduct, I will not take personal responsibility for his death. I do not think that a LOR is warranted and ask that you set it aside. Should you proceed with the LOR, I ask that you file it locally and not in my OMPF. I am proud to wear the uniform and want to continue to wear it, but I do not believe that the rights of anyone who poses a threat to American lives take precedence above my moral obligation to do everything I can to protect the lives of my fellow soldiers.

LEWIS E. WELSHOFER JR.
CW3, USA
3d Armored Cavalry Regiment

3

ARMED FORCES INSTITUTE OF PATHOLOGY
Office of the Armed Forces Medical Examiner
1413 Research Blvd., Bldg. 102
Rockville, MD 20850
1-800-944-7912

FINAL AUTOPSY REPORT

Name: (b)(6)-4

Alternate spellings: (b)(6)-4

Date of Birth: unknown

Date of Death: 5 April 2004

Date of Autopsy: 26 April 2004

Date of Report: 22 November 2004

Autopsy No.: ME 04-309

AFIP No.: 2924040

Rank: Civilian, Iraqi National

Place of Death: Mosul, Iraq

Place of Autopsy: Mosul, Iraq

Circumstances of Death: This approximately 27 year-old male civilian, presumed Iraqi national, died in US custody approximately 72 hours after being apprehended. By report, physical force was required during his initial apprehension during a raid. During his confinement, he was hooded, sleep deprived, and subjected to hot and cold environmental conditions, including the use of cold water on his body and hood.

Authorization for Autopsy: Office of the Armed Forces Medical Examiner, IAW 10 USC 1471

Identification: Visual, per detention facility records; postmortem fingerprints and DNA profile obtained

CAUSE OF DEATH: Undetermined

MANNER OF DEATH: Undetermined

MEDCOM - 6067

DOD 13279

(b)(6)-4

OPINION

Based on available investigation and complete autopsy examination, no definitive cause of death for this approximately 27 year-old male Iraqi civilian in US custody in Iraq could be determined. There is evidence of multiple minor injuries; however, there is no definitive evidence of any trauma significant enough to explain the death. The injuries include bilateral periorbital ecchymoses ("blackeyes"); abrasions and contusions of the face, torso, and extremities; contusion of the side of the neck; and subgaleal hemorrhage of the scalp.

There is evidence of restraint, consisting of "flexicuffs" around the wrists with associated minor contusions, and asphyxia from various means cannot be completely excluded in a restrained individual.

There are non-specific cardiac findings, including mild medial thickening of the sinus nodal artery and focal mild dysplasia of the penetrating branches of the atrioventricular nodal artery. However, there is no associated increased septal fibrosis, which can be a potential substrate for cardiac arrhythmia. There is no gross evidence of atherosclerosis of the coronary arteries. A cardiac arrhythmia related to various ion channelopathies or coronary vasospasm cannot be excluded.

The decedent was also subjected to cold and wet conditions, and hypothermia may have contributed to his death.

Therefore, the cause of death is best classified as undetermined, and the manner of death is undetermined.

MEDCOM - 6076

DOD 13288

04-629 [b)(6)-4 [_____]   *Death:*   8/18/2004

Date Autopsy   *Med. Examiner*   *Location*   *Autopsy Report:*   *Date DC Signed*

8/30/2004   [b)(6)-2 [_____]   Abu Ghraib   Prelim   8/30/2004

Manner: Homicide   *COD:*   Shotgun wound of the head

Circumstances: A group of prisoners at Abu Ghraib became unruly and the guards used lethal force to subdue the crowd. A shotgun was fired, killing the detainee.

04-630 [b)(6)-4 [_____]   *Death:*   8/18/2004

Date Autopsy   *Med. Examiner*   *Location*   *Autopsy Report:*   *Date DC Signed*

8/30/2004   [b)(6)-2 [_____]   Abu Ghraib   Prelim   8/30/2004

Manner: Homicide   *COD:*   Shotgun wound of the chest

Circumstances: A group of prisoners at Abu Ghraib became unruly and the guards used lethal force to subdue the crowd. A shotgun was fired, killing the detainee.

04-434 [b)(6)-4 [_____]   *Death:*   6/14/2004

Date Autopsy   *Med. Examiner*   *Location*   *Autopsy Report:*   *Date DC Signed*

6/19/2004   [b)(6)-2 [_____]   Abu Ghraib   Pending   6/23/2004

Manner: Pending   *COD:*   Pending

Circumstances: Made gasping sounds, found unconscious with no pulse.

04-435 [b)(6)-4 [_____]   *Death:*   6/10/2004

Date Autopsy   *Med. Examiner*   *Location*   *Autopsy Report:*   *Date DC Signed*

6/19/2004   [b)(6)-2 [_____]   Abu Ghraib   Pending   6/23/2004

Manner: Natural   *COD:*   Atherosclerotic cardiovascular disease

Circumstances: Collapsed while speaking to other detainees.

MEDCOM - 194

DOD 003321

04-386 (b)(6)-4 [   ]   **Death:**   5/22/2004

Date Autopsy **Med. Examiner** **Location** **Autopsy Report:** **Date DC Signed**

6/1/2004 (b)(6)-2 [   ]   Abu Ghraib Prelim   6/7/2004

Manner: Natural   **COD:** Atherosclerotic cardiovascular disease

Circumstances: Died in US custody

04-387 (b)(6)-4 [   ]   **Death:**   5/10/2004

Date Autopsy **Med. Examiner** **Location** **Autopsy Report:** **Date DC Signed**

6/1/2004 (b)(6)-2 [   ]   Abu Ghraib Prelim   6/14/2004

Manner: Natural   **COD:** Peritonitis of undetermined etiology

Circumstances:

04-388 (b)(6)-4 [   ]   **Death:**   5/24/2004

Date Autopsy **Med. Examiner** **Location** **Autopsy Report:** **Date DC Signed**

6/1/2004 (b)(6)-2 [   ]   Balad, Iraq Prelim   6/16/2004

Manner: Homicide   **COD:** Gunshot wound of abdomen
(Combat-related)

Circumstances: Iraqi male was shot in a firefight and died of wounds.

04-357 (b)(6)-4 [   ]   **Death:**   4/28/2004

Date Autopsy **Med. Examiner** **Location** **Autopsy Report:** **Date DC Signed**

5/18/2004 (b)(6)-2 [   ]   Baghdad, Ira Prelim   6/2/2004

Manner: Homicide   **COD:** Multiple gunshot wounds

Circumstances: Pending

MEDCOM - 195

DOD 003322

A-252

04-358 [b)(6)-4] **Death:** 5/11/2004

Date Autopsy **Med. Examiner** **Location** **Autopsy Report:** **Date DC Signed**

5/18/2004 [b)(6)-2] Abu Ghraib Prelim 6/2/2004

Manner: Natural **COD:** Severe atherosclerotic cardiovascular disease

Circumstances: Suspected MI

04-309 [b)(6)-4] **Death:** 4/5/2004

Date Autopsy **Med. Examiner** **Location** **Autopsy Report:** **Date DC Signed**

4/26/2004 [b)(6)-2] LSA Diamon Pending 5/14/2004

Manner: Pending **COD:** Pending

Circumstances: Q by NSWT, struggled/interrogated/died sleeping

---

04-110 [b)(6)-4] **Death:** 3/8/2004

Date Autopsy **Med. Examiner** **Location** **Autopsy Report:** **Date DC Signed**

3/10/2004 [b)(6)-2] Camp Cropp Final 5/13/2004

Manner: Natural **COD:** ASCVD

Circumstances: Reported to medics with chest pain

04-100 [b)(6)-4] **Death:** 2/7/2004

Date Autopsy **Med. Examiner** **Location** **Autopsy Report:** **Date DC Signed**

2/28/2004 [b)(6)-2] FOB Ironhor Prelim 5/13/2004

Manner: Natural **COD:** ASCVD

Circumstances: Found in bed during headcount unresponsive

MEDCOM - 196

A-253

04-101 [b)(6)-4 _____]   ***Death:***   2/19/2004

Date Autopsy   *Med. Examiner*   *Location*   *Autopsy Report:*   *Date DC Signed*

2/28/2004   [b)(6)-2 _____]   Abu Ghraib   Prelim   5/13/2004

Manner: Natural	*COD:* Acute Peritonitis secondary to gastric ulcer

Circumstances: Other detainees reported him in distress, unresponsive

---

04-038 [b)(6)-4 _____]   ***Death:***   1/16/2004

Date Autopsy   *Med. Examiner*   *Location*   *Autopsy Report:*   *Date DC Signed*

2/2/2004   [b)(6)-2 _____]   Abu Ghraib   Final   5/14/2004

Manner: Natural	*COD:* Myocarditis

Circumstances: Collapsed during morning prayers

04-012 [b)(6)-4 _____]   ***Death:***   1/8/2004

Date Autopsy   *Med. Examiner*   *Location*   *Autopsy Report:*   *Date DC Signed*

1/11/2004   [b)(6)-2 _____]   Abu Ghraib   Final   5/13/2004

Manner: Natural	*COD:* CV Disease

Circumstances: Brought to MPs by other Iraqis unresponsive

04-014 [b)(6)-4 _____]   ***Death:***   1/9/2004

Date Autopsy   *Med. Examiner*   *Location*   *Autopsy Report:*   *Date DC Signed*

1/11/2004   [b)(6)-2 _____]   FOB Rifles,   Final   5/13/2004

Manner: Homicide	*COD:* Blunt force injuries & asphyxia

Circumstances: Q by OGA, gagged in standing restraint

MEDCOM - 197

DOD 003324

03-571 (b)(6)-4 [_____]   *Death:*   11/26/2003

Date Autopsy   *Med. Examiner*   *Location*   *Autopsy Report:*   *Date DC Signed*
12/2/2003   (b)(6)-2 [_____]   FOB Tiger,   Final   5/12/2004

Manner: Homicide   *COD:*   Asphyxia due to smothering & chest compression

Circumstances: Q by MI, died during interrogation

A03-144 (b)(6)-4 [_____]   *Death:*   6/11/2003

Date Autopsy   *Med. Examiner*   *Location*   *Autopsy Report:*   *Date DC Signed*
11/13/2003   (b)(6)-2 [_____]   FOB Geresh   Final   11/13/2003

Manner: Homicide   *COD:*   Blunt force injuries complicated by rhabdomyolysis

Circumstances: Found unresponsive while under guard by Afghan Mil forces

---

03-504 (b)(6)-4 [_____]   *Death:*   11/4/2003

Date Autopsy   *Med. Examiner*   *Location*   *Autopsy Report:*   *Date DC Signed*
11/9/2003   (b)(6)-2 [_____]   Abu Ghraib   Final   5/13/2004

Manner: Homicide   *COD:*   Blunt Force Injury complicated by compromised respiration

Circumstances: Q by OGA and NSWT died during interrogation

03-367A (b)(6)-4 [_____]   *Death:*   8/22/2003

Date Autopsy   *Med. Examiner*   *Location*   *Autopsy Report:*   *Date DC Signed*
10/23/2003   (b)(6)-2 [_____]   Camp Sathe   Final   5/12/2004

Manner: Accident   *COD:*   Heat Stroke

Circumstances: Found on ground in EPW Camp, Body temp 102

MEDCOM - 198

DOD 003325

A-255

03-368 [b)(6)-4 ▢]   **Death:**   8/13/2003

Date Autopsy   **Med. Examiner**   **Location**   **Autopsy Report:**   **Date DC Signed**

8/25/2003 [b)(6)-2 ▢]   Abu Ghraib   Final   5/12/2004

Manner: Natural   **COD:**   ASCVD

Circumstances: Brought to MPs by other Iraqis unresponsive

03-385 [b)(6)-4 ▢]   **Death:**   8/7/2003

Date Autopsy   **Med. Examiner**   **Location**   **Autopsy Report:**   **Date DC Signed**

8/24/2003 [b)(6)-2 ▢]   Diwania, Iraq   Final   5/14/2004

Manner: Natural   **COD:**   Undetermined atraumatic cause

Circumstances: Distress during tranport by 115th MP - later died

---

03-386 [b)(6)-4 ▢]   **Death:**   8/8/2003

Date Autopsy   **Med. Examiner**   **Location**   **Autopsy Report:**   **Date DC Signed**

8/24/2003 [b)(6)-2 ▢]   Abu Ghraib   Final   5/14/2004

Manner: Natural   **COD:**   ASCVD/Diabetes

Circumstances: Chest pain following a fast.

03-369 [b)(6)-4 ▢]   **Death:**   8/20/2003

Date Autopsy   **Med. Examiner**   **Location**   **Autopsy Report:**   **Date DC Signed**

8/22/2003 [b)(6)-2 ▢]   Abu Ghraib   Final   5/12/2004

Manner: Natural   **COD:**   ASCVD

Circumstances: Taken to medics gasping for air

Thursday, September 23, 2004   *Page 6 of 8*

A-256

03-366B [b)(6)-4 _____] **Death:** 8/11/2003

Date Autopsy	*Med. Examiner*	*Location*	*Autopsy Report:*	*Date DC Signed*
8/11/2003	[b)(6)-2 ___]	Abu Ghraib	Final	5/12/2004

Manner: Natural   *COD:* ASCVD

Circumstances: No history

03-349B [b)(6)-4 _____] **Death:** 7/12/2003

Date Autopsy	*Med. Examiner*	*Location*	*Autopsy Report:*	*Date DC Signed*
7/13/2003	[b)(6)-2 ___]	Camp Cropp	Final	5/14/2004

Manner: Natural   *COD:* Massive hemoptysis due to tuberculosis

Circumstances: Pulmonary hemorrhage from TB

03-273 [b)(6)-4 _____] **Death:** 6/13/2003

Date Autopsy	*Med. Examiner*	*Location*	*Autopsy Report:*	*Date DC Signed*
6/17/2003	[b)(6)-2 ___]	Abu Ghraib	Final	5/14/2004

Manner: Homicide   *COD:* Closed head Injury; Cortical brain contusion and subdural hematoma

Circumstances: Died 12 hrs post escape attempt - subdued by force

---

A03-051 [b)(6)-4 _____] **Death:** 6/6/2003

Date Autopsy	*Med. Examiner*	*Location*	*Autopsy Report:*	*Date DC Signed*
6/10/2003	[b)(6)-2 ___]	Nasiriyah, Ir	Final	6/10/2003

Manner: Homicide   *COD:* Strangulation

Circumstances: Found unresponisvie outside isolation unit

MEDCOM - 200

DOD 003327

A-257

A02-095 (b)(6)-4 [_____]   **Death:**   12/10/2002

Date Autopsy   **Med. Examiner**   **Location**   **Autopsy Report:**   **Date DC Signed**

12/13/2002 (b)(6)-2 [_____]   Bagram, Afg   Final   12/13/2002

Manner: Homicide   **COD:** Blunt force injuries to lower extremities complicating coronary
                                          artery disease

Circumstances: Found unresponsive in his cell.

A02-093 (b)(6)-4 [_____]   **Death:**   12/3/2002

Date Autopsy   **Med. Examiner**   **Location**   **Autopsy Report:**   **Date DC Signed**

12/8/2002 (b)(6)-2 [_____]   Bagram, Afg   Final   12/14/2002

Manner: Homicide   **COD:** Pulmonary embolism due to blunt force injuries to the legs

Circumstances: Found unresponsive, restrained in his cell

MEDCOM - 201

A-258

6 "Unnatural Causes"

Case #	Circumstances	Autopsy Done?	Investigation / Disposition
A03-51	1 strangulation Found outside isolation unit	Yes	
03-273	1 closed head injury; Died 12 hrs after escape attempt	Yes	
03-504	1 blunt force trauma and choking Died during interrogation	Yes	
03-571	1 blunt force trauma and choking Died during interrogation	Yes	
04-014	1 blunt force trauma and choking Gagged in standing restraint	Yes	
None	1 gunshot wound to abdomen: "Shot without provocation"	No/not reported	

INFORMATION PAPER

DAJA-ZA   2 April 2004

SUBJECT: Allegations of Detainee Abuse in Iraq and Afghanistan

1. Purpose. To provide information on investigations into allegations of detainee abuse and/or death in Iraq and Afghanistan. New information added since the previous report is underlined.

2. Background.

    a. A total of sixty-two (62) cases of detainee abuse and/or death have been or are being investigated; forty-six (46) are being investigated by CID and sixteen (16) others are being investigated at the unit level.

    b. As noted in paragraph 3, of the forty-six (46) cases investigated by CID, twenty-six (26) cases involve detainee deaths and twenty (20) cases involve other allegations of detainee abuse (e.g., assault). Command dispositions in these cases are included, where known. Of the twenty-six (26) cases involving detainee deaths, twelve (12) investigations have been closed in cases where the death was determined to be due to natural causes or the cause of death was undetermined (i.e., no apparent evidence of abuse).

    c. As noted in paragraph 4, there have been sixteen (16) cases involving allegations of detainee abuse investigated at the unit level (e.g., AR 15-6 investigation).

    d. Command disposition, where known, is highlighted in the text.

3. Discussion of CID Investigations.

    a. Death Investigations[*]:

b7E

b7E

---

[*] There is one case summary of a death of a detainee that is missing. Efforts are underway to retrieve that summary.

DOD-054957

(5) On 3 Aug 03, at the Camp Cropper detention facility, an Iraqi detainee died while in US custody, no autopsy was conducted, and the body released for burial. The manner of death is currently classified as "undetermined" but since no forensic examination of the body was conducted, **no greater clarity as to the cause of death is expected. The case was closed on 4 Feb 04** (0025-03-CID919).

(6) On 8 Aug 03, an Iraqi detainee died at the Abu Ghraib Prison. An autopsy revealed that the detainee had died of a heart attack. **The investigation was closed on 24 Jan 04** (0136-03-CID259).

(7) On 10 Aug 03, an Iraqi detainee died at Abu Ghraib Prison. Initially, this investigation was classified as an undetermined death. An autopsy revealed that the detainee died of a heart attack. **On 1 Sep 03, the investigation was closed** (0139-03-CID259).

(8) On 13 Aug 03, an Iraqi detainee died at Abu Ghraib Prison. Initially, this investigation was classified as an undetermined death. An autopsy revealed that the detainee died of a heart attack. **Investigation was closed on 24 Jan 04** (0140-03-CID259).

(9) On 20 Aug 03, at the Camp Cropper detention facility, an Iraqi detainee died while in US custody. No autopsy was conducted and the body released for burial. The manner of death

2

030285

000245

000002

DOD-054958

is currently classified as "undetermined" but since no forensic examination of the body was conducted, **no greater clarity as to the cause of death is expected** (0147-03-CID259).

(10) On 11 Sep 03, at the Forward Operating Base Packhorse detention facility, an Iraqi detainee died while in US custody. An enlisted Soldier while on guard duty, failed to follow the ROE and shot the detainee who was throwing rocks. Case closed and referred to the command for appropriate action. **The Soldier was reduced to E-1 and administratively discharged in lieu of trial by court-martial** (0149-03-CID469).

(11)

b7E

(12)

b7E

(13) On 6 Nov 03, an Afghani detainee was found dead in his cell at FOB Gereshk, AF. He had bruising about his hips, groin, and buttocks. An autopsy could not establish a cause of death. The manner of death is currently classified as undetermined. **Investigation continues** (0174-03-CID369).

(14) On 24 Nov 03, four Iraqi detainees were shot and killed while trying to escape Abu Ghraib Prison. **Investigation determined the shootings were justified** (0264-03-CID259-61231).

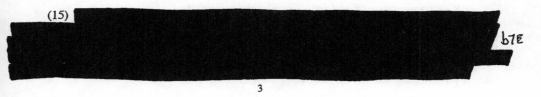

(15)

b7E

3

030286

000246

000003

DOD-054959

(16) On 9 Dec 03, at the 2d Brigade detention facility in Mosul, an Iraqi detainee died while in US custody. No autopsy was conducted, the body did not exhibit signs of abuse or foul play, and the death is currently classified by CID as "undetermined" with no greater clarity as to the cause of death expected. **Investigation was closed on 1 Jan 04** (0140-03-CID389).

(17) On 3 Jan 04, an Iraqi national was drowned after he was allegedly pushed off a bridge by Soldiers in Samarra. Further, the Soldiers are alleged to have conspired to cover up the incident. **Investigation continues.**

(18) On 8 Jan 04, an Iraqi detainee died of a heart attack at Abu Ghraib Prison. **Investigation was closed on 30 Jan 04** (0007-04-CID259).

(19) On 9 Jan 04, CID was notified of the suspicious death of an Iraqi detainee. The detainee, a former Iraqi Army LTC, was taken into custody on 4 Jan 04 and was subsequently placed in an isolation cell and questioned at least two times in ensuing days. An examination of the detainee's remains disclosed there was extensive bruising on his upper body. On 11 Jan 04, an autopsy was conducted by an Armed Forces Medical Examiner. His preliminary report indicates the cause of death as blunt force injuries and asphyxia, with the manner of death listed as homicide. **Investigation continues** (0009-04-CID679).

(20) On 16 Jan 04, at the Abu Ghraib Prison, an Iraqi detainee collapsed and died in his cell during morning prayers. To date, the results of the autopsy are unknown. The manner of death is currently classified as "undetermined." **Investigation continues** (0012-04-CID259).

(21) On 28 Jan 04, at Camp Cropper, an Iraqi Detainee, who was being treated for chest pains at the 28th Combat Support Hospital, fell out of bed, struck his head on the floor, and lapsed into a coma. A CAT scan and surgery revealed inter-cranial bleeding and signs of prior head injuries. The detainee subsequently died on 31 Jan 04. The cause of death was undetermined (body released prior to autopsy). **Investigation closed** (0020-04-CID259).

(22) On 7 Feb 04, a 61 year-old detainee died while in custody at a central collection facility in Iraq. The death was determined to be due to natural causes. **Investigation continues** (0025-04-CID469).

4

030287

000247

000004

DOD-054960

DAJA-ZA
SUBJECT: Allegations of Detainee Abuse in Iraq and Afghanistan

(23) On 19 Feb 04, an Iraqi detainee collapsed at the Abu Ghraib Prison, and died after CPR failed. An autopsy is pending. The manner of death is currently classified as undetermined. The death was determined to be due to natural causes (peritonitis). **Investigation continues** (0036-04-CID259).

(24) On 28 Feb 2004, a SGT attempted to detain an Iraqi; the Iraqi resisted when the SGT attempted to place flexi-cuffs on him. A PFC raised his weapon to protect the SGT. The SGT was able to complete the cuffing process and was leading the detainee away when the PFC believed that the Iraqi was lunging at the SGT. The PFC fired one round from his weapon which struck the detainee in the head and killed him. **CID is still investigating** (CID 004-04-CID469-79638-5HIA).

(25) On 7 Mar 04, a detainee died a Camp Cropper Detention Facility after complaining of chest pains. An autopsy indicated the death was due to natural causes (heart attack). **Investigation continues** (0050-04-CID259).

b. Other Abuse Allegations.**

(2) On 12 May 03, at Camp Bucca, Iraq, ten USAR enlisted MP Soldiers physically assaulted seven Iraqi detainees during in-processing at the facility. Case closed and referred to the command for appropriate action (0031-03-CID519). The command initiated court-martial charges against the four Soldiers – all in the 320th MP Group (USAR). All four Soldiers requested an administrative disposition of their case in lieu of trial by courts-martial. **All four Soldiers were administratively separated from the Army; three of these Soldiers also received nonjudicial punishment.**

** CID is currently tracking 20 cases of detainee abuse involving assault. Of those cases, four have not been summarized for this report. Efforts will be made to ascertain the specific facts of each case and report those facts in next week's report.

5

030288

000248

000005

DOD-054961

(3) On 12 May 03, at Camp Bucca, Iraq, an enlisted Soldier fired a shot at the feet of an Iraqi detainee instead of in a safe direction as required by the ROE, and the detainee suffered a facial wound as a result. Case closed and referred to the command for appropriate action. **The command disposition of this case (a PFC) is currently unknown** (0033-03-CID519).

(4) Between 1 – 22 Jun 03, two Soldiers (PFCs) detained two Iraqis for curfew violation and possible possession of small arms. It is alleged that one of the detainees became unruly, although their hands were "zip-tied." The two PFCs struck the detainee in the face several times breaking his nose. **Both PFCs were tried by a Summary Court-Martial. One received reduction to E-1; the other received a reduction to E-1, forfeiture of two-thirds pay for one month, and 45 days hard labor without confinement** (0049-03-CID899).

(5) On 13 Jun 03, a SGT punched, kicked and slapped a detainee. **SGT plead guilty at a BCD Special Court-Martial and sentenced to reduction to E-1 and 60 days confinement** (0046-03-CID899).

(6) On 13 Jun 03, the squad leader of the SGT mentioned in paragraph above, allowed his Soldiers to beat detainees. **SGT tried at a BCD Special Court-Martial and sentenced to a reprimand and forfeiture of $1000 per month for two months** (0046-03-CID899).

(7) On 20 Jun 03, a 1LT detained several individuals suspected of looting and placed them in the back of a truck. He later took one detainee, a young boy, from the truck, pointed his pistol at the boy's head, and fired a round away from the boy in an effort to scare him. **Case referred to a General Court-Martial; 1LT's request to resign in lieu of court-martial was approved by HQDA with OTH discharge** (0039-03-CID899)

(8) On 21 Jun 03, a SPC slapped a detainee who was seated on the ground with his hands behind his head. **SPC received a Field Grade Article 15 and was reduced to E-1** (0041-03-CID899).

(9) On 21 Jun 03, a SSG allegedly charged and placed a weapon next to a detainee's head. **SSG was found not guilty at a General Court-Martial** (0041-03-CID899).

(10) On 20 Aug 03, at Forward Operating Base Gunner, Iraq, an Iraqi being detained in US custody was physically assaulted and threatened by a battalion commander (LTC███, b6-5, b7c-5 three enlisted Soldiers and an interpreter after the detainee refused to provide information. Case

6

000249

000006

DOD-054962

closed and referred to the command for appropriate action (0152-03-CID469). **The enlisted Soldiers received Article 15 punishment; LTC** ▮▮▮ **was relieved of his command and, after** *b6-5, b7c-5* **an Article 32 hearing, received nonjudicial punishment. He also submitted a request to retire from active duty.**

(11) On 31 Aug 03, at the Bn HQs, 1/36th Inf, 1st Armored Div, Baghdad, Iraq, an enlisted Soldier committed the offense of assault when he threatened to kill Iraqi detainees in US custody in an attempt to obtain information from them. Case closed and referred to the command for appropriate action (0129-03-CID899). **Soldier received Field Grade Article 15.**

(12) On 1 Sep 03, at the Ammunition Collection Point, Baghdad, Iraq, enlisted Soldiers assaulted four Iraqi detainees who were in US custody. The four Iraqis, who were cuffed with their hands behind their backs, were kicked numerous times, then dragged from the detention area to another area where they were thrown against a wall and assaulted. Case closed and referred to the command for appropriate action (0117-03-CID899). **One Soldier (SSG) was tried by at a Summary Court-Martial and reduced to the grade of E-5. A second soldier (SPC) was convicted by a summary court-martial and sentenced to forfeitures and hard labor without confinement for 45 days. A third soldier (SFC) was convicted at a Summary Court-Martial and reduced to E-6. A fourth Soldier (SSG) was convicted at a Special Court-Martial and reduced to E-4 and given 30 days confinement.**

(13) On 8 Sep 03, at the Tikrit detention facility, an Iraqi detainee alleged he had been physically assaulted and struck repeatedly after being arrested by unknown 4th Inf Div Soldiers. **Investigation continues (0174-03-CID469).**

(14) On 7 Oct 03, at the Abu Ghraib detention facility, three active duty male enlisted Soldiers assigned to Co A, 519th MI Bn, Ft Bragg, NC allegedly sexually assaulted and threatened a female Iraqi detainee. **Investigation continues (0216-03-CID259).**

(15) On 31 Dec 03 during a "knock and search" operation, four Iraqi civilians were detained and guarded by an MP assigned to the 300th MP Co. The MP allegedly "butt stroked" one of the individuals when he refused to stay quiet and placed the muzzle of his M-4 rifle in the mouth of another detainee and "dry fired." He then removed the muzzle, charged the weapon, and fired the weapon into the ground near that detainee. **Investigation continues** (0006-04-CID259).

7

030290

000250

000007

DOD-054963

(16)

b7E

4. Discussion of Cases Investigated at Unit Level:

(1) In April 2003, a CPT abused detainees on two separate occasions. On one occasion, he pointed a loaded M9 pistol at an Iraqi child and wondered aloud whether he should kill the child to send a message to other Iraqis. In another incident, when a detainee approached one of the CPT's men for medical help with his arm, the CPT asked the Iraqi if he wanted to have the other arm cut off. **Officer reassigned to Fort Meade with charges preferred against him.**

(2) In Jul 03, several soldiers, including a SFC and a SSG, captured intruders into their outer perimeter. The detainees were stripped, beaten, and shocked with a blasting device. **SFC found guilty at a Summary Court-Martial and sentenced to forfeiture of 2/3 pay for one month and restriction for 30 days from MWR facilities; SSG is pending a General Officer Article 15.**

(3) On 13 Jul 03, two PFCs negligently discharged a pistol wounding a detainee. **Case awaiting unit disposition.**

8

030291

000251

000008

DOD-054964

(4) On 25 July 2003, a CPT pointed a 9 mm weapon at two Iraqi citizens who were handcuffed and then struck a detainee on the back of the head with the weapon. The next day, he handcuffed two Iraqi children and threw rocks at them. On 28 July, he ordered his Soldiers to detain Iraqi citizens who took water that had fallen from U.S. trucks. The CPT then threatened all of the detainees, who were blindfolded, by pointing his weapon at one of them. Finally, he approached two blindfolded detainees and pulled on the knots of their scarves causing them to choke. **Court-martial charges were preferred. The CPT has submitted a resignation for the good of the service; that action is pending approval by DA.**

(5) On 2 Aug 03, a SSG pointed a pistol at and punched a detainee during an interrogation. **SSG received an administrative discharge in lieu of court-martial. A SGT was present and also struck the detainee received a Field Grade Article 15.**

(6) On 24 Sep 03, a SPC struck a detainee on the feet, back and buttocks with an MP baton. **SPC received a Field Grade Article 15.**

(7) On 1 Oct 03, a CPT interrogated several detainees at gunpoint. He then fired the weapon six times to deflate the tires of the detainee's vehicle. **Officer received a General Officer Article 15 resulting in forfeiture of ½ of one month's pay for 2 months and relieved for cause.**

(8) On 15 Oct 03, two Soldiers (SSG and SPC) assaulted a detainee who had attempted to escape from his cell. Another Soldier saw, but failed to report the incident. **The SSG and SPC who assaulted the detainee received Field Grade Article 15s. The third Soldier (SPC) received a Summarized Article 15.**

(9) On 25 Oct 03, a SPC at the Abu Ghraib Prison slapped a detainee on the back of the head. **SPC received a Field Grade Article 15 and reprimanded.**

(10) In Nov 03, two SPCs and a PFC entered a unit holding facility at night and assaulted three detainees, punching them repeatedly. **Each soldier received a Field Grade Article 15. One SPC was reduced to E-3, forfeitures (suspended), and 45 days extra duty. The other SPC was reduced to E-3, forfeitures (suspended), and 45 days extra duty. The PFC was reduced to E-2, forfeitures (suspended), and 45 days extra duty.**

9

038292

000252
000009

DOD-054965

(11) On 22 Nov 03, five Soldiers (MAJ, CPT, 2LT, 1SG, SSG) were involved in detainees receiving head trauma. **All received written reprimands. Two other Soldiers (PFCs) who kicked or hit the detainees in the back of the head received Field Grade Article 15s.**

(12) On 10 Dec 03, an unknown Soldier fractured a detainee's jaw **The warrant officer operating the holding area received a General Officer letter of reprimand.**

(13) In Nov 03 and Dec 03, two detainees in Afghanistan made complaints to the ICRC of abuse at the outpost at Orgun-E. One detainee complained of being chained to a wall in a standing position for 10 days, kicked and beaten. A second detainee complained that he had been thrown from the back of a truck. **AR 15-6 investigation continues.**

(14) On 2 Mar 2004, Soldiers detained three individuals suspected of firing RPGs during a coordinated IED attack on a 1-37 convoy. The detainees were tested for explosive residue and tested positive. The detainees were held for approximately five hours at the platoon level then transported to the Brigade Holding Facility. Upon being interviewed, the detainees complained of being beaten by the platoon members; visible bruises and cuts corroborated the story. **An AR 15-6 investigation could not positively identify any culprits as all members of the platoon denied abusing the detainees. Several Soldiers, however, reported that the injuries may have occurred when the vehicle in which the detainees were traveling stopped abruptly; physicians examining the detainees determined that the injuries were consistent with sudden vehicle stops and starts. No further investigation was conducted.**

(15) On 18 Jan 2004, US SF personnel detained a man believed to be the head of a terrorist cell responsible for attacks against coalition forces. The commander of the SF unit indicated that the detainee began to resist which necessitated force to detain him. The detainee was brought to a short term holding cell and then taken outside by SF personnel for interrogation. Other US personnel alleged that the detainee was physically abused during the interrogation; the detainee, however, did not report any medical conditions during the medical screening process. **An AR 15-6 investigation was ordered by the Brigade Commander. The Brigade Commander ultimately determined that the allegations were false.**

(16) On 5 Feb 2003, a interrogator and counter-intelligence agent interrogated three detainees at Camp Bucca. During the interrogation, the Soldier struck one of the detainees in the face and back. **The battalion commander initiated an AR 15-6 investigation. Based upon the results of the investigation, the Soldier was given an Article 15.**

10

030293

000253

000010

DOD-054966

DAJA-ZA
SUBJECT: Allegations of Detainee Abuse in Iraq and Afghanistan

CID Input Provided by: CW3 ███████ /CIOP-COP/806-0296   66,7C
APPROVED BY: COL ███████   66,7C

TJAG Input Provided by: COL ███████ DAJA-CL ███████   66, 7C
APPROVED BY: MG Romig

11

030294

000254

000011

DOD-054967

A-270

Total as of 16 Jun 04: 10 Substantiated incidents; 10 Unsubstantiated incidents

1. <u>Substantiated</u>: 10 incidents - All 1stMARDIV – 8 OIF I, 2 OIF II.

      24 suspects: 9 Court-martial convictions – 1 General Court-martial, 5 Special Courts-martial; 3 Summary Courts-martial
                    2 Non-judicial Punishments (1 followed by Board of Inquiry & pending discharge)
                    6 - charges withdrawn or dismissed
                    7 cases pending:
                          3 pending General Courts-martial
                          2 pending Special Court-martial (1 of these may be GCM – TBD).
                          1 pending p.11
                          1 investigation ongoing

2. <u>Unsubstantiated</u>: 10 incidents; 7 known suspects & unknown number of other suspects (2 NJPs for false official statements alleging abuse).
3. <u>Other:</u>   One detainee death investigated with no allegation of abuse.
               Three investigations pending.

Unit	Date of Incident	Date Reported	Suspect, Location & Allegation	Type of Investigation	Disposition & Date	Curre Statu
			SUBSTANTIATED			
[1] 1st BN, 4th MAR, 1stMARDIV, 1 MEF *SUBSTANTIATED INCIDENT; I SUSPECT*	2 Jun 03	3 Jun 03	SUSPECT: LOCATION: TBD ALLEGATION: Beat detainees w/fists on various parts of their body	Command (JAGMAN)	SPCM: 2 Jun 03 Guilty of Art 92, violation of lawful order; Art 93, maltreatment; & Art 128, assault. SENTENCE: 120 days conf; red E-1; BCD	Closed

[2]
 	
3rd BN, 7th MAR, 1st MARDIV, 1 MEF
 	
SUBSTANTIATED INCIDENT; 3 SUSPECTS
	15 May 03	Originally reported 20 May 03; also reported it to CNN 11 May 04, & to WCQS reporter	SUSPECTS: (1)
			          (2)
			          (3)
			LOCATION: Karbala, Iraq (Logistics Base West of Karbala)
			ALLEGATION: ___ by mistreated a bound detainee (___ by holding a 9mm pistol to the back of the detainee's head while another Marine took a picture. ___ also admitted to pouring a glass of water on the detainee's head. ___ took a photograph of the detainee while an American Flag was draped over
				Command (JAGMAN)	(1) *SPCM 7 Jan 04*
					Guilty of dereliction, maltreatment, assault
					SENTENCE Conf 90 days, forf $500 x 3 mos, red E-1
					
					(2) SCM 2 Jan 04
					Guilty of Art 92
						Close

[3] 3rd BN, 5th MAR, 1st MARDIV, 1 MEF 3 *SUBSTANTIATED INCIDENTS; 4 ORIGINAL SUSPECTS; CHARGES WITHDRAWN AGAINST 1 SUSPECT*	1 Jun - 6 Jul 03	TBD	SUSPECTS: (1) ▮▮▮ (2) (3) (4) LOCATION: Adiwaniyah, Iraq ALLEGATIONS: (1) Locked two Iraqi male looters in an abandoned tank with a water bottle & hatch open. (2) Sprayed Iraqi looters w/fire extinguisher; (3) Ordered 4 juvenile Iraqi looters to kneel beside 2 shallow fighting holes & a pistol was discharged to conduct a mock execution.	NCIS	(1) Pending SPCM (2) SPCM 29Mar04 Guilty of dereliction SENTENCE: Red E-3; 30 days hard labor w/o conf (3) SCM 26 Jan 04 Guilty of detainee abuse (spraying detainee w/ fire extinguisher) SENTENCE: Red E-3; forf 2/3 pay x 1 mo; 14 days restr (4) Chrgs withdrawn
[4] ▮▮▮	6 Jun 03	▮▮▮	SUSPECTS: (1) ▮▮▮ (2) (3) (4) (5) LOCATION: ▮▮▮	NCIS	▮▮▮

(continued from previous row)

the detainee's body. ▮▮▮ failed to properly guard the detainee in the execution of his duties during these occurrences of maltreatment.

Ashville NC 23 Mar 04. ▮▮▮ is former 3/7 SSgt separated 31 Dec 03 on combat related physical disability)

SENTENCE Conf 30 days, forf 2/3 pay x 1 mo, red E-1

(3) SCM 15 Jan 04 FINDINGS Guilty of dereliction, maltreatment SENTENCE Conf 20 days, forf 2/3 pay x 1 mo, red E-1

(1) Pending SPCM-continue to 14Jun

(2) & (3 disciplin y action complete

(4) Clos

DODDON 000167

A-272

[handwritten: 197A]

	Date	Allegation		Disposition	Status
[5] 3rd BN, 23rd MAR, 1st MARDIV, 1 MEF (SNO is Reservist, Parent command is 4thMARDIV, MARFORRES) 2 *SUBSTANTIATED INCIDENTS; 1 SUSPECT*	Jun/Jul 03 (1) 23 Jun 03 (2) 29 Jun 03	ALLEGATION: [redacted] SUSPECT: [redacted] LOCATION: Al Kut, Iraq ALLEGATIONS: (1) 23 Jun 03 – SNO, as Combined Anti-Armor (CAAT) Platoon Commander, detained 4 Iraqi males for looting brass from the Ammunition Supply Point. After the 4th time of detaining them the same day, SNO had them searched, stripped of clothing except shoes & underwear, & released. SNO failed to account for their personal property & currency. (2) 29 Jun 03 – SNO's Platoon fired in self-defense at a semi-truck attempting to run a checkpoint on 28 Jun 03. The two occupants were injured & transported to the hospital for treatment of minor injuries. On 29 Jun 03, the Iraqis returned to recover their personal effects, but SNO denied them access & ordered his Marines to burn their property.	Command (JAGMAN)	CG's NJP 1 Aug 03 Guilty of Conduct Unbecoming an Officer, & Failing to Report & Turn Over Captured Property SENTENCE: Forf $2,034 for 1 mo & Letter of Censure. MARFORRES Board of Inquiry on 040406 substantiated misconduct & recommended separation w/ Hon discharge.	Closed a[...] to disciplin[a]ry actio[n] Separati[on] pending MARFC RES Report c[...] Board o[f] Inquiry; Dep CM Manpow[er] & Reser[ve] Affairs Rec[...] -da[...] SECNA[V] Final Action.
[6] 4thLARBn, 1st MARDIV, 1 MEF 1 *SUBSTANTIATED INCIDENT; 1 SUSPECT*	3 Aug 03	SUSPECT: [redacted] LOCATION: Al Mumudiyah, Iraq (LSA Dogwood) ALLEGATION: Mistreated detainee [redacted] by causing 2nd degree burns (blisters) to the back of the detainee's hands. Detainee requested to use hand sanitizer following a head call. As the detainee squatted down, resting his thighs on his heels, a Marine guard squirted some of the alcohol-based hand sanitizer into the detainee's hands; some of the excess hand cleaner formed a puddle on the floor. [redacted] lit a match & threw it onto the puddle of hand sanitizer. The liquid ignited, & flames burned the detainee's	Command (JAGMAN)	SPCM 5 Apr 04 Guilty of Art 128, assault with means likely to produce death or grievous bodily harm. SENTENCE: Confinement 90 days, Red to E-2	Closed

DODDON 000168

[7]			hands, causing large blisters.			
2nd Bn, 2d MAR, 1st MARDIV, I MEF

*SUBSTANTIATED INCIDENT;
5 SUSPECTS* | 13 Apr 04 | 15 Apr 04 | SUSPECTS: (1) ▇▇ shocked victim.
(2) ▇▇ helped ▇▇ operate transformer.
(3) ▇▇ escort for victim while he was ▇▇ shocked.
(4) ▇▇ET NCO, present during incident
(5) ▇▇ discussed shocking detainees before
LOCATION: Al Mahmudiya, Iraq (2/2 holding area)
ALLEGATION: ▇▇ reported he witnessed ▇▇ & ▇▇ shock an Iraqi detainee with an electric transformer; that ▇▇ held the wires against the shoulder area of the detainee & that the detainee "danced" as he was shocked. The detainee-victim was released on 14 April & cannot be located. | NCIS | (1) GCM 14 May 04 Camp Fallujah, Iraq Guilty of assault, cruelty & maltreatment, dereliction of duty, & conspiracy to assault an Iraqi detainee. SENTENCE: 1 yr conf; red to E-1; total forf; BCD

(2) SPCM 14 May 04 Camp Fallujah, Iraq Guilty of cruelty & maltreatment, dereliction, false official stmt, orders violation, & conspiracy to commit assault. SENTENCE: 8 months conf (PTA cap at 6 months), red to E-1, total forf, BCD

(3) Pending.

(4) Pending p11 (Art 32 complete). Evidence that SNM was not in room during incident, ordered Marines to stop when he heard the commotion, & reported it to others.

(5) Pending. | (1) & (2) disciplin ry actior complete

(3) Pending SPC 32 complete

(4) Pending p11 (Art 32 complete

(5) Pending GCM (Arraign ment 8 J 04, Cam Fallujah |

DODDON 000169

UNSUBSTANTIATED

[1] CTF-58 Suspects' ranks/units/service/ names were not provided by complainant 2 *UNSUBSTANTIAT- ED INCIDENTS; UNKNOWN # SUSPECTS*	No dates were provided	4 Jan 02	(1) Excessive force by guards when moved from transport aircraft to TF-58 Short Term Holding Facility (STHF) at Kandahar International Airport (2) Harsh physical treatment during interrogations – including interrogators hitting the head of a detainee on a table and squeezing testicles. Allegation made in Afghanistan to CTF-58, though unclear where interrogations occurred.	Preliminary Inquiry (Oral), which requested names of detainees/ suspects & dates but did not receive further information from complainant	Unsubstantiated Feb 02 -Guards use only that force necessary to control the detainee and provide adequate safety and security for the detainee and the guard force. No medical treatment was required or requested as a result of rough physical treatment from guards. -Physical abuse during any detainee's interrogation did not occur at TF 58 STHF.	Closed
[2] Task Force Tarawa, I MEF 1 *UNSUBSTANTIAT- ED INCIDENT; 1 SUSPECT*	29 Mar 03	30 Mar 03	SUSPECT: Marine Guard LOCATION: Detainee Collection Point An Nasiriyah, Iraq ALLEGATION: Detainee (Hamdan Shibey ISN 0408400C) was shot & killed by a Marine guard. Investigation determined that the detainee attacked the Marine guard and the guard acted in self-defense when he shot the detainee that was lunging for the guard's service rifle.	Preliminary Inquiry	Unsubstantiated 31 Mar 03	Closed
[3] 2nd BN, 23rd MAR, 1st MARDIV, I MEF 1 *UNSUBSTANTIAT- ED INCIDENT; 1 SUSPECT: NJP FOR FALSE OFFICIAL STATEMENT*	8 Apr 03	Jan 04 (open source – news article)	SUSPECT: ███████ USMCR LOCATION: Baghdad, Iraq ALLEGATION: ███ told Las Vegas Newspaper that he personally executed 2 Iraqis that were out of combat.	NCIS	Unsubstantiated for abuse/homicide Substantiated for False Official Statement, NJP 28 Apr 04 Guilty of False Official Statement – false allegation SENTENCE F orf 1 mo pay. SNM to retire.	Closed

DODDON 000170

[4] "U.S. Marines" 3/4, 1stMARDIV, 1 MEF *1 UNSUBSTANTIAT-ED INCIDENT; UNKNOWN # SUSPECTS*	9-12 Apr 03	2 Dec 03 CONGRINT	SUSPECT: "U.S. Marines" LOCATION: Baghdad/Umm Qasar, Iraq. ALLEGATION: ██████ alleged U.S. Marines "stole my belongings….and started torturing me" in Baghdad, Iraq. On 30 Apr 04, ████ filed a claim against the U.S. Army claiming abuse while at Camp Bucca, Umm Qasar, Iraq, an Army detention facility where he was transferred after being under Marine control for 3-4 days in Baghdad.	Command	Unsubstantiated Apr 03	Closed
[5] Combat Services Support Co 1st FSSG, 1 MEF *1 UNSUBSTANTIAT-ED INCIDENT; 1 SUSPECT*	Apr 03	13 Jun 03	SUSPECT: Cpl USMC. LOCATION: Iraq. ALLEGATION: Suspect told several other unit members that he had been ordered by his former ████ to execute 3 Iraqi EPWs while his unit was conducting combat ops near an abandoned Iraqi pharmaceutical factory south of Baghdad, & that his ████ threatened to kill him if he did not carry out the executions. Suspect claimed he killed 3 Iraqi EPWs & disposed of the bodies in an 8-ft deep hole.	NCIS	Unsubstantiated. Suspect claimed he was intoxicated, that he fabricated the entire story, & he then passed polygraph.	Closed
[6] 2/5, 1stMARDIV 1 MEF *1 UNSUBSTANTIAT-ED INCIDENT; 1 SUSPECT*	N/A False allegation	9 Jul 03	SUSPECT: LCpl USMC LOCATION: Iraq. ALLEGATION: Suspect was being treated at the Naval Medical Center San Diego, when he was overheard bragging about stabbing dead & wounded Iraqi EPWs.	NCIS Preliminary Inquiry & Command Preliminary Inquiry	Unsubstantiated. Suspect also told medical staff he was meritoriously promoted to Sgt, wounded in Iraq, awarded Purple Heart, honored by hometown ceremony, treated to dinner by Congressman, & assaulted 1 night in San Diego. In fact, suspect was assigned to chaplain's vehicle in Iraq, & there is no record of hometown ceremony or promotion.	Closed. Due to totality ████ fictitious stories b susp full held investig: tion deemed unwarra ted.

b6

[7] 1st BN, 4th MAR 1stMARDIV, I MEF 1 UNSUBSTANTIATED INCIDENT; 1 SUSPECT; NJP FOR FALSE OFFICAL STATEMENT	TBD	TBD	SUSPECT: ▉▉▉▉ LOCATION: Iraq ALLEGATION: SNM was medevaced with a broken hand. He told the BN surgeon that he broke it "punching an EPW in the face" & told another officer he broke it punching an EPW "in the back of the head." In CONUS, he recanted, stating he punched the ground.	Preliminary Inquiry (JAGMAN)	Unsubstantiated for detainee abuse. Substantiated for False Official Statement (false allegation) & infliction of self-injury. NJP Date TBD.	Closed
[8] Combined Anti-Armor Tm (CAAT), Wpns Co, 1st BN 1stMARDIV 1 UNSUBSTANTIATED INCIDENT; 1 SUSPECT	N/A False Allegation	Oct 03	SUSPECT: HM3 Navy Corpsman detailed from Naval Hospital Oak Harbor, Washington, in support of 1stMARDIV in OIF from 21 Feb 03 to 13 Sep 03. LOCATION: Iraq. ALLEGATION: That suspect claimed to have "roughed up some EPWs while in Iraq."	NCIS NAS Whidbey Island WA	Unsubstantiated. Suspect said he never abused or assaulted any EPWs, though admitted pushing one EPW's face in the dirt & tripping other difficult EPWs to put them on the ground while assisting USMC members conducting "pat-down" searches.	Close Case fo... to have ... prosecu- tive or disciplin... ry merit... Trial Sv... Office-... West N/... Whidbe... Isla
[9] 1st Intel BN, 1st MARDIV, I MEF 1 UNSUBSTANTIATED INCIDENT; 1 SUSPECT	12 Apr 04	15 Apr 04 Serious Incident Report, I MEF FWD 15 Apr 04	SUSPECT: SSgt, Counterintelligence Specialist LOCATION: Division Interrogation Facility, Camp Fallujah, Iraq ALLEGATION: That detainee was kicked & struck during screening.	Preliminary Inquiry	Unsubstantiated. Inquiry found evidence limited & conflicting. SIR indicated immediate medical exam of detainee found no associated injury.	Closed

DODDON 000172

USMC ALLEGED DETAINEE ABUSE CASES SINCE 11 SEP 01

# / Unit	Date	Date	OTHER	NCIS		
[1]	Apr 04	14 Jun 04	SUSPECT: (redacted) LOCATION: ALLEGATION: (redacted) _[handwritten: N/A]_		Investigation pending	Investigation pending
[2] 2d Bn, 2d MAR 1stMARDIV, I MEF	Apr 04	14 Jun 04	SUSPECT: (redacted) LOCATION: Iraq ALLEGATION: Death of 2 detainees who tried to attack the (redacted)	Command	Investigation pending	Investigation pending
[3] 3rd Bn, 7th MAR 1st MARDIV, I MEF NON-INCIDENT	19 Apr 04	19 Apr 04	SUSPECT: N/A LOCATION: Husaybah, Iraq (3/7 holding area) ALLEGATION: On 19 Apr 04, a detainee (suspected Muj martyr) captured during heavy combat operations died of unknown causes 36 hours after he was apprehended. The detainee is suspected to have died from head injuries suffered during one of over 20 escape attempts, including one in which he escaped from his restraints and threw himself through a window, landing on his head. Subsequent examination by a medical officer (MO) had him conscious, with good pupils, and responsive. However, a few hours later he took a turn for the worse and died with a Corpsman present. The examining MO surmised that the detainee died from internal cranial bleeding from the fall that was slow to kill him. The entire period of the detainee's captivity occurred during an intense combat engagement. Since the fall out the window did not appear to have caused any injury, the detainee was not evacuated due to military necessity.	Command/ Reportable Incident Assessment Team (RIAT)	N/A – No allegation of abuse	Closed
[4] 2nd Bn, 2d MAR 1stMARDIV, I MEF INVESTIGATION PENDING	Apr 04	2 & 6 May 04	SUSPECT(S): Unknown LOCATION: Iraq ALLEGATIONS: 2 detainees reported they were beaten & abused by U.S. military members.	Command	Investigation pending	Investigation pending

DODDON 000173

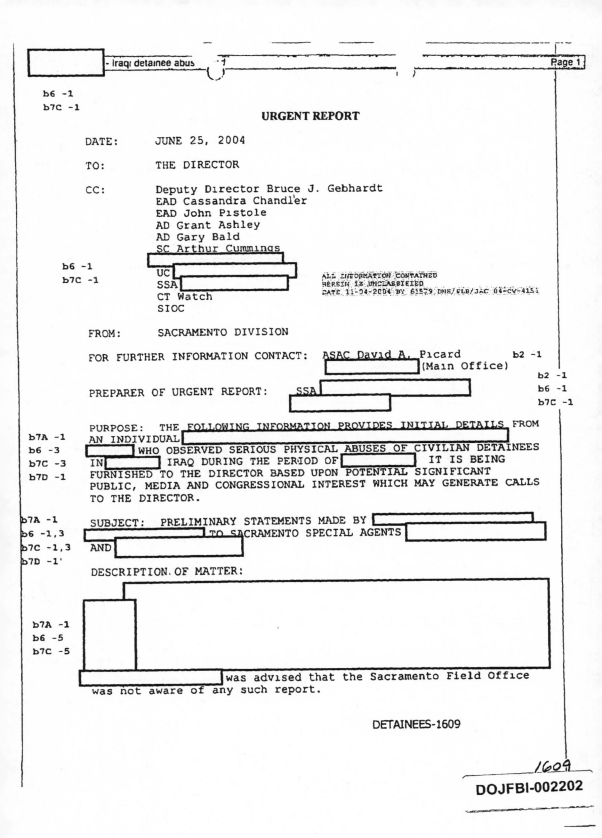

b6 -1
b7C -1

URGENT REPORT

DATE: JUNE 25, 2004

TO: THE DIRECTOR

CC: Deputy Director Bruce J. Gebhardt
             EAD Cassandra Chandler
             EAD John Pistole
             AD Grant Ashley
             AD Gary Bald
             SC Arthur Cummings

b6 -1
b7C -1
             UC
             SSA
             CT Watch
             SIOC

ALL INFORMATION CONTAINED
HEREIN IS UNCLASSIFIED
DATE 11-04-2004 BY 61579 DMH/PLB/JAC 04-CV-4151

FROM: SACRAMENTO DIVISION

FOR FURTHER INFORMATION CONTACT: ASAC David A. Picard   b2 -1
                                                (Main Office)
                                                                  b2 -1
PREPARER OF URGENT REPORT: SSA   b6 -1
                                                                  b7C -1

PURPOSE: THE FOLLOWING INFORMATION PROVIDES INITIAL DETAILS FROM
b7A -1   AN INDIVIDUAL
b6 -3   WHO OBSERVED SERIOUS PHYSICAL ABUSES OF CIVILIAN DETAINEES
b7C -3   IN   IRAQ DURING THE PERIOD OF   IT IS BEING
b7D -1   FURNISHED TO THE DIRECTOR BASED UPON POTENTIAL SIGNIFICANT
          PUBLIC, MEDIA AND CONGRESSIONAL INTEREST WHICH MAY GENERATE CALLS
          TO THE DIRECTOR.

b7A -1   SUBJECT: PRELIMINARY STATEMENTS MADE BY
b6 -1,3   TO SACRAMENTO SPECIAL AGENTS
b7C -1,3   AND
b7D -1'

          DESCRIPTION OF MATTER:

b7A -1
b6 -5
b7C -5

                            was advised that the Sacramento Field Office
          was not aware of any such report.

                                        DETAINEES-1609

                                        1609

                                   DOJFBI-002202

A-279

b6 -1
b7C -1

URGENT REPORT

b7A -1
b6 -3
b7C -3
b7D -1

_____ came into the Sacramento Field Office and provided
the following:

observed numerous physical abuse incidents of Iraqi civilian
detainees conducted in_____ Iraq.
He described that such abuses included strangulation, beatings,
placement of lit cigarettes into the detainees ear openings, and
unauthorized interrogations.

b7A -1
b6 -3,4
b7C -3,4
b7D -1

_____ was providing this information to
the FBI based on his knowledge that_____
_____were engaged in a
cover-up of these abuses. He stated these cover-up efforts
included

b7A -1
b6 -3,4
b7C -3,4
b7D -1

b7A -1
b6 -3,4
b7C -3,4
b7D -1

b7A -1
b6 -3,4,5
b7C -3,4,5
b7D -1

_____advised that
an individual did, in fact, make a complaint with Sacramento FBI
Office concerning Iraqi prisoner abuse.

b7A -1
b6 -3,4,5
b7C -3,4,5
b7D -1

DETAINEES-1610

b7A -1
b6 -3
b7C -3
b7D -1

1610

DOJFBI-002203

A-280

b6 -1
b7C -1

b7A -1
b6 -3
b7C -3
b7D -1

URGENT REPORT

b7A -1
b6 -3
b7C -3
b7D -1

The Sacramento Division is continuing to interview and will forward FBIHQ all details of his interview in future communications. Investigation in Sacramento is continuing.

DETAINEES-1611

1611

DOJFBI-002204

SWORN STATEMENT

For use of this form, see AR 190-45; the proponent agency is ODCSOPS

PRIVACY ACT STATEMENT

AUTHORITY: Title 10 USC Section 301:Title 5 USC Section 2951; E.O.9397 dated November 22, 1943 *(SSN)*.

PRINCIPAL PURPOSE: To provide commanders and law enforcement officials with means by which information may be accurately

ROUTINE USES: Your social security number is used as an additional/alternate means of identification to facilitate filing and retrieval.

DISCLOSURE: Disclosure of your social security number is voluntary.

1. LOCATION Abu Ghraib Detention Facility	2. DATE *(YYYYMMDD)*	3. TIME	4. FILE NUMBER
5. LAST NAME, FIRST NAME, MIDDLE NAME ████████	6. SSN		7. GRADE/ STATUS CIV
8. ORGANIZATION OR ADDRESS CACI, 504th Military Intelligence Brigade, Abu Ghraib			

9. ████████_____ WANT TO MAKE THE FOLLOWING STATEMENT UNDER OATH:

I arrived at Abu Ghraib in mid December. I was assigned as a screener, but for four weeks, I worked in the Hard site with interrogators. When I first arrived, we were told we needed to report any abuse and that if we did not report it, we were just as guilty. The CHIEF took us around the area and gave us a tour of the facilities. In reference to any detainee abuse, I know the following. I heard that a soldier took a female detainee and took her shirt off. The linguist did not report it and they both got charged. I never witnessed the use of dogs during interrogations nor did I witness any detainee abuse. I did not witness any detainees wearing women underwear. One day during a screening, one of the detainees was stripped of all his clothes. The detainee was in one of the rooms. For about 15 minutes, no one touched him. There was a MP female who worked during the in-processing of detainees. The female would hit the detainee on his legs to make him open his legs. She would first hit his left leg and then his right until he fell down. He was then pulled up and pushed to the wall.

A-282

The MPs were rough and having a female searching male is not right because that is against their religion. There were many detainees who came in abuse. While we were screening the detainees, they would ask us, "Are they going to beat us here too?" In the medical facility, they would start talking. Some would have broken shoulders, others came in on crutches. They do not know who beat them. They said they were beat at ASAMIYA PALACE. The detainees said that even the linguist beat them. They didn't know if Americans were involved. They were abused with cigarette burns and electric shocks. The doctor documented the bruises. I would say there were about 90 incident that took place in ASAMIYA PALACE. Some detainees would say they were beat up by Iraqis. ████████████ name was mentioned a lot by detainees. He was accused of bribing people for money and taking revenge on them. One detainee stated that ████████ would stick bottles up their rectum. The detainee couldn't sit down. This occurred at ASAMIYA PALACE. There was also a detainee who was handicap and was beat up very bad. ████████████ was a BA'ATH party member who would gather people up. He would arrest the people and turn them over to coalition forces. The Iraqis said that he was killed by the Iraqis and his body was hung. They say they have no more fear of him. A detainee said he was tortured for 7 days at night at the palace. They submitted two sworn statements. I heard this January or February time frame. There was a group that had been taken to the palace, they were two sisters, two brothers, and two uncles. One of the ladies does not want to talk about what happened to her. There was a detainee who said that he was given cold showers and was under sleep management in the isolation area. The MPs were there and they took orders to do it. The doctors didn't do anything. I checked into this and was told that cold showers was not abusive. The new unit that has taken over is much better and more organized. I spoke to every single woman and they said they spoke very highly of the soldiers. They would be taken out to get some sun. They were treated like brothers. even detainees who are leaving say there were not abused here.

Q. Do you have anything else to add to this statement?
A. No

End of Statement

10. EXHIBIT	11. INITIALS OF PERSON MAKING STATEMENT

Office of the Armed Forces Regional Medical Examiner
Landstuhl Regional Medical Center
Landstuhl, GE - APO AE 09180
DSN (314) 486-6781/7492
Comm 001 49 (0) 6371 86 6781/7492

FINAL AUTOPSY REPORT
(Addendum)

Name: [b)(6)-4]	**Autopsy No.: A03-51**
SSAN:	**Rank/SVC:** CIV Detainee
Date of Birth: UNK	**Org:** EPW
Date of Death: 6 JUN 03	**Place of Death:** Nasiriyah, Iraq
Date of Autopsy: 10 JUN 03	**Place of Autopsy:** Talil, Iraq
Date of Report: 22 OCT 03	**Investigative Agency:** NCIS

Circumstances of Death: Decedent is a reported 52 y/o Iraqi Male, Civilian Detainee, who was found unresponsive outside in isolation at Whitehorse detainment facility; Nasiriyah, Iraq. He was pronounced at 1230 hours.

Authorization for Autopsy: Office of the Armed Forces Medical Examiner, IAW 10 USC 1471

Identification: Visual recognition; fingerprints and specimens for DNA obtained

Cause of Death: Strangulation

Manner of Death: Homicide

Autopsy Diagnoses:

Head, neck and torso injuries:
1. Right hyoid bone fracture with associated recent hemorrhage
2. Rib fractures; right anterior 4-7, left anterior 4-5
3. Contusions; mid abdomen, back and buttocks extending to the left flank
4. Abrasions, lateral buttocks

Extremity injuries:
1. Contusions, back of legs and knees
2. Abrasions; knees, left fingers and encircling left wrist
3. Lacerations and superficial cuts, right 4th and 5th fingers

Toxicology: Negative

SUBSTITUTE FOR SF 503

MEDCOM - 37

DOD 003164

Opinion: Based on these autopsy findings and the investigative and historical information available to me, this believed to be 52 year old Male,  died as a result of asphyxia (lack of oxygen to the brain) due to strangulation as evidenced by the recently fractured hyoid bone in the neck with soft tissue hemorrhage extending downwards to the level of the right thyroid cartilage. Although the right superior horn of the thyroid cartilage was palpably intact prior to excision, an underlying hairline fracture cannot be entirely ruled out. Additional findings at autopsy include blunt force injuries, predominantly recent contusions (bruises), on the torso and lower extremities. The abrasions encircling the left wrist are consistent with the use of restraints. There is no evidence of defense injuries or natural disease. The alcohol detected on toxicologic analysis is most likely due to postmortem production. The manner of death in my opinion is homicide.

This is the second addendum report. The first addition has been made to reflect the presence of a second Forensic Pathologist at autopsy who concurs with the findings and opinions listed in this report. On the second addendum report, changes are made to clarify the descriptions of the larynx in the Internal Examination and Evidence of Injury Sections.

Original signed, on file

(b)(6)-2

LTC(P), MC, USA
ARMED FORCES REGIONAL MEDICAL EXAMINER

ARMED FORCES INSTITUTE OF PATHOLOGY
Office of the Armed Forces Medical Examiner
1413 Research Blvd., Bldg. 102
Rockville, MD 20850
1-800-944-7912

FINAL AUTOPSY REPORT

Name: (b)(6)-4
SSAN:
Date of Birth: 7 JAN 1957
Date of Death: 9 JAN 2004
Date of Autopsy: 11 JAN 2004
Date of Report: 30 APR 2004

Autopsy No.: ME04-14
AFIP No.: 2909185
Rank: (b)(6)-4 Iraqi Army
Place of Death: Al Asad, Iraq
Place of Autopsy: BIAP Mortuary, Baghdad, Iraq

Circumstances of Death: Iraqi detainee died while in U.S. custody.

Authorization for Autopsy: Office of the Armed Forces Medical Examiner, IAW 10 USC 1471

Identification: Identification by accompanying paperwork and wristband, both of which include his name and a detainee number, 3ACR1582

CAUSE OF DEATH: Blunt Force Injuries and Asphyxia

MANNER OF DEATH: Homicide

OPINION

This 47-year-old White male, (b)(6)-4 died of blunt force injuries and asphyxia. The autopsy disclosed multiple blunt force injuries, including deep contusions of the chest wall, numerous displaced rib fractures, lung contusions, and hemorrhage into the mesentery of the small and large intestine. An examination of the neck structures revealed hemorrhage into the strap muscles and fractures of the thyroid cartilage and hyoid bone. According to the investigative report provided by U.S. Army CID, the decedent was shackled to the top of a doorframe with a gag in his mouth at the time he lost consciousness and became pulseless.

The severe blunt force injuries, the hanging position, and the obstruction of the oral cavity with a gag contributed to this individual's death. The manner of death is homicide.

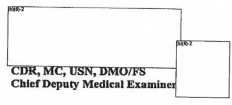

CDR, MC, USN, DMO/FS
Chief Deputy Medical Examiner

Office of the Armed Forces Regional Medical Examiner
Landstuhl Regional Medical Center
Landstuhl, GE - APO AE 09180
DSN (314) 486-6781/7492
Comm 001 49 (0) 6371 86 6781/7492

FINAL AUTOPSY REPORT

Name: [b)(6)-4]
SSAN:
Date of Birth: N/A
Date of Death: 6 NOV 03
Date of Autopsy: 13 NOV 03
Date of Report: 13 NOV 03

Autopsy No.: A03-144
Rank/SVC: Afghan Civilian
Org: Afghanistan Local National
Place of Death: Helmand Prov, Afghanistan
Place of Autopsy: Bagram AF, Afghanistan
Investigative Agency: USACIDC

Circumstances of Death: The decedent, an Afghan local national civilian, was found unresponsive while under guard by the Afghanistan Militia Forces at the FOB Gereshk, Afghanistan, approximately 1430 hours. An initial autopsy was performed by a FST, TF Warrior, KAF General Surgeon on orders of the local command.

Authorization for Autopsy: Office of the Armed Forces Medical Examiner, IAW 10 USC 1471

Identification: Visual recognition; fingerprints and specimens for DNA obtained

Cause of Death: Multiple Blunt Force Injuries Complicated by Rhabdomyolysis

Manner of Death: Homicide

Autopsy Diagnoses:
1. Multiple blunt force injuries
   a. Head injuries:
      i. Multiple abrasions, bilateral forehead and temporal areas
      ii. Bilateral scleral hemorrhages
      iii. Focal subgaleal hemorrhages, bilateral fronto-parietal areas
   b. Torso and extremity injuries:
      i. Crusted abrasions; anterior chest and abdomen, right upper arm and elbow, left knee and proximal lower leg
      ii. Focal contusions; left lateral shoulder, right posterior thigh and scrotum
      iii. Confluent contusions with subcutaneous and peri-muscular hemorrhages; lower back (L>R), buttocks, posterior thighs and knees, anterior thighs and both groin areas
      iv. Intramuscular hemorrhage with associated necrosis, left lower back
      v. Peri-testicular hemorrhage
2. Moderate pulmonary congestion and edema
3. Moderate pulmonary anthracosis
4. Moderate pulmonary hilar anthracotic lymphadenopathy
5. Mild cerebral edema with bilateral uncal and cerebellar tonsil herniation
6. Moderated hepatic fatty change
7. Moderate visceral autolysis

Toxicology: Negative

Special Studies: Urine chemistry positive for myoglobin

SUBSTITUTE FOR SF 503

MEDCOM - 44

DOD 003171

A-288

Opinion: Based on these autopsy findings and the investigative and historical information available to me the cause of death of this Afghan male believed to be [(b)(6)-4] is multiple blunt force injuries of the lower torso and legs complicated by rhabdomyolysis (release of toxic byproducts into the system die to destruction of muscle). The manner of death, in my opinion, is homicide. The decedent was not under the pharmacologic effect of drugs or alcohol at the time of death.

[(b)(6)-2]

LTC(P), MC, USA
Armed Forces Regional Medical Examiner

2

DOD 003172

Defense Intelligence Agency
Office of the Inspector General
Office for Investigations
Report of Conversation

(b)(3):10
USC
424,(b)(8)

Date: 19 May 2004	Project 9999(b)(2),(b)(3):10 USC 424	Time: 1300
Name of Contact: ███████	Office/Division: ████████	Phone ████████
Address of Organization: ████████	(b)(2),(b)(3):10 USC 424	
Employee Name: ██████████	Office/Division: IG	Phone #: ████
Circle One WE	VISITED	
Subject: Knowledge of incidents relating to IRAQ Prison Situation		

What was said:

████████████ and ████████ met with ████████ who was first asked if ████ had been interviewed by any other agency regarding the Iraq prison issues. ████████ stated that ███ had not been interviewed by anyone. ████ related that ████████ was TDY to Iraq from 23 October 2003 to 21 April 2004. During ████ time in Iraq ███ was the ████████████████ in which ████████ was in charge of a 3–4 man team that helped focused the interrogations. ████████ stated ████████ had the opportunity to visit the prison on two different occasions, during ████ 6 months in Iraq. During ████ last visit to the prison, ████ only observation of any prisoners was a single detainee being escorted by two guards, during which ██████████ did not observed anything but gentle handling of the detainee ██████████ was asked about any other DIA employees who may have been involved with the detainees, at which time ████████ stated that DIA had

(b)(2) no permanent representation at the prison until about February 2004, when a ██████████ reports officers arrived, there were two of them and they were contractors. ██████████ did not know the identities of the two individuals ██████████ went as to say that when ████ arrived, ████████ and three contractors arrive in Iraq, their DIA association stopped. They then reported directly to ████████

██████████ was asked about ████ knowledge of abuses specifically "Rape" that may have occurred against female detainees, ██████████ related that ███ personally know of none, however, ████ does remember in a meeting held by ████████████ during which ██████████ discussed an interview ████ had with BG TAGUBA, where BG TAGUBA had stated that there was allegations that some female detainees may have been raped by US Soldiers, and that the detainees had been tested for pregnancy with negative results. ████ stated ████ has no eyewitness or direct knowledge of abuses at the prison. ████████████ stated that the expectations of "Non Humantors" were that one had to break the detainees to get the information. ▮▮▮ stated that "HQ" wanted the interrogators to break the detainees. The interrogators

²)
were members of the ▮▮▮▮▮▮ based out of ▮▮▮▮▮▮▮ but (b)(2)
ᵊ)
▮▮▮▮ FBI also had interrogators working at the prison.

▮▮▮▮▮ was asked if the was some type of document, such as an SOP or regulation that stated what the interrogators could or could not do to the detainees. ▮▮▮▮▮ stated there is a 35 page document (Frag Order), which spells out the rules of engagement by which the interrogators were supposed to operate under. ▮▮▮ went on to say the people were encourage to go to the outer limits to get information from the detainees by people who wanted the information. ▮▮▮ was asked to whom ▮▮ was referring and ▮▮ stated LTG SANCHEZ ▮▮▮ said there was desperate need to get information from the detainees. ▮▮▮▮▮ did not have additional information to provide, and provided a contact number ▮▮▮▮▮ to reach ▮▮▮ until ▮▮ retires at the end of June 04.

(b)(3):10
USC 424

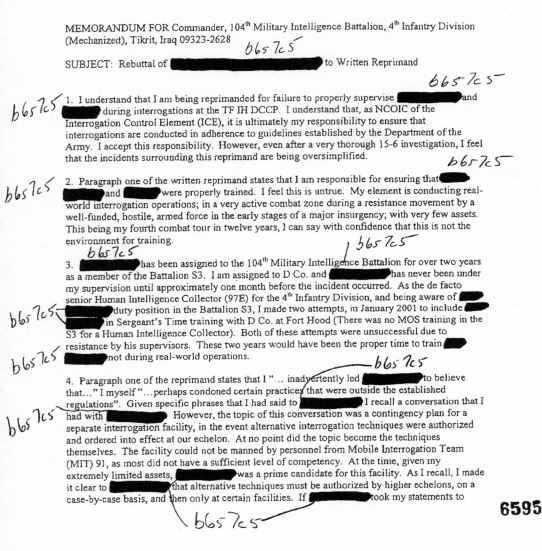

DEPARTMENT OF THE ARMY
104TH MILITARY INTELLIGENCE BATTALION
4TH INFANTRY DIVISION (MECHANIZED)
TIKRIT, IRAQ 09323-2628

AFYB-MIB-CDR   9 NOV 2003

MEMORANDUM FOR Commander, 104th Military Intelligence Battalion, 4th Infantry Division
(Mechanized), Tikrit, Iraq 09323-2628   b6 b7c5

SUBJECT: Rebuttal of ███████████████ to Written Reprimand

1. I understand that I am being reprimanded for failure to properly supervise ███████ and
███████ during interrogations at the TF IH DCCP. I understand that, as NCOIC of the
Interrogation Control Element (ICE), it is ultimately my responsibility to ensure that
interrogations are conducted in adherence to guidelines established by the Department of the
Army. I accept this responsibility. However, even after a very thorough 15-6 investigation, I feel
that the incidents surrounding this reprimand are being oversimplified.

2. Paragraph one of the written reprimand states that I am responsible for ensuring that ███
███ and ███████ were properly trained. I feel this is untrue. My element is conducting real-
world interrogation operations; in a very active combat zone during a resistance movement by a
well-funded, hostile, armed force in the early stages of a major insurgency; with very few assets.
This being my fourth combat tour in twelve years, I can say with confidence that this is not the
environment for training.

3. ███████ has been assigned to the 104th Military Intelligence Battalion for over two years
as a member of the Battalion S3. I am assigned to D Co. and ███████ has never been under
my supervision until approximately one month before the incident occurred. As the de facto
senior Human Intelligence Collector (97E) for the 4th Infantry Division, and being aware of ███
███ duty position in the Battalion S3, I made two attempts, in January 2001 to include ███
███ in Sergeant's Time training with D Co. at Fort Hood (There was no MOS training in the
S3 for a Human Intelligence Collector). Both of these attempts were unsuccessful due to
resistance by his supervisors. These two years would have been the proper time to train ███
███ not during real-world operations.

4. Paragraph one of the reprimand states that I "… inadvertently led ███████ to believe
that…" I myself "…perhaps condoned certain practices that were outside the established
regulations". Given specific phrases that I had said to ███████ I recall a conversation that I
had with ███████ However, the topic of this conversation was a contingency plan for a
separate interrogation facility, in the event alternative interrogation techniques were authorized
and ordered into effect at our echelon. At no point did the topic become the techniques
themselves. The facility could not be manned by personnel from Mobile Interrogation Team
(MIT) 91, as most did not have a sufficient level of competency. At the time, given my
extremely limited assets, ███████ was a prime candidate for this facility. As I recall, I made
it clear to ███████ that alternative techniques must be authorized by higher echelons, on a
case-by-case basis, and then only at certain facilities. If ███████ took my statements to

6595

A-292

mean anything more than what I said, that was not my intention. I do not feel that I said anything to ▮▮▮▮ that would lead a reasonable person to believe that I condoned any practices outside regulations.

5. ▮▮▮▮ is a 98G Voice Interceptor, attached to the 104th Military Intelligence Battalion as a linguist. He is neither trained, nor authorized to conduct interrogations. I trained ▮▮ ▮▮▮ on his duties as an interpreter during interrogation operations and he has always performed admirably and with dedication. There was no reason, whatsoever, to think that ▮ ▮▮▮ would harm the detainee or allow him to be harmed. During the incident in question, ▮▮▮ was under the immediate supervision of the team leader of MIT 91 and assistant NCOIC of the ICE, ▮▮▮▮▮ (223rd MI BN), who was supposed to be conducting the interrogation. My duties are such that I cannot supervise more than a small fraction of the interrogations or screenings carried out by my element. I am forced to delegate supervisory responsibilities during the majority of operations.

6. Paragraph two of the reprimand states that I "…assigned a known difficult interrogation task to a very junior and inexperienced interrogator". While this is true, the truth of it is rather relative. All interrogations at the TF IH CCP are difficult due to several factors that have been brought up, through Tac HUMINT Ops, many times. Suggestions made to rectify these problems have been, and continue to be, ignored. With the exception of myself, all interrogators at the TF IH ICE were, and most remain, inexperienced at actual interrogation. The intelligence exploitation of detainees at the TF IH CCP has been limited, largely, to cursory and in-depth screenings of detainees due to insufficient personnel, time and resources. Relatively speaking, few formal interrogations have been carried out, and all of these have been individuals targeted as being of potentially high intelligence value. After two to three weeks of observation and assessment of ▮▮▮▮▮ performance during joint screenings and interrogations, prior to the incident, ▮▮▮ was found to have a level of methodological proficiency above most of the other interrogators at the ICE and had, in fact (as I noted to ▮▮▮▮ on one occasion), exhibited a preference for "soft" approaches. In short, ▮▮▮▮ is, in reality, no less proficient, and possibly more talented, than most of the other interrogators at the ICE.

7. Paragraph two of the reprimand also states that I "…failed to discern what techniques ▮▮▮ would use during the interrogation". I do not feel that this is entirely accurate. When discussing the pending interrogation with ▮▮▮▮▮, he stated that he planned to use a "harsh approach". This is a term used frequently among interrogators to refer to such hostile approach techniques as "Fear-Up (harsh)" and "Pride and Ego-Down" or a combination thereof. Considering the approaches used previously against MP2496, and their relative ineffectiveness, I felt, and still feel, at that time, a "harsh approach" was in order. Additionally, interrogators are never required to have individual approaches approved by the ICE. An interrogation is an extremely fluid process that requires the interrogator to, in turn, be extremely flexible. While all interrogators must inform me as to the general approach they plan to use, as ▮▮▮▮ did, limiting interrogators to specific, preplanned approaches and techniques is not feasible during a proper interrogation. Some standard interrogation processes, which may be identified in FM 34-52 INTELLIGENCE INTERROGATION, are no longer applicable and may very well be counterproductive, due to this FM's application being Major Theater War operations. In many cases it is not applicable to the modern battlefield. I believe this is one of the reasons that it is no longer printed. To my knowledge, no FM covers counterinsurgency interrogation operations.

8. I firmly believe that ▮▮▮▮▮ took the actions he did, partially, due to his perception of the command climate of the division as a whole. Comments made by senior leaders regarding

6596

DOD 002822

A-293

detainees such as "They are not EPWs. They are terrorists and will be treated as such" have caused a great deal of confusion as to the status of the detainees. Additionally, personnel at the ICE regularly see detainees who are, in essence, hostages. They are normally arrested by Coalition Forces because they are family of individuals who have been targeted by a brigade based on accusations that may or may not be true, to be released, supposedly, when and if the targeted individual surrenders to Coalition Forces. In reality, these detainees are transferred to Abu Ghyraib prison and become lost in the Coalition detention system regardless of whether the targeted individual surrenders himself. I know that ███████████ has himself witnessed senior leaders at briefings, reporting that they have taken such detainees, with the command giving their tacit approval. In hindsight, it seems clear that, considering the seeming approval of these and other tactics by the senior command, it is a short jump of the imagination that allows actions such as those committed by ███████████, to become not only tolerated, but encouraged. This situation is made worse with messages from higher echelons soliciting lists of alternative interrogation techniques and the usage of phrases such as "...the gloves are coming off". The theory becomes even more plausible when one considers the facts surrounding a detainee such as MP2496—a known terrorist, insurgent and killer of American soldiers. While I do not condone ██████████ actions in any way, I am beginning to see how he might arrive at certain erroneous conclusions, despite my warnings that there is no detainee here worth any of my soldiers going to prison. I feel that this is a dangerous situation that should be confronted.

9. I agree that I am in a very delicate and perilous duty position. It is one for which none of my training has prepared me and was not supposed to exist. Additionally, numerous other issues inhibit our effective mission accomplishment. Our unit has never trained for detention facility operations because our unit is neither designed nor intended for this mission. Current detainee handling policies adversely effect operations in ways that eliminate any reasonable chance of successful interrogation. Other factors effecting mission accomplishment are more complicated. I spent over three years, between deployments, training my soldiers to operate in Tactical HUMINT Teams in a combat environment remarkably similar to the one in which our division is currently operating. Instead of allowing our soldiers to execute the mission which exists, for which they have trained, they are assigned a mission for which they have not trained, are not manned, are not equipped, are not supplied and, considering manning and the current policies effecting interrogation operations, cannot effectively accomplish at division level regardless. Unfortunately, the element's low production of IIRs supports this.

10. I agree that I have made some mistakes since being assigned this duty position. However, I feel that I have carried out my duties as well as, and in many cases better than, could be expected. I have been given scant resources, few supplies, and some of the attached collection assets could have only been considered mediocre at best. I have considered, at length, what more I could have done to prevent the actions of ███████ and ███████ while still conducting the element's assigned operations. Currently, I am still at a loss. ███████ was being supervised by a trained SSG Human Intelligence Collector, senior but subordinated to me, attached to the element, and supposedly in charge of his interrogation. ███████ is a Human Intelligence Collector whom I was not given the opportunity to properly train. However, due to limited organic assets, he was needed to help conduct operations. I feel I took what measures were available to me within the constraints of my mission and available support. I will continue to execute my assigned mission to the best of my ability.

███████████ b65 7c5

SSG, USA
NCOIC, TF IH ICE

6597

DOD 002823

A-294

DEPARTMENT OF THE ARMY
104th MILITARY INTELLIGENCE BATTALION
HEADQUARTERS 4TH INFANTRY DIVISION (MECHANIZED)
TIKRIT, IRAQ

REPLY TO
ATTENTION OF:

AFYB-MI-HHOC   6 October 2003

MEMORANDUM FOR RECORD

SUBJECT: Detainee Abuse Incident – 15-6 Investigation

1. REFERENCES

    a. Geneva Convention relative to the Treatment of Prisoners of War, 1949.

    b. Geneva Convention Relative to the Protection of Civilians in a Time of War, 1949.

    c. Hague Convention for the Protection of Cultural Property in the Event of Armed Conflict, 1954.

    d. FM 34-52: Interrogation Operations.

    e. FM 24-10: The Laws of Land Warfare.

2. FACTS   *b64 7c4*

    a. On 14 August 2003, █████████████████████ at Combined Joint Task
Force 7 (CJTF-7) Joint Human Intelligence Cell (J2X), V (U.S.) Corps, not further identified
(NFI), wrote an electronic mail correspondence (e-mail) to V Corps human intelligence
(HUMINT) exploitation elements (see Exhibit A). The e-mail addressed the relatively poor *b64 7c4*
success rate of intelligence collection from detainee interrogations. ████ provided the Judge
Advocate General's (JAG) list of definitions of "combatants", "lawful combatants", and
"unprivileged belligerents" or "unlawful combatants" and explained █ was unaware of any rules
of engagement (ROE) governing treatment of unprivileged belligerents, but was researching the
issue. ████ requested a creative "wish list" of what interrogators consider more "effective"
interrogation techniques, which the Staff Judge Advocate (SJA) would review for compliance *b64 7c4*
with the statutes of the Geneva Convention. ████ set a deadline of 17 August 2003, for "wish
list" submission. ████████ NFI, had grown frustrated with the lack of
interrogation success and wanted detainees "broken". "Broken" is a term interrogators use to
describe the interrogator's "successful application of approach techniques eventually induces the
source to willingly provide accurate intelligence information to the interrogator" (reference: FM
34-52, Chapter 3: Interrogation Process). ████ wrote, "The gloves are coming off...regarding
these detainees"; "[c]asualties are mounting and we need to start gathering info to help protect
our fellow soldiers from any further attacks."

b64 7c4

b64 7c4

b64 7c4

6611

b. ████████████████ 3rd Armored Cavalry Regiment, NFI, responded to ████████ e-mail (see Exhibit A) and stated ████ interrogation experience in Afghanistan had demonstrated ████████████████████████. As a result, the current detainee population in Iraq understands the use of physical force more than psychological manipulation or incentives. ████████ suggested the application of techniques used in Survival, Evasion, Resistance, and Escape (SERE) School and cited examples of "open handed facial slaps from a distance of no more than about two feet and back handed blows to the midsection from a distance of about 18 inches" as examples.

c. ████████ NFI, rebutted ████████ 501st Military Intelligence Battalion (MI Bn) response in a subsequent e-mail (see Exhibit A), stating international law could not be "just put aside when we find it inconvenient" and that, regardless of casualties sustained, no justification exists for dropping standards of ethics. ████████ concluded the e-mail stating "American soldiers…[are] heirs of a long tradition of staying on the high ground" and should remain there.

d. Shortly after that e-mail was sent, ████████████████████ of the Interrogation Control Element (ICE), Division Central Collection Point (DCCP), Forward Operating Base (FOB) Ironhorse, 4th Mechanized Infantry Division (4ID), Tikrit, Iraq, NFI, mentioned the e-mail to the soldiers assigned to the ICE and requested their suggestions for the interrogation technique "wish list" ████████ received no input from his soldiers. ████████ understood ████████ requested a list of interrogation techniques, both legal and illegal, which ████████ deemed more effective in obtaining intelligence information from detainees. ████████ spoke with ████████ of Tactical HUMINT Operations (THOPS), 104th MI Bn, 4ID, NFI, about the request. ████████ recalls (see Exhibits B and C) asking ████████ "Does this mean what I think it means?", to which ████████ replied, "I think so." ████████ compiled a list of ████████ own suggestions, named the document "Alternative Interrogation Techniques" (see Exhibit D), and saved it on ████████ computer's Desktop. ████████ subordinate soldiers have regular access to ████████ computer and any one of them are likely to have seen the document. It is not unreasonable to think curious soldiers may have opened the document and read the text. ████████ submitted ██ "wish list" document on 17 August 2003 (see Exhibit E). Nothing further is known about the "wish list" or what actions were taken with compiled lists at this time.

e. In late August 2003, ████████████████████ ICE, 104th MI Bn, 4ID, NFI, a HUMINT Collection Specialist, was reassigned from the Operations Office, 104th MI Bn, to the ICE, upon ████████ request for additional interrogators. ████████ completed HUMINT Collection Specialist (97E) Advanced Individual Training (AIT) approximately 2 years ago and has been assigned to the Operations Section, 104th MI Bn, in an administrative capacity until recently. Since ████████ needed skill refresher training, ████████ allowed ████████ to view interrogations ████████ or another experienced interrogator conducted. Eventually, ████████ allowed ████████ to conduct ██ own interrogations while supervised by ████████ or another experienced interrogator. When ████████ felt ████████ was ready, ████████ conducted

2

6612

DOD 002838

interrogations without supervision. It is unclear whether ████████████ discussed the
application of force in interrogations following the advent of ██████ e-mail. ████ recalls a
(see Exhibits F and G) discussion at the FOB Ironhorse dining facility in which █████ asked
████████ what sort of "alternate interrogation techniques" ██████ was suggesting.
allegedly suggested application of force, which did not leave bruises or scars on the detainee.
█████ recalls ██████ asked ████ whether █ was "up to it" and if █ could "handle it".
████ says █ replied ██████ could, though was ensure whether the interpreters could.

f. ████████ had conducted the initial interrogation screening of Detainee ████████
██████, and deemed ██████ much more difficult to "break" than most other detainees.
████ assigned ██████ to ██████ for interrogation. ████ felt ██████ imposing
physical size would intimidate ██████ greater than any of the other interrogators in the ICE
could and would likely yield results sooner. ██████ knew about ████ e-mail and agreed
with ██████ statement that "the gloves are coming off", likely encouraged by ██████
interpretation that this meant considering interrogation techniques heretofore unauthorized.
████████ identified ████████ as an accomplice in an attack against U.S. soldiers and led
American soldiers to ████████ ██ █ went into the interrogation viewing ████████ in
light of the information that ██████ had killed 3 American soldiers and did not deserve all
the rights and privileges he was afforded while at the DCCP. ██████ intended to interrogate
██████ employing "stress positions" and physical force to elicit a confession and time-
sensitive information of intelligence value, which could prevent future attacks against American
forces and save lives. "Stress positions" are body positions designed to cause physical
discomfort and fatigue. ████████ requested ████████, ICE, 104th MI Bn, 4ID, NFI,
for his interpreter for the interrogation. It is unclear why ██████ selected ██████ though I b
believe ████ likely told ██████ he would hit ██████ feet during the course of the
interrogation. ██████ a Voice Interceptor (98G) Arabic linguist ██████
descent and ████████████████████████████ describes the
interpreter in this interrogation as an ██████████ sworn statement (Exhibit H).
████████ likely knows very little about interrogation legal and ethical guidelines, since he has
worked at the ICE only since late August 2003. I suspect ██████ knew of ██████ intentions
to hit ████████ feet and ██████ a young and junior-ranking soldier, likely went along with
the idea (see Exhibits I and J).

g. In mid-afternoon on 23 September 2003, ██████ approached ████████,
4th Military Police (MP) Company, 4ID, and requested
████████ presence in ██████ interrogation later that day. ██████
intended to "turn it up a notch" or "soup up" ██████ interrogation (see Exhibits K and L).
██ he wanted the use of a room with solid walls for ██████
interrogation, as the walls would provide for a wider variety of stress position options. An
interrogation at the DCCP normally occurs in one of three tents, or "booths", set up outside the
east wall of the DCCP high-security area. It is unclear whether ████████████████
intentions, though I strongly suspect ██████ had full knowledge. ██████ sworn statement
indicates he not only told ██████, but ██████ and ██████ conspired together to assault
████████ also states he and ██████ agreed they would be discreet in their

3

A-297

b647c4

b65 7c5 / b657c5

handling of the interrogation, telling only ████████████ consented to being present at the interrogation and told ████████ would request permission from ████ 4th MP Company, for use of one of the rooms in the DCCP high-security holding area.

b657c5

b657c5

b657c5

h. ████████ accompanied by ████████ went to the ICE Operations Office and told ████ would interrogate ████████ using a "Fear-Up (Harsh)" approach technique. A "Fear-Up" approach means the interrogator identifies a stimulus that causes fear in the subject and exploits the stimulus to elicit information. A "Fear-Up (Harsh)" approach involves the added psychological stress of the threat of physical violence on the subject. ████████ also told ████ intended to use one of the rooms in the DCCP high-security holding area to be able to choose from a variety of stress positions. ████████ consented. Interrogators are required to adapt to the changing needs of the interrogation and must remain flexible. As a result, interrogators do not usually seek approval for an interrogation plan. ████████ left for the MP Headquarters, where ████ was asking permission to use one of the rooms in the DCCP high-security area. ████████ plan to raise the level of fear in the interrogation to "break ████" was not specific about what tactics ████ intended to use. ████ (Exhibits M and N) recalls ████ told ████ had a "bad feeling" about the interrogation, though ████ did not mention ████ had said so in ████ sworn statement. ████ agreed ████ would remain in the room during the course of the interrogation and would brief ████ about the interrogation later.

b647c4

b647c4

b657c5

b647c4

b647c4

b657c5

b657c5

b647c4

b657c5

b647c4

b657c5

b65 7c5

b647c4

b647c4

b647c4

b657c5

i. ████████ walked to the DCCP high-security area. Once inside, ████████ moved ████ from ████ cell and put ████ the detainee temporary holding area. Inside ████ cell were two metal folding chairs and ████ bedding. ████ walked into ████ cell and ████ escorted ████ into the room ████ wore a dishdasha [traditional Arab garment], sandals, and shackles on his wrists and ankles. The interrogation began immediately ████ questioned ████ a loud, angry voice, which ████ translated, mimicking ████ demeanor and tone. ████ paced the room as ████ yelled ████ stayed near ████ and ████ stood against the north wall of the room. (Exhibit O is ████ drawing of how the room was set up and where participants stood.) It is unclear how ████ obtained the MP riot baton, though ████ likely received it from ████ told ████ to lie on ████ back and put his legs on the chairs, which ████ arranged such that they faced each other. (Exhibit P is ████ drawing of how the room was set up and where participants stood at this point in the interrogation.) ████ asked ████ about his involvement in attacks against American soldiers, where ████ received ████ funding and weapons, and ████ associates. When ████ did not receive the answers ████ wanted, ████ hit ████ feet. ████ the soles of ████ sandals individually, for a total of about 10 to 30 times. Neither ████ or ████ objected. ████ spent approximately 15 minutes in this position.

b657c5

b647c4

b647c4

b657c4

b6525

b657c5

b657c5

b647c4

b657c5

b647c4

b657c5

b657c5

b657c5

j. ████ grabbed ████ by ████ and pulled him to ████ feet. ████ suggested removing ████ wrist restraints, though it is unclear to whom ████ suggested the idea. ████ unlocked ████ wrist shackles, likely one side remained locked.

b657c5

b657c5

b647c4

4

6613

DOD 002840

A-298

████ instructed ████ to stand with ████ arms out at ████ sides, knees bent, and head tilted back so ████ faced the ceiling. ████ stood in that position for approximately 15 minutes. ████ told ████ to stand a few feet from the wall, forehead pressed to the wall, arms out at his sides and parallel with the floor, such that ████ body stood at approximately a 70-degree angle to the floor. At some point, ████ moved from ████ position against the north wall to just inside the door against the south wall, likely to get a better view. ████ continued to question ████ and ████ maintained ████ innocence. Not receiving the answer ████ wanted, ████ hit ████ across his buttocks and possibly ████ lower back as well. ████ likely did not intend to hit ████ on his buttocks or lower back when he began the interrogation. I believe this was a spur-of-the-moment idea ████ had. Again, neither ████ objected. ████ approximately 10 times. ████ concluded the interrogation and ████ led ████ back to ████ cell. ████ states ████ walked in and out of the interrogation, as it was time to feed other detainees. I believe ████ spent much more time in the interrogation than the 50% ████ states, nor was ████ notably absent each time the baton was used against ████. I also believe ████ not only consented to giving ████ baton, but condoned using the baton on ████ and ████ was likely even a co-conspirator with foreknowledge when ████ approached him originally.

k, ████ remained in ████ cell while ████ moved ████ back. ████ then interrogated ████ with ████ remaining in the room. Shortly after the interrogation began ████ arrived and joined the interrogation. This interrogation was much quieter than the preceding one. I do not feel anything significant occurred during the course of ████ interrogation. Later that evening, ████ went to ████ and explained ████ had seen nothing of note during the interrogation and that ████ was only put in stress positions. ████ demonstrated three stress positions ████ used (see Exhibit J).

l. Neither ████ said anything about the events of ████ interrogation to ████ went to dinner later that evening and sat with ████ 104th MI Bn, NFI (see Exhibit Q). ████ asked ████ how ████ interrogation of "MP ████" had gone that evening and whether ████ had been able to "break" ████ said ████ was thus far unsuccessful and had beaten ████ with an MP "control stick". "Control stick" refers to the MP riot baton and is the terminology ████ used in ████ interview and the same terminology ████ quoted in ████ sworn statement ████ looked at each other, unknowing whether to believe ████. Neither questioned ████ further about the incident. At approximately 0900 or 1000 hours on 24 September, ████ and told ████ to restrict ████ access to detainees until further notice. ████ refused to explain over the telephone and asked ████ to come to ████ office ████ woke ████ and asked ████ what had happened the previous evening. ████ told ████ about ████ hitting ████ feet. ████ did not ask further and went to ████ office ████ went upstairs to discuss the matter. Following this conversation, ████ drafted a counseling statement for ████ on 25 September and counseled ████ on 26 September. The counseling statement (see Exhibit R) detailed ████ punishment of 10 hours of one-on-one Geneva Convention training with ████, as

6614

DOD 002841

well as suspended access to detainees at the DCCP. ████████ suffered two days of significant discomfort on his buttocks and lower back as a result of the assault.

m. ████████ stated in ████████ statement ██ was mistreated in another interrogation at the FOB Ironhorse DCCP. ████████ recalls an interrogation (see Exhibit H) conducted on 29 September in which ████████, ICE, 104th MI Bn, 4ID, NFI, served as interrogator and ████████ served as interpreter. ████████ recognized ████████ as the same ████████ interpreter from the previous interrogation. As ████████ was led into Booth 1, ████████ ordered ████████ to kneel and walk around the tent on ██ knees with his hands clasped behind his head ████████ is under the impression ████ was in control of the interrogation, as ████████ was not very loud, did not say much, and allowed ████████ to have some degree of control. ████████ crawled around the table in the middle of the tent approximately 15-20 times. Either ████████ realized detainees in the juvenile detention cell were able to see the events in Booth 1 (see Exhibit J). ████████ moved the interrogation to Booth 2, where ████████ resumed crawling around the table in the tent. ████████ was dizzy, tired, and his knees hurting and tried to lean back against his calves. On one of these occasions, ████████ pushed or prodded ████████ with the half-filled water bottle ██ carried. ████████ recounts (see Exhibit H) ████████ hitting ████ once with the water bottle. As a result of this interrogation, ████████ has open sores on both knees which precludes ████ from participating in proper Muslim worship practices. I alerted ████████ about ████████ wounds; ████████ since been seen by a medic. I am inclined to believe no further abuse occurred during this incident.

n. No further details are known about the events under investigation.

2. VARIABLES

a. I am considering six variables in my assessment; that is, six uncorroborated events which will assign, aggravate, or mitigate culpability. First, if ████████ did, in fact, request ████████ be released from ██ administrative duties for skill refresher training and the chain of command denied the request (see Exhibit C). Second, if ████████ did hold a conversation with ████████ in which they discussed whether ████████ would be able to "handle" using physical force against detainees (see Exhibit G) and if statements were taken out of context or intended as worded. Third, if ████████ agreed to beat ████████ with a riot baton and intended not to discuss the incident with anyone besides ████████ (see Exhibit G). Fourth, if ████████ his riot baton with specific intent to assault ████████ (see Exhibit G). Fifth, if ████████ did not clearly explain to ████████ role in an interrogation (see Exhibits G and J). Sixth, if ████████ was, in fact, not present in the room during the alleged assault (see Exhibit L).

b. The outcome of these unknowns may change culpability of the persons involved.

6

6615

DOD 002842

3. FINDINGS b657c5

b647c4

a. ██████████ is a trained HUMINT Collector and has had instruction on interrogation/procedures, with special emphasis on abiding by the statutes of the Geneva Convention. Since ██ work depends greatly upon adherence to the Geneva Convention regulations, ██████ should have a sense of the tremendous responsibility ██ has to follow them, if not for ethical reasons, at least to avoid the potential consequences of violations. I find ██████ liable for premeditated assault on ████████████████ guilt is exacerbated by ████ use of an MP riot baton, which constitutes "aggravated assault" in criminal court proceedings. ██████ bears less guilt as it is clear ██ felt encouraged by ████████ even if "are you up to it?" and "can you handle it?" were taken out of context. His guilt is mitigated further by his lack of skill training and his short time in service, much of which was spent performing duties other than the work for which he was trained. Moreover, ██████ was unclear what definition applies to the majority of the detainee population of the DCCP, as ██ states ██ sees them as unlawful combatants who had murdered 3 of ██ brethren soldiers. 4ID Commanding General Major General Raymond Odierno's memorandum regarding treatment of enemy prisoners of war and detained unlawful combatants was released at about this time and did not reach all soldiers before this incident occurred. According to his statement, ████████ would have reconsidered ██ intentions, had he seen the memorandum before going into the interrogation room with ████████ on 23 September.

b647c4   b657c5   b657c5   b657c5

b. ████████████████████████████████ Military Policeman with ████ of active duty service. Intrinsic to the duties of a Military Policeman is ████████ responsibility for the security and welfare of enemy prisoners of war, including adherence to the statutes of the Geneva Convention. I find ████████ liable for ██████████ abuse of ████████ guilt is exacerbated if ██ did, in fact, partake in planning and not just offer tacit consent once in the room. ████████ guilt is further exacerbated if ██ lied about his involvement and knowledge of the incident on his sworn statement. As an ████████ of ██ service, ██████ knew what ██████ was doing was wrong. ██████ guilt is mitigated if he was, in fact, absent from the room during ████████ assault on ████████.

b657c5   b647c4   b657c5

b657c5

c. ████████████████████████ an interpreter who has only worked with the ICE for the ████████ knowledge of the Geneva Convention and interrogation operations is limited to what ██ has experienced while working at the ICE and what ██ has been told by interrogators with whom he has worked. ████████ is most likely a scared junior enlisted soldier who was convinced ██████ knew what ██ was doing. ████ guilt is mitigated ██ was not informed about ██ intentions prior to entering the interrogation room. ████████ guilt is exacerbated by ██ intervention in the interrogation, which is outside the scope of his interpreting duties. ████ intervention in ████████ 29 September interrogation was also out of line, for which ██ should be held liable, if he authorized it.

b657c5   b647c4   b657c5

d. I feel ████████████████████ is a good soldier and ████████ who runs the DCCP with diligence and efficiency. ████████ took necessary steps to ensure soldiers were properly trained and had sufficient experience before conducting interrogations of

b657c5

7

b657c5

6616

b647c4   b657c5   b647c4

detainees. ████ e-mail did not explain fully the intent of the "wish list" and, as a consequence, implanted ideas neither ████ nor any of his interrogators would have considered before. ████ references to "gloves coming off" and ████ desire to have detainees "broken" quickly lead one to believe ████ wanted suggestions of less-than-ethical or less-than-legal nature. I believe ████ and ████ had a discussion about ████ e-mail and ████ likely read ████ statements as an endorsement of more violent interrogation methods, based upon opinions in ██ sworn statement. b647c4

b657c5   b657c5

e. I do not feel First Lieutenant ████ is culpable for any part of this incident. A Field Artillery officer by training, ████ became a Military Police officer only within the past month. ████ seems to be learning her duties and understanding DCCP operations quickly. ████ is a diligent officer and has a good understanding of most operations in her purview.

b647c4   b657c5

f. Although ████ account of events differs slightly from the other three in the interrogation room on 23 September, ██ story is highly credible and plausible. I do not feel ████ intentionally altered the events of that interrogation, though ██ account of his 29 September interrogation lends itself to mild exaggeration.

b647c4   b647c4

4. RECOMMENDATIONS

b657c5

a. At a maximum, I recommend ████ be subject to military court martial and be prosecuted for first degree aggravated assault and violation of Geneva Convention articles 13, 17, 20, 42, and 87, which govern the humane treatment of prisoners of war. I recommend ████, be subject to military court martial and be prosecuted for conspiracy to commit aggravated assault. I recommend ████ b657c5 be given a company grade Article 15, Uniform Code of Military Justice, for his involvement in the aggravated assault of ████ I recommend no charges be proffered against ████ or ████ b657c5

b657c5   b647c4   b657c5

b. At a minimum, I recommend ████ be given a Field Grade Article 15. I recommend ████, be given a Field Grade Article 15. I recommend ████ be given a letter of reprimand.

b657c5   b657c5

c. Since 4ID Commanding General Major General Raymond Odierno has already published specific guidance about treatment of enemy prisoners of war, no further memoranda or orders need be published. Commanders should ensure all personnel who may have contact with enemy prisoners of war understand the tenets of the Geneva Convention completely.

b657c5   b647c4

d. Additionally, I recommend ████ be questioned about his involvement in the 29 September 2003 interrogation of ████. Although I have no belief ████ or ████ had any intention of causing physical harm to ████ during this interrogation, ██ bear some culpability for explaining his expectations in the interrogation. ████ should have informed ████ about his

b647c4   8   b657c5

6617

665 7c5

responsibilities in an interrogation and stopped ▮▮▮▮ from conducting duties of an interrogator. Further investigation may be required for this incident.

66 2/7c2

CPT, MI
Investigating Officer

9

6618

DOD 002845

AFYB-MI-CDR   30SEP03

b627c2

MEMORANDUM FOR: ████████████████████

SUBJECT: Appointment as AR 15-6 Investigating Officer

1. You are hereby appointed an investigating officer to
conduct an informal investigation IAW AR 15-6 surrounding
the possible use of excessive force by ██████████ while *b657c5*
interrogating a internee at the Division Consolidated
Collection Point.

2. In your investigation, gather sworn witness statements
to the alleged event described in the enclosed statement
b647c4 from ████████ Your purpose is to determine the facts of
what happened and recommend to me if additional
investigation is needed.

3. No charges are being preferred at this time. If in the
course of your investigation you come to suspect that
certain people may be responsible for actions that could be
subject to UCMJ or prosecution, you must advise them of
their rights under the UCMJ, Article 31, or the Fifth
Amendment, as appropriate. In addition, you must provide
them a Privacy Act statement before you solicit any
(further) personal information. You may obtain assistance
with these legal matters from the office of the Staff Judge
Advocate.

4. Submit the statements and your findings IAW AR 15-6
within 10 days.

                                    ██████████████ *b62-7c2*
                          ████████████████████
                          Commanding

Encl
1 - Sworn statement, ████████████ *b647c4*
2 - Counseling statement 26Sep03

6619

DOD 002846

A-304

REPLY TO
ATTENTION OF:

AFYB-MI-HHOC   6 October 2003

MEMORANDUM FOR RECORD

SUBJECT: Detainee Sworn Statement

b647c4

1. [redacted] Detainee [redacted] provided [redacted] sworn statement on 1 October 2003 through [redacted] a Category II Civilian interpreter. [redacted] was provided by the Interrogation Control Element (ICE), Division Central Collection Point, 4th Mechanized Infantry Division.

b647c4

2. I transcribed [redacted] b647c4 statement using most nearly the language [redacted] used during the course of the interview. I presented the statement to [redacted] on 2 October and had [redacted]

b647c4 — [redacted] a Category II Civilian interpreter, also provided by the ICE. [redacted] verified [redacted] statement through [redacted] before signing. — b647c4

3. Point of contact for this memorandum is the undersigned at DNVT [redacted]

b627c2

Investigating Officer

6620

DOD 002847

A-305

From:
Sent: Thursday August 14 2003 11:26 AM
To:
Cc:

b627c2

Subject: RE: FW: Taskers

All:

Regarding the tasking—I am not a legal expert, but seems to me that everyone we are detaining at this point is an unpriviledged belligerent, since we have taken over the country and there is no longer any force opposing us that 1) wears recognizable uniform; and 2) bears arms openly. So I think everyone we detain is in that category.

As for "the gloves need to come off..." we need to take a deep breath and remember who we are. Those gloves are most definitely NOT based on Cold War or WWII enemies—they are based on clearly established standards of international law to which we are signatories and in part the originators. Those in turn derive from practices commonly accepted as morally correct, the so-called "usages of war." It comes down to standards of right and wrong—something we cannot just put aside when we find it inconvenient, any more than we can declare that we will "take no prisoners" and therefore shoot those who surrender to us simply because we find prisoners inconvenient.

"The casualties are mounting..." we have taken casualties in every war we have ever fought—that is part of the very nature of war. We also inflict casualties, generally many more than we take. **That in no way justifies letting go of our standards.** We have NEVER considered our enemies justified in doing such things to us. Casualties are part of war—if you cannot take casualties then you cannot engage in war. Period.

BOTTOM LINE: We are American soldiers, heirs of a long tradition of staying on the high ground. We need to stay there.

 b62/7c2

Psalm 24 3-8

——Original Message——
From:
[mailto
Sent: Thursday August 14 2003 3:58 PM   b62/7c2
To:
Cc:

Subject: Re: FW: Taskers

I sent several months in Afghanistan interrogating the Taliban and al Qaeda. Restrictions on interrogation techniques had a negative impact

EXHIBIT A   1   **6621** on our ability to gather intelligence. Our interrogation doctrine is based on former Cold War amd WWII enemies. Todays enemy, particularly those in SWA, understand force, not psychological mind games or incentives. I would propose a baseline interrogation technique that at a minimum allows for physical contact resembling that used by SERE instructors. This allows open handed facial slaps from a distance of no more than about two feet and back handed blows to the midsection from a distance of about 18 inches. Again, this is open handed. I will not comment on the effectiveness of these techniques as both a control measure and an ability to send a clear message. I also believe that this should be a minimum baseline.

Other techniques would include close confinement quarters, sleep deprivation, white noise, and a litnany of harsher fear-up approaches...fear of dogs and snakes appear to work nicely. I firmly agree that the gloves need to come off.

V/R

 b62/7c2

—— Original Message ——
From: ▮▮▮▮▮▮▮▮▮▮▮▮▮▮▮▮▮▮▮▮▮▮▮▮▮▮▮▮▮▮▮ b62/7c2
Date: Thursday, August 14, 2003 2:51 pm
Subject: FW: Taskers

> Sounds crazy, but we're just passing this on.
>
> —— Original Message ——
> From: ▮▮▮▮▮▮▮▮▮▮▮▮▮▮▮▮▮▮▮▮▮▮ b62/7c2
> [mailto▮▮▮▮▮▮▮▮▮
> Sent: Thursday, August 14, 2003 1:51 AM
> To: ▮▮▮▮▮▮▮▮▮▮▮▮▮▮▮▮▮▮▮▮▮▮ b62:7c2
> Cc: ▮▮▮▮▮▮▮▮▮▮▮▮▮
> Subject: Taskers
>
>
> ALCON
>
> Just wanted to make sure we are all clear on the taskers at hand
>
> 1- A list identifying individuals who we have in detention that
> fall under
> the category of "unlawful combatants" I've included a definition
> form the
> SJA folks:
>
> In order to properly address your request for a legal definition of
> the term "unlawful combatant," I must first provide you with a
> framework of definitions with which to work. According to the Law
> of Land Warfare,
> the term "combatant" is defined as anyone engaging in hostilities
> in an
> armed conflict on behalf of a party to the conflict. Combatants are
> lawful targets, unless out of combat. With that said, "lawful
> combatants" receive protections of the Geneva Conventions and
> gain combat
> immunity for their warlike acts, as well as become prisoners of
> war if
> captured. In comparison, "unprivileged belligerents," commonly
> referred to as "unlawful combatants," may be treated as criminals
> under the
> domestic law of the captor. Unprivileged belligerents may
> include spies,

2

6622

> saboteurs, or civilians who are participating in the hostilities.
> The
> term "unlawful combatant" is not referenced, nor is it defined.
> The term
> that properly described these type of individuals is "unprivileged
> belligerents," and as stated before they may be treated as
> criminals under
> domestic law.
>
>   As far as an ROE that addresses the treatment of enemy combatants,
> specifically, unprivileged belligerents, we are unaware of any
> but we will
> continue to research the issue for you. I hope this information
> has been
> helpful.
>
> 2- An additional list identifying who we have detained who are
> "Islamicextremist"
>
> 3- Immediately seek input from interrogation elements (Division/Corps)
>   concerning what their special interrogation knowledge base is
> and more
>   importantly, what techniques would they feel would be effective
> techniques
>   that SJA could review (basically provide a list).
>
>   Provide interrogation techniques "wish list" by 17 AUG 03.
>
> The gloves are coming off gentleman regarding these detainees, ▮ b627c.2
> ▮▮▮▮has
> made it clear that we want these individuals broken. Casualties
> are mounting
> and we need to start gathering info to help protect our fellow
> soldiers from
> any further attacks. I thank you for your hard work and your
> dedication.
> MI ALWAYS OUT FRONT!
>
>
> V/r
> ▮▮▮▮▮▮▮▮▮▮▮▮▮▮   b627c2
> ▮▮▮▮▮▮▮▮▮▮▮▮▮▮▮▮
> ▮▮▮▮▮▮▮▮▮▮▮▮▮▮▮▮▮
> ▮▮▮▮▮▮▮▮▮▮▮▮▮▮▮▮▮
> ▮▮▮▮▮▮▮▮▮▮▮▮▮▮
> ▮▮▮▮▮▮▮▮▮▮▮
> ▮▮▮▮▮▮▮▮
> ▮▮▮
>

6623

3

A-308

Alternative Interrogation Techniques (Wish List)
4Th Infantry Division, ICE

Open Hand Strikes (face and midsection) (no distance greater than 24 inches)

Fairly self-explanatory.

Pressure Point Manipulation

Manipulation of specific points on the human body can cause acute temporary pain but cause no long term effects or damage.

Close Quarter Confinement

Confinement of subject in extremely close quarters. Discomfort induces compliance and cooperation.

White Noise Exposure

Overexposure of subject to noise found to be meaningless and many times monotonous to subject. Often used in conjunction with Sleep Deprivation.

Sleep Deprivation

An initial period of total deprivation (usually 12 to 24 hours) followed by regular and irregular sleep patterns over several days.

Stimulus Deprivation

The human mind requires stimulation, however small, to maintain resistance to suggestion, mental and emotional manipulation and self will. Subject is deprived of this stimulation for 12 to 24 hours during initial stages. Effects on subject's resistance are monitored with short intense interrogations (15-60 minutes at most). Subject's resistance will usually rapidly decay after 36 to 48 hours. This technique requires no physical pressure to be applied. However, subject must be carefully monitored.

*There are a number of "coercive" techniques that may be employed that cause no permanent harm to the subject. These techniques, however, often call for medical personnel to be on call for unforeseen complications. They include but are not limited to the following:

Phone Book Strikes
Low Voltage Electrocution
Closed-Fist Strikes
Muscle Fatigue Inducement

EXHIBIT D

6627

DOD 002854

SWORN STATEMENT

For use of this form, see AR 190-45; the proponent agency is ODCSOPS

LOCATION DCCP, FOB Ironhorse, Tikrit, Iraq	DATE 01 October 2003	TIME 1430 hours	FILE NUMBER
LAST NAME, FIRST NAME, MIDDLE NAME b64/7c4	SOCIAL SECURITY NUMBER		GRADE/STATUS
ORGANIZATION OR ADDRESS			

I, b64/7c4 _____ WANT TO MAKE THE FOLLOWING STATEMENT UNDER OATH:

During the evening hours on approximately 23 or 24 September 2003, I was removed from my detention cell for an interview. This was my fourth interview during my detention at this facility. I was taken to an interview room, where I was questioned for approximately 15 to 20 minutes by an American soldier whom I describe as a tall, skinny male with a light facial complexion and black hair. He was accompanied by two other soldiers, a Military Police (MP) officer whom I describe as "white skin" and "not too tall or short" [Affiant indicated a soldier outside approximately 5'7" to 5'9" tall, wearing military fatigue pants and a brown tee-shirt; a large tattoo on his upper left arm was exposed. Though there were other soldiers present, this was likely the soldier Affiant meant], and an interpreter whom I describe as darker skinned and having an Egyptian accent when he spoke. The Tall American led me inside the interview room. I was wearing a dishdasha [an Arab garment much like a nightshirt], my sandals, handcuffs, and ankle shackles. The Tall American made me stand with my forehead against the wall, my hands behind my head, my feet planted several feet from the wall, such that my body was positioned at a 45-degree angle. The Tall American was in control and was very angry. The Tall American shouted at me, asking if I was the person who had killed Americans. The Egyptian Interpreter was also very angry and yelled at me. I said I was not involved and did not know anything about any weapons. The Tall American had in his hands a yellow wooden MP baton I describe as approximately 2 to 3 feet in length and 1 inch in diameter. When I did not give the answer the Tall American wanted to hear, he hit me with the baton on my lower back and buttocks "about 10 times". The baton hurt me, though it did not leave any bruises or break the skin. I do not know how long I was in that position. The Tall American then told me to lie down on my back with my legs up on a chair. I did as I was told and the Tall American questioned me again about my alleged involvement in an attack against Americans. I said I did not know anything about it. When the Tall American did not like my response, he hit my feet with the baton "almost 15 times". Again, the baton hurt me, though it did not leave any bruises or break the skin. I do not know how long I was in that position. During the entire interview, the Military Police officer stood in

the corner of the room, said nothing, and did nothing but observe. I have had no problems with him before or since. My fifth interview was during the evening hours of about 2 or 3 days ago [Affiant indicated 28 or 29 September 2003], I was removed from my detention cell for another interview. During the interview, the Egyptian Interpreter was present again, though it was a different American who was questioning me. I cannot recall any details about his appearance or distinguishing features. As soon as I entered the tent [Affiant indicated Booth 2], the Egyptian Interpreter moved the box upon which I usually sit during my interviews. The Egyptian Interpreter ordered me to get on my knees, put my hands behind my head, and move around the table in the middle of the tent, during which the Egyptian Interpreter yelled at me and asked me who was shooting Americans, who was with me, and what kind of weapons I had. I said I did not know anything. I crawled around the table about 10 to 15 times before the Egyptian Interpreter and the Unidentified American Interviewer moved me to the other tent [Affiant indicated Booth 3]. There, the interpreter ordered me to kneel again and move around the table. I told the Egyptian Interpreter and the Unidentified American Interviewer I was tired, dizzy, my knees hurt, and I could not go around the table anymore. When I told the Egyptian Interpreter I "could not handle it", he said, "Keep going" and hit me once on my lower back with a water bottle. The water bottle was nearly half full with what I recall might have been an orange-colored juice. It appeared to me the Egyptian Interpreter was in control during the course of this interview, as he did all the yelling. The Unidentified American Interviewer asked questions only once in a while. I was in the first tent a total of about 10 minutes and in the second for a total of about 15 minutes. There was no MP guard or anyone else present in the tent, though there may have been a witness. [Affiant indicated a man dressed in yellow in the 'Juvenile detention cell']. At no time during this interview did the Egyptian Interpreter or the Unidentified American Interviewer push me or strike me with anything other than the water bottle. As a result of crawling on my knees in the tent, my knees are bloody and I still have open sores, which are exposed to flies. I have not been given the opportunity to see a doctor for my injuries. The injuries I sustained in the first-mentioned interview did not produce any bruises or break the skin and the pain went away after 2 days. The injuries I sustained in the second interview are confined to my knees. My right knee has 3 open wounds ranging in size from 1 inch to 1.5 inches across. My left knee has 2 open wounds approximately 1 inch across. These wounds make daily prayer difficult. In the other 3 interviews I have had, I have not been abused in any way. The guards and interviewers have been otherwise good to me. I have nothing further to add to this statement.
b64/7c4

Nothing Follows

EXHIBIT	INITIALS OF PERSON MAKING STATEMENT
	b64/7c4

AGENT'S INVESTIGATION REPORT   0106-04-CID259-80185

CID Regulation 195-1   Page 3 of 12

he described as he was just caught in a lie. Mr. ███████ provided this office with a
photograph and medical evaluation of Mr. ███████ (See documents)

About 1328, 12 May 04, SA ███████ reviewed the medical records on file of Mr. ███████
which reflected an incident when Mr. ███████ faked a heart attack. Nothing else remarkable
was seen.

About 0930, 15 May 04, SA ███████ and SA ███████ interviewed Mr. ███████
███████ AKA ███████, Interpreter, 1st Cavalry Division DIF, Titan Corporation, APO AE
09342 who stated he was the interpreter for Mr. ███████ when Mr. ███████ was
interviewed. He reiterated what Mr. ███████ stated in that Mr. ███████ related a man he
claimed to be an Iraqi abused him when he was detained at the Al-Azimiyah Palace. Mr.
███████ stated the man's name could also have been ███████. Mr. ███████ related he was
not familiar with ███████ and has not heard anyone mention his name. Mr.
███████ further related this was the only detainee he talked to which mentioned being abused
in the Al-Azimiyah Palace. Mr. ███████ stated sometime in Aug 03, while he was working in
Abu Ghraib Prison, he witnessed a female soldier he believed to be U.S. Army Military Police,
make a detainee jump up and down and then roll left to right on the ground in what he believed
to be a 150 degree Fahrenheit temperature clothed in only his underwear. He stated this went on
for about twenty minutes and the detainee was at the point where he collapsed several times and
when the detainee attempted to drink water he would vomit. Mr. ███████ related he knew the
female soldier's first name as ███████ (NFI) and she always worked with an interpreter named
███████ (NFI) who was also employed by Titan Corporation. Mr. ███████ stated Mr.
███████ would know exactly who ███████ was and would be able to give more details on this
incident and possibly other incidents.

About 0900, 20 May 04, this office received the final Information Report from the Baghdad
Correctional Confinement Facility (BCCF), Abu Ghraib, IZ, APO AE 09342. The report
included the AIR from SA ███████ which detailed the interviews of Ms ███████ Ms.
███████ and Mr. ███████ (See AIR for details)

About 1015, 20 May 04, SA ███████ and SA ███████ this office interviewed Mr.
███████ date of birth ███████ Place of Birth ███████
███████ (NFI) with
assistance from Mr. ███████ Linguist, Titan Corporation, 1st CAV Detention
Interrogation Facility (DIF), Baghdad International Airport (BIAP), Baghdad, IZ, who re-
interated his previous statement he provided to Mr. ███████ on a prior interview. Mr.
███████ also provided additional details. Mr. ███████ described ███████ (Iraqi interrogator) as a
white male, combed, gray hair, no mustache, light, white beard, who wore a white t-shirt, brown
trouser, sneakers, and rubber gloves. Mr. ███████ stated after he was apprehended from his

SA ███████   78th MP DET Forward (CID)   DODDOACID-005496
Special Agent, ███████   Baghdad, Iraq APO AE 09342
Signature: Date: 6 Jun 04   Exhibit:
                    LAW ENFORCEMENT SENSITIVE
CID Form 94   FOR OFFICIAL USE ONLY   Exhibit ___   10
                    Law Enforcement Sensitive

ARMED FORCES INSTITUTE OF PATHOLOGY
Office of the Armed Forces Medical Examiner
1413 Research Blvd., Bldg. 102
Rockville, MD 20850
1-800-944-7912

FINAL AUTOPSY REPORT

Name: (b)(6)-4
SSAN:
Date of Birth: Unk
Date Found: 04 NOV 2003
Date of Autopsy: 09 NOV 2003
Date of Report: 09 JAN 2004

Autopsy No.: ME 03-504
AFIP No.: 2903283
Rank: CIV, Iraqi National
Place of Death: near Baghdad, Iraq
Place of Autopsy: Mortuary
Affairs, Camp Sayther, Baghdad
International Airport

Circumstances of Death: This Iraqi National male was captured by Navy Seal Team #7 and died while detained at Abu Ghraib Prison in Iraq.

Authorization for Autopsy: Office of the Armed Forces Medical Examiner, IAW 10 USC 1471

Identification: Visual Identification as per Investigating Agency

CAUSE OF DEATH: Blunt Force Injuries Complicated by Compromised Respiration

MANNER OF DEATH: Homicide

MEDCOM - 85

DOD 003212

A-313

[b)(6)-4

<u>OPINION</u>

[b)(6)-4   , an Iraqi National, died while detained at the Abu Ghraib prison
where he was held for interrogations by government agencies. According to an
investigative report, Mr. [b)(6)-4   was captured by Navy Seal team #7 and resisted
apprehension. External injuries are consistent with injuries sustained during
apprehension. Ligature injuries are present on the wrists and ankles. Fractures of the ribs
and a contusion of the left lung imply significant blunt force injuries of the thorax and
likely resulted in impaired respiration. According to investigating agents, interviews
taken from individuals present at the prison during the interrogation indicate that a hood
made of synthetic material was placed over the head and neck of the detainee. This likely
resulted in further compromise of effective respiration. Mr. [b)(6)-4   was not under the
influence of drugs of abuse or ethanol at the time of death. The cause of death is blunt
force injuries of the torso complicated by compromised respiration. The manner of death
is homicide.

[b)(6)-2

CDR MC USN (FS)
Deputy Armed Forces
Medical Examiner

SWORN STATEMENT

For use of this form, see AR 190-45: the proponent agency is ODCSOPS

PRIVACY ACT STATEMENT

AUTHORITY: Title 10 USC Section 301: Title 5 USC Section 2951: E. O. 9397 dated November 22, 1943 *(SSN)*

PRINCIPAL PURPOSE: To provide commanders and law enforcement officials with means by which information may be accurately

ROUTINE USES: Your social security number is used as an additional/alternate means of identification to facilitate filing and retrieve.

DISCLOSURE: Disclosure of your social security number is voluntary.

1. LOCATION Coraopolis, PA	2. DATE (*YYYYMMDD*) 2004/05/26	3. TIME 1525 [VIP]	4. FILE NUMBER
5. LAST NAME, FIRST NAME, MIDDLE NAME ███████████		6. SSN ██████	7. GRADE/STATUS 05
8. ORGANIZATION OR ADDRESS 320th MP Bn. Ashley, PA			

9. I ███████████ _____. WANT TO MAKE THE FOLLOWING STATEMENT UNDER OATH:

I am currently assigned to the 320th Military Police (MP) Battalion (BN) in Ashley, PA, having been the 320th Commander from 1 Jun 02 until 1 May 04. The 320th was mobilized for Operation IRAQ FREEDOM on 10 Feb 03 and assembled at the mobilization point at Fort Dix, NJ, on 19 Feb 03. On 12 Mar 03, we departed Fort Dix and deployed to Camp Arifjan, Kuwait where we remained for about two weeks before crossing into Iraq. Our first mission was to take over operations from the British at Camp Freddy, which later became Camp Bucca. HHC 320th was at Camp Bucca and had about 140 of the authorized 154 personnel. The 314th and 447th MP Companies were assigned to the 320th. On 24 Jul 03, the 320th advance party went to Abu Garayb (AG) to establish operations, and I personally arrived at AG on 28 Jul 03. My Rater was the 800th MP Brigade (BDE) Commander, initially BG Paul HILL until the end of May 03, and then BG KARPINSKI. Upon my arrival at AG, the 72nd MP Co, an Army National Guard (ANG) unit from Las Vegas, NV, was the only MP unit there, and it had arrived at AG at the end of May 03. It was subordinate to the 400th MP BN headquartered at BIAP. Since the 72nd was already in place, the decision was made to reassign the 72nd to the 320th, and the

314th, which had been assigned to me at Bucca, was "traded" to the 400th in exchange. The 447th MP Co arrived AG together with the 320th. The next MP unit to arrive at AG was the 229th MP Co, an ANG unit from Virginia Beach, VA, and they arrived about the Aug 03 timeframe. The 372nd MP Co arrived on 1 Oct 03, followed shortly thereafter in early Oct 03 by the 870th and 670th MP Co, and then the 320th MP Co toward the end of Oct 03. The 72nd MP Co, which had been deployed for approximately 13 months, was then redeployed and departed AG during the first couple of days in Nov 03. The conditions at AG upon my arrival on 28 Jul 03 were not favorable. AG covered a grid square and was divided into four compounds. Local Iraqis had thoroughly looted and striped AG after Saddam Hussein fell, and there was no infrastructure to speak of. The 72nd had only cleared and occupied one area. The Coalition Provisional Authority (CPA) was funding the reconstruction of AG and had hired local contractors to refurbish the facilities. However, there were never any CPA representatives at AG, there was no CPA project officer, and there was not, until much later, CPA oversight of the Iraqi Correctional Officers. One of the compounds became Camp Vigilant, and was designated as the holding area for suspected Saddam Fedayeen members that were to detained as a result of Operation VICTORY BOUNTY, which began in early Aug 03. Camp Ganci, which would eventually occupy one compound, did not yet exist. Elements of A Co, 519th Military Intelligence (MI) BN were already on the ground when I arrived at AG, and my thinking was that they must be there in preparation for VICTORY BOUNTY. ██████ was already there and it was with ██████ that I had my first conversation about the delineation of MP and MI roles at AG. ██████ arrived shortly thereafter. ██████ was the Operations Officer that ran and managed interrogation operations, she was the highest-ranking MI officer at AG at that time, and it was with her that I would coordinate any MI related issues. The hard site was still being remodeled and MI interrogations were taking place in tents at Camp Vigilant. I would go to ██████ to ensure we were accomplishing our mission and that we were appropriately separating high and low value detainees. It became obvious to me that the majority of our detainees were detained as the result of being in the wrong place at the wrong time, and were swept up by Coalition Forces as peripheral bystanders during raids. I think perhaps only one in ten security detainees were of any particular intelligence value. It appeared that there was an extreme reluctance to release these low value inmates because of the fear that one of them might return to attack Coalition Forces. ██████

10. EXHIBIT	11. INITIALS OF PERSON MAKING STATEMENT
	██████

PRIVACY ACT STATEMENT

AUTHORITY:	Title 10 USC Section 301; Title 5 USC Section 2951; E.O. 9397 dated November 22, 1943 (SSN).
PRINCIPAL PURPOSE:	To provide commanders and law enforcement officials with means by which information may be accurately identified.
ROUTINE USES:	Your social security number is used as an additional/alternate means of identification to facilitate filing and retrieval.
DISCLOSURE:	Disclosure of your social security number is voluntary.

1. LOCATION ARMY G2 PENTAGON, WASHINGTON DC	2. DATE (YYYYMMDD) 2004/05/18	3. TIME 12:30	4. FILE NUMBER

5. LAST NAME FIRST NAME MIDDLE NAME	6. SSN 633-22-9845	7. GRADE/STATUS SGT

8. ORGANIZATION OR ADDRESS
B/CO 470TH MILITARY INTELLIGENCE GROUP, CAMP BULLIS, TX 78254

9. _____ WANT TO MAKE THE FOLLOWING STATEMENT UNDER OATH:

I arrived at Abu Ghraib as an Individual Augmentee from the 470th MI Group on or about 16 October 2003. I was assigned to the Detainee Assessment Board (DAB). My DAB Supervisor was _____ When I first arrived, we didn't receive any training for working in the DAB. We received the IROEs and I believe I signed them. The IROEs I would say were only vaguely understood due to the speed at which operations had to be conducted. Since the focus of the initial groups was on maintaining a steady stream of intelligence reports answering PIR's, methodology took second stage to volume of output. The IROE's were clarified three months later when we received updated IROEs which we signed again. We were shown the Geneva Conventions and told to adhere to them. They were on the wall along with the IROEs and other memorandums from various commanders within theater for the perusal of anyone who wished to review them. There was some controversy in relation to what the school taught and the environment we were in. The school is an environment where you have some overwatch and where the ambience wherein interrogations are being conducted in a safe place with no additional stresses involved, but at Abu Ghraib, we were so busy there was no oversight on most of the interrogations being conducted as everyone was busy trying to hold up their part of the process. Most individuals arrived one day and were conducting operations the following day. Additionally, because of the additional stresses and due to the detainee's cultural and religious upbringing, many of the things taught at the school house were nearly useless or even irrelevant, which is why experienced or flexible interrogators were so absolutely necessary. Many of the interrogators should not have been conducting interrogations on their own. Most were young, inexperienced, and reservists who did not have the sufficient training nor the experience needed to achieve the necessary mindset of an interrogator in a combat zone. They did not know what to do so they reverted to screaming and throwing things, in other words, harsh approaches. After they didn't get what they wanted, they could send the detainee to isolation for thirty days or more as long as they wrote the right memo. The focus was on intelligence, and the fast tempo dictated that oftentimes the individual interrogator or direct line supervisor had to be trusted to make the right judgment, but unfortunately not everyone was equipped to make the right decisions. The memos were being approved by COL PAPPAS or whatever individual had the authority at the time. No one was checking to ensure the recommendations were sound with any sort of regularity. At the beginning even a memo was not required as far as I knew but as I was not there during the first few weeks of the reorganization of Abu Ghraib into an interrogation facility, I cannot speak with any certainty. We were standing up the JIDC, being mortared daily, and the gate guards were being attacked. The DAB was not part of the Interrogation Control Element (ICE) and there was no SOP in place on how to run one. We began developing one based on the GTMO concept, but the environment was different than GTMO. We were in a combat environment and the numbers of detainees requiring processing was higher so we had to make a lot of changes to the SOP. We were responsible for debriefing all detainees interrogated by the ICE. When a detainee arrived, he was screened and was either identified as being of intelligence value or not. Those with intelligence value were placed in CAMP VIGILANT. Eventually, CAMP VIGILANT became overcrowded some detainees having intelligence value were sent to one of the GANCI camps. A lot would go into isolation to prevent them from corruption of intelligence. I would say that the DAB identified about 85% to 90% of detainees were of either no intelligence value or were of value but innocent and therefore should be not have remained in captivity. We debriefed all the detainees considered to having some intelligence value to ensure intelligence was not getting lost and determined if detainees required to be held longer or recommend release of detainee. At the beginning, the initial group at Abu Ghraib became overwhelmed with the number of detainee being delivered by lower echelon units. The prison went from 200 one day to thousands during the following days. We did not have enough personnel to conduct the screenings and interrogations and determine the value of each detainee on a timely manner. When a detainee was able to answer a Priority Intelligence Requirement (PIR), he would get interrogated numerous times and therefore, others would go without being interrogated for months. The DAB would identify those who had not been interrogated and question the JIDC why it hadn't been done. An interrogation would then be conducted but this didn't always occur because of the shortage of interrogators and due to their focus on detainees of intelligence value. This of course changed for the better after the JIDC was more established and more direct oversight began to be conducted by higher echelon commanders. We would then get the detainee once the interrogator finished with the detainee. We would conduct a thorough debriefing of the detainee. The

10. EXHIBIT	11. INITIALS OF PERSON MAKING STATEMENT _____ PAGE 1 OF _____ PAGES

ADDITIONAL PAGES MUST CONTAIN THE HEADING "STATEMENT OF _____ TAKEN AT _____ DATED _____

THE BOTTOM OF EACH ADDITIONAL PAGE MUST BEAR THE INITIALS OF THE PERSON MAKING THE STATEMENT, AND PAGE NUMBER MUST BE BE INDICATED.

DA FORM 2823, DEC 1998 _____ DA FORM 2823, JUL 72, IS OBSOLETE. _____ USAPA V1.00

AG0000772

DOD 000859

1   Q. Did anybody ever tell you--any of your MPs ever tell

2 you about any of those issues, such as naked detainees in the

3 cells or any of those other things?

4   A. In the cells? No. But the MPs would say to me

5 sometimes, you know, this prisoner wanted to be on a hunger

6 strike, but that lasted for a day, and then he heard the rattle

7 of the MREs, as they said, so instead of being on a hunger

8 strike, he decided that he was going to take his clothes off.

9 So he's refusing to wear his clothes and the MI people took them

10 away so he doesn't hang himself. But we gave him an extra

11 blanket.

12   I specifically talked to the juveniles, because after

13 one time that they brought some in, I saw a kid that was--he

14 looked like he was 8-years old. He told me he was almost 12. I

15 asked him where he was from. He told me his brother was there

16 with him, but he really wanted to see his mother, could he

17 please call his mother. He was crying.

18   So, I never saw anything that was abuse or could be

19 considered abuse. When a prisoner was refusing to eat, he was--

20 he was "mentally ill," he was refusing to eat, they took

21 everything--the MPs took everything out of the cell that could

22 possibly hurt him or that he could use, and they were just--they

23 were considering taking out his bunk for fear that he would

92

PRIVACY ACT STATEMENT

AUTHORITY: Title 10 USC Section 301; Title 5 USC Section 2951; E.O. 9397 dated November 22, 1943 (SSN).

PRINCIPAL PURPOSE: To provide commanders and law enforcement officials with means by which information may be accurately identified.

ROUTINE USES: Your social security number is used as an additional/alternate means of identification to facilitate filing and retrieval.

DISCLOSURE: Disclosure of your social security number is voluntary.

1. LOCATION OSJA, DAMSTADT, GERMANY	2. DATE (YYYYMMDD) ▮▮▮ 2004/05/13	3. TIME ▮▮ 1535	4. FILE NUMBER
5. LAST NAME, FIRST NAME, MIDDLE NAME ▮▮▮	6. SSN ▮▮▮▮▮		7. GRADE/ STATUS
8. ORGANIZATION OR ADDRESS A/302nd MILITARY INTELLIGENCE BATTALION, HEIDELBERG, GERMANY APO AE 09102			

9. ▮▮▮▮▮▮ WANT TO MAKE THE FOLLOWING STATEMENT UNDER OATH:

I arrived in Kuwait on 12 February 2003 and was assigned to the targeting cell in the Intelligence Fusion Center at Camp Victory. This was a Coalition operation and we were conducting Support and Stability Operations. Sometime in January, I was sent to Abu Ghraib to interrogate a ▮▮▮▮▮ I had developed a linked diagram on this GENERAL who had over 100 members. I was working the targeting folder for the general and knew more about him than most people. I was sent by ▮▮▮▮▮ in order to verify or validate ▮▮▮▮▮ link diagram I had created. I was to possibly develop more targets from this interview. When I arrived at Abu Ghraib, I asked to speak to the GENERAL. They tried to find the GENERAL because they did not know where he was. Some interrogators told me, do not know who they were (a SFC about 5'9, balding light brown hair, in his mid 40's and possibly wore glasses.) that I could not interrogate the GENERAL because he had just endured a 14-hour interrogation and had been broken. They did not want me to jeopardize their interrogations. I was told that the GENERAL was very concerned about his son due to his age, 17yrs old. The interrogators (not sure what type of soldier did this -MP, Intel, or exactly what MOS) took his son and got him wet. They then put mud on his face and drove him around in the back of the Humvee. The boy was very cold. They placed the son in an area where his father could observe him. The GENERAL thought he was going to get to see his son but they just allowed him to see his son shivering and this broke the GENERAL (this incident supposedly took place the day before I interrogated the General's son). The son also verified this account in my interrogation of him. ▓▓▓▓▓▓▓▓▓ was with me as my analyst and took notes while I interrogated the son. The son said he wanted to go to another tent where his brothers were because he was afraid of the other men in his tent.

Q. Is there anything else you would like to add to your statement?
A. No.

End of Statement

10. EXHIBIT	11. INITIALS OF PERSON MAKING STATEMENT
	▓▓▓▓▓▓▓▓▓▓▓▓▓▓

HEADQUARTERS
MULTINATIONAL FORCE–IRAQ
OFFICE OF THE DEPUTY COMMANDING GENERAL
DETAINEES OPERATIONS
BAGHDAD, IRAQ
APO AE 58343-1400

REPLY TO
ATTENTION OF

MNFI-D   15 June 2004

MEMORANDUM FOR RECORD

SUBJECT: Detainees Basic Tenant Rights IAW Geneva Convention and Army Regulations

1. Ar 190-8, Enemy Prisoner of War, Retained Personnel, Civilian Internees, and Other Detainees, outline the minimum standard of living for detainees in permanent internment facilities, but does not addressed temporary holding facilities of a capturing unit.

2. FM3–19.40, Internment/Resettlement Operations, identifies the basic safeguards that are mandated for all types of detainees.
   a. Provide first aid and medical treatment for all detainees that are equal to the treatment that would be given to US causalities.
   b. Provide food and water. These supplies must be commensurate to those for US and allied forces.
   c. Provide firm, humane treatment.
   d. Allow captives to use protective equipment in case of hostile fire or NBC threat.
   e. Do not locate captives near obvious targets (e.g. ammunition sites, fuel points, etc.)

3. The Geneva Convention Relative to the Protection of Civilian Persons in Time of War, 12 August 1949, deals with the status and treatment of civilian internees, in that it must be humane in nature. The capturing unit is responsible for proper and humane treatment of detainees from the moment of capture or other apprehension.

4. FM 3–19.40 does not articulate the minimum standard a capturing must provide in form of shelter or manner of detention, thus the standard must be relative to that of a forward collection point. A forward collection point as a minimum has a guard force based on METT-TC, food and water, latrine facility, trench or overhead cover, and concertina wire establishing a perimeter. It is understood that all these requirements are based of METT-TC and security for both the detainees and capturing unit must be a planning consideration. The guard force is necessary to monitor the detainees, especially in the event of a medical emergency (e.g. heart attack, seizure or stroke) that could result in permanent

injury or death if not treated immediately by medical personnel. These tenants fall under the preamble of humane treatment in the Geneva Convention.

5. FM 3–19.40 provides suggestions of a detention facility but does not limit the ground commander on other types of detention methods or means to secure the detainees, as long as the method or means does not violate the Geneva Convention and meets the basic safeguards outlined in FM3–19.40. AR 190–8 specifically prohibits any measure of such character to cause physical suffering or extermination of the Civilian Internee.

1.4(a)

a. Use of chains bolted to the floor as a means of securing detainees for a short period of time that allow the detainee the ability to stand, sit, or lay down is acceptable as long as the minimum requirements/safeguards listed in paragraphs two and four are adhered to. (A short period of time is defined

B2

as not to exceed 14 days, as outlined in ███████████ for the amount of time a detainee can be held prior to evacuation to a Coalition Holding Facility, Baghdad Central Collection Facility.)

b. Securing detainees in a cement cell with dimensions of 4 feet long, 3.10 feet high, and 1.5 feet wide secured by a sliding metal door is acceptable for a short duration not to exceed 24 hours. The cell does not provide for good ventilation, lighting, or observation by guard force. In addition, long periods of detention in this type of facility would cause physical suffering to the detainee violating AR 190–8 and the provisions of the Geneva Convention. In addition, the minimum requirements/safeguards listed in paragraphs two and four apply here also.

B6

6. Point of contact for this memorandum is the undersigned a ███████
█████████████████

█████████████████
█████████████████ B6

CPT. MP
MNF-1 Detainee Operations

U.S. NAVAL CRIMINAL INVESTIGATIVE SERVICE

INVESTIGATIVE ACTION   07OCT03

CONTROL: 06OCT03-NWWH-0193-7GNA

I/NAS WHIDBEY ISLAND WA/ALLEGED ASSAULT OF IRAQI PRISONERS OF WAR

RESULTS OF INTERVIEW WITH ▮▮▮▮▮▮▮▮▮▮▮▮▮▮▮▮▮▮

1. On 07OCT03 at approximately 1400, Reporting Agent (RA)
interviewed ▮▮▮▮▮▮▮▮▮▮▮▮▮▮▮▮, USN (SSN ▮▮▮▮▮▮▮▮▮ in
regards to ▮▮▮▮▮ knowledge of the abuse of Enemy prisoners of war
(EPW) in Iraq.

2. ▮▮▮▮ advised that ▮▮▮▮ was part of nine corpsmen stationed at
Naval Hospital Oak Harbor (NHOH), WA to volunteer to deploy to Iraq
from 21FEB03 to 16JUN03. ▮▮▮▮▮ stated that the nine corpsmen first
went to San Diego then on to Iraq where the nine corpsmen were
separated in different areas of Iraq. ▮▮▮▮▮ went to the 1st
Battalion, 7th Marine Division where ▮▮▮▮▮ was attached to the
Headquarters and Service Company, Battalion Aid Station (BAS).

3. ▮▮▮▮▮ duties as part of the BAS consisted of transporting
injured American soldiers and Iraqi citizens, helping to train the
Iraqi police force and providing supplies to the first line. ▮▮▮▮▮
advised that when an Iraqi would become injured and require aid,
▮▮▮▮▮ would treat the Iraqi under an armed guard at the Regimental
Aid Station then would take the Iraqi to the "Head Team" who would
process the Iraqi as an EPW as deemed appropriate. ▮▮▮▮▮ advised
that upon being declared an EPW, the EPW would be taken to an area
that contained an empty swimming pool. The EPW would be handcuffed,
leg cuffed and have a burlap bag placed over their head. ▮▮▮▮▮
further advised that the EPW would remain in the kneeling position
for no longer than 24 hours while the EPW was awaiting interrogation.

4. ▮▮▮▮▮ stated that he never saw any instances of physical abuse
towards the EPWs. ▮▮▮▮▮ stated that the EPWs would be yelled at or
jerked into an upright position if the EPW were misbehaving but that
▮▮▮▮never saw an EPW beaten.

5. ▮▮▮▮▮ advised that since returning to NHOH, all of the corpsman
have experienced some form of problem from what they observed in
Iraq. ▮▮▮▮▮ has suffered from nightmares and has been treated by a
counselor.

REPORTED BY: ▮▮▮▮▮▮▮▮▮▮▮▮▮ Special Agent
OFFICE: NCISRA Whidbey Island, WA

b7c

DODDON 000008

EXHIBIT (3)

WARNING

SWORN STATEMENT

For use of this form, see AR 190-45; the proponent agency is ODCSOPS

PRIVACY ACT STATEMENT

1. LOCATION METRO PARK, SPRINGFIELD, VA	2. DATE *(YYYYMMDD)* 2004/05/23	3. TIME	4. FILE NUMBER
5. LAST NAME, FIRST NAME, MIDDLE NAME ███████████████	6. SSN ████████		7. GRADE/STATUS SGT
8. ORGANIZATION OR ADDRESS 66th MILITARY INTELLIGENCE GROUP, DARMSTADT, GERMANY			

9. I _____, WANT TO MAKE THE FOLLOWING STATEMENT UNDER OATH:

After reading about and seeing pictures of some of the incidents of possible detainee abuse on the internet I want to mention some recollections of matters I observed while assigned at Abu Ghraib. The first pertains to a picture on the internet of a detainee with a hood over his head handcuffed to a railing on the top floor. (I am not able to identify the detainee in the picture). I observed a similar incident on one occasion when I was in the area to pick up a detainee for interrogation. I observed a detainee hooded and handcuffed to a railing. I asked the MP what it entailed and was informed that since the MPs were short handed they often had to "park" a detainee somewhere if they could not immediately return him to his cell. I do not remember the identity of the detainee or the MP. I did not report this to anyone as the explanation by the MP was plausible and this was a common practice due to the shortage of MPs. The second matter pertains to a picture on the internet of a MP ███████████ standing next to a detainee in a hallway. The detainee (reportedly) had a brown substance spread over his body. Police observed a detainee we commonly referred to as "shitty" because he would often defecate in his cell and throw the feces around, at time throwing it at the MPs. (This particular detainee appeared to act very strangely at times and might have had a mental condition). On this particular occasion at night I saw him sleeping on a mattress on the floor in the hallway, handcuffed and covered with a blanket. I asked the MP what was going on and was informed that the detainee had defecated in the cell, covered himself with feces and thrown feces around the cell and at the MPs. The MPs had to take him to the showers to clean him up and clean his cell—that was shy he was sleeping on a mattress on the floor. Again I did not report this, as similar matters were a common occurrence with this particular detainee. A similar situation could have been the precipitation behind the photo on the internet. The night of the shooting. I was sent in to help with guarding of the Iraqi Police (IP). My duties were to keep them from talking to one another ▇▇▇▇▇▇▇▇▇▇▇▇▇ and ▇▇▇▇▇▇▇▇ were there as well. When I arrived to the Hard Site ▇▇▇▇▇▇▇ was the senior person on site. The interrogators had been going on for 3-4 hours already. The dogs were being used at the time as well. There was one cell the dog went into. The dogs barked but was not close enough to hurt the detainee. I do not remember who the interrogator was but I do remember that the interpreter was ▇▇▇▇▇▇ The dogs were authorized before but by this time, any approval had to go through LTG Sanchez. During this particular incident, there was a sense of urgency to conduct simultaneous interrogations of the police that had been identified as being involved and word circulated around that LTG Sanchez had given blanket approval for somewhat harsher interrogation methods for the police interrogations. (I did not see any written blanket approval and do not remember any one individual specifically telling me that we had a blanket approval—it was just accepted by all of us). During this time, there was an IP who was taken into isolation and into the shower room to keep him away from the other IPs. He was left there for about half an hour. We were directed to go back in with the IP. When we got to the cell, he was falling asleep and one of the MPs ▇▇▇▇▇▇▇ threw a bucket of water to wake him up. I asked if this was necessary, he said ▇▇▇▇▇▇ indecipherable that the IP was falling asleep and had to keep him awake. The IP was given a blanket to keep him warm. ▇▇▇▇▇▇ also pertained to ▇▇▇▇▇▇▇ occurred after the shooting incident, possibly two to three days after, where in a detainee had a gun in his cell and had it had to be taken by force. We had an informant (one of the detainees) who had tipped us to Iraqi police smuggling weapons and other contraband into the detainees so after the shooting incident, the Iraqi police were rounded up and put into cells. As this was done, the informant pointed out which of the police were involved and which were not. In this particular instance ▇▇▇▇▇▇ was working with a civilian interrogator ▇▇▇▇ I observed ▇▇▇▇ interrogating one Iraqi policeman and ▇▇▇▇▇▇ alternated between coming into the cell and standing next to the detainee and standing outside the cell. ▇▇▇ apparently using the MP as an intimidation tactic with the detainee and would tell him to answer questions or he would bring ▇▇▇▇▇ back into the cell. At one point ▇▇▇▇ put his hands over the nose and mouth of the policeman, cutting off his air flow and not allowing him to breathe, this lasted for a few seconds. At another point

████████████ his collapsible nightstick to push and possibly twist the policeman's arm causing some pain. when ██████ walked out of the cell at one point he commented to me that he knew how to do this without leaving any marks. When ██████ made that statement I wondered why he would say such a thing. I did not report the matter to anyone for two reasons. First, ██████ was an interrogator who knew the IROEs and ██████ was a SSG-therefore, both should have known what was allowed and what was not.

Second, it was commonly understood that LTG Sanchez had given blanket approval for somewhat harsher interrogation methods (not specified) for use against the Iraqi police as a result of the shooting incident. The interpreter with ██ was ██████ supervisor was ██████. The last matter concerns treatment of a detainee who was accused of shooting an Army Colonel in the head (just walked up to him on the street and shot him). The detainee was in an isolation cell and one or two MPs and a male dog handler with a leashed but unmuzzled dog outside the cell. The detainee was handcuffed to the cell door on the inside and the dog was allowed to jump up at the door and bark and snarl. The dog was on the leash at all times and was not allowed to get close enough to bite the detainee. I did not report this because it did not seem to be abuse. I do not remember the identity of any of the personnel involved. I mention these incidents at this time only as a result of reading and seeing pictures on the internet bringing the matters to mind.

Q. Is there anything else you would like to add to this statement?
A.

10. EXHIBIT	11. INITIALS OF PERSON MAKING STATEMENT

AFFIDAVIT

I, _____, HAVE READ OR HAVE HAD READ TO ME THIS STATEMENT WHICH BEGINS ON PAGE 1, AND ENDS ON PAGE 2. I FULLY UNDERSTAND THE CONTENTS OF THE ENTIRE STATEMENT MADE BY ME. THE STATEMENT IS TRUE. I HAVE INITIALED ALL CORRECTIONS AND HAVE INITIALED THE BOTTOM OF EACH PAGE CONTAINING THE STATEMENT. I HAVE MADE THIS STATEMENT FREELY WITHOUT HOPE OF BENEFIT OR REWARD, WITHOUT THREAT OF PUNISHMENT, AND WITHOUT COERCION, UNLAWFUL INFLUENCE, OR UNLAWFUL, INDUCEMENT.

_____
(Signature of Person Making Statement)

WITNESSES

Subscribed and sworn to before me, a person authorized by law to administer oaths, this <u>23</u> day of <u>MAY,</u> <u>2004</u> at Metro Park, Springfield, VA

_____

_____

ORGANIZATION OR ADDRESS

████████████

(Signature of Person Administering Oath)

_____

_____

ORGANIZATION OR ADDRESS

(Typed Name of Person Administering Oath)

<u>UCMJ. ARTICLE 136</u>

(Authority To Administer Oaths)

PRIVACY ACT STATEMENT

1. LOCATION CRYSTAL CITY, VIRGINIA	2. DATE *(YYYYMMDD)* 2004/05/18 ▮▮▮	3. TIME 1224 ▮▮	4. FILE NUMBER
5. LAST NAME, FIRST NAME, MIDDLE NAME ▮▮▮	6. SSN ▮▮▮		7. GRADE/ STATUS SGT

8. ORGANIZATION OR ADDRESS B/CO, 470th MILITARY INTELLIGENCE GROUP, CAMP BULLIS, TX 78234

9. I, ▮▮▮▮▮ WANT TO MAKE THE FOLLOWING STATEMENT UNDER OATH:

I arrived at Abu Ghraib in Mid October 2003. When I first arrived, I was asked if I wanted to work in the Fusion Analysis Cell (FAC). There were only a few soldiers with Top Secret Clearances and I was one of them. I agreed to work in the FAC. There were a total of five individuals working in the FAC. My focus was on the Foreign Fighters and Extremist Cell. We would bring together all intelligence on these groups from the interrogation reports. From the reports, we would develop link analysis and analytic assessments. I didn't really do interrogations, but did sit in on a few. I was asked to help the interrogators and better guide them with specific questions to assist in gathering intelligence. When I first arrived, I didn't receive training on the Interrogation Rules of Engagement (IROEs) or the Geneva Convention. There was one time when ▮▮▮▮ held a formation and told everyone to read the IROEs and sign them (this was prior to the CID investigation). We were then given updated IROEs and a class on them when the 202d MI BN assumed responsibility of the JIDC. This was sometime in February 2004. At the time I arrived, I believe LTC JORDAN was in charge. Once my ▮▮▮▮ left, I was placed in charge of the FAC. I worked in the FAC the entire time I was at Abu Ghraib with the exception of six weeks when I left to work in a Tactical HUMINT Team at the entry control point. I never witnessed or heard of any detainee abuse. The only thing close to it was: when we first arrived, The GTMO SGT took us on a tour of the facility. While in the Hard Site, we saw the MPs had two detainees in the middle of the cell. They were naked with a bag over their head, standing on MRE boxes and their hand spread out each holding a bottle in each hand. I asked if this was right. I was told by the GTMO (NCO) that this was the MP's way of disciplining detainees and that it was normal. Apparently the detainees had tried to stab some other detainee. I believe that ▮▮▮▮▮ (600th MI in Japan) was also with me. I have never seen or heard of pictures and videos of detainees prior to the CID investigation. After the investigation, ▮▮▮▮▮ a girl he believed to be an MP with pictures of detainees. He came to me to tell me about it. I told him to take it to CID and report it. I saw dogs being used a few times. The detainees were in the back of a Humvee with the dog handlers and the dogs. The detainees were sitting on one side while the dog handler was sitting on the opposite side. The dogs were next to the dog handler. I know the drivers and passengers were MI, interrogators and/or analysts. I recognize one civilian. He had blond hair, a goatee, was chunky, about 27-28 years old, and about 5'7 or 5'8. From my understanding, they would always have prior approval to use the dogs. Dogs were also used for crowd control along the concertina wire. There were two analyst who were transferred into my section because they were no longer allowed to inter-rogate. These two, ▮▮▮▮▮ were great analyst and outstanding soldiers. These two individuals came to me (separately) with concerns of some-thing they had done. ▮▮▮▮▮ told me that ▮▮▮▮▮ wasn't involved that he went to the JIDC and asked ▮▮▮▮▮ go with him because he wanted to show him something. They went to the hard site where the MPs had several detainees naked on the floor and a nerf ball was being thrown at the detainees. Apparently ▮▮▮▮▮ got into it and threw a nerf ball at the detainees After they left, ▮▮▮▮▮ asked ▮▮▮▮▮ he was okay because he looked concern. They told me they were afraid and they wanted my advice. I told each that they needed to get some legal advice. I told ▮▮▮▮▮ They told me they knew about it and that I should not have been told about this. I went ahead and reported it to CID just in case they had not heard. They said they knew about it. The only other incident that I heard of which might have been considered humiliation was when a detainee wanted to smoke. The MPs let him smoke but they made him smoke the entire pack within 30 minutes while he did PT. In reference to OGA detainees, I only dealt with this situation once. I wanted to speak to one of their detainees who was a foreign fighter and belonged to OGA. I asked and was told he would not come to me but that I would be able to see the report OGA wrote up on SIPR. I never got it or saw it. One of the problems we had was sharing information or obtaining information with other units conducting interrogations. The reports would be posted on the portal or a similar site, but the interrogator notes were not posted. One time I saw a report that would have been very helpful to me a month previous. I began to make back channels to share information with other interrogators. This worked out great but my leadership got mad for doing that. I kept doing it because there was information they had which helped us develop link analysis diagrams and write analytic assessments I was shown some photos. Photo #23 show ████████ and ████████ looking at naked detainees. Photo #11 in file named CG Lapmark shows a female interpreter (name unknown) and ████████ a CACI interrogator. There was another photo which showed ████████ an interpreter working with one of the Military Police.

10. EXHIBIT	11. INITIALS OF PERSON MAKING STATEMENT
	████████

LOCATION	DATE	TIME	FILE NUMBER
30th Military Police Detachment (CID), Fort Stewart, GA	14 Nov 03	1223	

NAME	SSN	GRADE/STATUS
b7D		b7D

ORGANIZATION/ADDRESS:

b7D

I, _____, want to make the following statement under oath:

BETWEEN 25 APR 03 – 15 AUG 03, I WAS DEPLOYED TO IRAQ. WHILE IN IRAQ, I SAW WHAT I THINK WERE WAR CRIMES ON THE PEOPLE OF IRAQ. IN MY MIND, MY CHAIN OF COMMAND DID NOTHING TO STOP THESE WAR CRIMES, AND ALLOWED THEM TO HAPPEN. MANY TIMES HARSH TREATMENT WAS GIVEN WITH MY 1SG THERE WATCHING OVER. ONE PLACE I ALWAYS SAW THE TREATMENT WAS IN THE AREA 1ST PLT'S (CAMP RED) WAS. I'D SEE IRAQI CITIZENS MISTREATED. SOMETIMES THERE WOULD BE PRISONER'S WITH SAND BAGS ON THEIR HEADS, STANDING ON A BRICK WITH THEIR HANDS BEHIND THEIR HEAD, AND CONCERTINA WIRE ALL AROUND THEM. IF THEY GOT OFF THE BRICK THEY WERE MANHANDLED. A LOT OF PICTURES WERE TAKEN AT THE TIME THAT 1ST PLT WAS AT CAMP RED. MANY SHOW THE MISTREATMENT OR CRIMES AGAINST THE PEOPLE THAT WERE CAUGHT AT CAMP RED. WHEN PRISONERS WERE WITH HEADQUARTERS PLATOON, THEY WERE PUT OUT IN THE OPEN PAVEMENT WHERE THEY WOULD BE MADE TO SIT FOR 6 TO 12 HOURS AT A TIME IN THE HEAT AND SUN. THEIR HANDS WOULD BE TIED BEHIND THEIR BACKS, SOMETIMES TURNING THEIR HANDS PURPLE. WE WERE TOLD BY OUR 1SG NOT TO GIVE THEM FOOD OR WATER BECAUSE THEY WOULD JUST KEEP COMING BACK FOR IT. IF WE DID GIVE THEM ANYTHING BY THE 1SG, HE WOULD YELL AT US.

Q. Where is Camp Red located?
A. Baghdad, Iraq.
Q. Who was the person in charge at Camp Red?
A. CPT _____ he is the Battalion Maintenance Officer for 3/7 Infantry. b7C 3, b6-3
Q. How long were you at Camp Red?
A. I was not actually at Camp Red, I just went there everyday _____
Q. These people you feel were mistreated, were they military or civilians?
A. I don't know for sure.
Q. Why were these people being detained at Camp Red?
A. For trespassing. If they were caught inside 1st Platoons area, they were detained.
Q. What exactly did you see happen to these people?
A. I saw them get pushed and kicked by soldiers in 1st Platoon.
Q. How many times did you see these people being pushed and kicked?
A. Every day I went down there.
Q. Why were sandbags placed on the heads of the detainees?
A. I have no idea.
Q. When you say the detainees were manhandled if they got off the bricks, what do you mean by that statement?
A. They were jerked up.
Q. Who was the person in charge of the detainees?
A. SFC _____ he is the Platoon Sergeant of 1st Platoon. b7C-3, b6-3
Q. Was he aware the detainees were being pushed and kicked?
A. Yes.
Q. How do you know he was aware?
A. I saw him there.
Q. Did you see him push or kick the detainees?

EXHIBIT- 2

Initials of Person Making Statement _____

Page 1 of 5 Pages   5

DA Form 2823 (Automated)

b7D

Statement of ████████████████████, taken at the 30ᵗʰ Military Police Detachment (CID), Fort Stewart, GA 31314, dated 14 Nov 03, Continued:

A. Yes, I saw him push their heads down while they were sitting on the ground. Sometimes the detainees would look up at him and he would push their heads down.
Q. What would happen to the detainees after being at Camp Red?
A. After 72 hours they would release them.
Q. You have provided three pictures to this office, where did these pictures come from?
A. They were given to me by other soldiers in 1ˢᵗ Platoon.
Q. I am showing you one of the pictures of a building, what does this picture depict?
A. That is the main building at Camp Red. This is where 1ˢᵗ Platoon stayed and where they kept the detainees.
Q. I am showing you one of the pictures of a soldier standing between two detainees, what does this picture depict?
A. It shows how the detainees were put inside the wired in area with bags over their heads.
Q. I am showing you one of the pictures of individuals lying on the ground, what does this picture depict?
A. That is what I was told the detainees were put on the ground and then a Bradley was backed up on the sidewalk to spook the people on the ground.
Q. Were you at Camp Red when the Bradley was backed up on the sidewalk while detainees were lying on the ground?
A. No.
Q. In the picture you can see what appears to rucksacks in the upper right hand corner. Is this correct?
A. Yes.
Q. Was it common for rucksacks to be hung on the outside of the Bradleys?
A. Yes.
Q. Do you know if there is a Bradley parked in the upper right hand corner of the picture?
A. Yes there is.
Q. Was this a common area for the Bradleys to be parked?
A. Yes.
Q. Could this Bradley have been parked prior to the individuals being placed on the ground beside it?
A. I have no idea.
Q. Do you know why the Bradley was backed up on the sidewalk?
A. I was told it was to spook the detainees.
Q. Were the detainees given food and water?
A. I saw them with water. I never saw them eat.
Q. Did you see any soldiers shoot any of the detainees?
A. No.
Q. Did you see any soldiers stab any of the detainees?
A. No.
Q. Did you see any soldiers cut any of the detainees?
A. No.
Q. Did you see any soldiers choke any of the detainees?
A. No.
Q. Did you see any soldiers place a noose around the necks of detainees?
A. No.
Q. Did you see any soldiers sexually assault any of the detainees?
A. No.
Q. Did you see any soldiers throw urine or feces on any of the detainees?
A. No.
Q. Did you see any of the detainees being dragged by a vehicle?
A. No.
Q. Did you see any of the detainees being physically harmed?
A. No.
Q. How were the hands of the detainees tied behind their backs?
A. Sometimes with zip-ties or 550 cord.
Q. Were zip-ties or 550 cord the only means of restraining detainees by your unit?
A. Yes.
Q. Is there anything you would like to add to this statement?

EXHIBIT_ ∠

Initials of Person Making Statement ████ b7D

Page 2 of 3 Pages

⌐JJ 6

DETAILS

About 0900, 21 Oct 03, this office was notified by the Staff Judge Advocate (SJA), 4ID, Camp Iron Horse, Tikrit, Iraq, APO AE 09323, of a possible detainee abuse incident involving Mr ▇▇▇▇ b(6)4 b(7)(c)4
b(6)1 b(7)(c)1

About 1020, 21 Oct 03, SA ▇▇▇▇▇ coordinated with the Detention Confinement Facility, Camp Iron Horse, Tikrit, Iraq, APO AE 09323, and obtained Mr ▇▇▇▇ personal records. In his capture data, Mr ▇▇▇▇ claimed when he was captured, he was hit in the stomach by several soldiers in civilian clothes, causing blood to be in his urine and stool. Mr ▇▇▇ was seen by medical personnel and no injuries were seen. According to the detainee information, Mr ▇▇▇▇ was captured by 1-22 Infantry, 4ID personnel and possibly Task Force 20 soldiers.

b(6)1 b(7)(c)1

About 0945, 22 Oct 03, SA ▇▇▇▇ coordinated with S-2, Task Force 20 unit on Camp Iron Horse and discovered the previous group re-deployed on 1 Oct 03. He was unsure of their current location.///LAST ENTRY///

TYPED AGENT'S NAME AND SEQUENCE NUMBER	ORGANIZATION
b(2) b(6)1 b(7)(c)1	43rd Military Police Det (CID)
SA ▇▇▇▇▇	APO AE 09323

SIGNATURE	DATE	EXHIBIT
▇▇▇▇	22 Oct 03	1

CID FORM 94   FOR OFFICIAL USE ONLY

10

A-334

Law Enforcement Sensitive FOU   0174-03C10469   ①

0174-03C10469-60225

b(6)H
b(7)(C)H

LAW ENFORCEMENT SENSITIVE

FOR OFFICIAL USE ONLY

I live in [redacted] Nieghberhood (Yoth $)N. I was arrested by the American forces 9/7/2003 they raided my house and broke the door, the wall and the interior door they searched the house they asked me if I have the weapons. I said No. at 7:30 they Put me in the Hamves then American Solder aproched me and beated me with his rifle on my head too many Time, and they took me the prison in Tikrit North location, I stayed there three days they took me out at gov prob and they beat me up on my head and my stomich many Time

LAW ENFORCEMENT SENSITIVE - FOR OFFICIAL USE ONLY

FOR official USE ONLY — LAW Enforcement Sensitive

0174-03C10469 ②

after they tied me up on the chair then they dislocate my both arms. He asked to admit befor. I kill you then he beat me again and start bleeding, and he asked me are you going to report me? you have no evidence then he hit me very hard on my Noise then too he steped on my Noise until he borkeded. blood I start bleeding on my clothes then he brought spray and wash my face with water, he took me to the Jail after then next night came the same solder told me I'am sorry for beating you up, because I thought you were bad person therefore I apologize, I told him I dont accept you appologize.

encl 4

EXHIBIT 10

27

DODDOACID 005914

EXHIBIT 10

28

0130-04-CID769 ④

he took me back to the jail
after two days later he came
back to me and he asked.
me are you going to admit
then he lay me down in the
Floor and he kicked
me on my left leg with
baseball stick. (I couldn't walk
he told me this is your last
beating. So you can stay all
your life in prison. then he
start hiting me on my head
until I Past out then he carried
me to the car then he threw me
in the Floor then my Freind
prisoner throw water in my face
and took me to the other
Hospital they checked me out
and they gave me medicen. then
I stay for 12 days in Owja
prison then they took back to
the another prison in the school
(Tikrit) then I was interrogated

Inc/4

0130-04-CID769 ③

and he told me it is today.
will be the last day in your
life. he came out 1:00 AM
and he appoligize he told me
that I appoligized to you
but you didn't accept my
appology then he pulled his
out his pistol and he sticked
on my mouth and discharge
the pistol but the pistol was
out of bulets or (empty)
so he said it to -
The bolt it's no good. I will
tried again and then he pul
his pistol on the tabel and
he hanged me with the robe
till I stop breathing out then
he left me he threw water in
my face he repeated this until
I passed out and Fell in the
ground.
end Page 2

Inc Y

0136-04-C1046 9 (5)

by one of the Solder, I told him
that I have ~~problems~~ health
problems then he took me
to the hospital in the air
force Acadmy then they examined
me and the doctor said these
disease caused by beating
severly not ~~by~~ diseases. Then
the doctor told me to press
Charges against those who beat
you up and destroyed your
life. then he send me back
to the prison School (Tikrit)
after they give me medication
but the medication it did not
help, then they send me to
Abo Ghreeb I stayed ~~there~~ there
for two months in the Fourth
camp prison, one of the American
solder took me to the computer
room and he asked me are you
the one who pressed charge
against american, I said I didnt

Encl 4

0136-04-C1046 9 (6)

press Charge against anyone
But one of the solder in Tikrit
press Charge, he asked me do
you want to be released. from
the prison? I said yes, then
he said write in this paper
(with all my mind I drope the
charge.) after I wrote this
he told me it's done you will
stay in the prison for long
time and you will never get
out until you get 50 years old
Then they transfer me to Um-Qaser
but the treatment was very good
they treated my health in the
prison, then I get back to my
normal health but I was still
suffer from my Noise and leg
it was hurting me, One
of the doctor recommedd me
to have operation to be good.

Encl 4

EXHIBIT 10

29

EXHIBIT 10

0136-04-CID469 ⑤

30

Q- Do you remember what the man looked Like who beat you?

A. The Solder was six feet tall. He wears Glasses, his Face was red and scratched. He has a Red and green Tatoo on his right arm., he was 28 years old bald head, blue eyes., blond hair.

- Why didn't you make a complaint at Abo prison.?

A. Because I was scare of torturing.

Q. How many different People were they beating you.?

A. They were Four People, one of them was Iraqi. dark color wears Jeans and red shirt he use to Tie me on the chair and beat me on my head. His hair was Gray medium size hight he use to wear militry uniform and all. He was daily change his clothes

End 4 ⑦

he was cursing me with a bad words and beating me.

his eyes was Hazel. has short very light beard. he was [redacted] calling himself.

The third one was civilian had long goat beard, blue eyes., very slim, long hight, his Face was very red

Q- were there any other detainees with you when you were beat?

A- I was Alone

Q- Is there any thing else you would like to add to this statment?

A- There is nothing.

The fourth one medium size hight, wears yellow shirt and blue Jean, blond hair, he use to role his nick many times and gets nervous.

End of the statment   End 4

0174-03-CID469-00035

A-337

b(6)4
b(7)(c)4

STATEMENT OF SSG ▮▮▮▮▮▮▮ TAKEN AT FHTX CID DATED 9 Jul 04 CONTINUED

A. YES, NOT ALLOWED TO ENTER CELLS

Q. What condition was the ▮▮▮▮▮ in when you dropped him off?

A. GOOD CONDITION, TIRED

Q. Do you remember what he had in his possession?

A. NOT OTHER THAN ID

Q. Who were your interpreters?

A. ▮▮▮▮▮▮▮   b(6)6   b(7)(c)6

Q. Any one report to you that an interpreter had abused a detainee?

A. NO

Q. Did your platoon leader ever mention detainee abuse?

A. NO

Q. Did your S-2 or support personnel at the detention facility ever mention detainee abuse?

A. NO

Q. Do you know who interviewed detainees after you released them to your S-2?

A. I NEVER SAW ANY PERSON TALK TO HIM BUT WAS TOLD THAT OUR S-2 AND TF+20 QUESTIONED HIM

Q. Who manned or supported the detention facility?

A. THE TF 1-22 MORTAR AND SMOKE PLATOONS

Q. Was that their mission in Iraq?

A. GAURD CELL AND FORCE PROTECTION

Q. Who did you see around the FOB in civilian clothes?

A. TF 20 AND SF(ODA)

Q. Did you ever see TF20 or SF personnel in the detainee cells?

A. YES, THE WOULD PULL THE DETAINEE OUT AND TAKE HIM TO ANOTHER ROOM BEHIND THE CELL.

Q. Did you ever observe any detainee abuse in the room behind the cell?

A. NO

Q. Do you know any of the TF20 or SF personnel who interviewed the ▮▮▮▮▮▮▮

b(6)4
b(7)(c)4

INITIALS OF PERSON MAKING STATEMENT: ▮▮▮▮   PAGE _3_ OF _4_ PAGES

EXHIBIT _15_

DODDOACID 005930

b(6)4
b(7)(c)4

STATEMENT OF 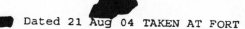 Dated 21 Aug 04 TAKEN AT FORT
HOOD, TX 76544

A: Yes, just rumors. Mainly from prisoners. When the Task Force
20 would come pick them up to interview them, they'd complain
when they got back but I never saw any bruises when the prisoner
would try to show me.

Q: Do you know any names of the Task Force 20 personnel?   b(6)3
b(7)(c)3
A: They only give their first name. I think his name was

Q: Did any prisoners ever leave your custody?
A: Yes. Sometimes the Task Force 20 would come and pick up
prisoners from the cell without letting me know they were taking
the detainee. The prisoner would have intel the Task Force
needed. When I would go down in the morning to check on the
prisoners, the guard personnel would tell me that the Task Force
20 had come and got someone and hadn't brought them back yet. I
would be upset because I would still have this guy's property.

Q: Who conducted interrogations at your facility?
A: We had our own team but I can't remember the chief's name.
If it was a joint between TF 20 and 1/22 then a lot of the
interrogation was done by them on the ground. They would
determine if the information the detainee provided was good
enough for them to be brought back.

Q: Did you ever witness any prisoner abuse?
A: No.   b(6)4   b(7)(c)4
Q: How long was Mr.   in your custody?
A: Maybe two weeks or so.

Q: Where did he go after he left your custody?
A: He went to Division Detention center, on the same compound,
just up a little farther then us. Tikrit, Iraq. I think it was
the Ironhorse compound.

Q: Did you have rooms behind the cells where prisoners would be
taken to be interrogated?
A: No.

Q: Who was the Commander of S-2?
A: CPT   b(6)4
                b(7)(c)4
Q: Do you have anything you wish to add to this statement?
A: No.///END OF STATEMENT///

----

b(6)4 4
b(7)(c)4   AFFIDAVIT

I,   , HAVE READ OR HAVE HAD READ TO ME THIS
STATEMENT WHICH BEGINS ON PAGE 1 AND ENDS ON PAGE 3.   I FULLY
UNDERSTAND THE CONTENTS OF THE ENTIRE STATEMENT MADE BY ME.   THE
STATEMENT IS TRUE.   I HAVE INITIALED ALL CORRECTIONS AND HAVE
                          INITIALS   Page 2 of 3
FOR OFFICIAL USE ONLY
                                              EXHIBIT 2D

DODDOACID 005944

REPLY TO
ATTENTION OF

CIRF-ZC-OP.

19-May-04

MEMORANDUM THRU

Commander, 6th Military Police Group (CID), ATTN: CIRF-OP, Mail Stop #84, P. O. Box 339500, Fort Lewis, WA 98433-9500

Commander, 3rd Military Police Group (CID), ATTN: CIRC-OP, 4699 N. 1st Street, Forest Park, GA 30297-5119

FOR Commander, USACIDC, ATTN: CIOP-COP-CO, 6010 6th Street, Fort Belvoir, VA 22060-5506

SUBJECT: Operation Review of CID Report of Investigation (0174-03-CID469-60225)

1. On 17 May 04, this office received a Request for Investigation (RFI 0212-04-CID001) from Headquarters, USACIDC, via 3rd Military Police Group (CID), Forest Park, GA to conduct an operation review of all detainee death/abuse investigations to ensure standards of timeliness, thoroughness, and timely reporting are met.

2. On 19 May 04, the undersigned conducted an operational review of the above referenced Report of Investigation (ROI) to determine if it was operationally sufficient. This ROI was initiated on 20 Jul 03 by the 43rd Military Police Detachment (CID) (FWD). When the 43rd MP Detachment redeployed from Tikrit, Iraq to Fort Hood, TX, this case file was brought back for distribution to the Crime Records Center (CRC), Fort Belvoir, VA. The case file is maintained at the Fort Hood Resident Agency, Fort Hood, TX in accordance with applicable regulations.

3. This investigation was initiated upon notification by the Staff Judge Advocate (SJA), 4ID, that Mr. ████████ was the possible victim of detainee abuse. Mr. ████ was apprehended during a raid on 8 Sep 03, and alleged he was blindfolded and taken to an unknown location in northern Tikrit, Iraq where he was confronted by five Americans dressed in civilian clothing and an Iraqi interpreter, ████████ and was beaten and choked. After being transferred to Al-Oja for four days, then to the DCCP. Mr. ████ was at the DCCP for ten days before being examined by medical personnel. This investigation was closed 5 Feb 04 as a Final (C) as determined the complainant/victim's cooperation is necessary for the satisfactory resolution of the investigation, and such cooperation is not forthcoming. Remaining leads include the identification of the persons involved in the interrogation and the canvass of the soldiers involved in the raid. However, during the operational review, the following investigative leads were identified:

48

DODDOACID 005993

a. The investigation was initiated based on the allegations submitted by the SJA, 4ID, some 40 days after Mr. ██████ capture. There were no medical treatment exhibits or explanation for the lack thereof included in the ROI.

b. 1LT ██████████ RECON, 1-22 Inf, 4ID was identified as the platoon leader at the time of the capture of Mr. █████ No concerted effort was made to locate, identify and interview 1LT ████ regarding the capture or identify the personnel involved.

c. On 25 Nov 03, Mr. █████was interviewed while detained at Abu Ghruyeb Prison Complex by SA ██████ with the assistance of Mr. ██████████ Category II, Civilian Linguist of Titan Industries. Mr. █████translated statement states in part," I do not want to file a complaint against the American Forces so I can get released.... I was not forced or threatened by anyone to write this statement." This statement, alone, is a prima facie indication of threats.

d. There was no effort to prove or disprove the allegations of Mr. █████as presented by the SJA, 4ID.

4. This ROI will be reopened to complete the above-identified leads and/or follow other investigative leads that may be developed during the investigation.

5. The point of contact for this action is the undersigned at DSN████████ COM███████ or email: ██████████@hood.army.mil.

CW4, MP
Assistant Operations Officer

2

49

DODDOACID 005994

A-341

OTY-03-~1D467-6022S

TRANSLATION OF STATEMENT PROVIDED BY ▓▓▓▓▓ b(6)4 b(7)(c)4
1040/25 NOV 03:

"I am ▓▓▓▓▓ I swear under oath that I do not want to file a complaint against the American Forces so I can get released. I was given the opportunity by the Criminal Investigation to think about this matter and I did not want to file a complaint and I swear that was my own decision. I was not forced or threatened by anyone to write this statement. This is my sworn statement."

TRANSLATED BY: ▓▓▓▓▓   VERIFIED BY: ▓▓▓▓▓

b(6)4   b(6)6
                                           b(7)(c)6

Mr. ▓▓▓▓▓   Mr. ▓▓▓▓▓
Translator, Category II b(7)(c)4   Translator, Category II
Titan Industries   Titan Industries
Assigned to:
    Prisoner Interview/Interrogation Team (PIT)(CID)(FWD)
    10TH Military Police Battalion (CID)(ABN)(FWD)
    3rd Military Police Group (CID), USACIDC
    Abu Ghruyeb Prison Complex (ABPC)
    Abu Ghruyeb, Iraq APO AE 09335

0174-03-CID 469-60225

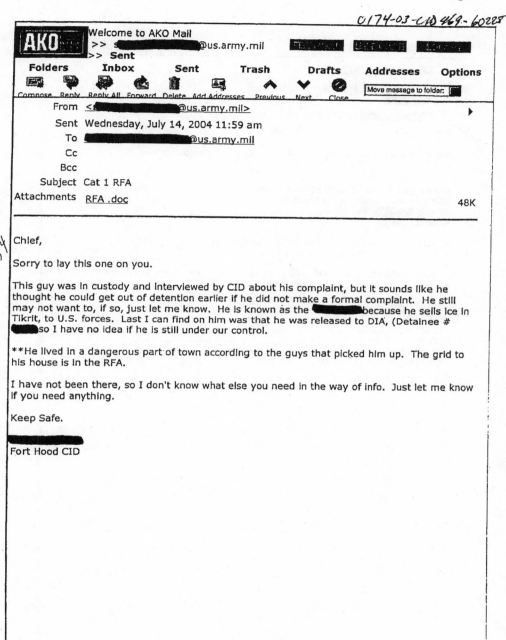

AKO Welcome to AKO Mail
>> s███████@us.army.mil
>> Sent

Folders   Inbox   Sent   Trash   Drafts   Addresses   Options

Compose Reply Reply All Forward Delete Add Addresses Previous Next Close   Move message to folder:

From <s███████@us.army.mil>
Sent Wednesday, July 14, 2004 11:59 am
To ███████@us.army.mil
Cc
Bcc
Subject Cat 1 RFA
Attachments RFA .doc   48K

Chief,

Sorry to lay this one on you.

This guy was in custody and interviewed by CID about his complaint, but it sounds like he thought he could get out of detention earlier if he did not make a formal complaint. He still may not want to, if so, just let me know. He is known as the ███████ because he sells ice in Tikrit, to U.S. forces. Last I can find on him was that he was released to DIA, (Detainee # ███ so I have no idea if he is still under our control.

**He lived in a dangerous part of town according to the guys that picked him up. The grid to his house is in the RFA.

I have not been there, so I don't know what else you need in the way of info. Just let me know if you need anything.

Keep Safe.

███████

Fort Hood CID

https://webmail.us.army.mil/en/mail.html?sid=LEn69hdUAMWw&lang=en&cert=false   7/14/2004

DODDOACID 006014

_____ SA CID (PKI)   0174-03-CID469-60225

From: _____ SA CID
Sent: Sunday, August 15, 2004 5:05 PM
To: _____
Cc: _____ SA CID (PKI)
Subject: RE: CAT I

Outstanding!. Now we (read you more than likely) have to ID the subjects from TF 20.

    -----Original Message-----
    From: _____ [mailto:_____@us.army.mil]
    Sent: Sunday, August 15, 2004 4:29 PM
    To: _____@us.army.mil
    Subject: CAT I

    Interviewed your guy today and his father; we got an 8 page statement and he supposedly got his ass kicked. Once the statement is translated I will email you a copy. He gave a pretty detailed statement and good descriptions. Hope this doesn't convolute your investigation, but he was pretty shaken up and also provided medical records as well. Will give you more details when the statement is translated. Also attached photos of the guy if you need them.

    _____
    SPECIAL AGENT
    1ST MP CO (CID); 1ST ID
    FOB DANGER; OIF II
    APO AE 09392
    TIKRIT, IRAQ

b(6))
b(7)(6))

8/16/2004   65

DODDOACID 006010

A-344

DEPARTMENT OF THE ARMY
UNITED STATES ARMY CRIMINAL INVESTIGATION COMMAND
48TH MILITARY POLICE DETACHMENT (CID) (FWD)
3RD MILITARY POLICE GROUP (CID)
CAMP VICTORY, BAGHDAD, IRAQ
APO AE 09342

17 JUN 2005

(U) MEMORANDUM FOR SEE DISTRIBUTION
(U) SUBJECT: CID REPORT OF INVESTIGATION – FINAL
SUPPLEMENTAL/SSI-0213-2004-CID259-80250 –5C2B/5Y2E

(U) DATES/TIMES/LOCATIONS OF OCCURRENCES:
    1. 4 JAN 2004, 2330 – 5 JAN 2004, 0800; SADDAM INTERNATIONAL
AIRPORT (BAGHDAD INTERNATIONAL AIRPORT (BIAP)), BAGHDAD, IRAQ
(IZ).

(U) DATE/TIME REPORTED: 13 JUL 2004, 1200

(U) INVESTIGATED BY:
    SA
    SA
    SA
    SA
    SA
    SA
    SA
    SA
    SA
    SA
    SA
    SA
    SA

b(7)(C)-1, b(2)-1

(U) SUBJECT:
    1. UNKNOWN; ASSAULT (UNFOUNDED), CRUELTY AND
MALTREATMENT (UNFOUNDED) (NFI)

b(7)(c)-4

(U) VICTIM:
    1. ███████████████████████ CIV; IRAQI; INTERNMENT SERIAL
NUMBER (ISN): ███████████ 15 MAY 1985; TIKRIT, IRAQ; MALE; WHITE;
XZ; DATE OF CAPTURE: 5 JAN 2004; AKA: ████████████████████████
██ ISN: ██████████ DOB: ████████

1

000 ᴗ1

DOD-044418

A-345

b(7)(c)-4

███████ ASSAULT (UNFOUNDED), CRUELTY AND MALTREATMENT
(UNFOUNDED) (NFI)

(U) INVESTIGATIVE SUMMARY:

(U) Investigation by this office and review by Headquarters, U.S. Army Criminal
Investigation Command (USACIDC), determined there was sufficient credible
information to believe the offenses of Assault and Cruelty and Maltreatment did not
occur as alleged.   b(7)(c)-4

(U) Investigation determined ███████ was captured on 4 Jan 04, and detained by
members of Task Force (TF) 6-26 ███████ alleged he was detained in Tikrit, IZ, and
was then taken to BIAP, where, over the course of one evening, he was forced to take off
all of his clothes, made to walk into walls blindfolded, punched in the back, kicked in the
stomach, drug around the room, and forced to assume uncomfortable positions, such as
lying down with his hands on the floor and his legs on top of a meal-ready-to-eat (MRE)
box. ███████ further alleged during this time he had cold water poured on him and was
forced to stand in front of a running air conditioner.

(U) All attempts to identify, locate and interview personnel associated with ███████
arrest and interrogations prior to his arrival at the Baghdad Central Confinement Facility
(BCCF), Abu Ghraib, IZ, have met with negative results. There was no medical
documentation found in ███████ detainee files and all attempts to locate his medical
records have met with negative results.   b(7)(c)-2

(U) This investigation was coordinated with MAJ ███████ Staff Judge
Advocate, 10th Special Forces Group, Special Operations Command, Forward Operating
Base (FOB) Central, Baghdad, IZ, who opined there was no probable cause to believe the
offenses occurred as alleged; therefore, they are unfounded.

(U) STATUTES:

(U) ARTICLE 128, UCMJ: ASSAULT (UNFOUNDED)
(U) ARTICLE 93, UCMJ: CRUELTY AND MALTREATMENT (UNFOUNDED)

(U) EXHIBITS/SUBSTANTIATION:

(U) ADDED ATTACHED: b(7)(c)-1

(U) 13. Agent's Investigation Report (AIR) of SA ███████ 48TH Military
Police Detachment (CID), Camp Victory, Baghdad, IZ, 17 Jun 05, detailing receipt of
Request for Correction (RFC), completion of supplemental report, forwarding of case file
to USACIDC for review, and coordination with SJA.

2

022694

000 02

DOD-044419

A-346

(U) 14. Biometrics Automated Toolset (BATS) File, 31 Jan 04 through 16 Jul 04, pertaining to ███████ containing: Detainee Dossier; Interrogator Reports; Related Interrogators Reports; and a Related Interrogations Report.   b(7)(C)-4

(SECRET) 15. Classified documents in the BATS File of ███████ 31 Jan 04 through 6 Jul 04, including: Personal Data Report and Interrogation Reports (USACRC and File copies only).

(SECRET//NOFORN) 16. Interrogation Report, 16 Feb 04, pertaining to ███████ (USACRC and File copies only).

(U) ADDED NOT ATTACHED:

None.

(U) The originals of Exhibits 13 through 15 are forwarded with the USACRC copy of this report. The original of Exhibit 16 is maintained in the files of 66th Military Intelligence Group, Darmstadt, Germany.

(U) STATUS: This is a Final Supplemental Report. Commander's Report of Action (DA Form 4833) is not required.

(U) Report Prepared By: Report Approved By:

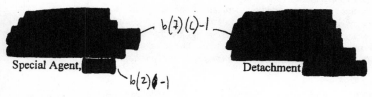

Special Agent, ███████   Detachment ███████

b(7)(C)-1
b(2)(?)-1

(U) DISTRIBUTION:

1-DIR, USACRC, 6010, 6th Street, Fort Belvoir, VA 22060-5506 (original)
1-Thru: CDR, 11TH MP BN (CID) (FWD), APO AE 09342
  Thru: CDR, 3RD MP Group (CID)
  To: CDR, USACIDC, ATTN: CIOP-ZA, Fort Belvoir, VA 22060
1-Chief, Investigative Operations Division, USACIDC
1-Deputy Chief of Staff for Operations, USACIDC
1-CID Current Operations, USACIDC
1-PMO, MNC-I (e-mail only)
1-SJA, MNC-I (e-mail only)
1-Chief of Staff, Detainee Operations, MNF-I
1-Detachment Sergeant, 48TH MP Det (CID) (FWD)
1-CDR, 48th MP DET (CID) (FWD)
1-File

3

022695

000 03

DOD-044420

A-347

DETAINEE ASSESSMENT TASK FORCE
CASE FINDING STATEMENT

Date Reviewed: 26 Feb 05

Reviewer: ███████████████ b(7)(c)-1

Case number: 0213-04-CID259-80250

Offense: Assault / Cruelty & Maltreatment

Status: Closed as a Final (C) on 27 Oct 04

FINDINGS OF DATF REVIEW: b(7)(c)-4

1. No effort was made to identify and interview the interrogators and screening personnel who were working at the Temporary Screening Facility (TSF) during the time period of the alleged incident (4-5 Jan 05). The detainee provided **very** good descriptions of the interpreter ███████ as well as other individuals who were involved or present during the abuse and it may be possible to identify suspects based on his descriptions.

2. The "lost records" explanation is unacceptable. Capture reports and interrogation reports do not just sit in a database on a local hard drive. They are submitted to higher echelons as well as other intelligence activities in an expeditious manner. The bottom line is this detainee's circumstances were rather unique, due to his relationship to another high value detainee (as detailed in the case file). Because of this relationship, the interrogators would have prepared and submitted a report to higher echelons. There is not indication that we had MI or the TSF search the available databases for any reports pertaining to this detainee.

3. During his interview with CID, the detainee stated he agreed to show the interrogators where the person lived who provided his fake passport. The detainee stated he was taken by helicopter to show the interrogators the location and then he was taken to Abu Ghraib. Again, more information that can be used to distinguish this detainee from other detainees and assist in identifying the individuals who interrogated him.

b(7)(c)-2

(same)

(same)

4. The ███████████████ explanation of the pseudonyms ███████████████ and ███████████████ does not make sense. He stated the pseudonyms were used for operational security purposes to protect the identity of the **capturing** personnel and the personnel who captured the detainee would not have been the same personnel who interrogated him. In the statements of ███████████ and ███████████████ they both stated, "It **was reported to me** that Detainee was detained because he was at the home of....". This clearly demonstrates that ███████████ and ███████████ were not capturing unit personnel. Further, the memorandum attached as Exhibit 10 to the ROI states "The Temporary Screening Facility administrative staff has used the following pseudonyms during that time period: ███████████████████████ It is clear that ███████████ and ███████████████ were TSF personnel.

022769

000 78

DOD-044494

5. Exhibit 9 (AIR) contains a paragraph that states interrogation reports were reviewed that had variations of the detainee's name; however, the date of birth on the reports did not match the detainee's date of birth. The AIR does not indicate whether or not the dates of birth were close to the detainee's date of birth. We have found that the same detainee may have numerous dates of birth listed in his records due to a variety of reasons, including admin errors or even because the detainee simply does not know his exact date of birth. Also of note in this case is the fact that the detainee's father was detained during the same time period and the detainee and his father have very similar names. The questioned interrogation reports should have been reviewed for content and compared with subsequent reports that we do have from when the detainee was at Abu Ghraib. The detainee was questioned concerning a very specific issue and the circumstances of his capture were similarly unique.

    b(7)(C)-4

6. The case file contained a copy of _____ statement; however, it was not attached to the ROI as part of Exhibit 2, which include the detainee records as well as a copy of _____ statement.

7. Exhibit 5 contained several aliases that were not listed in the VICTIM BLOCK o the ROI, i.e. _____ and _____ (apparent misspelling of detainee's actual name).

8. Exhibit 4 reflects that the detainee had another Internment Serial Number _____ apparently from a previous capture. Should have been listed in the VICTIM BLOCK.

RECOMMENDATION: Reopen this investigation and address the aforementioned issues.

b(7)(C)-4   (b(7)(C)-4

022770

000 79

DOD-044495

0213-04-CID259-80250 (DATF)   b(7)(c)-4   Reviewed: 11 Feb 05

Occurrence: 0001/5 Jan 04-2359/5 Jan 04
Location: Unknown location, BIAP, Baghdad, IZ, APO AE 09342
Subject: Unknown: (NFI)
Victim: ████████████████ Civilian, Internment Serial Number (ISN)
████████████

Offense: Aggravated Assault, Cruelty and Maltreatment (Same)

This investigation was initiated upon receipt of RFI 0332-04-CID001, from
HQUSACIDC, which indicated a review of ████████████ interrogation reports revealed
he was allegedly abused while detained by us Coalition Forces.

A review of this case file and investigative reports revealed this detainee was captured
and detained by Task Force 6-26. Task Force 6-26 is stationed out of Fort Bragg, NC. A
Request for Assistance was sent to the CID assest with this Task Force. An Information
Report was provided to this office which stated fake names were used by the 6-26
members. The only names identified by this investigation were determined to be fake
names utilized by the capturing soldiers; however, the abuse allegedly occurred during
the interrogation of the detainee. The 6-26 CID agent related that the capturing soldiers
would not know who the interrogators were. 6-26 also had a major computer
malfunction which resulted in them losing 70 percent of their files; therefore, they can't
find the cases we need to review.

This investigation meets the necessary requirements and does not need to be reopened.
Hell, even if we reopened it we wouldn't get anymore information then we already have.

022771

000 80

DOD-044496

SECRET//NOFORN//20290625

INFO MEMO

S-0517/DR   June 25, 2004

FOR: UNDER SECRETARY OF DEFENSE FOR INTELLIGENCE

FROM: L. E. Jacoby, Vice Admiral, USN. Director, Defense Intelligence Agency

Subject: (S//NF) Alleged Detainee Abuse by TF 62-6 Personnel

(S//NF) During the afternoon of 24 June 2004, we were notified that DIA personnel serving with TF 6-26 in Baghdad had informed their ISG seniors of the following:

- (S//NF) Two DIA, Directorate for Human Intelligence (DIA/DH) interrogators/debriefers assigned to support TF 6-26 (SOF) have observed:

    - Prisoners arriving at the Temporary Detention Facility in Baghdad with burn marks on their backs. Some have bruises, and some have complained of kidney pain.

    - One of the two DIA/DH interrogators/debriefers witnessed TF 6-26 officers punch a prisoner in the face to the point the individual needed medical attention. This record of treatment was not recorded by TF 6-26 personnel. In this instance, the debriefer was ordered to leave the room.

    - One DIA/DH interrogator/debriefer took pictures of the injuries and showed them to his TF 62-6 supervisor, who immediately confiscated them.

- (S//NF) TF 6-26 personnel have taken the following actions with regards to DIA/DH interrogators/debriefers:

    - Confiscated vehicle keys

    - Instructed them not to leave the compound without specific permission, even to get a haircut at the PX

    - Threatened them

Classified by: Multiple Sources
Reason: Paragraph 4?
Declassify on: 25 Jun 2029

SECRET//NOFORN//20290625

DODDIA-000155

~~SECRET//NOFORN//20290625~~

- – Informed them that their e-mails were being screened

- – Ordered them not to talk to anyone in the US

- ~~(S//NF)~~ The two DH strategic debriefers assigned to TF 62-6 reported the above information to the Operations Officer. He immediately contacted DIA IG Forward and asked that both individuals be interviewed. The IG representative made the recommendation that VADM Church's group be immediately apprised in order to get this into official IG channels as the issue fell directly under its charter. The Church IG Team senior investigating officer is conducting interviews of the interrogators/debriefers today. The DIA IG was informed and concurred with this course of action.

- ~~(S//NF)~~ The ISG Operations Officer contacted and briefed the Director of the ISG, who was in Qatar attending a Commander's Conference. The ISG Director informed the Deputy Commander for Detainee Affairs, MNF-I. He subsequently contacted the Commander of TF 6-26 and directed him to investigate this situation. In turn the TF 6-26 Commander informed his superior, the Commander JSOC. The Commander. CENTCOM has also been informed of this situation.

- ~~(S//NF)~~ The two interrogators/debriefers were directed to return to the ISG compound at Camp Slayer due to these events.

(b)(3)

~~SECRET//NOFORN//20290625~~   2

DEPARTMENT OF THE ARMY
22D MILITARY POLICE BATTALION (CID)
UNITED STATES ARMY CRIMINAL
INVESTIGATION COMMAND
BIAP, IRAQ APO AE 09342

CIMPL-ZA

20 May 04

MEMORANDUM FOR Commander, USACIDC, ATTN:
CIOP-COP-OP, 6010 6th St., Fort Belvoir, VA 22060

SUBJECT: RFI (0212-04-CID001)

1. The review of ROI # 0235-03-CID259 determined the investigation was operationally insufficient and was administratively insufficient. This investigation was reported as an SSI only report of death.

2. The review disclosed the following deficiencies. The investigation did not conduct a crime scene examination or explain why such an examination was not conducted. The investigation did not conduct any interviews to determine the circumstances surrounding the death. There was no investigative effort made to obtain the victim's medical records that could have been used to determine if he was under medical care prior to his death. The investigation was closed without opening a full Report of Investigation (ROI). The case file was closed without any preliminary or final autopsy report, or any information as to whether or not an autopsy was conducted. There was an email in the case file that the SSI ONLY email message was received, however, there was no paper or electronic copy of the SSI report in the case file.

3. The point of contact is the undersigned at ███████████
@ us.army.mil, DNVT ████████   b7e-1, b6-1

████████████
                                          b7e-1, b6-1
                                          CW4, MP
                                          Special Agent

FOR OFFICIAL USE ONLY

DATE: 16 SEP 03

FROM: SAC, 43rd MP DET (CID)

TO: DIRECTOR, USACRC, USACIDC, FORT BELVOIR, VA
      CDR, HQUSACIDC //CIOP-ZA//
      CDR, 10TH MP BN (CID)(ABN)(FWD)//OPS//
      CDR, 3D MP GROUP(CID)//OPS//
      LNO CID, CJTF-7 (FOR FURTHER DISTRIBUTION)

SUBJECT: CID REPORT - INITIAL/SSI - 0149-03-CID469-60209-
5H1H

DRAFTER: ███████████████████ ⟩ b7C, b6 1
RELEASER: ███████████████████

              UNCLASSIFIED - FOR OFFICIAL USE ONLY

1. DATES/TIMES/LOCATIONS OF OCCURRENCES:
   1. 11 SEP 03/2315; GRID 38S LD 79352220 (DETAINEE
COLLECTION POINT, FORWARD OPERATING BASE PACKHORSE, TIKRIT,
IRAQ)

2. DATE/TIME REPORTED: 15 SEP 03/1600

3. INVESTIGATED BY: SA ██████████████████; SA ████ ⟩ b7C, b2, b6 1
████████████████████

4. SUBJECT: 1. ████████████████████SPC; ████████ b7C, b6 5
██████████ M; BLACK; D CO, 4TH FORWARD SUPPORT BN,
1BCT, 4ID, APO AE 09323; FC; [MURDER]

5. VICTIM: 1. RADAD, OBEED HETHERE; DETAINEE NUMBER 0019;
M; OTHER; AD DWAR, IRAQ; (NFI); [MURDER]

6. INVESTIGATIVE SUMMARY: THE INFORMATION IN THIS REPORT IS
BASED UPON AN ALLEGATION OR PRELIMINARY INVESTIGATION AND
MAY CHANGE PRIOR TO THE COMPLETION OF THE INVESTIGATION.

THIS IS AN "OPERATION IRAQI FREEDOM" INVESTIGATION.

PRELIMINARY INVESTIGATION DISCLOSED SHORTLY AFTER SPC
███████████ WAS PLACED ON DUTY AT THE ENEMY PRISONER OF
WAR (EPW) FACILITY, HE HAD BEEN OBSERVED BY GUARDS AND EPWS
ALIKE, EXHIBITING BELLIGERENT AND AGGRESSIVE BEHAVIOR TOWARD
RADAD AND HAD ENGAGED IN A YELLING SPREE WITH RADAD THE
NIGHT BEFORE THE INCIDENT. SPC ████████████ HAD ONLY BEEN
DETAILED TO GUARD DUTY AT THE FACILITY FOR THREE DAYS AND
WAS BRIEFED ON THE USE OF DEADLY FORCE WHICH CONSISTED OF
SHOOTING EPWS IF THEY APPROACHED THE WIRE WITHOUT

b7C b65 (left margin)

b7C b65 / b7C, b6 (right margin)

01066

PERMISSION, AND ONLY AFTER VERBAL WARNINGS AND OTHER
MEASURES WERE FIRST CONSIDERED BEFORE APPLYING LETHAL FORCE.
ON 8 SEP 03, RADAD, WHO WAS DETAINED IN A RAID IN AD DWAR ON
31 AUG 03, WAS PLACED IN AN ISOLATION CELL WITH HIS HANDS
FLEXI-CUFFED IN FRONT OF HIM AND HELD FOR QUESTIONING FOR
POSSIBLE TIES TO MRS ███████████ (WIFE OF ███████)
███████ UPON HIS ARRIVAL, MR RADAD WAS INSTRUCTED TO
REMAIN SEATED AND TO STAY AWAY FROM THE CONCERTINA WIRE, OR
HE WOULD BE SHOT.

SPC ██████████████ WHO WAS THE ON-DUTY GUARD FOR THE
ISOLATION CELL, REPORTED DURING THE INITIAL INQUIRY THAT
DURING HIS DETAINMENT, MR RADAD WAS "FIDDLING" WITH HIS
FLEX-CUFFS AND ATTEMPTING TO SPEAK WITH ANOTHER DETAINEE IN
AN ADJACENT HOLDING CELL. AT THE TIME OF THE INCIDENT, SPC
███████████ REPORTED HE HAD MOMENTARILY TURNED AWAY
FROM MR RADAD AND WHEN HE TURNED BACK TO THE ISOLATION CELL,
HE SAW THAT MR RADAD HAD SAT UP AND WAS LEANING OVER THE
STRAND OF CONCERTINA WIRE. SPC ██████████████ WHO STATED HE
THOUGHT MR RADAD WAS ATTEMPTING TO ESCAPE, LOWERED HIS M-16
RIFLE AND SHOT MR RADAD. THE ROUND WENT THROUGH MR RADAD'S
FLEXI-CUFFED ARM AND INTO HIS ABDOMEN.

SPC ██████████████ DID NOT FOLLOW PROPER PROCEDURE WHEN HE
FIRED HIS M16 AT MR RADAD, DELIBERATELY SHOOTING AND KILLING
HIM. PRIOR TO THE SHOOTING, SPC ███████████████ USED NO
VERBAL WARNING NOR DID HE FOLLOW INSTRUCTIONS FOR THE
GRADUATED USE OF FORCE AS RELATED IN 4ID FRAGO 422, 16 MAY
03, WHICH PROVIDES GUIDANCE FOR THE USE OF GRADUATED FORCE
AND SPECIFICALLY IDENTIFIES A "SHOUT, SHOW, SHOVE, SHOOT,
SHOOT" METHODOLOGY, BUT AIMED HIS WEAPON WITH THE INTENT TO
KILL MR RADAD BASED ON MR RADAD'S ACTIONS.

MR RADAD WAS TRANSPORTED TO E COMPANY, 4TH FORWARD SUPPORT
BN MEDICAL AID STATION WHERE MEDICAL AID WAS GIVEN. MR
RADAD DIED FROM HIS WOUNDS AND WAS PRONOUNCED DEAD BY
UNKNOWN MEDICAL PERSONNEL AT APPROXIMATELY 2330, 11 SEP 03.

THE CLO IS CW3 ████████████████████ SAC, 43RD MP DET (CID)
(FWD), DNVT 302-534-████████

INVESTIGATION CONTINUES BY USACIDC.

*** REQUEST A USACRC NAMECHECK BE CONDUCTED ON SPC ███████████
████████

7. COMMANDERS ARE REMINDED OF THE PROVISIONS OF AR 600-8-2
PERTAINING TO SUSPENSION OF FAVORABLE PERSONNEL ACTIONS AND
AR 300-67 FOR THE SUSPENSION OF SECURITY CLEARANCES OF
PERSONS UNDER INVESTIGATION.

01067
JJJ123

DODDOACID 007180

8.   CID REPORTS ARE EXEMPT FROM AUTOMATIC TERMINATION OF
PROTECTIVE MARKINGS IN ACCORDANCE WITH CHAPTER 3, AR 25-55.

AGENT'S INVESTIGATION REPORT

CID Regulation 195-1

ROI NUMBER
0149-03-CID469-60209

PAGE 1 OF 1 PAGES

DETAILS

BASIS FOR INVESTIGATION: About 1600, 15 Sep 03, this office was notified by the Staff Judge Advocate, 4ID, Camp Iron Horse, Iraq, that Mr ▓▓▓ detained Iraqi Local National, was shot and killed at Camp Packhorse, Iraq, by SPC ▓▓▓▓▓.

About 1900, 15 Sep 03, SA ▓▓▓▓ obtained a Serious Incident Report (SIR), and a 15-6 investigation packet conducted by MAJ ▓▓▓▓▓ 720th Military Police Bn, Camp Iron Horse, Iraq, which disclosed SPC ▓▓▓▓▓ was in violation of the U.S. Army Use of Force policy and Task Force Iron Horse directives concerning the use of deadly force. (See SIR and 15-6 investigation packet for details)

About 23 Oct 03, SA ▓▓▓▓ advised SPC ▓▓▓▓▓ of his rights, which he invoked and requested a lawyer.

About 20 Nov 03, SA ▓▓▓▓ coordinated with CPT ▓▓▓▓ SJA, 4ID, who opined there was probable cause to believe SPC ▓▓▓ commited the offense of Murder when he failed to obey SOP and fire his rifle at Mr RADAD, killing him. CPT ▓▓▓▓ stated there was already an article 32 hearing where SPC ▓▓▓▓ was being charged for the offense of Voluntary Manslaughter. She stated the results of the hearing concluded that SPC ▓▓▓▓ would not be tried at a courts-martial. She stated that on 12 Nov 03, SPC ▓▓▓▓ was reduced to the grade of E-1 and received a Chapter 10 Discharge from the U.S. Army.///LAST ENTRY///

TYPED AGENT'S NAME AND SEQUENCE NUMBER	ORGANIZATION
SA ▓▓▓▓	43rd MP Det (CID)(FWD), Camp Iron Horse, Iraq APO AE 09323-2647

SIGNATURE	DATE	EXHIBIT
▓▓▓▓	20 Nov 03	1

CID FORM 94
1 FEB 77

FOR OFFICIAL USE ONLY

01057

A-357

DEPARTMENT OF THE ARMY
11TH MILITARY POLICE BATTALION (CID)
6TH MILITARY POLICE GROUP (CID)
P. O. BOX V
FORT HOOD, TEXAS 76544-0740

REPLY TO
ATTENTION OF
CIRF-OP

19 May 04

MEMORANDUM THRU

Commander, 6th Military Police Group (CID), ATTN: CIRF-OP, Mail Stop #84, Box 339500, Fort Lewis, WA 98433-9500

Commander, 3rd Military Police Group (CID), ATTN: CIRC-OP, 4699 N. 1st Street, Forest Park, GA 30297-5119

FOR Commander, USACIDC, ATTN: CIOP-COP-CO, 6010 6th Street, Fort Belvoir, VA 22060-5506

SUBJECT: Operational Review of 0149-03-CID469-60209

1. On 17 May 04, this office received a Request for Investigation (0212-04-CID001) from Headquarters, USACIDC, via 3rd Military Police Group (CID), Forest Park, GA, to conduct an operational review of all detainee deaths and other crimes against detainees by U.S. Military personnel during Operation Iraqi Freedom (OIF) and Operation Enduring Freedom (OEF1)

2. On 17 and 18 May 04, the undersigned conducted an operational review of the above referenced Report of Investigation to determine if it was operationally sufficient. This ROI was initiated on 15 Sep 03. When the 43rd MP Detachment (CID), Ft Hood, TX was re-deployed from Tikrit, Iraq, they brought the case file back for distribution to Crime Records Center (CRC), Ft Belvoir, VA. The case file is maintained at the Ft Hood RA in accordance with applicable regulations.

3. This investigation was initiated upon notification that detainee Mr. Obeed Hethere RADAD was shot and killed by SPC ███████████████████████ On 23 Nov 03, the investigation was closed as a final(C) under the provisions on CIDR 195-1, chapt 4-17(6) (SAC prerogative). However, on 20 Nov 03, coordination with SJA revealed on 12 Nov 03, SPC ████████ ████ was reduced to E1 and received a Chapt 10 discharge in lieu of court martial. The following information was extracted during the review:

    a. CID was notified of the incident after a 15-6 determined SPC ██████████████ did not follow regulations governing the use of deadly force. The notification occurred 4 days after the fact.

b7C, b65

b7C, b65

2 0

01080

DODDOACID 007193

A-358

b. Three witness statements and SPC ███████████ confession during the 15-6 *b7C, b6S* *b7C, b6S* (without rights advisement) substantiated the CID investigation and 15-6. SPC ███████ ███ requested a lawyer when advised of his rights by the unit and CID.

c. The delay in reporting prevented the recovery of forensic evidence, specifically:

1. the projectile was not recovered from the deceased nor the scene (although agents did conduct a CS exam upon notification)
2. no autopsy was conducted of the remains
3. the M16 rifle was not collected as evidence.

4. Subsequent to the case review, I discussed with the former SAC why the rifle was not collected as evidence. The former SAC responded that the rifle was not collected because there was no projectile to compare it to. I explained fingerprint evidence could have been a key to the investigation since the subject confessed without rights advisement, which would have meant, if this had gone to court martial, the confession would have been thrown out. Further the witness testimony could have been under question by a good defense attorney. Fingerprint evidence would have supported the events under investigation (and possibly *only* his fingerprints on the weapon verses the defense tactic "it wasn't my client and someone else"). The former SAC rebutted by saying the subject's prints would have been on the weapon anyway, since it was his assigned weapon.

5. The issues addressed in paragraph 4 above will be addressed in training during the upcoming staff (site) assistance visits.

6. Although not completely thorough (i.e. collection of the weapon for fingerprint analysis) this ROI will be NOT be reopened as further investigation would not change the outcome of the investigation. The subject received non-judicial punishment for the offense and is no longer in the military.

7. POC for this action is the undersigned at DSN: 738-████ Comm: (254) 288-████ or email: ███████████@hood.army.mil

b7C, b6S

b7C, b6S

CW3, MP
Battalion Operations Officer

DRAFT

21

01081

FACTS:

1. Detainee ▮▮▮ was either struck or fell at about 110530DEC03, and broke his jaw.
2. The BHA was under the supervision of ▮▮▮▮▮▮ at this time.
3. There were soldiers from 1/502, 3/327, 2/44, and 311 MI at the BHA at this time, serving as either guards or in other MI roles.
4. The detainees were being systematically and intentionally mistreated (heavy metal music, bullhorn, hit with water bottles, forced to perform repetitive physical exercises until they could not stand, having cold water thrown on them, deprived of sleep, and roughly grabbed off the floor when they could no longer stand).
5. The detainees had sand bags on their heads with "IED" written on them, the infantry soldiers stated they felt this was done to make them angry at the detainees, and it had exactly this effect.
6. The IO could determine if ▮▮▮ was hit or simply fell to the ground.
7. The IO could not determine who might have struck ▮▮▮ if he was struck.
8. The 3d & 4th Geneva Conventions were violated in regard to the treatment afforded to these detainees.
9. The IO made no recommendation as to potential disciplinary action.
10. All deficiencies at the Strike BHA have been corrected.

RECOMMENDATION: That ▮▮▮▮▮▮ be issued a GOMOR.

SYNOPSIS OF WITNESS STATEMENTS:

▮▮▮▮ 1/502: We "always harassed the hell out of the detainees." They always told us to "smoke the detainees, but to not physically harm them."

I saw the Chief throw them down, put his knee in his neck and back and grind them into the floor. He would use a bull-horn and yell at them in Arabic and play heavy metal music extremely loud, they got so scared they would urinate on themselves. He was very aggressive and rough with the detainees

We were told to only feed them crackers & water (may have been because of late hour)

▮▮▮▮ 1/502: They were setting it up to make the infantry guys angry by writing IED on the sand bags over their heads.

▮▮▮▮ of Guard Detail) 3/327: We would force them to stay awake, by banging on metal doors, playing loud music, screaming at them all night - those were our instructions. We were told to not strike them.

▮▮▮▮ & ▮▮▮▮ 3/327: Our instructions were to keep them awake, smoke them, yell at them, but to not hurt them.

001168

████████████ 2/44: We "hazed" the detainees – we had a lot fall and hurt themselves

████████ 1/502: ████ had IED on the sandbag over his head, the guards were all over him, screaming at him things like "you like to use IED's motherfucker), and smoking him extra. They were smoking him really hard when I heard him cry in pain (he could have been hit or fell).

████████ 3/327: A lot of detainees had IED written on their bags. I was near ████ when he fell and I helped him up. Interpreters (ICDC) blew cigarette smoke up their sand bag hoods. They also poured water on them to get them up, after the were exhausted from being smoked.

████████ 3/327: "We were yelling in a bullhorn at the detainees, making them do PT, things like flutter kicks, ups and downs, stuff like that." We knew we were supposed to do these things because MI was already doing this stuff when we got there. He did not say it was part of the SOP. He stated, "we were briefed to keep them awake, do not let them talk, and to not hurt them." I had seen "detainees collapse before because of the intensive physical training."

001169

The following is an exact transcription of the statement of █████████████

By the Name of God, the Most Merciful and Gracious,

My name is █████████████ a student in high school. On Wednesday 10/12/2003, me and my family were sleeping at home when we heard a knocking at door. Then, soldiers from coalition forces entered the house and commenced searching our house. (It was 5 in the morning). After that, they tied my brother and father and my hands and took us to their quarters. There, they put bags on our heads and took us to a room which contains a vocal device (so big recorders) and rised its voice so loudly and started torturing us with many kinds of torture like stand and sit down, pour cold water on our bodies at night and beat us during the day and didn't give us food and even water except one time for two days. (The period of our torture).

During the time of torture, the bag was on my head, when one of the soldiers drew me till I came near the wall, then he kicked me a very strong kick on my face even my teeth were broken. Also my down jaw brake (several fractures). After I are injured, they took me to another room and told me to say that I've fallen down and no one beated me. Then, they transferred me from Mosul to Baghdad without treatment of my wounds.

Now, for eight day, I am in the hospital for remedy. I am from a poor family. I have two brothers, one is a child and the other is 25 years old, but he is very sick. He suffers from three disease that are kidney, stomach, and windpipe. He is incapable to work. I also have 5 sisters. I used to work as a carrier of pebbles and sand after my duration in school. My father is an old man. The coalition forces took him with my brother and I don't know where are they, or in which detaition they are. I hope to release so I can go to my school because it's my last year in high school. Also, to work and help survive my family (my mother and sisters).

Be so kind to review my case

█████████████
18/12/2003

001185

b(6)

REPLY TO
ATTENTION OF

AFZB-JA-CAL   31 December 2003

MEMORANDUM FOR RECORD

SUBJECT: AR15-6 Investigation Into the Broken Jaw Injury of ███████████

1. On 19 December 2003, at 0900 hours I was notified that I would soon be appointed as the investigating officer in an AR15-6 investigation into the broken jaw injury of a detainee named ██████████████ detainee #0672753, to determine the cause of his injury while in the custody of the 2ⁿᵈ BCT holding facility. My instructions were to determine if the injury was the result of intentional acts by coalition forces and to develop all the factors surrounding the injury.

2. The exact cause of the broken jaw injury to ██████████ is blunt trauma to his lower mandible: How exactly he sustained this blunt trauma is uncertain. Two explanations that have been offered by the parties involved are that he either fell directly onto his face while trying to get up, or he was struck by a US soldier while he was bent over, see Findings for a complete discussion.

3. What factors contributed to his injury?

   A. Safety of the detainees was not a priority.

      1. ████████ was harassed and exercised without stopping for at least three hours, while he was flex-cuffed and while he had a sand bag over his head.

      2. The guards who were on duty were infantry enlisted personnel that were either told to keep the prisoners awake, silent, and moving, or were not given any guidance at all and just followed the lead of the guards they were joining or replacing.

      3. All the guards on duty at the brigade holding are (BHA) were yelling at the detainees and were making them do flutter kicks and knee benders.

      4. Some BHA personnel were striking the detainees with water bottles.

      5. There is evidence that suggests the 311th MI personnel and/or translators engaged in physical torture of the detainees.

001198

b(6)

B. The atmosphere in the detainee holding room was tense, emotional, and encouraged the guards to engage in abusive, out of control behavior.

1. The guards who were guarding the detainees in the holding room were not properly briefed or properly trained on handling detainees, and were shown abusive behavior toward the detainees by the MI personnel and the interpreters.

2. The noise level was tremendous. A stereo with approximately three-foot floor speakers was blasting music. The guards were encouraged to yell at the detainees and they beat against metal doors and probably empty ammunition cans.

3. The detainees had sand bags over their heads that were marked with different crimes, leading the guards to believe that the particular detainee committed that particular crime. ███ ███ bag was labeled "IED", a particularly hated crime by infantry soldiers patrolling the streets.

4. The MI personnel were abusive to the detainees and these personnel set the example for the inexperienced guards.

C. There were not enough US personnel on duty.

1. There were too few personnel on duty from 311th MI when the detainees arrived, resulting in ███████ not being interrogated prior to the incident.

2. ████████ was one of approximately seventy detainees brought in that night as a result of Operation Reindeer Games. If he had been interrogated it would have been determined that he was not the target and should have been released after questioning.

3. Many of the guards made statements to the effect that they did not know what the other guards in the room were doing or where they were when the incident occurred. More guards would have allowed the guards to supervise eachother.

001199

19 December 2003

E X 6
3.2.1.6

At approximately 0900 hours ████████████ of OSJA informed me that I was to be appointed as an AR 15-6 investigating officer involving an incident that occurred in the 2ⁿᵈ BCT holding area. I first contacted 2ⁿᵈ BCT trial counsel ████████████████ to get a brief synopsis of what had occured. I was informed that a commander's inquiry had already been completed and that a brigade 15-6 investigation was underway. I was told that the point of contact for the brigade 15-6 was ████████ of 327ᵗʰ infantry regiment. I attempted to contact ████████ but was unable to reach him by DNVT. I telephone the DMAIN in an attempt to get a signed appointment memo.

20 December 2003

E X 6
3.2.1.4

Made several attempts to contact ████████ in order to obtain a copy of the commander's inquiry information that he was given and to see if had any new evidence to add from his investigation. Left several messages. Was unable to make contact.

21 December 2003

E X 6
3.2.1.6

Telephoned 2ⁿᵈ BCT trial counsel and spoke at length about the background on this incident. I learned from ████████ that a detainee had died in that same holding area just 2 days prior to the incident I was investigating. I was given the name of the IO for the death incident and attempted to make contact to see if he had any information that might assist me. Also made several attempts to contact ████████. No success with either contact attempt. Contacted DMAIN about getting a signed appointment memo and was told it would be forth coming later in the evening.

22 December 2003

E X 6
C3.2.1.6

I interviewed ████████████, the company commander of 108ᵗʰ MP Company. I obtained information about what types of changes her company made to the brigade holding area (BHA) since they took over operating it.

23 December 2003

ε √ 6
c 3.2.1.6

I visited the BHA for the first time. Viewed the facility, spoke with ████████ the B Company, 311ᵗʰ MI company commander, and spoke with ████████ Got the background information about the events of 10-11 December, the circumstances surrounding the incident, and about the procedures they had in place at the time of the incident. While here, ████████ arrived to conduct his investigation. We spoke and I obtained the information contained in the file from the commander's inquiry. Went back to the 108ᵗʰ MP Company to see if there were any diagrams of the facility. Obtained a copy of the signed appointment memo from the DMAIN.

1

001200

b(6), b(3)

24 December 2003

Obtained a list from the BHA of the guards that were purported to be on duty the night of the incident and who had signed an acknowledgement of understanding of what they were to do. Asked MI personnel if they knew who was on duty at the exact time of the incident and was told no.

25 December 2003

Christmas Day. No investigation.

26 December 2003

Went back to the BHA with a camera and took pictures. Went to the 21st CSH and interviewed ████████. Obtained a copy of the x-ray of ████████

27 December 2003

Went to AO Glory. Interviewed ████████ at approximately 1000 hours. Interviewed ████ at approximately 1100 hours. Interviewed ████████ and ████████ who were the replacement guards for ████████ and ████████ Also interviewed ████████ Returned to the airfield to type the statements.

28 December 2003

Interviewed ████████ Had ████████ and ████████ sign their statements. Visited the BHA and talked off the record with ████ the ████ from 108th MP Company. Went to ██ Company 2-44 ADA to interview the guards that were present on 10-11 December at the BHA. They were unavailable but I spoke with their ████ and set up an interview appointment for later that night at the DREA for 1830 hours. Returned to the DREAR. At 1830 waited for the ADA guards to arrive. They never came.

29 December 2003

Went to 1/502nd CP at AO Glory and interviewed ████████, ████████, ████████ ████████, and several other 502nd soldiers who were thought to have relevant information but in fact did not. Went to the BHA and obtained a written MFR from ████████

30 December 2003

Returned to 1/502nd CP to have ████████ ████████ ████████, and ████████ sign their statements. Interviewed ████████ one more time.

2

001201

31 December 2003

From 0830 to approximately 1500 wrote this report

3

b(6), b(3)

Factual Summary

1. ████████████ was detained and removed from his house along with his 25 year old brother and his father as a result of Operation Reindeer Games sometime late 10 December 2003. His father, ███████████████████████ was the person targeted in their house. He is suspected to be an officer in the Fedayeen. ████████████ and his brother were captured as sub-targets. Sub-targets are male Iraqi citizens found inside a target's home.

2. All three detainees were brought with approximately seventy other detainees to the 2nd BCT Holding Area. This holding area is a prison like facility located on AO Glory and operated by B Company, 311th MI battalion.

3. Upon arrival at the BHA, all detainees were made to stand in formation in the courtyard in the center of the compound and await in-processing. The detainees were flex-cuffed, and some had bags over their heads.

4. ████████ was in-processed by the MI personnel. He was given a detainee number (#0672753), and had a bag placed over his head that had "IED" written on it. He was then placed in a large detention room with the other detainees.

5. In the detention room ████████ was made to perform excessive amounts of exercises like flutter kicks and knee benders for a period ranging in length from three to four hours. Loud music was blasting in this room. ████████ was yelled at and was subjected to bullhorns in his face and cold water being poured on him. The guards in the room were roaming among the detainees pounding on metal doors, shouting at the detainees to perform exercises, and physically grabbing detainees up if they were slow getting to their feet. If the detainees attempted to lift the bags over their heads, the guards pulled the bags back down and spent extra time in front of that detainee making them do exercises.

6. The guards that were guarding the detainees changed at various times depending on what unit they were from. There were guards from 1/502nd, 3/327th, and several interpreters from the 311th MI personnel that guarded this group of detainees. The group of detainees that were already being held in the BHA prior to the arrival of the detainees from Operation Reindeer Games had been moved to a different room and they were being guarded by 2-44 ADA guards. Those detainees were told to sleep. Several of the infantry guards guarding the detainees from Operation Reindeer Games were on this detail for the first time.

7. Only three guards were positively identified as being in the room at the time of the incident. They were ████████ from ████, ████████ from ████, and ████ ████████ of ████ Both ████ and ████ have stated that they never saw what happened to ████. In his very first statement, ████████ claimed to have been assisting ████ get up when he suddenly fell. In every statement thereafter he denies seeing ████ fall.

Exc 2.1.6

001203

b(6), b(3)

8. At approximately 0545 hours, ▮▮▮▮▮ began crying and bleeding from under his bag. ▮▮▮▮▮ and ▮▮▮ go approached ▮▮▮▮▮ and both were present when either an interpreter or an MI soldier removed his bag. He was bleeding from his mouth.

Ex 6
C3.2.1.6

9. ▮▮▮▮▮ was taken to an interrogation room where he was asked what had happened. The first person to ask him what had happened was an Arabic speaking US soldier, ▮▮▮▮▮ He translated that ▮▮▮ said he fell down.

Ex 6
C3.2.1.6

10. When the Arabic translator, ▮▮▮▮▮, asked ▮▮▮▮▮ what had happened, he claims ▮▮▮▮▮ told him he was punched or something similar.

11. ▮▮▮▮▮ was returned to the detention room and the guards were told to leave him alone. He was subsequently examined and x-rayed by ▮▮▮▮▮ from ▮▮▮▮▮. She found he sustained a fractured lower jaw and recommended he be sent to the 21 CSH.

Ex 6
C3.2.1.6

12. ▮▮▮▮▮ arrived at the 21st CSH at approximately 1450 hours. He was again x-rayed and was examined by ▮▮▮▮▮ Dr. ▮▮▮▮▮ found that ▮▮▮▮▮ sustained a fractured lower jaw and malocclusion. He arranged for ▮▮▮▮▮ to be sent to the 28th CSH in Baghdad for treatment. Eventually ▮▮▮▮▮ was transferred to the 28th CSH and is still there as of the date of this AR 15-6.

Ex 6
C3.2.1.6

001204

DODDOA 026618

A-369

b(6), b(3)

FINDINGS

1. Was ▊▊▊▊▊▊ injured?

Finding: Yes, ▊▊▊▊▊ was injured. He was not injured when he came in to the BHA. There are no indications that he had any injuries when he was in-processed. He was injured and bleeding from his mouth when he left the BHA. He suffered a mandible fracture, or broken lower jaw. ▊▊▊▊▊▊, the first medical person to thoroughly examine ▊▊▊▊▊ ordered x-rays taken of his jaw and found a clear mandible fracture to the lower jaw. (Exhibit G-3) Dr. ▊▊▊▊▊▊ ordered his own x-rays taken of ▊▊▊▊▊▊ at the 21st CSH and determined that ▊▊▊▊▊▊ sustained a fractured lower jaw as well as malocclusion (teeth not lining up). (Exhibits C-1, C-2) I attempted to locate ▊▊▊▊▊ and was told by ▊▊▊▊▊▊ of the Division Provost Marshall's Office that he was still at the 28th CSH in Baghdad because his mouth was wired shut and he needs to be fed through a straw.

2. Was the broken jaw injury of ▊▊▊▊▊ the result of an accident or intentional acts by coalition forces?

Finding: ▊▊▊▊▊▊ **injury was the result of intentional acts.** After examining the evidence, I am unable to definitively determine the actual injury-causing event. Every single guard I interviewed on duty in the room where the incident occurred that night testified that they did not see the injury occur. (Exhibits D-5, E-5, F-1) ▊▊▊▊▊▊ is the guard most consistently placed close to ▊▊▊▊▊ at or around the time the injury occurred. He has two inconsistent statements. In his first statement taken just hours after the incident, he states that he was helping to pick up ▊▊▊▊▊ from a laying down position when he fell. In every statement thereafter he states that he did not actually see ▊▊▊▊▊ fall. It is my opinion that ▊▊▊▊▊ was somehow involved in ▊▊▊▊▊▊ injury, but I do not have conclusive evidence to prove this. ▊▊▊▊▊▊ claim that ▊▊▊▊▊ fell is neither plausible nor credible.

Regardless of whether the injury was the result of a blow by a US soldier or was the result of a collapse due to muscle fatigue or muscle failure, it was an intentional act that led to the injury. If we accept the explanation that ▊▊▊▊▊▊ fell face down while trying to get up, the evidence undeniably shows that he was intentionally, excessively exercised by US soldiers for at least three hours prior in such a way that would have resulted in complete leg-muscle fatigue and failure. If his injury was the result of an unassisted fall and not a blow, in order to fall completely on his face while his hands were cuffed in front of him, and with enough force to completely fracture his jaw, the fall would have had to have been the result of a complete collapse. ▊▊▊▊▊▊ stated that the lack of abrasions to ▊▊▊▊▊▊ face, and the contusions on his body, suggest that his testimony of being beaten is more likely the truth of what happened, but excessively exercising the detainees to the point of complete muscle failure is still the result of an intentional act by US soldiers.

3. What were the events leading up to the incident?

Finding: ▊▊▊▊▊ had been brought into the BHA at approximately 0100 hours on 11 December 2003, as the result of a large target operation called Operation Reindeer Games. He

001205

was among approximately 70 detainees brought in at this time. They were all flex-cuffed at this time. He was downloaded from the vehicle that brought him in, lined up in a formation in the courtyard of the BHA, and awaited in-processing. He was eventually in-processed where he was given a target number, was briefly questioned about background information, and had a bag placed over his head whereon was written a suspected offense. He was taken to the large detainee holding room along with the other detainees from the operation, and was subject to very loud music from a stereo. He was exercised without stopping for approximately three hours, was made to do flutter kicks and up-downs, and was subject to being hit by water bottles. He had cold water poured on him and was yelled at repeatedly by roving guards. The evidence suggests that he was harassed more than most of the other detainees. At some point approximately 0545 hours, the guards were told that a certain detainee was requested for interrogation. The guards began organizing the detainees in formation. At some point during that attempt ▇▇▇▇▇▇ began crying and bleeding from his face, under the bag.

4. Was there evidence of any misconduct on the part of coalition forces?

Finding: Yes. Supervision and training of the guards was almost non-existent at the Brigade Holding Area (BHA) under B Company, 311th MI control. Abuse of the detainees in some form or other was an acceptable practice and was demonstrated to the inexperienced infantry guards almost as guidance. Evidence clearly indicates that detainees were excessively exercised to the point of complete muscle failure and collapse (Exhibits D-3, D-5, E-3, F-1, H-4, J-1, K-1), that detainees were struck with half-filled water bottles (Exhibits D-5, J-1, J-2), that detainees had cold water poured on them while in the stone-walled detention room where there was no heat (Exhibits K-1), and were subject at times to direct physical abuse (Exhibits K-1).

In addition, at the time the detainees were brought into the BHA there were not enough MI staff on duty to conduct the interrogations. As a result, even during in-processing, the detainees waited for a long time. When MI personnel started conducting interviews, the fact that there were not many personnel on hand resulted in longer periods of exercise for the detainees before they could break to be interrogated. It also meant that sub-targets were not readily segregated out of the target population and had to endure the harassment for many hours. There were also too few guards. There were approximately 5 guards tasked with guarding approximately 70 detainees and tasked with keeping the detainees awake, silent, and moving. In addition, the detainees were marked with suspected offenses on the bags that covered their heads, and there is no indication that there was a rational basis for this labeling. Since the detainees were not interrogated and since many were sub-targets, the markings of suspected offenses seem to be arbitrary. The detainees were marked in such a way as to illicit anger from the poorly briefed and minimally trained infantryman-turned-guards.

5. What were ▇▇▇▇▇▇ actions while he was detained?

Finding: There is little evidence that addresses this question directly. To many of the guards, the detainees were indistinguishable. Evidence shows that ▇▇▇▇▇▇ was arrested as a sub-target in the capture of ▇▇▇▇▇▇▇▇▇ (Exhibit A-4). He was in-processed in accordance with B Company, 311th MI procedures. His picture was taken (Exhibit A-1) and he was assigned a detainee target number (Exhibit A-4). According to B Company, 311th MI personnel, the biographical information taken at the in-processing interview was sent with ▇▇▇▇▇▇ to the

21st CSH and is not kept at the BHA. ▮▮▮▮▮▮▮ was kept with in the large holding room with the general population of detainees from Operation Reindeer games prior to his injury and was not individually interrogated. He stayed in this large holding room almost the entire time he was at the BHA except for the time spent outside in the courtyard waiting to be in-processed. He participated in exercising along with the other detainees and may have been more than most. His hands were cuffed in front of him the whole time, and the detention bag that was placed over his head was labeled "IED", indicating his suspected offense. For this reason he may have drawn more attention from the infantry guards than most of the other detainees.

6. What is the SOP at 2nd BCT for processing detainees?

Finding: The standard operating procedure for processing detainees is that when a detainee is captured, the capturing unit completes a CPA in-take form, the detainee is entered into the BDE target database if they are not released to the local police, and they are processed by the BHA. Processing by the BHA means that B Company, 311th MI is responsible for collecting biographical information from an in-process interview and his belongings are tagged and kept in an evidence room. If the detainee is not the target, he is released shortly after the interview.

7. Was the SOP followed during ▮▮▮▮▮▮▮ detainment (approximately 10 to 12 December 2003)?

Finding: No. There are no records on ▮▮▮▮▮▮ except for the front of an OCPA detention form. He does not appear in the detainee log for 2nd BCT under the primary target number, as he should, and he does not have a completed initial intake form from the BHA. He was not a primary target and should not have been there in the first place. Since he was detained, he should have been released shortly after the in-process interview but was not.

8. Did the failure to follow any policies or procedures contribute to the alleged incident?

Finding: Yes. If the policy had been followed of quickly in-processing detainees and releasing those who were detained incident to the specified target but were not actually targeted, then ▮▮ ▮▮▮▮ may very well have been released prior to the injury. In addition, if B Company, 311th MI had observed proper detention procedures of not allowing abuse of detainees, he certainly would not have sustained a fractured jaw. Did the failure to follow the documentation procedures contribute to ▮▮▮▮▮ injury? The answer to that question is no.

Recommendations:

1. Remove control of the BHA from 311th MI and replace that unit with an MP unit.
    -MP units are better trained and better equipped for the task of processing, managing, and handling detainees. They have been trained to identify and address critical elements in this process and have experience doing it.
    -This recommendation has already been implemented.

2. Institute a safeguard that will allow detainees who are not targets to be released much sooner in the process or not detained at all.
    -This recommendation will require more precise seizure operations, but it may eliminate the large percentage of incidental detainees, thus reducing the overcrowding in the detention facility and allow for greater supervision of the detainees.

3. Eliminate all physical harassment of detainees.
    -This will have the effect of eliminating the possibility that the harassment might become criminal or injurious to the detainees.
    -This recommendation has already been implemented.

4. Increase the number of guards.
    -The guard-to-detainee ratio should be greater.
    -At critical times when larger numbers of detainees are present at the BHA, the number of guards on duty to guard them should be increased.
    -This recommendation has already been implemented.

5. The Company Commander for B Company, 311th MI should be disciplined for allowing abuse of detainees as standard operating procedure, as well as anyone else that was involved in the decision to allow the abusive behavior to be SOP for the BHA.

6. The BHA facility should be repaired, heat should be added to the detention rooms, and better lighting should be installed for the rooms and for the courtyard.
    -The detainees have been kept in extremely cold conditions, which could lead to their inability to react or to cooperate quickly with guard demands. Heat will help them stay warm, stay healthier, and keep them safe during their detainment.
    -Better lighting would help guards keep better visibility of detainees and help deter misconduct of the guards themselves. It will help the guards keep better visibility of each other.
    -This recommendation has already been implemented.

7. Ensure that all guards are well trained and are familiar with proper procedures for handling detainees.
    -This recommendation is already being implemented.

8. Establish set schedules for when detainees are allowed to eat, what they can eat, what they are allowed to do while being detained, and ensure that all guards are aware of this information.
    -This will allow the feeding of detainees to better monitored so that it is not overlooked
    -This will also help reduce any abusive behavior in the future.

001208

b(6)

-This recommendation has already been implemented.

9. ████████ should be compensated for his injury and for his suffering.

-According to his statement, his family is impoverished and he is the only male that can work.

-He is a fulltime high school student and is missing valuable class time that may affect his ability to graduate on time.